Translating
the West

Translating the West

Language and Political Reason in Nineteenth-Century Japan

Douglas R. Howland

University of Hawai'i Press
■ Honolulu

© 2002 University of Hawai'i Press

All rights reserved

Printed in the United States of America

07 06 05 04 03 02   6 5 4 3 2 1

Library of Congress Cataloging-in-Publication Data

Howland, Douglas.

    Translating the West : language and political reason
in nineteenth-century Japan / Douglas R. Howland.

      p. cm.

    Includes bibliographical references and index.

    ISBN 0–8248–2411–3 (cloth : alk. paper)—
ISBN 0–8248–2462–8 (pbk.)

    1. Political science—Japan—History—19th
century. 2. Liberalism—Japan—History—19th
century. 3. Japan—Civilization—Western influences.
I. Title.

JA84.J3 H68 2001

320'.0952'09034—dc21   2001035134

University of Hawai'i Press books are printed on
acid-free paper and meet the guidelines for permanence
and durability of the Council on Library Resources.

Designed by Chris Crochetière, B. Williams &
Associates, Durham, North Carolina

Printed by The Maple-Vail Book Manufacturing Group

To Rob and the guys

Contents

Acknowledgments

Since the initial inspiration for this study long ago in graduate school, a number of scholars have graced me with their wisdom and generosity. Among the many individuals who assisted my work in Japan, I am especially grateful to Professor Hida Yoshifumi, formerly of the National Language Research Center and now at International Christian University, who first welcomed me into the Modern Language Research Seminar and spent long hours responding to my questions and tempering my interpretations; if I can approximate the rigor with which Professor Hida pursues his scholarship, I will have accomplished something. I would also express special gratitude to Professor Igarashi Akio of Rikkyō University, who put his command of research on Japanese law and politics at my disposal and made innumerable introductions essential to the success of my research. Dr. Maeda Kazuo of Rikkyō University instructed me on the history of Tokyo University and Japanese education; Mr. Nakamura Kikuji of the Center for Textbook Research guided me through the history of textbook research in Japan; and Mr. Oikawa Kiyohide of Kanagawa University provided indispensable answers to my questions about language use and reference materials.

A number of libraries and archives made their collections available to me with unflagging goodwill and assistance. I remain indebted to Mr. Koizumi Toru at the Rikkyō University Law Library, for his vast knowledge of Japanese collections and technological access, and to the supreme generosity of Professor Ōkubo Toshiaki for making his personal archive available to a novice. I would also thank the staffs of the Inoue Tetsujirō Archive at the Tokyo Chūō Library, the Library of the National Education Research Institute, the Tokyo University Law Library, the Tokyo University Archive for Meiji Periodicals, the Tōyō Bunkō, and Waseda University Library Special Collections. At the Harvard-Yenching Library, Mr. Timothy Connor kindly provided access to and instruction for the Maruzen microfilm collection of National Diet Library Meiji Era Books.

The research and writing of this work were made possible through the generous support of several organizations and individuals. I began this research in tandem with my dissertation in the 1980s, funded by a research fellowship from the Japanese Ministry of Education. A professional fellowship from the Japan Foundation allowed me to continue research in Tokyo in 1992, and a grant from the Northeast Asia Council of the Association for Asian Studies facilitated another trip to Japan in 1994. Preliminary writing was supported by research grants from the Social Science Research Council and DePaul University's College of Liberal Arts and University Research Council. Working the research into book form was made possible by a fellowship at the Woodrow Wilson International Center for Scholars during the 1997–1998 academic year. A number of friends and peers have offered critical suggestions; in addition to my comrades at the Wilson Center—Charles Briggs, David Gilmartin, Akhil Gupta, James Hevia, and Luise White—I would also thank Ken Alpern, Andrew Barshay, Linn Freiwald, Howard Kaplan, James Ketelaar, Richard H. King, Elizabeth Lillehoj, Joseph Murphy, Luke Roberts, Karen Scott, Ronald Toby, David Tucker, Ann Wehmeyer, and George M. Wilson. Throughout this long project, Kevin Doak and Stefan Tanaka gave me the benefit of their wide learning and expertise, and I am grateful to both for the eminent favor of reading the entire first draft and offering their insights and suggestions.

Earlier forms of sections of this book appeared elsewhere in "Nishi Amane's Efforts to Translate Western Knowledge: Sound, Mark, and Meaning," *Semiotica* 83(3–4) (1991):283–310; "Society Reified: Herbert Spencer and Political Theory in Early Meiji Japan," *Comparative Studies in Society and History* 42(1) (January 2000):67–86; and "Translating Liberty in Nineteenth-Century Japan," *Journal of the History of Ideas* 62(1) (January 2001):168–181.

Finally, special thanks to Harry Harootunian and Gregory Kozlowski for professional support; to Patricia Crosby of the University of Hawaiʻi Press for her confidence and enthusiasm; to my dean, Michael L. Mezey, for encouraging the leaves of absence necessary to my writing; to Noriko Aso, Alan Christy, and Leslie Pincus for a myriad kindnesses in Tokyo; to Jason Jones for computer graphics; to Alexis Dudden for Mitsukuri's biography; to Lee K. Pennington for research assistance in Washington; to Franz and Wolfgang for all the sonatas during the long winter; to Linn and Howard for precious intellectual engagement; to Karen for the voice of reason; to my parents for their mix of discipline and tolerance; and to Rob, for making so much possible.

A Note
on Conventions

The romanized pronunciations in this book are typically Japanese terms. When I have occasion to give both Chinese and Japanese pronunciations of a term, I use the according notation: C: *gongyi* / J: *kōgi*.

I have relied on Ōkubo Toshiaki's dating of the early issues of the *Meiroku zasshi* in making citations from that journal; when I supply a missing date, I do so in square brackets. See Ōkubo Toshiaki, *Meirokusha kō* (Tokyo: Rittaisha, 1976), pp. 29–30.

Because of the problematic numbering of early Meiji periodicals and the occasional disarray in which I found them, my citations include as much information as possible: volume and issue numbers, as well as dates. I have not westernized Japanese month names, but I have converted reign years to Gregorian calendar years, so that the fourth month of Meiji 6 is indicated: 4/1873.

And in keeping with the Japanese habit of giving precedence to Meiji translators of works over their "original" authors (legally mandated in the Publications Regulations of December 1887), I cite Nakamura Keiu rather than J. S. Mill as the main entry for *Jiyū no ri*, Katō Hiroyuki rather than J. K. Bluntschli as the main entry for *Kokuhō hanron*, and so on. See W. W. McLaren, ed., *Japanese Government Documents* (1914; repr. Tokyo: Asiatic Society of Japan, 1979), p. 553. I cite a host of short works in Chapters 5 and 6 for examples of word use; only the collections from which they are taken appear in the bibliography.

Translating
the West

1

Introduction

This study concerns the transmission of political concepts from Western Europe and the United States to Japan in the latter half of the nineteenth century. The specific concepts that I examine in this book—liberty, rights, sovereignty, people, and society—were introduced to Japan in a largely English context of "liberalism" and its enlightenment model of civilization. The political terrain marked by liberal terminology is familiar to readers of a text such as John Stuart Mill's *On Liberty* (1859): the people join together in opposition to the despotic monarch, force upon him the law that transforms his privileges into their rights of individual freedom and participatory government, and thereby reconstruct themselves as a self-governing society of citizens. As this civil society and body politic develop, those rational individuals of superior understanding—who rightly rule—undertake the education of their social inferiors, granting the political franchise to greater numbers. As participation expands, so too does the potential advancement of all humankind.

This ideal scenario, however, was not a predetermined and simple undertaking. One purpose of this study is to demonstrate, for the case of Japan, that westernization was not a linear process—unlike the tree that arrives with its roots secured in soil and burlap, there was no transplanting of the West in a neat package. The concepts that defined the content of westernization did not translate well; they did not have a natural fit with existing Japanese concepts. Hence the adoption of a new and Western political discourse in Japan necessitated the invention of new terminology with which to engage in the new political discourse. Japanese efforts to translate the West must be understood both as problems of language—the creation and circulation of new concepts—and as problems of action—the usage of new concepts in debates about the policies to be implemented in a westernizing Japan.

Accordingly, a second purpose of this study is to clarify the connections between translation and political practice as westernization was introduced into nineteenth-century Japan. Japanese political, educational, and intellectual leaders were much more enthusiastic about translating political concepts than they were about practicing them; like their European counterparts, they were cautious about establishing liberal institutions. As in Europe, where older republican theories informed nineteenth-century interest in liberalism and democracy, the majority of Japanese leaders advocated a constitutional system with guardedly representative institutions. The people required political and moral tutelage before they would be capable of representing themselves; and such a perspective has informed perhaps all national variations of westernization in the past century.

Hence this study offers a new lens for looking at Western liberal theory and its transmission in the nineteenth century. Central to my argument is the difference between westernization and modernization. By westernization, I draw attention to the early Meiji phenomenon of *bunmeikaika:* the Japanese effort to create a strong and wealthy Japan after the example of the West—from industrial technology and scientific knowledge to the educational system informing a self-governing entrepreneurial society. As I explain in Chapter 2, *bunmeikaika* came to mean both westernization—becoming more like the West—and development, the active work of attaining that Western state of enlightened civilization. In this book I focus on the adoption of political language and modes of reasoning that informed Japanese efforts to reproduce Western political structures.

But "becoming civilized" or more like the West does not necessarily mean to become more modern. My focus on *bunmeikaika* is a deliberate alternative to modernization theory, which problematically conflates a historiographic theory and the process of "becoming modern." The former, an explanation of how societies changed as they industrialized, can be described and debated. The latter, however, is extremely contentious because of its implicit values and assumptions: who or what determines "being modern"? Prominent among the assumptions of modernization theory is a mode of idealism that seeks a common pattern of development for modern and modernizing nations; the experience of England persistently serves as a normative point of comparison in examining capital accumulation, bureaucratization, and rational methods of production, transportation, and communication—phenomena that modernization theory evaluates as modern, progressive, and socially good.

Here I am less interested in identifying the modern or Western content of *bunmeikaika* than I am motivated to examine the intellectual dynamics of the scholars and educators who conceptualized *bunmeikaika* and engaged the political and moral conflicts it raised. Hence a specific shortcoming of the idealism of modernization theory has been its inability to grasp the contingencies and differences of meaning between European and Japanese descriptions of "being Western," particularly in regard to political concepts. Modernization theorists have persistently presumed that a liberal democracy duly follows in the wake of industrial capitalism; although Japan was initially slow to institute a liberal order, its progress has improved markedly since 1945. But as we shall see in Chapters 4 and 5, "liberty," "law," and "right" are not stable terms with meanings common to Dutch, English, French, German, and Japanese: they have been as highly contestable in Japanese as in English. This study engages Japanese translations of the West not in terms of an ideal liberalism but in terms of the historical Western models selected by Japanese westernizers. A model like Mill's *On Liberty*, for example, is not a timeless representation of liberalism—most self-styled liberals in the United States today would not endorse Mill's elitism and his skepticism of democratic institutions. Where previous scholars have tended to interpret, say, the Meiji Japanese debate over freedom of the press as an instance of liberalism and its opposite, I insist on a careful reading of the debate to see how "liberty" is constructed in the process of debate, with reference to both European arguments about freedom of the press and Japanese claims about appropriate moral behavior. I seek to replace the political idealism assumed in modernization theory with an account of Japanese historical development.

If this study thus returns our attention to debates over nineteenth-century European political theory that formed the ground of Japan's engagement with westernization, it also returns to the fundamental issues of the ethical choices that accompanied Japan's westernization. Indeed, the materials I examine force us to put values at the forefront, because Japan's leaders deliberately empha-sized the moral content of political thought. Much of the earlier scholarship on Japan's westernization assumed that constitutional democracy and indus-trial capitalism contain a universally credible and implicitly superior ethics. But in fact the individualism and freedom of action advocated by nineteenth-century English liberalism were specifically contested by Japanese intellectu-als, educators, and politicians. In translation, a word like "liberty" connoted a measure of selfishness that restricted its ready acceptability; in the arena of political action, liberty posed an anarchic threat to social stability—thus the ethical decision to restrict liberty seemed reasonable.

This is not to argue that key elements of political relations in Japan con-tinued uninterrupted through much of the nineteenth century. My point is not that restrictions on personal freedoms were a constant condition from the "feudal" or "early modern" Tokugawa regime (1603–1867) into the western-izing Meiji regime (1868–1912). Rather, in the transition from Tokugawa to Meiji, a new vocabulary for describing political relations was invented and used to interpret the new social and political relations under construction. This book shows how the new vocabulary, borrowed largely from English lib-eralism, was both transformative and transformed in the process of translation.

To some extent, of course, Western political theory and language were trans-formed because the Japanese setting differed from its European counterparts. From the demise of the Tokugawa shogunate, the Meiji Restoration produced a political confrontation that necessarily transformed the liberal paradigm. The point of political argument from the 1860s through 1880s was not royal privilege but government power in the hands of a self-appointed oligarchy. Precisely because of the overlordship of the Tokugawa shoguns, the imperial sovereign was never perceived as a despotic monarch against whose arbitrary rule the people contended. Rather, the dominant confrontation that reappears between the 1860s and 1880s was that between the oligarchic government and the people; most often, it was specified as the government's administrative power and authority versus the people's autonomy and right to constitute a government. In this struggle, the emperor proved to be a key to political solu-tions. As many scholars have demonstrated, with the emperor's granting of the Meiji Constitution in 1889 the people were given a share of administra-tive right to be actualized in an elected national assembly. But in the interests of the social unity that signified their imperial subjecthood, the people had to relinquish sovereignty to the emperor and civil rights to the government. A key development facilitating this transaction was the new concept of society: the enlightenment model, which justified the political tutelage of the people on the basis of the greater rationality of their enlightened superiors, was replaced by an evolutionary model that justified political tutelage on the basis of natural developmental stages of society.

Nonetheless, this study is more than a contribution to Japanese political history, for its focus is the way in which the translation of European political concepts constituted a social infrastructure for Western political thought in Japan. The liberal paradigm and its constituent concepts were transformed in translation, and my initial point is that between 1860 and 1890, as Japanese versions of concepts like rights, liberty, and society were under construction, both their form and meaning were unsettled. Scholars, educators, officials, journalists, regional parties, and local associations—the various segments of literate society—debated the meaning of words and their inherent claims to authority and action. This work of translation and debate thus involved both the description of a received world and the construction of a new one. If intellectuals like J. S. Mill in nineteenth-century England believed that one could discuss "individuals" as if they were separate from "society," we must remember—as Norbert Elias pointed out in his pathbreaking work, *The Civilizing Process*—that such an intellectual was reflecting his own experience in a given social position and, moreover, that such a representation was nonetheless contestable.[1] The class basis of political constructions such as the liberal paradigm deserves careful examination, particularly in the Japanese setting where, in the absence of a bourgeoisie, several coalitions of former samurai—the elite class privileged by the Tokugawa shogunate—and commoners were struggling over the meaning of the Meiji Restoration of 1868 and the creation of a political structure to replace the Tokugawa regime.

Accordingly, this book pursues two parallel lines of argument. One, I examine Japanese translations of Western concepts largely from the perspective of semiotics, which theorizes translation as the problem of transcoding material from one linguistic context into another. Rather than understand meaning as a fixed attribute of words, independent of language or usage specificity (the problem of semantic transparency), I examine the processes whereby new words (and new uses of existing words) generate meaning. As I describe in Chapter 3, there were two basic forms for generating meaning in 1860s and 1870s Japan: loanwords (phonic transcriptions or phonic translations), which attempted to reproduce the *sound* of foreign words; and translation words, which attempted to render the *meaning* of foreign words into Japanese signs—and Chinese characters were the standard vehicle for translation words during the nineteenth century. To give an example: when Japanese scholars translated the English word "liberty," they produced both the loanword *riberuchi* and the translation word *jiyū*. (The latter is still the standard translation for "liberty.") Quite often, however, both loanword and translation word were juxtaposed together in a form unique to Japanese, which I call the "compound sign" or "analog"—in effect, a sign form that instructed the reader to understand *jiyū* as *riberuchi* (liberty).

This semiotic approach critiques the widespread assumption of semantic transparency operating in nearly all historical studies of this period of Japanese history. In criticizing semantic transparency, I draw attention to the fact that previous studies of this material have not problematized the language of concepts; intellectual and political historians of Japan have been satisfied to discuss texts written by European authors and to assume that language is not bound by its historical context—that what a text meant to a nineteenth-century reader, European or Japanese, is what it means to anyone reading it today. This cannot be. Take, for example, a concept central to the Japanese translation of German constitutional thought, *soziale Recht*. In what is still the best study of the intellectual construction of Japanese constitutionalism, its author makes no mention of how *soziale Recht* was translated into a Japanese idiom or whether its translation had any consequences for the meaning of the concept. Instead, language stands outside its historical context, so that *soziale Recht* has a universal and fixed meaning for—is semantically transparent to—German advisers to the Meiji government, their contemporary Japanese advisees, historians writing in the early 1960s, and those of us considering the issue today. As any commentor on the German tradition of *Recht* would admit, an understanding must begin by unraveling the difference between traditions of legal conceptions, since *Recht* encompasses what in English we know as both "law" and "right."[2] In other words, we cannot make transparent references to "the impact of Western thought" and assume that Japanese unproblematically absorbed an assortment of alien intellectual traditions in foreign languages. We cannot hold meaning constant and note "mere" shifts in forms of expression and, in an abstract manner, their accuracy or inaccuracy. For such an analysis offers only the unsatisfying but prevalent conclusion that when a scholar or translator did his work well, the Japanese acquired knowledge of some concept or text. If he did his work badly, then Japanese misunderstood as a result of mistranslation. These conclusions not only attribute an inordinate measure of political power to intellectuals, but also ignore the concrete problems of transmitting and reconstructing meaning from one language context to another.

As a second line of argument, because words do not exist in isolation (the dictionary perhaps the one exception), I examine this new terminology as it was used in Japanese political debate in order to understand the pragmatic meaning asserted in textual records. In Chapters 4, 5, and 6, I examine specific usage of words in a number of political debates: the nature of Japanese sovereignty, the appropriateness of popular rights, the acceptability of freedom of religion, and so on. This process necessitates a close examination of context, for the meaning of words is produced not in a dictionary but in usage.[3] This study emphasizes the fact that attempts to transmit to Japan European theories about the relationship between society and representative institutions, for example, were problematic for two reasons, both of which deserve our attention. Not only was there no Japanese word for an English abstraction like "society," but if Europeans were not unanimous about what they meant by "society," then the Japanese too would have to work at constructing some meaning for "society" themselves.

In relating these two lines of argument—the work of translation and political debate with translation words—I have benefited from the insights of the interdisciplinary historiographic approach developed in Germany, *Begriffsgeschichte* (conceptual history). *Begriffsgeschichte*, which combines lexical field theory (from historical linguistics) with the histories of philosophy, political thought, and society, identifies multiple temporalities in the rise of modernity: the parallel development of political and epistemological changes. In the words of Melvin Richter, *Begriffsgeschichte* relates conceptual history to social history—in particular, it relates thought, once social or political change has been conceptualized, to changes in the structure of government and society.[4] Reinhart Koselleck, director of the multivolume historical dictionary of political concepts that best exemplifies the work of *Begriffsgeschichte*, has organized the work around the rise of modernity in Germany, defined as a *Sattelzeit* or "watershed" between 1750 and 1850. He argues that, with modernity, the tensions between experiences and expectations generate a new, modern sense of historical time, and, in the process, political concepts become more abstract and more oriented toward the future. Of particular relevance to my project is the shift in political categories, traceable to the French Revolution, that opened up new spaces of experience and new horizons of expectation: Aristotelian forms of rule—monarchy, aristocracy, and democracy—were replaced by a compulsory alternative: despotism or republicanism. About the new concept, republicanism, Koselleck notes: "Whatever constitution might be in force, it was necessary in the long run to displace the rule of men by men with the rule of men by law; i.e., to realize the republic." Modern humankind invoked political concepts that promised political forms dependent on future action.[5]

Such a description of new horizons of expectation opened by, and opening, new spaces of experience fits the introduction of Western political thought to Japan. For in describing Japan's aspirations to Western civilization, Japanese writers frequently employed a spatial metaphor that recalled Japan's relation to its earlier model: Chinese civilization. All the related expressions for Western civilization discussed in Chapter 2—*bunmei, kaika, kaimei,* and so on—were paired with the spatial expression *iki,* as in *bunmei no iki*: the region or borderland of civilization, which extends metaphorically to mean the stage or level of civilization. As with Japanese modeling after the example of China, this spatial metaphor necessitates a peculiar shift of perspective. In terms of territory or borderland, one approaches such an *iki* from a posited center; *iki* lies at the edge of civilized space. In antiquity, when Japan borrowed much of Chinese civilization, Japan was such a borderland from the point of view of China. Japan entered Chinese civilization from its edges. Hence in terms of level or stage, the metaphor commonly used in the 1870s, the standard or point of reference was again elsewhere—in Europe—and Japan approached this new center again from afar: Japan was a borderland on its way to becoming westernized space. This fractured gaze, with which Japan regards itself in relation to others, is the opening for new space of experience, a space filled with the new horizons of republicanism, industrial wealth, and technological power.[6] Koselleck's example would urge us to attend to at least two temporalities at play in nineteenth-century Japan: on the one hand, the chronological developments of political action in the name of westernization; on the other hand, the epistemological changes taking place with the incorporation of Western political concepts.

Japanese Westernization in the Nineteenth Century

When the U.S. Navy arrived in Edo Bay in 1853, Japanese officials were not surprised by the appearance of the West, for some Japanese had undertaken careful study of Europe for well over a century. Even though the Tokugawa shogunate (1603–1867) had decreed a policy of seclusion in 1641, to prohibit contact between Japanese and foreigners, interaction persisted on the island of Deshima (or Dejima) in Nagasaki harbor, where Chinese and Dutch merchants continued their exclusive trade with Japan for more than two centuries.

Communication between the Dutch and their Japanese hosts was facilitated by a guildlike hereditary corps of "Nagasaki interpreters"—Japanese who cultivated the ability to speak Dutch but who were initially prohibited from possessing texts in the Dutch language and hence unable to study the written language. Because of the potentially seditious effects of Christian texts brought to Japan by Portuguese and Spanish Catholics during the sixteenth and early seventeenth centuries, the shogunate banned European books in 1641, except those concerning pharmacology, surgery, and navigation. The necessity of linguistic competence, however, meant that officials turned a blind eye to the gradually increasing circulation of Dutch dictionaries and grammars. Finally, in 1720, the eighth shogun Yoshimune (r. 1716–1745) allowed the importation of Dutch books.[7]

In addition to Dutch medical knowledge, to supplement the work of his doctors trained in Chinese medicine, Yoshimune was motivated by an interest in Dutch mathematics for its applications in astronomy and the related work of producing accurate calendars. He commissioned scholars to study the Dutch language, to collect Dutch books, and to develop the expertise to translate them, thereby sanctioning a nucleus of scholarly activity in his capital, Edo (now Tokyo); by the end of the eighteenth century, this set of studies became known as "Dutch learning." Apart from mathematics, astronomy, and medicine, Japanese students of Dutch learning pursued knowledge of world geography, natural history, perspective painting, and other related crafts and branches of learning.[8] Although Dutch learning in the eighteenth century was markedly amateur, it became increasingly professional in the nineteenth century with the establishment of an official Translation Bureau in 1811 under the auspices of the shogunate's Observatory. During the first half of the nineteenth century, as American, British, and Russian ships encroached into Japanese waters, the shogunate added military science, gunnery, and ordnance to the content of Dutch learning.

Great Britain's Opium War with China (1839–1842) and the Perry intrusion into Japan (1853–1854) created a new set of circumstances for Japanese officials and scholars interested in Europe. First, Japanese realized that not all Westerners spoke Dutch—that, in fact, Japanese must quickly master the English and French languages—and, second, the shogun and his advisers realized that they must immediately engage their scholars in studies specific to managing the Americans and Europeans: international law, diplomatic protocol, and the professional work of interpreting. It is largely on the basis of this immediately practical orientation of the study of the West after 1854, along with the reconstruction of the shogun's Translation Bureau as the Bansho shirabesho (Institute for the Study of Barbarian Books) in 1856, that historians identify a second phase of Japanese study of the West in the final years of the Tokugawa shogunate (the Bakumatsu period, 1853–1867): a shift from Dutch learning to "overseas" or "Western learning" (*yōgaku*). Western learning expanded quickly after 1856, and its primary official institution (renamed the Yōsho shirabesho or Institute for the Study of Western Books in 1862) participated in official visits to the United States and Europe, sent students abroad for extended periods of study, trained a younger generation of scholars fluent in Dutch, English, French, and German, and sponsored the translation of a number of key texts discussed in Chapters 4 and 5—including Henry Wheaton's *Elements of International Law* and a trilogy of books based on the Dutch lectures of Simon Vissering regarding international law, constitutional law, and natural law. The Bansho shirabesho, whose personnel increased from about two hundred in 1860 to fifteen hundred by 1866, produced a nucleus of reform-minded officials, many of whom figured as educational and intellectual leaders in the early Meiji period and served prominently in Meiji government positions.[9]

In 1868, the Meiji Restoration was proclaimed. Largely the work of a self-appointed oligarchy composed of members of the imperial court in Kyoto and samurai from southern domains, the two groups united in opposition to the overlordship of the Tokugawa shogun. Thus the Meiji Restoration was in fact a revolution carried out in the name of the Meiji emperor and intent on utterly altering the political structure of Japan. Within the first decade of "restored" imperial rule, the lords were divested of their domains and the samurai of their hereditary stipends and exclusive military function; the peasants were freed from the land and the townspeople from their guild associations. To replace these institutions, the new central government in Tokyo established a prefectural system with a centralized bureaucracy as well as a national and conscript army; it instituted the free sale of land and a national land tax; and it removed restrictions on occupational choice and domestic trade and travel. "Public administration," a major slogan of the day, meant government by public discussion as opposed to the exclusionary habits of the former regime. Although the Meiji oligarchs, in overthowing the Tokugawa shogunate, wanted especially to replace the political principle of hereditary hierarchy with the potentially more egalitarian principle of rewarding talent and ability, they left open the question of whether or not public discussion implied a national representative assembly.

Foremost in the minds of the Meiji revolutionaries was the failure of Tokugawa policy toward the foreign powers, which they judged to have been guided by weakness and ultimately disrespectful of imperial rule. Given the international political situation in the second half of the nineteenth century—marked by an expanding European capitalism and colonialism based on aggressive military policies—the oligarchy emphasized national unity under the Meiji emperor. At the same time that the oligarchs struggled both to centralize political power and to acquire the political legitimacy necessary to a revolutionary regime, they were repeatedly assailed by samurai complaints and regional demands for exceptions to the ongoing centralization. Kido Takayoshi, one of the leaders of the restoration, recounted in his diary his frustration over the embattled position of the oligarchy; particularly galling to him were the divisions among his fellow oligarchs, which destabilized the first decade of the Meiji reign with a number of political crises and military conflicts.[10]

The first irreparable fracture among the oligarchy occurred at the end of 1873. And in due course it prompted not only a heated debate over whether or not a Western constitutional government was necessary but also the most serious military rebellion against the authority of the oligarchy. Disgruntled over its failure in promoting an invasion of Korea (to chastise the Koreans for their rudeness in diplomacy), one faction resigned their government offices in protest; they had imagined the military adventure an appropriate solution to declining morale among segments of the samurai and preferred external expansion to the majority's policy of internal development. Some of this faction, led by Itagaki Taisuke, issued a "white paper" in January 1874 urging the establishment of a national assembly to check the authoritarian power of the oligarchy. Although Itagaki and his allies are sometimes dismissed as samurai spoilers, their action inaugurated what was at the time known as the movement to establish a national assembly. The movement, which lasted somewhat over a decade, first spawned an urban and regional exercise in petition drives and the formation of political parties; in some regions, it soon joined ranks with an increasingly violent set of rural protests for tax justice and local rights. The first phase was partially co-opted in 1881 with the oligarchy's promise of a national assembly to convene in 1890; the second phase, which peaked in 1884, was thoroughly repressed with military force. Others of the resigning faction took to military uprisings; the gravest challenge to the oligarchy, the Satsuma Rebellion, erupted in 1877 under the leadership of former oligarch Saigō Takamori, who had been central to planning the frustrated military expedition to Korea. Saigō led an army of ex-samurai disgruntled with the loss of their stipends, privileges, and livelihoods, and only after months of protracted battle did the new government troops defeat the rebels. To Kido and the majority in power, this was yet another plot by dissidents and malcontents to foment opposition and destroy the government.[11]

Scholars have long debated the degree to which the oligarchy was committed to the kind of popular participation inherent in a national assembly. Certainly Kido Takayoshi imagined such a development, but it was tempered by concern for the security of the monarchy and the well-being of the people. He saw the role of government in the light of Confucian paternalism—to combine centralization with responsibility for the people. Hence he repeatedly expressed concern for the hardships of peasants and samurai and understood that the oligarchy's goal should be a "people's government," made capable and responsible through the promotion of men of talent. After his trip to Europe with the Iwakura Mission (from December 1871 to July 1873), an official delegation sent abroad to investigate both Western technology and political, economic, and scientific institutions, Kido concluded that the best way to counter regional or other divisions among the people was "to cultivate a respect for law in the public mind," because such a "spirit of law" (referring to Montesquieu) would ultimately protect the people. He noted that a system of law must be based on a "despotic" fundamental law (a constitution), especially to maintain discipline in education and military institutions. But it must also include local assemblies and, gradually, a national parliament—and most important, it must be committed to impartial administration in order to eliminate the favoritism that marked the first decade of Emperor Meiji's rule.[12]

Central to the political and social restructuring of Japan was the work of cultural change or westernization. Given the widespread alarm over Japan's international vulnerability, the oligarchy and its supporting intellectuals were determined to create a strong and wealthy Japan after the example of the West, a new Japan capable of resisting the Western aggression reported in China, India, and Africa. This new program of westernization, or, as it was called at the time, "enlightened civilization" (*bunmeikaika*), included not only the industrial technology necessary for manufacturing ships and guns and mechanizing Japan's cotton industry but also the scientific knowledge informing that technology. The problem facing such a Japanese undertaking was the expansiveness of nineteenth-century European science. At a time when the formal divisions among academic and technological disciplines were only beginning to be established in Europe and the United States, science was inseparable from metaphysics, political economy, and industry—and those in turn inseparable from religion, ethics, and politics. Each thread in the weave of west-ernization led to the synthetic whole, and Japanese intellectuals spent a great deal of mental effort discussing one or another causal sequence that might enable them to replicate the Western pattern. If some insisted that Christianity was the starting point for Western civilization, others insisted it was science. Clearly, all agreed, industrialization and a Western university system were imperative for Japan's progress.

The most famous site of public discussion over cultural change was the Meirokusha or "Meiji Six Society"—so named after its founding in the sixth year of the Meiji emperor (1873). This group of self-styled educators, most of whom were samurai, saw their task as threefold: to advance learning and moral-ity, to establish patterns of leadership (that is, to assert a role for themselves in the new Japan), and to develop a forum for public speaking and debating that would serve as an example for their unenlightened peers and common-ers. In the manner of a European or American scholarly society, the Meirokusha would encourage both the discussion of ideas and the propagation of these ideas through the publication of their proceedings as the *Meiroku zasshi* or "Meiji Six Journal"—the first such scholarly journal of opinion. The society included many leading philosophers, educators, legal scholars, and political economists, all of whom had started their careers in the Tokugawa schools for Western learning. One of these men, Katō Hiroyuki, had been the first to systematically introduce the theory of constitutional government in 1861. Two others, Fukuzawa Yukichi and Nakamura Keiu, had introduced Anglo-American liberal theory through several popular works—in particular Naka-mura's widely read translations of Samuel Smiles' *Self-Help* and John Stuart Mill's *On Liberty*. Among the countless issues first debated by the Meirokusha were religious liberty, the need for a popularly elected assembly, the equality of women, the free travel of foreigners in Japan, and freedom of the press. Hence the writings of the Meirokusha constituted a significant political agenda in laying the groundwork for public discussions of social and political questions.[13]

As I explain in Chapter 2, an initial argument among the Meirokusha con-cerned the starting point for the educational work of promoting enlightened civilization. Some members, led by Nishi Amane and Shimizu Usaburō, urged that the society concentrate on reconstructing the Japanese language so as to facilitate communication among Meirokusha members and the people at large, who were divided by regional dialects, class differences, and a cumbersome system of writing. But a vocal majority felt that such a project was too grandiose; they instead identified the people's ignorance as the main obstacle to progress—

a diagnosis that conveniently placed society members in a position to undertake the education and civilization of the people. Implicit in this analysis, of course, was an assumption of class differences. With the telling exception of Shimizu, the son of a *sake* brewer, these men were all former samurai and objectified the "people" as an inferior class. They typically looked upon the lowly people—composed, in the Tokugawa formulation, of farmers, craftsmen, and merchants—with an often arrogant paternalism that had accrued to their commanding position. While they understood that theoretically all men of all classes were free and equal, and nearly all of the Meirokusha scholars would have agreed that the authoritarian Tokugawa shogunate had unfortunately encouraged servility among the people, this sympathetic argument could not alter the fact of existing conditions.

Nonetheless, to the credit of these former samurai, two points should be borne in mind. In the first place, they were able to include a commoner like Shimizu among their ranks because they generally did share a belief in the principle articulated by Nakamura Keiu in his translation of Smiles' *Self-Help* and by Fukuzawa Yukichi in his *Encouragement of Learning*: since heaven did not create men above or below each other, high and low in human society were entirely a product of education and self-improvement. All men were capable of bettering themselves. In the second place, these men did not often represent themselves in their writings as former samurai. Rather, based on a key element of their shared samurai upbringing—that the samurai had been the politically privileged class—the word typically used in their debates is "government" (*seifu*). In texts like the *Meiji Six Journal*, these scholars represent Japan as an opposition between the government and the people, and the Meirokusha scholars implicitly speak on behalf of government. Indeed, numerous connections linked the Meirokusha and the oligarchy: Fukuzawa Yukichi was a personal friend of oligarch Kido Takayoshi; Mori Arinori, Kanda Takahira (Kōhei), Katō Hiroyuki, and Tsuda Mamichi were members of the "steering committee" of the Kōgisho (Gijisho), an early "public assembly"; Kanda also served as governor of Hyōgo prefecture and in that capacity played a central role in the Prefectural Governors' Assembly; Katō served as tutor to the emperor; and several of these men later in their careers served as central government officials—Mori as minister of education; Katō as president of Tokyo Imperial University and minister of education; Nishi Amane as minister of the army.

These men spoke on behalf of the government because, given their knowledge of civilization and participation in government, it was they who were best qualified to represent the government's position publicly. The work of westernization, in other words, proceeded with the help of a powerful sympathy linking the elite social standing of the former samurai and the meritocratic elite imagined by Western liberalism. Hence when the ruling oligarchy decreed an extensive press censorship law in 1875 to curb the people's meddling in government affairs, the Meirokusha demonstrated its solidarity with the government by voluntarily ceasing to publish its journal. Within two years, other deliberately apolitical journals resumed the work of the *Meiji Six Journal.* Most prominent of these were *Gakugei shirin* (Annals of Science and Art, 1877–1885), published by the faculty of the new Tokyo Imperial University, and *Tōkyō gakushi kaiin zasshi* (Journal of the Tokyo Academy, 1880–1901), the publication of the new honorary society of scholars established by the Ministry of Education. Both of these journals included articles by the same nucleus of Meiji educators.[14]

At the same time, the strong identification between the Meirokusha scholars and the government and its goals meant that the former supported the latter during the political conflicts of the 1870s and 1880s. In a word, the Meirokusha and the government oligarchy were united in a policy of gradualism: the preference for social stability over political participation and the maintenance of elite rule over expanding popular representation. I show in Chapters 4 and 5 that a majority of the Meirokusha and their allies valued loyalty over liberty and the state's right over personal rights. By the mid-1880s, I argue in Chapter 6, a new explanation of social evolution justified continued political tutelage on the basis of developmental stages of society, and gradualism became more firmly rooted in the putative certainty of scientific ground.

The Historiography of *Bunmeikaika*

Virtually every scholar who has commented on the early Meiji phenomenon of *bunmeikaika* has treated it as an aspect of "the rise of modern Japan"—as a moment within Japan's national history or the history of Japan's modernization. Perhaps the earliest systematic treatment of *bunmeikaika* was that of Japanese Marxists working in the 1930s and 1940s. In this perspective, which sought to write the history of the Meiji Restoration as a bourgeois revolution, scholars like Hattori Shisō, Miyagawa Tōru, Tōyama Shigeki, and, in English, E. H. Norman worked to explain the peculiar development of Japan's revolution. Most often they identified the error of "Meiji absolutism," that expansion of bureaucratic powers after 1885, such that the imperial bureaucracy became the main arm of an autocratic state with wide powers and unaccountability to the electorate and legislature. Along with the slogan "enrich the country, strengthen the military," Marxists treat *bunmeikaika* as a bourgeois policy employed by would-be reformers in their efforts to transform Tokugawa society along the path of development suggested by modern European civilization. Unfortunately for the liberal reforms usually connoted by *bunmeikaika* civilization, these reformers were more committed to industrial capitalism and its ideology of progress than to civil liberties and elected institutions; hence would-be reformers became the very absolutist officials responsible for misdirecting the revolution toward the fascism of the 1930s.[15]

Modernization theorists, who engaged Japanese historiography in the late 1950s in direct opposition to Marxism, treated *bunmeikaika* in much the same way as Marxist historians. In modernization theory, *bunmeikaika* is again a slogan that publicizes the policy and programs intended by the government to introduce the technological innovations of the modern West. Unlike Marxism, however, modernization theorists narrate an ultimately successful triumph, for they see continuous and beneficial development from Meiji to the 1960s—an interpretation that begs the question of 1930s "fascism." Most modernization theorists treat the unfortunate period of fascism and war as an aberration; some construe a positive interpretation by suggesting that Japanese nationalism offers lessons for broadly defining patterns of modernization.[16] The rare contributions to modernization theory that express some unease over the trajectory of Meiji development point to a "reactionary" response in the 1880s by Meirokusha intellectuals like Nishimura Shigeki, who perceived a lamentable absence of attention to standards of behavior in the "civilization and enlightenment" programs.[17] In any case, this largely positive approach to long-term trends is marked by the fact that modernization theorists routinely equate civilization (*bunmeikaika*) and modernization (*kindaika*)—a conflation that reduces the problem of explaining *bunmeikaika* civilization to an account of intellectual factors in the modernization process, particularly the rationality and scientific thought characteristic of "enlightenment." In the same way that political institutions become secondary phenomena, so too the issues of meaning and translation become secondary to the development of industrial capitalism.[18]

Both Marxism and modernization theory have contributed to what is now a standard treatment of *bunmeikaika* in Japanese intellectual history, exemplified by such seminal works as Carmen Blacker's *The Japanese Enlightenment*, Carol Gluck's *Japan's Modern Myths*, the many publications of eminent historians Ōkubo Toshiaki and Matsumoto Sannosuke, and the 1979 studies produced by Hayashiya Tatsusaburō and the Tokyo University Humanities Research Institute: *Bunmeikaika no kenkyū*. Most historians now comfortably equate civilization and modernization (or modernity), both of which refer to the technological progress achieved by Japan during the Meiji period—in particular the intellectual and sociological underpinnings sponsored by *bunmeikaika:* rationality, utility, science, a modern educational system, and the promise of national unification provided by common language habits and textbooks. Above all, *bunmeikaika* represents the practical impetus for modernizing Japan. As I describe in Chapter 2, references to the eighteenth-century French Enlightenment suggest a Japanese parallel and essentialize "enlightenment"—albeit anachronistically—as *keimō shisō* (enlightenment thought), whose setting and manpower can be cleanly chronicled during the early Meiji period. To Blacker, for example, the "enlightenment movement" in Japan signifies the acquisition of a scientific worldview, which is thus the occasion for rethinking traditional knowledge in the manner of the French *philosophes.*[19]

A majority of historians of Japan follow Marxism in closing the period of *bunmeikaika* around 1884 with the demise of the popular rights movement and the intellectuals' putative abandonment of liberal values as they rallied behind oligarchic leadership—echoing what Marxists identified as the rise of Meiji absolutism. Indeed, it is difficult today either to treat as aberrant or to remain silent about the joint development of Japanese capitalism and authoritarianism—a linkage that has been central to the development of modern industry throughout the non-Western world. Hence while most Japanese historians working on the Meiji period today would agree with modernization theory that Japan is the beneficiary of successful industrial development, they must at the same time acknowledge the issue of value judgments made by Meiji oligarchs and would-be reformers. Tetsuo Najita has described Meiji enlightenment as a "highly pluralistic" set of ideas indicative of the tensions "between radical and unexpected disruption in history . . . and the continuing psychological attachment to loyal action as a social value"; Carol Gluck judges "civilization and enlightenment" a temporary diversion from a longstanding and more compelling interest in *kokutai*, Japan's unique body politic defined by the imperial line; and Yamamuro Shin'ichi describes *bunmeikaika* as an international and systemic "indoctrination" on behalf of the construction of a Japanese nation-state.[20] But rather than locate *bunmeikaika* in a national history of Japan, I am instead interested in describing the dynamics of "civilization" as Japanese intellectuals created the linguistic material needed to represent the Western model and worked out its meaning in translation, scholarship, and debate. It is the characterization that *bunmeikaika* represents a liberal movement, followed by a conservative reaction, with which I take issue here. For rather than portray early Meiji intellectuals beginning their careers as liberals and undergoing some middle-aged conservative reversal, my position in this book is that theirs was a nineteenth-century liberalism committed more to an elite republicanism than to populist democracy and more to law and order than to personal freedoms and rights. As a self-appointed elite, they chose rational and state control instead of popular initiative. In this book I examine the conceptual and semantic bases for these choices.

The Problem of Semantic Transparency

The primary difficulty with previous studies of the conceptual foundations of Japan's westernization is, as I stated above, the error of semantic transparency. While I am certainly not the first historian to draw attention to this problem, readers are perhaps familiar with earlier critiques that phrased the problem differently. Semantic transparency was assumed in the practice of "the history of ideas" as normalized by Arthur O. Lovejoy's *The Great Chain of Being*, a mode of historiography that both John Dunn and Quentin Skinner criticized thirty years ago as unduly abstracting ideas from their contexts and turning the activity of thought into "reified reconstructions" too often embedded in biographical approaches to thinkers or simplistic classifications of ideas intended to impart to them universal themes.[21] Although intellectual historians have in recent decades substantially revised their methodologies, the problems that Dunn and Skinner associate with "the history of ideas" linger in studies of Japan's westernization. At the risk of belaboring this perhaps familiar issue, I would point out two significant ways in which the historiography of ideas has impeded a better understanding of the conceptual foundations of Japan's engagement with Western civilization: the abstraction of ideas from their contexts and the simplistic classification of ideas, both of which contribute to this central problem of semantic transparency.

Joseph Pittau's *Political Thought in Early Meiji Japan* merits close scrutiny because it remains the single best discussion of the development of constitutionalism in Japan despite methodological shortcomings typical of an earlier generation of scholarship. In his introduction, Pittau observes that ideas, as they "unfold in history," are by nature abstract; they are expressed in a more concrete fashion in institutions (which is one purpose of leaders).[22] Accordingly, the tension that ideas face in their reified existence as historical agents is the disjunction between their position in a political philosopher's system, where they are whole or original, and their selected and rationalized position as politicians use them in one or another living system. Pittau's understanding of ideas is committed to the continuity and identity of ideas over time. Or, to put the point another way, Pittau is committed to a principle of the semantic transparency of words—it does not much matter when or in what language an idea is expressed. To Pittau, a German idea like *Rechtsstaat* in the philosophical system of Rudolf von Gneist is the same idea when used by Itō Hirobumi in his selective adaptation of Gneist for the Japanese constitution. Any non-German reader (let alone non-Japanese reader) who might not understand *Rechtsstaat* must resort to Pittau's parenthetical note ("legal state")—even if another translator might render it "constitutional state." Instead of explaining how Gneist's meaning of *Rechtsstaat* was translated into Japanese and how Japanese statesmen interpreted it, Pittau simply presents *Rechtsstaat* in the context of Gneist's system and asserts that Gneist's "doctrine" exerted its influence on Itō. *Rechtsstaat* is abstracted from its historical context and treated as a timeless idea.[23]

A variation on this abstraction of ideas from their concrete contexts of translation has been the reduction of ideas to values—a problem that arose from the engagement between modernization theory and sociology, largely under the example of Talcott Parsons.[24] In the service of a systemic study of values, concepts are abstracted from their immediate contexts in order to identify, first, those values that have been generally conducive to policies of modernization and, second, the degree of commitment to such values on the part of their advocates. Democracy, for example, is understood less as a political institution than as one of several presumably modern values that motivates individuals and societies in the modern and modernizing worlds.[25] As such, democracy is best studied for its ability to foster social mobilization, and thus its key function is the election, the means by which societies engage in the rational choices that guide policies.[26] Because this modernization approach to values is largely informed by functionalism, which identifies the functional parts of posited systems, ideas are reducible to maxims operational according to instrumental reason. The consequence for historiography is that, again, with intellectual history written as a history of ideas, concepts are reified and removed from their historical context and questions instead address, at one level, the relation of values to the systemic changes wrought by modernization and, at a second level, the understanding or intentionality of agents in a position to rationally choose some value and its corresponding policy.[27]

Robert Bellah and Robert Scalapino, for example, describe Japan as having a rather fixed "value-institutional structure" that facilitated Japan's modernization. Where Bellah sought to identify a "central value system" in Japan and to chart the integration of central values such as loyalty among the political, religious, and economic spheres in order to explain how such central values of the Tokugawa period encouraged Japan's modernization, Scalapino identified stages of modernization in terms of a series of "ideologies" that are animated by a persisting structure of values.[28] Scalapino's first stage, national unification, corresponds to the Meiji period and to the ideology of liberalism; together this nexus of stage, period, and ideology—national unification, the Meiji period, and liberalism—fostered nationalism, mass mobilization, and modern economic development. Even though this stage of national unification was beset by an internal division between so-called radicals (like Itagaki Taisuke) and moderates (like Fukuzawa Yukichi), the key value of imperialism, supported by both groups and motivating national unification, persisted throughout the other stages of Japan's modernization.[29]

As one of the few modernization theorists willing to note the problem of conceptual or semantic differences, Scalapino is confident of the Japanese ability to understand and make use of foreign ideology—a process that, in his view, depends mainly on the adequate selection of keywords. Perhaps because Scalapino is aware that "these words will bear different connotations from those in the place of their origin" and that there exists an "omnipresent gap between ideas and the social environment to which they had been brought," he focuses not on meaning but on the use that Japanese politicians made of foreign ideas. When Meiji intellectuals "diverged in terms of emphasis or interpretation, it was ordinarily a conscious or unconscious effort to meet the demands of indigenous conditions."[30] For Scalapino, the force of ideas matters in situations that call for political action whereas the meaning of ideas—because they refer to a modern and Western standard—is temporarily problematic and of secondary concern. Japan, a "follower nation," was forced to follow the universal stream, for which it was aided by its ideological proclivities. Because Japan emphasized a traditional way of life, "its relatively higher particularist quotient" of values like Japanese imperialism assisted the introduction of "the purely technological facets of Westernism."[31]

But this "sociology of values" generates an interpretive problem that is based on an internal contradiction between the universal and the particular. When modernization is construed as a linear process determined by universal values—especially rationalization—the particularity of Japan's success, in light of particular Japanese values such as imperialism, prevents Japan from attaining the ideal and universal state defined by modernization. One difficult point of interpretation, for example, was whether or not authoritarianism, as a particular Japanese value that facilitated Japan's successful modernization, was "good" for modernization—to reason instrumentally. How were scholars to evaluate Japan's successful modernization if it had been attained by means presumably neither ideal nor universal?[32]

This conundrum is expressed in histories of Japan's westernization in a peculiar fashion: misplaced apologies on the part of postwar historians for "antidemocratic" attitudes among Meiji intellectuals. As it figures in modernization historiography, Parsonian sociology redefined the significance of ideas as the degree of commitment on the part of those who give voice to them. Simply put: sociology diverted attention to the question of intentions. As Pittau asked in his study of constitutionalism, was the imperialist ideology of the 1930s really what intellectuals of the early Meiji period wanted? To few readers' surprise, Pittau's answer is no, but this reader is troubled that so many scholars of Japanese intellectual history in the 1950s and 1960s felt compelled to apologize for "illiberal" ideas in the works of their subjects. Clearly Pittau's asking a question that holds little interest for scholars today—"is this really what they wanted?"—reflects the ideological conundrum central to modernization theory as the United States entered the Vietnam War: it seemed contradictory that the model of modernization being offered to Third World leaders was Japan's joint program of industrialization and political authoritarianism. Japanese historians betrayed their complicity with Cold War policy by keeping silent about modernization theory's propensity to defer the goals of liberalism and democracy—putting themselves in the odd position of having to apologize for the untoward attraction of values like authoritarianism by invoking the reverse, the unintentionality of their subjects. As Pittau puts it, modernization was the Meiji leaders' goal—a good goal even if it was the occasion for authoritarian methods whose consequences were unintended.[33] This is an especially peculiar conclusion when we remember, as I show in this book, that liberalism in the nineteenth century confidently asserted the authority of a social and educational elite.

Apart from this problem of abstracting ideas from their contexts, semantic transparency is implicit too in the simple classification of ideas. One common habit is the identification of contrastive elements in a man's thought: traditional versus modern, Japanese versus foreign, or conservative versus progressive.[34] Surely the most problematic manifestation of such simplification in relation to the topic of this book is the confusion of an ideal definition of liberalism with the actual construction of liberalism in Japan during the early Meiji period as well as the substitution of this history with a false and anachronistic opposition between liberalism and conservatism. The liberalism of J. S. Mill, for example, who was central to the Japanese construction of liberalism, was essentially libertarian in its commitment to both minimal government and the leadership of an educated elite. As a number of scholars have pointed out, drawing on Michel Foucault's exposition of "governmentality," the political reason of liberalism is best defined by the rule of law and the participation of the governed in the elaboration of that law; at the same time, liberal law is committed both to general forms of government intervention exclusive of individual or exceptional measures and to limiting government intervention in a social economy best left to a self-governing civil society. Graham Burchell has aptly concluded: "To the extent that the objective of government is to provide the regulatory framework which will secure the more or less automatic functioning of civil society, the state's exercise of governmental power can be seen as in continuity with, or as grafted onto, society's immanent relations of power."[35] Society's immanent relations of power in the nineteenth century, in England as well as Japan, emphasized the principle of tutelage on the part of an educated elite over their social inferiors. As Uday Singh Mehta has persuasively argued, tutelage informed both British liberalism and imperialism and rendered the two entirely compatible.[36] The same is true of Japan.

Take, for example, Fukuzawa Yukichi, who has been praised as a "liberal unto the end" and criticized for supporting "policies that were in conflict with the liberal ideas [he] had earlier espoused"—policies like oligarchic rule and government control of the press.[37] Fukuzawa and his Meirokusha associates are said to exemplify liberalism because they embodied these ideas in their personal lives. For evidence, one often reads the now hackneyed anecdote about Fukuzawa's encounter with a peasant on a horse: On vacation at the beach near Kamakura, Fukuzawa encountered a peasant riding a horse, who, oblivious of the new elimination of class differences, dismounted and knelt before Fukuzawa, mortified to be riding in the presence of someone clearly a samurai. As Mikiso Hane, Ivan Hall, and others have interpreted the story, "Fukuzawa reprimanded the peasant for his servility and made him get back on the horse."[38] Observe how Fukuzawa told that part of the story:

The poor fellow was afraid to mount before me.

"Now, get back on your horse," I repeated. "If you don't, I'll beat you.

According to the laws of the present government, any person, farmer or merchant, can ride freely on horseback without regard to whom he meets on the road. You are simply afraid of everybody without knowing why. That's what's the matter with you."

I forced him to get back on the horse and drove him off.[39]

Although scholars rightly read this passage as evidence of Fukuzawa's commitment to the new equality of classes under the Meiji government, they ignore the fact that Fukuzawa invokes both the force of law and the threat of personal violence in order to make another do what he arrogantly knows is best. This is evidence of the liberalism that insisted upon paternalistic tutelage in promoting enlightened civilization. But Hane and others have instead excised tutelage from liberalism, explaining instead a demise of liberalism in terms of a biographical shift; they suggest that early Meiji intellectuals embraced liberalism in their progressive youth and then underwent middle-age transformations to conservatism.[40] In a similar but larger context, Hane sees liberalism in early Meiji as "losing its popularity" with the ugly but necessary and simultaneous rise of nationalism.[41] Indeed, Japanese interest in liberalism and constitutionalism was matched by the need for Japanese strength and wealth, and I would agree with Hane that these men were committed to supporting the government and of course fell into line with changing policies. But one can explain their rather consistent perspective without invoking simple oppositions or a false biographical shift.[42] The concepts supplied by liberalism and its enlightenment project separated both politics and epistemology from the hereditary forms of the Tokugawa regime and placed them in the new categories of Western knowledge. But liberalism in Japan was concerned less with democracy or equality than with the work of reconstituting political power in the hands of a broader but still elite group.

We must take care, then, in identifying a Japanese "liberalism" of the 1870s, when "liberty" so strongly connoted selfishness that, in the interests of social stability, intellectuals close to the ruling oligarchy defined liberty as pertaining not to public speech, assembly, or the press but to the internal domain of thought and religious belief. This is one reason why I insist on repositioning the so-called popular rights movement in its Meiji context in Chapters 5 and 6. Twentieth-century scholarship has tended to see a democratic movement—which, for the most part, it was not. During the 1920s heyday of "Taishō democracy," Japanese scholars and activists sought precedents for their own activities in what they called the Meiji "freedom and popular rights movement." And in the postwar period, a subsequent generation cited this Meiji movement as a precedent for the "democratization" of Japan under the postwar constitution. But to contemporaries in the 1870s, the movement was known as the movement "to establish a national assembly."[43] In print media descriptions of agitation for "popular rights" through the 1880s, "freedom" is increasingly— but "democracy" never—part of the description. Aside from occasional activists in local political societies and branches of national parties, Ueki Emori seems to have been alone on the national (Tokyo) stage in suggesting that all the people deserved some role in political decisions. Instead, as in Europe, the majority of intellectuals advocated a constitutional system with guardedly representative institutions.[44]

That postwar American scholarship has thus framed a study of Japan in familiar but misleading terms—liberal versus conservative—is especially evident when we look at nineteenth-century commentaries on Japan. In an editorial printed in 1881 in the *Japan Weekly Mail*, for example, the English writer identified Japan's political conflict in terms of conservatism versus nationalism. By nationalism, he meant the specific form that Japan's would-be reformers had advocated in calling for reform: a national assembly that would "multiply the bearing points of responsibility." The danger that Japan faced, according to that writer, was not some demise of liberalism as its followers turned conservative; rather, he worried that nationalism would cease to be seen as an honorable patriotism and be redefined as treason. That is, would the conservative government honor the nationalist sentiments of patriots' calls for reform, or would it label them traitors? In either case, the Meirokusha intellectuals sit in the conservative camp, for in the eyes of the *Japan Weekly Mail*, the nationalists were the reform-minded local organizations largely allied with Itagaki Taisuke's Liberty Party.[45]

Rather than succumb to a discussion of commitment to liberalism or whether Japanese values are conducive to liberalism, I would instead examine concepts and their evaluations. Or as Dipesh Chakrabarty phrased the issue in a recent discussion of the "ideological" and the "political," rather than differentiate what is real from what is merely ideological, I would engage political concepts as they are involved in historical debate over meaning and policy.[46] What passes through these earlier studies of Japan's modernization as "central values" is better examined in terms of what Japanese at the time called "moral character"—the persisting problem of ethics. As Kido Takayoshi noted in his *Diary* in late 1868, the technology at the basis of the change required by Japan's national emergency called for a change of attitude, but the cultivation of moral character was still most essential for families through-out the land.[47]

The Historicity of Concepts in Translation

In seeking to reposition Japanese westernization within the historicity of "enlightened civilization" and its translated terminology, I have taken my lead from both *Begriffsgeschichte* and intellectual history "after the linguistic turn," which William J. Bouwsma once described as a history of meaning that seeks to link intellectual history to cultural and social history.[48] Although the new intellectual history is well represented in the study of Tokugawa Japan, par-ticularly through the "Chicago school" of H. D. Harootunian and Tetsuo Najita and their students and associates, there have been few contributions to the intellectual history of Meiji Japan apart from prominent works by Carol Gluck and Stefan Tanaka.[49] The new directions in research represented by the 1994 Meiji Conference at Harvard University do not engage westernization or intel-lectual history; rather, these papers pursue nation building instead of mod-ernization and local resistance instead of the imposition of elite prerogatives.[50] In Japan, the new intellectual history of Meiji Japan is perhaps best repre-sented by Ishida Takeshi, whose analysis of Japan's importation of Western political concepts traces the work of prominent intellectuals in introducing key ideas to Japanese political debate. As the mechanism by which transla-tion coordinates "Eastern" or Japanese culture and that of the West, Ishida borrows the notion of language symbols from Ernst Cassirer's *Philosophy of Symbolic Forms*, which problematically opens the door to language universals—concepts semantically transparent to cultural and temporal differences.[51] In this book I undertake a concrete study of words in translation in order to bring linguistics back into an intellectual history after its turn.

Perhaps most prominent in the Anglo-American practice of new intellec-tual history is Quentin Skinner, whose work is exemplary for its effort to engage historical process. Skinner examines word usage in order to grasp the inten-tions of past contributions to political thought—an intentionality he describes in terms of action. Skinner wants to be able to describe what "authors were *doing* in writing" texts, for then

> we can begin to see not merely what arguments they were presenting,
> but also what questions they were addressing and trying to answer, and
> how far they were accepting and endorsing, or questioning and repudiat-

ing, or perhaps even polemically ignoring, the prevailing assumptions and conventions of political debate.[52]

In theory, Skinner provides a sophisticated alternative to R. G. Collingwood's understanding that history is the history of past thought and that the way to study it is to understand what questions thinkers were asking in the past. But in addition, Skinner not only corrects the idealism implicit in both Collingwood's insistence that one can rethink the thoughts of the past and Lovejoy's abstract method of isolating the unit ideas of universal themes, but he also potentially remedies charges of reductionism leveled against the new intellectual history—that in keeping with a long-standing Euro-American assumption that meaning explains action, the new intellectual history reduces experience to meaning.[53] Rather than study political events by referring to political texts, Skinner would have us study the words in which ideas are represented and the ways in which they are used in the past argument that constitutes political event.

It is precisely upon this methodological point that advocates of Koselleck's *Begriffsgeschichte* assert common ground: they all share a commitment both to treating thought within its context and to addressing "the question of what historical actors thought was at stake when they disputed the meanings and uses of abstract terms."[54] The prominent degree of abstraction in Koselleck's idea of "basic concept," however, risks reproducing the idealism of conventional history of ideas. According to Koselleck, concepts are to be detached from their situational context so as to order them according to a temporal sequence. Hence Koselleck differentiates concepts from words: "A word presents potentialities for meaning; a concept unites within itself a plenitude of meaning."[55] Although one might argue, in support of Koselleck, that this abstraction of concepts is in fact the nature of modernity—that this recognition of experience in concepts is precisely an effect of modern temporality—I am struck that his focus is this reified notion of meaning:

> The meaning of the word always refers to that which is meant, whether a train of thought or an object, etc. The meaning is therefore fixed to the word, but it is sustained by the spoken or written context, and it also arises out of the situation to which it refers. A word becomes a concept if this context of meaning in which—and for which—the word is used, is entirely incorporated into the word itself. The concept is fixed to the word, but at the same time it is more than the word.[56]

That is: as linguistic signs, the conceptual signification of a word exceeds its material signifier; concepts are abstracted from multiple significations and thus can be considered thought detached from the material sign. Or as Hans Erich Bödeker represents the point: Koselleck distinguishes the meaning of a word from its referential relation and introduces the word-to-thought relation as the third pole of a triangle of meaning. Hence a concept is defined by three points: the word, the object(s) to which it refers, and the meaningful content intended by thought.[57] It is perhaps this aspect of Koselleck's theory that has led Melvin Richter to the idealist conclusion that "an individual or group may possess a concept without having a word by which to express it"—a surprising position that mimics the abstract idealism of semantic transparency.[58]

A more materialist way to understand this relation between concept and word is the semiotic relation between type and token—a word in its abstracted and general existence (as in a dictionary) and the word as it appears in a particular instance of usage. As I explain in Chapters 2 and 3, a sign type like *bunmei* carried with it the meaning of "universal (Chinese) civilization," which enabled Fukuzawa Yukichi to use the word (a sign token), by metaphorical extension, to mean "universal (Western) civilization." In the process, the type began to assume the new meaning derived from the new token; the meaning of *bunmei* shifted from Chinese to Western civilization. To Koselleck, concepts are abstract summations of meaning—like sign types—whereas words present ambiguous or potential meanings—actualized in use, like sign tokens.[59] My own reliance on type and token corresponds to the terminology of the materialist linguist V. N. Voloshinov, who describes this relation as meaning and theme—respectively, the abstract word (type) and the word in use (token). But like Quentin Skinner, Voloshinov insists that these two aspects of words remain united in the singular word. This insistence forces two conclusions: first, we are dealing not with a material word and its mental or ideal meaning but a material word whose meaning is "multi-accentual" and depends on usage and user; second, language must be considered as a synchronic totality available to users, whose language usage—in the form of "utterances" or "statements"—is examined in terms of what both Skinner and Voloshinov call "understanding."[60] We understand words by examining how they are used in a language context.

But Koselleck does not enlist the language of sign type and token; rather, he explains his work—with a structuralist vocabulary—as a combination of synchrony and diachrony (or structures and events), which produces a curious combination of materialism and idealism.[61] Koselleck resolutely grounds his work in the animal materiality of human life, from which he generates a fascinating description of different levels of reality (or multiple temporalities) moving at different speeds: on the one hand, the repeatability and circulation of linguistic phenomena; on the other hand, unique sequences of events. The fact that the two series change independently of each other, at different rates, produces multiple ways of understanding changes that involve both linguistic and sociopolitical phenomena.[62] At times this materialist grounding may be located in the word—as when he asserts that *Begriffsgeschichte* addresses the "ever-present diachronically pre-existing language" in relation to the "spoken word in a specific, synchronic, case."[63] Hence:

> A new term may be coined which expresses in language previously non-existent experiences or expectations. It cannot be so new, however, that it was not already virtually contained in the respective existing language and that it does not draw its meaning from the linguistic context handed down to it.[64]

The materiality of words appears to govern the capacity of language users to create new concepts or expand existing concepts in new directions—my position in this book.

Koselleck's recent interpreters, however, remind us that the linguistic grounding of *Begriffsgeschichte* is derived from the largely structuralist study of semantic or lexical fields. This includes a number of different attempts by historical linguists to examine the (synchronic) structure of a language (what Saussure called *langue*) in order to compare onomasiology, the study of different terms available for designating the same or similar concepts, to semasiology, the study of all the different meanings of a given term, in order to identify the semantic field pertaining to a set of related terms.[65] Although historical linguists are divided as to whether or not a semantic field is lexical or conceptual, Koselleck's interpreters repeatedly settle on the idealist interpretation that a concept is a position within a semantic field and not a lexical item.[66] Indeed, Koselleck recently grounded his linguistic views in semantics, which, when treated analytically by linguistics, typically reifies meaning as elemental markers, features, or components of words that are somehow associated with words and hence provide meaningful distinctions among words. It is this analytic procedure of identifying components that affords the reification of concepts—as a pure semantics—independent of their material basis in words. Hence the project of *Begriffsgeschichte* appears to emerge from material social history to engage in the philosophical mentalism of semantics and then return such meaning to the social realm—a point its critics have noted.[67]

It is this potential independence of concepts from their linguistic contexts, I believe, that most divides *Begriffsgeschichte* from the work of intellectual historians such as Skinner and J. G. A. Pocock, who insist on grounding an analysis of political thought in discourse and language. According to Iain Hampsher-Monk, Skinner in particular attempts to avoid this pitfall by attending to the multiplicity of the meanings of *words* in circulation among a given society of language users.[68] Pocock himself has recently stated that he would find it more appropriate to proceed from the history of discourses and the people who have used and been used by them to a history of concepts, rather than the reverse, which he understands to be the method of Koselleck and his followers. *Begriffsgeschichte* runs the risk of imposing an ideal construct upon history when it ascribes "the same concept, or the components of variations of the same concept, to the same word or cognates of the same word wherever they occur in the historical record."[69] Similarly, Dutch conceptual historian Willem Frijhoff has recently stressed the link between conceptual history and social history in order to advocate a renewed focus on "how semantic changes were rooted in new forms of social representation, in changing social relations, or in the updating of old schemes of perception or cultural models of social organization."[70] And Hans-Jürgen Lüsebrink has advocated extending interest in concepts to their materiality of communication, their use by political or social groups, and their intercultural transfer through processes of translation.[71]

This book is meant to contribute to such efforts. At the same time, the need in *Begriffsgeschichte* for a long-term view of conceptual development is displaced, in my case, by the action of translation, which occurred within two to three decades but which nonetheless established the "horizon of expectations" on the part of Japanese intellectuals and activists and began to work the changes theorized by Koselleck and followers as having occurred during Europe's modernity. Koselleck notes in a discussion of the different approaches toward democratization in Britain, France, and Germany: "The concrete concepts around which the political debate turned were bound to the historical experiences that had made their way, at one time or another, into these concepts."[72] Here I engage that process of mediating concept and experience with three different examples. Chapter 4 examines *jiyū*, the quickly standardized translation word for "liberty" and "freedom," whose perhaps easy standardization was accompanied by a series of debates over the proper meaning of "liberty." Chapter 5 examines *ken*, a term used to translate "right," "sovereignty," "power," and many other words; hence *ken* posed the problem of creating meaningful distinctions in Japanese for such distinctions perceived in the source languages. And Chapter 6 examines "society," a new and borrowed concept for discussing the people of Japan, which necessitated the creation of a neologism, *shakai*.

But I am also moved to note the claims of *Begriffsgeschichte* to serve as a critique of the present by affording a point of entry to actual historical discontinuities, which are reflected in language and shifts in semantics. As Melvin Richter and Terence Ball have argued, conceptual history has consequences for the present; if history helps us to perceive how available concepts push us to think along certain lines, this history may enable us "to conceive of how to act on alternative and less constraining definitions of our situation."[73] Two conclusions follow: first, the critical impulse of *Begriffsgeschichte* urges us to free historical scholarship from the idealist anachronisms of, for example, modernization theory; second, as Koselleck has argued, it makes us aware that the translation of concepts into other languages extends conceptual and political structures elsewhere—precisely the subject of this book.[74]

2

The Project
of Enlightened
Civilization

In seeking to transfer Western civilization to Japan, Japanese leaders found a convenient point of departure for their efforts. The enlightenment model of Western civilization dovetailed with the moral assumptions of Tokugawa hierarchy: both maintained that a social and intellectual elite propagated civilization by way of education and behavioral modeling. For both, the problem in spreading civilization was especially the ignorance of the masses, whose education was prerequisite for participation in the social and political order anticipated by Western civilization. This tutelary function was central to Japan's importation of Western technology and institutions in the nineteenth century.

But in a process best described as dialectic, the reorientation of Japanese attention toward the West produced two antithetical developments. In the face of Western imperialism, scholars agreed that the pressing business at hand was to augment Japan's wealth and power in accord with Western models and thereby secure Japan's independence in international affairs. Accordingly, an outspoken number perceived that the engagement with Western civilization meant that Japan must sever its historical and especially intellectual connections to China. Although Japan had borrowed Chinese characters to write the Japanese language beginning in the fifth century, and Japanese scholars had achieved fluency with literary Chinese during the Tokugawa period, many Western-learning scholars in the nineteenth century argued that China was categorically different, and they repeatedly advocated that Japanese literate culture and education eliminate Chinese characters, literary Chinese as a written form, and Chinese learning generally.[1] If they hoped to simplify the Japanese language in order to educate the people more quickly and thereby advance Japan's progress at civilization, proposing such radical measures not only opened a proverbial Pandora's box of problems but ensured that only minimal adjustments would be made. The stubborn fact remained that, until the 1880s, the dominant habit of translation was to create translation words for Western concepts and things in Chinese characters. For all its alleged difference, Chinese learning proved impossible to eliminate from Japan.

At the same time that efforts to educate the people raised this question of language and targeted the heritage of Chinese culture as an obstacle to unified efforts at education, a second antithetical development arose within ruling class ranks. The 1874 fracture among the ruling oligarchy, marked by Itagaki Taisuke's demand for a national assembly and largely perceived by educators and intellectuals as a betrayal of collective efforts, raised the issue of how to proceed with the work of civilization and yet maintain some measure of unity. Fukuzawa Yukichi urged his fellows in the Meirokusha to work outside of government. As we shall see in this chapter, his attack on "duty" was an attempt to wrench from the samurai past a key concept that would help reorient his samurai fellows to their new role as recommended by Western civilization— to pursue personal goals as a contribution to national progress. Fukuzawa's recommendations begged the question of Itagaki's faction's motives: Were they purely selfish, motivated by jealousies among the samurai oligarchy? Or were they a matter of public honor, motivated by the urge to advance civilization?

However one resolved this confusion, one point was clear: if Western civilization intended to empower the political and economic autonomy of the people, then the development of individual autonomy had to be conditioned by a reliable form of ethics instruction that would encourage the people to be responsible. Unlike Tokugawa authoritarianism, which had merely encouraged the people to be servile before authority, some new program of ethics instruction would have to prepare the people for their future political participation by encouraging unity before division and loyalty before selfishness. Hence—contrary to the many historians who have argued that this early Meiji generation of leaders underwent a conservative conversion in the 1880s and 1890s and thus revised their youthful enthusiasm for westernization—this chapter demonstrates that the program of westernization included from the start so-called conservative proposals such as the call for ethics instruction.

As we shall see, Chinese learning was central to Japan's new synthesis of Western civilization, for China was a point of mediation between the West and Japan. The critiques of Chinese language and Chinese learning on behalf of Western civilization would ultimately serve two purposes key to the development of Japanese culture as it entered the twentieth century: one was the formation of ethics instruction on behalf of improving "national character" as a supplement to the technical and political content of Western learning; the other was the formation of a "national language" that could comfortably accommodate Japanese syllabaries, Chinese characters, and Western loanwords.

Bunmeikaika: Enlightened Civilization

Let us begin with a clarification of terminology. The expression I have been using, "civilization" or *bunmeikaika*, entered the Japanese lexicon as somewhat of a double entendre—as both "universal civilization" and, more narrowly, "westernization." Moreover, the consequence of Fukuzawa's critique of duty was to fracture this "civilization" into two related but different programs: one was the goal of universal civilization according to European theories; the second was the goal of development undertaken pragmatically by government officials. These shifts in meaning have gone largely unobserved in previous histories of Meiji Japan.

Although *bunmeikaika* has become the standard representation for the slogan, movement, policy, or historical period to which it is habitually attached, it is but one of a set of synonyms used in Japanese during the 1870s and 1880s.[2] These included the constituent parts *bunmei* and *kaika;* those parts reversed, *kaikabunmei;* and a pair of abbreviations, *kaimei* and *bunka.* All of these served as translation words for the nineteenth-century English and French term "civilisation," introduced to Japan through such works as the histories of civilization by Thomas Henry Buckle and François-Pierre Guizot and popularized through the work of the Meirokusha intellectuals and their critics.[3] As Norbert Elias has recounted in *The Civilizing Process*, this nineteenth-century "civilisation" was the self-conscious representation of the European bourgeoisie, who applauded the superiority of their political, economic, religious, technical, moral, and social institutions. They understood civilization to be the orderly development of the human community patterned by social forces that could be assisted by human intelligence. Social existence was accordingly understood as the process of progress, inaugurated by the eighteenth-century bourgeois takeover of the state, which displaced the decadent aristocracy and their inefficient barriers to trade and development.[4]

The first such uses of *bunmeikaika* and its variations occurred in Fukuzawa Yukichi's *Seiyō jijō* (Conditions in the West), the first two volumes of which appeared on the eve of the Meiji Restoration. Fukuzawa opened the work with a discussion of "civilized political administration" (*bunmei no seiji*), which summarized his observations of Western governments: they promote liberty, religious toleration, the trades and arts, roads, schools, the education of human talent, peace and security, and benevolent institutions for the poor, the sick, and the needy. Fukuzawa also included a section on "world civilization" (*yo no bunmeikaika*), which outlined a commonplace nineteenth-century theory of social progress from savage to half-civilized to fully civilized stages.[5] Given the ease with which Chinese-character words can be metaphorically extended, these were not surprising choices when Fukuzawa sought translation words for civilization, since in the Chinese textual tradition familiar to educated Japanese, *bunmei* and *kaika* referred to the self-conscious patterns defining Chinese civilization.[6]

In short, the compound expression *bunmeikaika* was not completely foreign to Fukuzawa's educated contemporaries, and it took advantage of the familiar pretensions of Chinese claims to universality. From the start it carried a double reference: on the one hand, to a pattern of civilization that deliberately presented an alternative to the long-standing Chinese model and did so with equally universal pretensions; on the other hand, to the promise of Western civilization, its wealth and power produced by the European bourgeois political community. Fukuzawa Yukichi was the most prominent advocate of *bunmeikaika* as a universal civilization; his early works outlined *bunmei* as a universal development—the second volume of *Seiyō jijō* (1867), for example, the series of pamphlets assembled as *An Encouragement of Learning* (1872–1876), and his *Outline of a Theory of Civilization* (1875). To Fukuzawa, it was incidental that this new universal civilization had first been achieved in Europe. He saw evidence that the West was not necessarily going to maintain its lead— if, for example, it insisted on pursuing profit at the expense of public welfare. Fukuzawa was confident he had isolated a set of key determinants of civilization that would serve as goals to encourage Japan's development in such a direction: personal intelligence and morality, collective knowledge and mental advancement, and social order and progress, all of which contributed to the defining aspect of civilization, the spirit of independence. With this set of goals, any nation could aspire to attain civilization.

Most of Fukuzawa's contemporaries, however, were less visionary and more attentive to the desired technology and institutions. Hence Fukuzawa's enthusiastic endorsement of universal civilization was largely eclipsed by the second point of reference implicit in *bunmeikaika:* Western political society and its technological benefits. In this regard, civilization carries the nuance of westernization (*seiyōka*), the process of adopting Western institutions and technology and thereby making Japan more like the West. Such an approach was encouraged during the 1870s in the wake of the Iwakura Mission, which returned to Tokyo in 1873 from an investigation of Europe and the United States. In the course of visiting the United States, England, France, Belgium, Holland, Germany, Russia, Denmark, Sweden, Italy, Austria, and Switzerland, and taking the opportunity to visit government legislatures and courts, mines, foundries, factories, printing offices, navy yards, schools, and trade and industrial organizations, members of the mission gained a comprehensive knowledge of institutional goals for Japan's adoption of Western civilization. Equally important, they returned with firsthand experience of the West—a familiarity shared with those Meirokusha intellectuals who had spent time in Europe and the United States as overseas students. The new leadership and intelligentsia thus had a common understanding of what was required in Japan as they set to work.[7]

As a survey of the development of such civilization in Japan during the 1870s, take, for example, the first "history of Meiji civilization," written by Watanabe Shūjirō and published in 1880. Watanabe sytematically described major accomplishments in the ten areas of political administration, foreign relations, the military, law, political economy, business, "things" (technology), literate culture, religion, and popular customs; each section is largely a narrative of recent events, highlighting government policies and new institutions. "Political administration," for example, covers the moving of the capital from Kyoto to Tokyo, the abolition of the domains and creation of a national administration of prefectures, the political disruptions of the plan to send a punitive mission to Korea, the rise of a political opposition under Itagaki Taisuke, the pressure to establish a national assembly, and the creation of local assemblies. "Literate culture" surveys the development of foreign studies from the Dutch learning schools of the Tokugawa period, the growth of language schools for diplomatic purposes, the creation of the Ministry of Education in 1871, the establishment of schools for commoners and women, normal schools for training teachers, the university for advanced study, museums, libraries, newspapers and the key development of movable type, the problematic effects of the 1875 press laws, and the growth and popularity of public speaking.[8]

Of course, Watanabe's history privileges the official view from Tokyo. The new civilization at the level of daily life—confined largely to major cities through the 1880s—is strikingly revealed in a number of popular lists circulating the streets. One, for example, was a children's rhyme to impress upon youngsters the importance of Western technology. Invented as a ball game, the point of the "civilization ball song" was to have a child recite the names of ten things that would improve Japan—one for each bounce of the ball: "gas lamps, steam engines, horse-drawn carriages, cameras, telegrams, lightning conductors, newspapers, schools, letter post, and steamships."[9] Another such list, composed in the spirit of a comedian's limerick, highlighted telegraphs, steam engines, post offices, elementary schools, newspapers, the national bank, gas lamps, military conscription, the Tomioka silk factory, crude oil, overseas students, meat shops, Sundays, patrolmen, photographs, expositions, brick buildings, rickshas, bankruptcies, steamships, noncirculating gold, horse-drawn carriages, and "everlasting" bridges (built of stone rather than the traditional wood).[10]

As this second list illustrates, the people whose lives were forever changed by the new developments reacted sometimes with irony and parody. Alongside proud reports about the striking progress in civilization and its spread to regional centers, the newpapers of the day include many comical stories that play on the absurd tension between the grand concept of civilization and its more mundane manifestations. A fellow named Okano Kinpei has set up a stand in Ueno Park where he sells confections made of beef and beef hide, which he advertises as "Great Treasures from Mr. Civilization"—hence his creations are labeled "civilized confections." Another report lauds the latest advance—painted lavatories with kerosene lamps. The most common butt of jokes is the new short haircut called *zangiri*; one ditty compares it to the bamboo whisk used in the tea ceremony, while another mocks the "clip clip" of hair-cutting as knocking the head to produce the sound of civilization.[11] In their parodies of changing customs, Japanese critics of civilization resisted the dogmatic criticism of old ways and the thoughtless endorsement of the new. Katō Yūichi, whose *Bunmeikaika* (1873) was the first formal parody to appear, includes a dog's apprehension that civilized dogs are moving next door to his uncivilized neighborhood; the newcomers imitate the ways of Westerners with their food, their freedom, their cleanliness. But Katō's point is explicit in an illustration—whether bareheaded or sporting a bowler, it's a dog's life.[12]

In this regard, the historian Kimura Ki, who has collected a vast array of often hilarious anecdotes about these quotidian manifestations of civilization, described the 1870s as a Don-Quixote-like, mixed-up age: Japanese did not wear the clothes of Europeans, they wore Western clothes; they did not wear Western haircuts, they covered their short hair with bowlers; they spoke English, assuming the French and Germans did too. The Meiji emperor's first handshake occurred with the official visit of the Duke of Edinburgh in 1869; the emperor was first kissed on the occasion of the Italian king's visit in 1880—the former etiquette endured, while the latter induced panic and was not repeated.[13] Irony and absurdity aside, Kimura does point out, much like Elias' description of the "civilizing process" in Europe, that civilization in Japan meant a significant softening of manners and a changed perception regarding such behavior as mixed public bathing, prostitution, and certain aspects of lower-class dress—the *fundoshi* (loincloth) alone on workingmen became no longer acceptable.[14]

Whether universal civilization or westernization, both references for *bunmeikaika* animate two persistent tensions surrounding the importation of Western civilization into Meiji Japan. In the first place, many Japanese were aware that the universal pretensions of Western particularism were precisely the claims of the powerful against the weak. Kido Takayoshi, an initial member of the Meiji oligarchy, observed in 1868 that international law depended on military force; hence the Western nations use the cloak of international law to pursue their own interests in dealing with weaker nations.[15] More than any other issue, the matter of revising the unequal treaties that Japan had been forced to sign with the Western powers at the end of the Tokugawa regime was a controversial reminder for the next five decades that "universality" was an effect of Western interests. In the second place, this importation was debated and resisted on many fronts. Japanese negotiated the degree to which Western ways should be imitated: some resented that the West claimed to be superior in all respects; others like Fukuzawa sought to go further and reformulate civilization beyond its Western particularism toward a truly universal form. If members of the Meirokusha argued the relative merits of introducing romanized script, permitting unrestricted travel by foreigners within Japan, and the equal rights of men and women, others, as we have seen, satirized the witless imitation of Western forms. Two decades later, in the 1890s, resistance to civilization in Japan would be organized in a manner largely borrowed from German resistance to France in the wake of the Napoleonic wars. The nineteenth-century German critique of the dominance of French "civilisation," reified in the German concept of *Kultur*, was taken up by some Japanese intellectuals in the 1890s as *bunka*, which accordingly shifted in meaning from "civilization" to "culture." Where civilization was overly material and technical, *Kultur* was intellectual, artistic, and religious. Where civilization and *bunmeikaika* were allegedly universal, *Kultur* and *bunka* would represent the collective products of national significance.[16]

An Aside: "Civilization and Enlightenment"

But if early Meiji contemporaries referred to *bunmeikaika* and all of its variants as "civilization," one might well wonder why American historians of Japan have typically translated *bunmeikaika* as "civilization and enlightenment" in the postwar period. The current habit is misleading, for the word "enlightenment" per se does not appear in Japanese texts of the 1870s. Instead a variation of the term, "enlightened," appears first in writings related to the Iwakura Mission to Europe and the United States (1871–1873). Iwakura Tomomi noted in his diary during 1871 that the knowledge being transmitted to Japan was "what in English is called *enlightened civilization*, which we translate as *bunmeikaika*." Similarly, Mori Arinori, Japanese ambassador to the United States when Iwakura and his entourage reached Washington, D.C., in 1872, described the West as the "enlightened nations of the earth" characterized by "civilization, or enlightened state of human society." Clearly, early Meiji intellectuals were aware of the pairing of "enlightened" and "civilization." But for both Iwakura and Mori, "enlightened" is attributive and qualifies the independent noun that is properly the basis of attention: civilization.[17]

"Enlightenment" does not appear until the 1880s—and then as a gloss for "civilization." Inoue Tetsujirō added the word to his second edition of *A Dictionary of Philosophy* in 1884, where he translated it as *daikaku*, a "religious" (that is, Buddhist) term for the "great realization" of enlightenment; he also glossed enlightenment as *bunka* (civilization). James Hepburn included "enlightenment" as a secondary translation for *bunmei* (civilization) in the 1886 edition of his famous Japanese-English dictionary. The largely eighteenth-century and French event, the Enlightenment, does not figure in the writings of Meiji intellectuals in the 1870s and 1880s; Fukuzawa Yukichi, for example, does not mention it in his history of France in *Seiyō jijō*.[18] Inoue's third edition of his dictionary in 1912 included an entry for the German word for enlightenment, *Aufklärung*, but explained it as "the elimination of superstition." Hence our current use of *keimō* for "enlightenment" is a later, twentieth-century invention, and the now common reference to Meiji "enlightenment thought" *(keimō shisō)* does not appear to have been given wide credence until the 1954 roundtable discussion sponsored by the journal of social and political commentary, *Shisō*.[19] In fact, the rare usage of *keimō* in early Meiji is in keeping with its meaning in the Chinese tradition, the "opening of childhood intelligence," and thus it appears in the titles of textbooks for children, one of which I describe in Chapter 3, "A Circle of Knowledge for Childhood Instruction" (*Keimō chie no kan*).

This is not to say that all Japanese were unaware of the term "enlightenment," for "civilization" and "enlightenment" functioned as synonyms among some English-speakers in Japan at the time. Translators and editors at the Yokohama English-language newspaper, the *Japan Weekly Mail*, introduced the translation of *bunmeikaika* as "civilization and enlightenment" in the 1870s. Their translations of government pronouncements, memorials to the government, and commentaries on current events in the 1870s and 1880s exhibit a variety of translations as unsystematic as the original Japanese terms—from "civilization and enlightenment" to "enlightenment and civilization" and each term alone.[20]

It is curious, however, that other translators and the academic community were slow to pick up this excessiveness. In a systematic but by no means exhaustive examination of English-language works on Japanese history and culture published between 1890 and 1950, I have not found one usage of "civilization and enlightenment"; scholars routinely translate *bunmeikaika* and its variations as "civilization"—the one curious exception is "Enlightenment and Civilization" in Anesaki Masaharu's *History of Japanese Religion* (1930). Although Nobutaka Ike's *Beginnings of Political Democracy in Japan* (1950) seems to inaugurate the postwar habit of "civilization and enlightenment," not until the appearance of "Studies in the Modernization of Japan" (1965–1971) did American scholars begin to habitually translate *bunmeikaika* as "civilization and enlightenment," and I suspect the reason has to do with an aspiration to "thorough" translation. The English scholar Carmen Blacker, whose biography of Fukuzawa Yukichi, *The Japanese Enlightenment* (1964), is routinely cited for further reading on the matter of "civilization and enlightenment," reproduces the understanding of terms standard among Japanese historians of Japan: "civilization" is the translation for *bunmeikaika* and its variations; "enlightenment" is the translation for *keimō*, that anachronistic choice informed by the wish to find an Enlightenment in Meiji Japanese history analogous to the European Enlightenment and thereby confirm a universal standard of development in Japan's modernization.

My point with this aside is not that translating *bunmeikaika* as "civilization and enlightenment" is a gross error, but that it is misleading, for it masks a critical debate among Meiji intellectuals about how to best introduce "civilization" to Japan—an issue I treat in the following section.

Enlightened Civilization and the Duty of Scholars

By 1873, when the Meirokusha intelligentsia established their forum for debate, the Meiji oligarchy's program of westernization was well under way with the first railway, the beginnings of a national telegraph system, shipyards and model factories, and the reorganization of the military. But the observations made by the Iwakura Mission—as well as by early overseas students and founding members of the Meirokusha—underlined the point that reproducing technology was not enough. Japan was going to have to adopt the educational system and many more Western institutions if it was going to act as an independent nation in international affairs.

Hence the question faced by Meiji leaders and intellectuals was how to set the progress of civilization in motion. To nineteenth-century European theorists of civilization, its development had been largely a natural outgrowth of expanded trade and manufactures—assisted with the creation of overseas colonies for sources of raw materials and markets for the sale of finished goods and, at home, legislative bodies to represent the will of bourgeois "civil society." Progress had a dynamism of its own and was clearly an end in itself. Although Japanese scholars had begun to analyze Western expansion in the eighteenth century—one obscure Dutch learning scholar, Honda Toshiaki, had imagined as early as 1798 a plan of development that linked gunpowder, metallurgy, and gun production to shipping, foreign trade, and colonization— the initial goals of the Meiji Restoration were essentialized in the desire for an "enriched domain and strengthened military" *(fukoku kyōhei).*[21]

These goals were sufficient for initiating the Meiji oligarchy's plans for westernization, but the comprehensive nature of *bunmeikaika* necessitated a more sophisticated linkage of wealth and power to the whole of Western institutions. In rethinking the radical project of reorienting Japan toward the West, the Meirokusha scholars emphasized three goals for importing the new civilization. First, in order to avoid the colonization experienced by India, China, and Africa, Japan needed to reconstruct itself as an independent state based on wealth and power—independence became the end to which wealth and power served as means. Second, to displace the main obstacle to Japan's advance toward such an independent state, namely, the tradition of Tokugawa despotism, Japan would have to introduce a constitutional government and some form of deliberative assembly. Third, in order to prepare the largely backward masses for participation in representative political institutions, schools and programs of education were needed.[22]

At the heart of this set of three goals lies a causal series productive of the whole. In tracing the connections from education and individual productivity to collective governing and to wealth and power, Meirokusha scholars like Fukuzawa Yukichi, Nakamura Keiu, and Mitsukuri Rinshō sought to grasp pragmatic links between the parts and the whole of civilization. Such an understanding of civilization is, I believe, best described as an enlightenment model of progress because the basis of human civilization rests on developing the human mind through education. As people are educated and begin thinking for themselves, they become increasingly capable of independent thought and action. Secure in their rational autonomy, these enlightened individuals pursue their personal interests and develop their individual talents in commerce, manufactures, education, communications, and the arts, and the cumulative results of their labors not only advance national independence but also push all humankind one step further in the development of civilization. Grounding this theory is the principle that human reason gives humankind the power to control both nature and political tyranny, the two major obstacles facing human progress. Hence actualizing this project of civilization depends on the principle of tutelage, overt in the work of the Meirokusha and quite compatible with the former samurai leaders' assumptions of social superiority.

In taking upon themselves the responsibility for enlightening the masses, the Meirokusha scholars—many of whom had earlier served as Western learning scholars under the Tokugawa regime—proceeded with a pedagogy that implicitly reflected key structures of Western society. As we shall see in Chapter 4, their translations and works on Western civilization began with international law in order to establish the roles of states, rights, and sovereignty in international relations; they proceeded with constitutional law, political economy, and civil law in order to explain how political society was formed around free economic activity with some government facilitation or supervision; and they then turned to the "motor" of the system: the initiative of free individuals aware of their social duties and personal interests.[23] Such a project of civilization, Meirokusha scholars noted, recommends that government recognize the personal freedoms and rights bestowed upon each individual by heaven. For only when we secure our rights to freedom of thought, expression, assembly, and property can we support ourselves and engage in the debate that clarifies understanding, ascertains metaphysical truth, advances knowledge, and promotes the progress of human civilization.[24] As I describe in Chapters 5 and 6, the movement for a national assembly would make a fundamental issue of causal sequencing. Is an enlightened state of mind prerequisite to political participation, as the oligarchy and Meirokusha would argue, or does enlightened reason develop with participation, as political rights activists would insist?

Thus the central problematic in promoting civilization in Japan—and one that guided political developments during the early and mid-Meiji periods—was the relationship between the people and the government. Where the European example had been promoted by a new social class of trading and manufacturing entrepreneurs, who in time constituted a new ruling class, the Japanese case—as in every country seeking to industrialize after the model of the West—began with a despotic government attempting to initiate the entire sequence of institutions. There was, in other words, a conflict of interests in the project of civilization: between the government that took charge of development and a people that anticipated participating in government decisions. Eventually, the Meiji Constitution of 1890 would define the people as imperial subjects and minimize their participation, but to the members of the Meirokusha in 1873, it was a question of who should take the initiative—the government or the people? In particular, Fukuzawa Yukichi challenged his fellows by wondering where they, the scholars and educators, fit. In this regard there is a direct connection between the issue of initiative and the movement to establish a national assembly, which erupted as a pertinent test case shortly after the founding of the Meirokusha.

This debate over the duty of scholars is important for two reasons. On the one hand, it was one of the first debates sponsored by the Meirokusha—and one of the first public debates in Japan altogether—and hence the rebuttals to Fukuzawa are interesting both for their content and for their rhetorical strategies.[25] On the other hand, the debate had the momentous consequence of fracturing *bunmeikaika* into two approaches to promoting civilization. Although both *bunmei* and *kaika* continued to mean civilization, and everyone agreed on the principle of tutelage of the people, *bunmei* became the word preferred by Fukuzawa for indicating the universal civilization, cultivated privately by scholars and entrepreneurs, in which Western and Japanese progress would eventually coincide. *Kaika*, by contrast, became the word used by nearly all of his fellows to indicate the public cultivation of civilization through government policy. Hence in the hands of the Meirokusha, *kaika*—the constituent characters of which are active verbs meaning "opening" and "transforming"— had a strong connotation of "civilizing" and "developing." To put it another way: *bunmei* was routinely used as a noun—civilization—and implied the ongoing and total progress of humankind whereas *kaika* was used as an active verb and, when used as a noun, implied the civilizing process directed toward its projected end.[26]

In opening the debate, Fukuzawa argued that in order to support the collective goal of Japan's independence in the world, a balance of power must be achieved between government and people. Fukuzawa compared the nation to a human body, the health of which is maintained by internally managing external stimuli (heat, cold, pain); likewise, the nation tries to maintain political activity by equalizing the internal power of the government and the external power of the people. In other words, the government is like the "life force" while the people provide the "stimulation of external things"; both are necessary to maintain independence. Fukuzawa complained that Japan's progress in civilization had been slow because the government's current approach—to take upon itself the work of instructing the people in the three key areas of learning, law, and commerce—merely reinforced Japan's long-standing authoritarian habits of government. To advance civilization more quickly, the correct alternative was to work at changing the minds and spirits of the people. Fukuzawa systematically dismissed the government, merchants, farmers, nativist scholars, and Chinese learning scholars as inadequate to the task. The one capable group, however, the Western learning scholars, were so busy offering their skills to the government that Fukuzawa judged them unreliable. Hence he challenged his fellow Western learning scholars to become reformers and examples to the people, to keep themselves out of government service and assume a private position from which to pursue learning, law, and commerce—and thereby work to equalize the powers of government and people in support of Japan's independence.[27]

Key to Fukuzawa's argument is his assault on the traditional concept of duty (*shokubun*). His fellow scholars, he argued, no longer owed allegiance to lords and masters, or the government—as had been the case with Tokugawa ethics teachings. Rather their duty was properly directed toward the people—and in a manner that would have once been considered selfish. Fukuzawa insisted that in serving the people and the nation, it was far more important that his fellow scholars act as private persons and pursue personal goals, which would cumulatively contribute to the advance of civilization. It is this last point that helps to distinguish Fukuzawa's position from one more traditionally "Confucian." Both emphasize duty to the people, but Fukuzawa stresses the fact that a scholar too is one of the people, and thus his personal goals coincide with the interests of the people.

Four of Fukuzawa's colleagues responded—Katō Hiroyuki, Mori Arinori, Tsuda Mamichi, and Nishi Amane—and all of them justified their public employment, in effect maintaining the received understanding of duty to government. Katō and Tsuda specifically took issue with Fukuzawa's analogy of "internal life force" and "external stimulation." Katō chose instead to speak of the government as "internal cultivation" and the people as "external stimulation." Given the recent call for a national assembly, he recast the issue as the state's rights versus the people's rights and insisted that internal cultivation was more important at present. Tsuda, by comparison, rejected Fukuzawa's analogy of the nation as a body, reminding him that the people were both external and internal. Hence he recast the analogy in terms of the government as the nation's spirit and the people as the body. The spirit does not command the body; instead, because the body strengthens or weakens according to nurturance, it tires or energizes the spirit. If Tsuda was more willing than Katō to grant the government and people an equal importance, both concluded that Western learning scholars, they themselves, could choose either course of action, in government service or in private undertakings.

Mori Arinori's tactic was novel by comparison. He found fault with Fukuzawa's desire for equal standing between government and people, since the "people" included officials, aristocrats, commoners—everyone. By insisting that government and people are one and the same, and hence obviating any significant difference between a scholar acting as a private person or as an official, Mori shifted the ground of the argument away from a balance of power for the sake of national independence to "public interest," which he explained as the progress of civilization. While Mori concluded the same point about government service and private action, his argument was a powerful and striking attempt to rethink the dichotomy of government and people and to fuse the two in a manner much more in keeping with the mutuality and cooperation implicit in the Western ideal of representative government.[28] The point was wasted on

Nishi Amane, who merely reiterated the position of the oligarchy. Fukuzawa was indifferent to actuality, he claimed; it was entirely appropriate that authoritarian government continue to manage the ignorant people, whose "external stimulation" was a potential problem. Even if Western learning scholars' knowledge was rudimentary, they were a vast improvement upon the hereditary retainers of Tokugawa times, and it was crucial that they serve in government.[29]

In response to his colleagues' rebuttals, Fukuzawa specifically addressed the fears of Katō and Nishi that private persons outside of government would come to rival the power of government as an assembly akin to government. Such a fear, he said, was a small-minded person's theory. Ultimately, private persons and government officials are all Japanese working together for the independence of the nation—exactly what Mori had concluded. In due course, Mitsukuri Rinshō too echoed such an endorsement of civil society, quoting Buckle's *History of Civilization in England* to the effect that the social and public world provides a common denominator: government and its leaders are products of society, and public opinion is the moving force for reform and change.[30] As I describe in Chapter 6, a new conception for society—some way to unite the long-standing opposition between government and people— was slow to develop in Meiji Japan.

Civilization and Language

By determining that the most appropriate way to foster civilization in Japan was to concentrate on educating the masses, the Meirokusha intellectuals begged the question of "the people." Although outspoken members like Nishi Amane and Nishimura Shigeki denounced the people in terms of character— they were "stupid" or "degenerate"—the majority focused on the problem of ignorance. In a somewhat surprising move, several members identified language as the main obstacle to educating the people and proposed reforms that would simplify the written language. The first issue of the *Meiroku zasshi* began with Nishi Amane's famous proposal, "On Writing Japanese with the Western Alphabet," in which he enumerated a set of problems that would occupy Japanese language reformers for well over a century. Indeed, Meirokusha proposals were reiterated a decade later in the successor journals to the *Meiroku zasshi*, and some of these points have continued to circulate into the 1990s. Hence my purpose here is not to recount a history of language reform but to account for the connections between civilization and language as understood by Japanese intellectuals in the 1870s and 1880s.[31]

According to Nishi Amane, the Japanese language in 1873 placed an onerous burden on the student. Nishi deplored the unsystematic state of written Japanese, an admixture of Chinese characters (*kanji*) and the pair of Japanese syllabaries (*kana*): the "square" form *katakana*, akin to our habit of printing, and the "cursive" form *hiragana*, similar to our handwriting.[32] He lamented the arcane variations in pronunciation: one Chinese character may have as many as three standard pronunciations, and *kana* are often not pronounced the way they are written—"*omoshiroshi*," for example, is pronounced "*omoshiroi*." (The final syllable is the effect of an archaic written form.) The written Japanese language included too many different stylistic forms, there was too little connection between writing and speaking in Japan, and the spoken Japanese language was fragmented among regional variations. Unless these daunting obstacles were overcome, there seemed to be little promise of success in educating the people.[33]

Implicit in this argument was the collective personal experience of this group of would-be educators. As members of the former samurai class, nearly all had, at an early age, undertaken the study of literary Chinese at the "Chinese schools" that provided a foundation for the education of the samurai class during the Tokugawa period. They had also acquired a competence with *sōrōbun*, a style particular to letters and formal proposals to superiors, *wabun*, the written form of Japanese poetry, tales, and expository prose, and *wakan konkōbun*, a mixed form of Chinese and Japanese used in medieval war tales and other expository prose.[34] Moreover, in the interests of learning something about the West in the wake of the U.S. Navy's visit in 1853, they had all undertaken Dutch studies, which not only afforded a familiarity with Japanese works about the West but also meant, in most cases, the acquisition of fluency in Dutch, English, French, or a combination thereof. This group shared, then, an exposure to very different and seemingly simpler forms of language and usage—and some accordingly argued that in the interest of reducing the time required to master writing and promoting Japan's progress, Japan's various languages and scripts would have to be somehow simplified in order to construct a Japanese language that would serve as a medium for educating the people.

Apart from the repeated complaints that the written Japanese language encompassed too many forms and was too difficult to master quickly, there was another common complaint: unlike Western languages, Japanese writing bore little connection to Japanese speech. This purported link between writing and speaking in the civilized West was in large measure a consequence of

Japanese scholars' experience with Dutch and other European languages from the sixteenth century on. Japanese learned to read European languages through the mediation of European grammars, dictionaries, and occasional native speakers, and in the process they became acquainted with the European conception of grammar as a unified description of a language defined as a set of speech practices.[35] This desire to unite Japanese speech and writing runs through many proposals for language reform in the 1870s and 1880s. As I have demonstrated elsewhere for the case of Nishi Amane, the logic of the argument relies on a systematic analysis of language as sound, written mark, and meaning, which Nishi derived by juxtaposing Japanese nativist theories of language, which equated sound and meaning, to comparative grammar (encountered in the Netherlands in the 1860s), which equated the written sign and meaning. Nishi's goal was to discover a means of writing Japanese that would conform to the European relation between written characters and meaning.[36]

The practical consequence of this analysis was that when they compared Japanese to Chinese and Western languages, Japanese scholars noted a fundamental pair of differences that threatened the utility of Japanese for importing Western civilization. In the first place, sounds and words are not identical in Japanese, as they allegedly were in English. In the second place, the Japanese *kana* syllabaries (and Chinese characters as well) were a synthetic form that awkwardly joined consonants and vowels. English, it was argued, had the advantage that unified sounds could be constructed from consonants and vowels and function as words. So, for example, the word "march" in English (spoken as one sound and one word) could only be approximated in Japanese with a combination of three Japanese *kana*, "ma-ru-chi"—three separate sounds that, first, failed to sound like one word and, second, failed because *kana* did not distinguish consonants from vowels. (The *kana* syllable "ma" combined what in English is a paired consonant "m" and vowel "a.")

If this argument seems arcane or absurd—which it did to such critics of Nishi as Nishimura Shigeki and Fukuzawa Yukichi—remember that the argument arose from a preoccupation with loanwords, those words borrowed from one language by another. In the same way that "Volkswagen" or "Toyota" has become a word in English today, so too Japanese-speakers were borrowing a great many words for things and ideas in the nineteenth century. But when, for example, they tried to render into Japanese the English loanword "civilisation," which English had already borrowed from French (and some Japanese overlooked the fact that, although the "same" word, its pronunciation differed from French to English), "civilisation" became "shi-bi-ri-ze-sho-n"—a conglomeration of *kana* so awkward that they concluded the Japanese language was inadequate to the task of creating loanwords for borrowing civilization. Hence, as I describe in Chapter 3, Japanese translators in the early Meiji period relied less on loanwords like *shibirizeshon* and more on translation words like *bunmeikaika* that used Chinese characters. These concerns may seem excessive, but because scholars such as Nishi, Shimizu Usaburō, Yatabe Ryōkichi, and Toyama Shōichi (Masakazu) believed there was an essential connection between Western languages and civilization, they analyzed the Japanese language to safeguard against too great a divergence from what was in effect a Western norm. Foremost in their concern was that Japan and the West share a familiar linguistic basis.[37]

The two main strategies for simplifying Japanese that were suggested in the 1870s and 1880s promised a better link between Japan and the West. Both, it was claimed, would help to unify speaking and writing, regularize Japanese pronunciation and grammar, save time in education, spread learning widely among the people, and promote practical learning and progress in civilization. The first of these, advocated by Nishi, Yatabe, Toyama, and others, was to replace Japanese writing with the Western alphabet—or, as it came to be known, to write Japanese with *Rōmaji* or "Roman characters." The use of *Rōmaji*, in light of the interest in loanwords, promised the additional advantage of linking Japanese directly to Western languages, for if Japanese were written with the Western alphabet, Western words could be borrowed directly into Japanese, exactly as they were spelled in English or French, thus permitting Japan to directly incorporate the terms of Western civilization.[38] The alternative, advocated by Shimizu Usaburō and Toyama and more widely endorsed in the 1880s, was simply to write Japanese in *hiragana*, the cursive syllabary. The only difficulty they saw was the occasionally large number of homonyms in Japanese, but they were confident that context would clarify all ambiguities. As in speaking or listening, when one saw a noun like *hashi* in writing, the context would obviously determine whether it meant "bridge" or "chopsticks." To demonstrate that Japanese could be written without Chinese characters altogether—and that the alleged shortcomings of *kana* as a writing system were negligible—Shimizu translated a European chemistry textbook into Japanese using only *hiragana*.[39]

A majority of scholars, however, found both of these proposals unworkable. To write Japanese with *Rōmaji* would overlook national character and history; to write Japanese with *kana* alone simplified nothing unless other reforms were undertaken, such as the revising of archaic written forms. Both proposals promised tremendous inconvenience and inefficiency, and in any case the concern over coordinating sounds and words or consonants and vowels was irrelevant. Fukuzawa Yukichi, Shimizu, and other members of the Meirokusha simply proposed that, for the time being, the leaders of education—themselves—agree to substitute colloquial expressions for arcane Chinese words and constructions and reduce the number of Chinese characters used in writing Japanese. Speaking on behalf of what was to become the de facto practice of forgoing a collective attempt at language reform, Nishimura Shigeki based his opposition on a contrary causal analysis. The problem, he insisted, was not a problem of language; it was a problem of ignorance. As he put it: "Nishi states that when we reform our script, we will smash the ignorance of the people; but I say that if we smash the people's ignorance, we will be able to reform our script." The people must be pushed to set their minds to scholarship, be it native learning, Chinese learning, or Western learning, for a foundation in any school would eventually open the mind to the shortcomings of Japanese speech and writing. Only then might it be appropriate to collectively address the question of reform.[40]

The practical consequence of this decision to refrain from radical language reform was to encourage the Meirokusha intellectuals to persist in writing their form of mixed Japanese, termed *wakan konkōbun* or *kanamajiribun*, which was based on the Tokugawa practices of reordering Chinese writing and translating from European texts into Japanese. It was this form that, from the start, had been the medium for the Meirokusha journal, and it continued to be the primary form of written Japanese used in educational and civilizing texts (see Chapter 3). Through their participation in the central institutions of publishing, journalism, education, and government—and especially at private academies or Tokyo Imperial University—the Meirokusha intellectuals defined by default the terms by which language and learning would proceed during the early Meiji period. It was their language that was educated language—and their learning that was civilized learning—for they produced models and established standards that were in time reproduced widely across the new society under formation. Certain popular texts like Nakamura Keiu's translation of Samuel Smiles' *Self-Help* and Fukuzawa Yukichi's *Encouragement of Learning* were used in schools as textbooks, encouraging in students not only this new ideology of self-improvement through education but also the very style of writing used by Nakamura, Fukuzawa, and their peers in the Meirokusha.[41] Indeed, this somewhat simplified and colloquialized style was identified in the late 1880s as a *futsūbun*, or "common written style," and thereafter became the basis for a national language (*kokugo*).[42]

The Debate over Chinese Learning

But the concern over coordinating Japanese and Western habits of language in the interests of importing Western civilization continued to preoccupy a number of scholars, and increasingly, this concern was not limited to language alone. For implicit in both these plans to reform the Japanese language was a wish to eliminate Chinese characters from Japanese; increasingly the call was raised to eliminate Chinese learning from Japan. In the effort to make Japan more like the West, some Japanese scholars judged China and Chinese learning a handicap to Japan's progress at civilization.

Fukuzawa Yukichi had been largely alone among Western learning scholars in publicly condemning China and Chinese learning in the 1870s. Although Fukuzawa did not advocate eliminating Chinese characters altogether, he voiced a strong opposition to Chinese learning in his popular works of the mid-1870s. Chinese learning was irrelevant to the new civilization of commerce and equality, for it was impractical and directed toward the past. Worse, it was a hindrance to progress because it promoted hierarchy and encouraged a morality that perversely valued self-conceit, insincerity, flattery, slavishness to others, and greed. It minimized intelligence. If anything demonstrated the failure of Chinese learning, it was China's submission at the hands of foreigners.[43] Because of comments like these and widespread public criticism of China in the course of international conflict over the Taiwan Incident in 1874, Nakamura Keiu spoke out in defense of China in the *Meiroku zasshi* in 1875, commending China for its history of great men, its useful inventions and manufactures, and pointing out that Japan had long imported Chinese goods, not least of which was Chinese language. Because it set standards for composition and was conveniently concise, literary Chinese was an excellent medium for expressing ideas and translating foreign texts. Who was to say that the Chinese did not show good judgment in their foreign relations—indeed that China would not one day surpass the West?[44]

Fukuzawa's and Nakamura's preliminary exchange of 1875 was repeated by many more who spoke out against Chinese characters and especially Chinese learning in the 1880s. Three events served as pretexts for the renewed scholarly attack against China: the establishment of Tokyo University in 1877, which created a formal course of study in Chinese learning; the beginning of Japanese conflict with China in 1882 over influence in Korea; and the Sino-French War of 1884 over control of Vietnam. An indication of the rhetorical weakness of the arguments against Chinese characters is their nonspecificity—they were largely inverses of the arguments in favor of writing Japanese in romanization or exclusively with *kana*. Chinese characters, it was alleged, vastly increased the time required for a child's education and thus restricted the spread of learning among the people; they would prolong the disjunction between speaking and writing; and because they created an educational hierarchy that favored students with better capacities merely to remember characters, they inhibited practical learning and progress in civilization. Chinese characters were faulted for being ideographs and thus representations of thoughts—yes, they represented words, as did the units of Western languages, but they were indifferent to the phonic requirements of language properly conceived as analytical units of sound.[45]

Nonetheless, as Fukuzawa and others had already admitted, learning Chinese characters was inconvenient but eliminating them was more inconvenient. A greater problem was the alleged perniciousness of Chinese learning, and the attack against it was led by a number of noted professors at Tokyo University, foremost among them Ariga Nagao, Inoue Tetsujirō, and Toyama Shōichi. Their arguments shared two critical points. In the first place, they saw an essential connection between the Chinese language, the content of Chinese learning, and the kind of civilization China produced. Although Japan had once borrowed this entire complex of culture from China, it no longer served a purpose useful to Japan; and since Japan had set itself the goal of mastering Western civilization, Chinese learning and civilization were no longer relevant. In the second place, by way of causal explanation, the Chinese language and learning exhibited certain inherent patterns of thought that were fundamentally contrary to the needs of Japan and demands of Western civilization: Chinese literate culture was lacking in detail and precision, unable to move from theories and principles to laws, and was thus unscientific.[46]

Inoue specifically targeted the content of Chinese learning, which privileged poetry and history. Chinese poetry, Inoue maintained, emphasized the imagination at the expense of actual affairs, while Chinese history, which ostensibly concerned actual affairs, emphasized antiquity and was hence committed to a certain impracticality for present conditions. According to Inoue, the brevity of Chinese writing—perhaps appropriate for poetry and historical narrative—minimized the need for depth and detail central to Western learning. This inability to grasp depth and detail, and the related shortcoming that

Chinese learning focused primarily on literature, meant that Chinese learning tended to rest content with theories and did not take the next logical step to a description of laws; at the same time, it could discuss principle but could not develop science.[47]

Ariga Nagao offered a deeper analysis of this alleged failure of Chinese learning to comprehend science. He cited a pair of criteria that tainted the totality of Chinese language, learning, and civilization: the "individual" and the "particular," by which he critiqued a Chinese habit of emphasizing the individual thing, in its concrete and idiosyncratic manifestation, at the expense of classes of things. To Ariga, the most obvious problem presented by the Chinese preference for the individual and the particular lay in China's political structure, which lacked fixed systems or regulations and thus endorsed arbitrary rule—demonstrated by centuries of military conquest and dictatorial, hereditary rule. As Fukuzawa, Inoue, and others had already observed, Ariga too noted that Confucianism valorized the unique acts of ancient kings rather than promoting a unified principle like freedom or general systems like constitutionalism as in the West. But even more important was the not-so-obvious. Ariga located the origins of this distortion of the individual and particular in the Chinese language, where Chinese characters relied on physical form to indicate the abstract. To write "a woman in the house" to signify "peacefulness," for example, or to write "a child at an elder's feet" to signify "filiality," was to employ individual and particular physical forms in an effort to attain abstractions.[48] In other words, where another scholar might praise the Chinese language for its capacities to engage in metaphorical extension, Ariga faulted Chinese characters for relying inappropriately on physical metaphors to reach that which has no form: motives, relations, and so on. As a consequence of this writing system, Chinese learning lacked the capacity to state generalizations or describe abstract relations and hence to develop science and foster progress. As Ariga put it: Chinese scholars could competently describe the melting of gold, silver, copper, and iron in terms of their differences, but they could not generalize a unified rule about the melting of metals. Their one success in antiquity, astronomy, was typically a science of individual and particular phenomena.[49]

If the recurring sentiment in these critiques of Chinese learning is that China poses an "old world" obstacle to Japan's growing identification with the new civilization of the West, the response of Chinese learning scholars was in large measure a case of "beating the opposition at their own game." For among the rebuttals by prominent Chinese learning advocates like Nakamura Keiu,

Kawada Kō (Takeshi), and Shigeno Yasutsugu, two points recur. One is the significant utility of Chinese characters as a medium of thought and expression; the other is a series of similarities aligning China and the West. In much the same way that government officials and Western learning scholars always underlined the "practical use" or advantage of *bunmeikaika* civilization, it was a rather simple matter for Chinese learning defenders to refer to common sense when they promoted the usefulness of Chinese characters and literary Chinese— the Japanese writing system already employed Chinese characters and literary forms. As several newspaper editors and advertisements pointed out in reports of a rise in the popularity of Chinese in the late 1870s, every child needed to learn literary Chinese in order to know how to read newspapers and write letters. It was an essential tool for national administration and could only benefit students wanting to pursue careers in government.[50]

But more important, as advocates pointed out, Chinese learning taught a discipline of models or rules that served young minds as a foundation for further branches of learning. Literary Chinese offered a student familiarity with the transmission of meaning in languages generally; or as Shigeno put the matter, it demonstrated with great advantage the structure of language and the analysis of meaning. Nakamura Keiu added further that the structure of Chinese was comparable to English (indeed, both are Subject → Verb → Object languages) and argued that early study of literary Chinese would assist in the study of English and other European languages.[51] Shigeno made perhaps the best case for an eminently practical use for Chinese: if Japan were to create a professional group of translators, by combining Chinese learning with the work of the former Nagasaki translators (Japanese who learned spoken Dutch in order to translate for Dutch merchants during the Tokugawa period), then Japan could only benefit from their services in the course of relations with China—as might have happened during the Taiwan Incident of 1874.[52]

In addition to the similarities observed between Chinese and European languages, the defenders of Chinese learning further noted that specialized studies in the West had their precedents in China: ethics and religion; politics and law; and history, literature, and the arts.[53] Although Kawada voiced the largely discredited opinion that Western learning had originated in China (what was lost in ancient China developed into Western learning through contacts between China and Rome), Shigeno and Nakamura were content to stress the comparative and foundational possibilities of Chinese learning.[54] In what was perhaps the definitive defense of Chinese learning, Nakamura Keiu articulated in 1887 pursuasive conceptual foundations for the value of Chinese learning for Japan. Drawing on his earlier rebuttal of Inoue's criticisms, in which he pointed out the relativity of the categories "imaginary" and "actual," Nakamura extended his analysis to the opposition of "truth" and "delusion," which, he contended, had been equated respectively with, on the one hand, science and Western learning and, on the other hand, religion and Chinese learning. Nakamura asserted that just as science and religion each contain a measure of truth and delusion—truth for a scientist is, after all, only unchanging certainty, which describes the faith of a religious believer—so too do Chinese and Western learning. Nakamura's goal was to overturn the alleged opposition between the two: the truisms that science and religion were enemies, that Chinese and Western learning were incompatible. In the same way that truth and delusion mix with each other, so too did scientific observations in China and the West, as well as religious sentiments in China and the West, mingle their contents and appear the same instead of different.[55]

If one man's scientific truth is another's religious truth, the criterion that would help one to distinguish civilized truth from barbarian delusion is "the human heart and morality." To Nakamura, civilized people express the greatest need for, and give greatest weight to, the benefits of heart and morality in distinguishing truth from falsity. In opposition to Ariga's claim that Chinese sacrificed abstract thought to physical form, Nakamura pointed out that the ultimately significant needs of religion and ethics were precisely formless— and identical in China, the West, and even Japan. Drawing on his command of English and Chinese, Nakamura noted the parallel terminology uniting Western and Chinese religious and ethical sensibilities: God, heaven, spirit, providence, desire, and conscience. Both Chinese and Western philosophers urged humankind to respect heaven, to love one's fellow man, to use one's conscience to fulfill one's duty, and to love one's person and country. Ultimately, according to Nakamura, scientific and religious truth were united in morality, which is why Chinese and Western learning shared three fundamental impulses: the "way of heaven," which pursued knowledge of the origin of heaven, earth, and all things; the "innate principle of human nature," which pursued the moral knowledge of human society and government; and natural science or "the examination of things," which pursued a perfect knowledge of natural principles. Nakamura's syncretic sensibility, however, did not limit him to advocating only points in common. He faulted small-minded Confucians for limiting themselves to the traditional branches of Chinese learning—statecraft, political economy, and moral values—and insisted that Chinese learning in the new age of civilization would have to attend to matters of liberty, rights and duties, the joint rule of constitutional government, and republican political administration. In other words, Nakamura imagined that a synthesis of Chinese and Western learning would be most beneficial to the new Japan.[56]

Civilization and Moral Character

Nakamura Keiu's lone defense of Chinese learning among the Meirokusha scholars was not a sign of his fellows' indifference. Indeed a number of them were keenly aware of the contributions Confucianism had made to social order and stability during the rule of the Tokugawa shogunate. Although they agreed with Fukuzawa that Confucianism had encouraged a deplorable subservience among the people, at the same time they recognized that it had also promoted the virtues of mutuality, sincerity, honesty, and loyalty. The eruption of conflict among the ruling oligarchy in late 1873 over the punitive expedition to Korea—manifested in a series of localized samurai rebellions and the movement to establish a national assembly in 1874—convinced some of Nakamura's peers that the growth of bad behavior among segments of the Japanese people was a sign that the new civilization needed to do more than focus on technology and material things. And the problem was not limited to dissenters alone, for the oligarchy and its civil servants frequently acted with the arrogance and despotism that the Meiji Restoration had been intended to eradicate. Given that former samurai, who should know better, were so selfishly disrupting the nation, measures should be taken to promote everyone's good behavior. As Nishimura Shigeki lamented in 1875, Confucianism was on the decline but nothing had been introduced from the West to replace it.[57] It was very clear to the Meirokusha scholars that Western civilization too encompassed systems of ethics; in addition to Christianity, the West included a number of other philosophical and religious teachings that preserved the excellence of peoples and nations, maintaining their wealth, power, and independence.

Hence, aside from the mere momentum of Chinese learning as an established department at Tokyo Imperial University and the mainstay of a number of private academies, Nakamura and his fellow advocates salvaged Chinese learning precisely on this point of its utility for ethics education. Generally two approaches to the problem of moral instruction were pursued by Meiji intellectuals: ethics teaching and national character. The first of these, which would ultimately define the terms of ethics in Meiji Japan, was largely the work of Nishimura Shigeki and Sakatani Shiroshi, both of whom were responding to two important debates that ensued between 1872 and 1874: on the separation of government and religion and on religious freedom (see Chapter 4). Although the majority of the Meirokusha supported the division of church and state in order to safeguard religious freedom, both Nishimura and Sakatani sought to preserve a place for state encouragement of ethical behavior. Both realized the risk in advocating Confucianism at a time when Chinese learning was generally under attack, and so their strategy was identical to that of Nakamura—to define fundamental ethical principles common to China, Japan, and the West. By minimizing significant differences between one or another tradition, Nishimura and Sakatani appealed strongly to all parties regarding the need for ethics education.[58]

Nishimura took a position like that of Nakamura Keiu: a country's customs and people's behavior were the criterion for determining whether the country was civilized or not. Hence, he asserted, the improvement of customs was a matter of national concern. Both Western and Chinese learning understood man to be a creature formed of "animal instincts" (or desires) and "rational instincts" (heaven's reason); the latter informed the conscience that governed individual behavior. As in China and Japan, Westerners too saw the cultivation of individual behavior as the foundation of a good nation, for good individuals meant that families were well managed, that a country was properly administered, and that peace reigned among the people. Hence, Nishimura concluded, both ethics and government administration were united in the work of promoting rational behavior.[59]

Sakatani too framed his discussion in terms of human self-mastery by means of moral principles, but he was especially interested in discussing behavior in terms of good and evil. Evil led to barbarism; good was the foundation of a nation; and the foundation of the good, in turn, is a deep integrity. Sakatani developed this concept of *shin*, "living up to one's word" and hence truthfulness or integrity, to demonstrate a link between ethics and religion. Sakatani was alarmed by Nishi Amane's discussion of *shin* as belief or faith in the context of religion, which Nishi defined as utterly personal and intuitive and thus beyond human comprehension and heaven's reason. But at the same time, Nishi declared that belief is "the source of human virtue and the foundation of conduct"—one must have belief in order to be benevolent and loyal. To Sakatani this seemed to disengage *shin* and other Confucian virtues from reason altogether, and hence he recalled Confucius' statement that "without integrity, people cannot be upright." Without integrity, passion flourishes, conscience withers, and the human community experiences disorder—

disharmony in republics and disagreement in parliaments. Rather than leave the moral foundations of a good society to religious teaching alone, he advocated ethics teaching to cultivate good conduct, character, and customs. Agreeing with the majority of his peers, he acknowledged that the enlightened countries of the West had separated government and religious doctrine to avoid the harm produced when governments attempted to compel their subjects to one or another religious belief. Accordingly, when he observed that Japan's corrupt leaders ignored their own habits and conduct—that the very implementers of civilization mistook liberty for license, thus threatening Japan with the national decline experienced by Athens and Rome—Sakatani appealed to his fellows and leaders to support, not religious teaching, but a broad program of ethics teaching to cultivate good conduct and character. Ultimately, both Sakatani and Nishimura agreed, it is the leaders and upper classes of a society who set the standard for customs and conduct, as the people below look up to them. Their vision of ethics education relied on a traditionally Confucian equivalent of tutelage quite compatible with the enlightenment model of civilization.[60]

A second way in which Meirokusha scholars phrased the need for moral instruction was in terms of "popular" or "national character." Nakamura Keiu questioned whether a mere change of government like the restoration was expected to reform the character of the Japanese people, to rectify their subservience, their ignorance, their dependence, their general lack of virtue. He reasoned that civilization could not improve degenerate customs if it were confined to the materialism of arts and techniques alone. Nishi Amane echoed this skepticism in a critique of despotic government, which he claimed had produced the servility of the people and had perverted loyalty into cruelty and directness into deviousness. Both Nakamura and Nishi recommended an educational program that would impart knowledge and develop character. Nakamura insisted that in addition to Western learning in the arts and sciences, some form of moral or religious instruction was necessary. Nishi, for his part, imagined that national character could be improved through the study of law, which would produce the individual autonomy that grounded political and moral character and served as a foundation for constitutional government.[61]

Although Nakamura seems to have limited his interest in ethics education to the general goal of improving the people's customs, the path charted by Nishi, Nishimura, and Sakatani proved more compelling in the long run, for they imagined a program of moral education that created a national character useful to the nation by promoting virtues which would serve the nation's interests. If Nakamura's defense of Chinese learning paved the common ground for a discussion of ethics education, Sakatani's contributions to the Meirokusha opened the door to values that would inform the Meiji Constitution of 1889 and the Imperial Rescript on Education in the subsequent year. In two public speeches, "An Opinion on Nurturing Human Spirit" and "On Descending from Heaven," Sakatani laid the groundwork for a theory of nationalism that both endorsed and challenged the universality of *bunmeikaika* civilization. "On Descending from Heaven" drew attention to the issue of multiple perspectives on the world and the work of rational thought in making distinctions among things. Those who take the position of heaven's reason and try to see things rationally from a universal point of view do attempt to practice a morality that values justice, but at the expense of making no distinction between, for example, their own fathers and the fathers of others. Like Zen Buddhists or Daoists, they end up denying the difference of good and evil; at worst, their behavior becomes libertine—they would not even be bothered by the destruction of family and nation. By contrast, those who take the utterly human perspective on this world may fulfill their duties to fathers and lords honorably but at the risk of missing the vastness of reason and sinking into self-centeredness. The middle ground that Sakatani proposes recalls Reinhart Koselleck's discussion of the new space of modern experience: the country in which one is born, which gives us our parents, families, friends, and rulers, and which promises a reasonable position for making the important distinctions in human life—that one honors one's own ruler more than the rulers of others, that one honors one's own father more than the fathers of others. The universal point of view affords an understanding of the principles at work in the world, but after "descending from heaven" to one's nation, one grasps the course of action necessary to maintain one's own nation's independence in the world.[62]

To be sure, Sakatani is proposing little more than Fukuzawa had already advanced in his *Outline of a Theory of Civilization*—that the reforms introduced with *bunmeikaika* were collectively directed toward the goal of national independence. Like Fukuzawa, Sakatani observed that the progress of civilization was prompted by warfare and other forms of struggle and consolidated by scholarship and wealth.[63] But Fukuzawa faulted Japanese development at the point where Tokugawa despotism discouraged samurai retainers from developing the individuality so central to Western struggle and progress, while Sakatani criticized despotism for inhibiting the expression of human power, which he understood to be the dynamic cause nurturing the human spirit.

To Sakatani, everything depends on the creation of technology ("tools and machines"): education in the technical arts develops thinking and skills, which encourage the production of technology, which forms the ground of morality. Only after a people have a division of labor based on available technologies do they reach a level of civilization in which morality can develop; hence moral instruction in Japan could be expected to proceed in tandem with the development of technology through Western learning. But Sakatani broadened the expression of human power beyond the expansion of minds and development of tools to include training in martial arts, which would safeguard the individual and nation from external injury. He recognized that he might be criticized for advocating barbarism and thinking contrary to the goals of civilization, but he assured his fellows that he was not simply another samurai lamenting the demilitarization of his former class; rather, he applauded the fact that military specialization was now the prerogative of the new army and navy. But in the same way that physical training was central to general education in Germany, so too should Japanese students undertake both gymnastics and the martial arts. The latter would assist in nurturing their spirits, would foster courage and patriotism, would serve the people well on the battlefield, and would create the foundations for Japan to emerge as the great civilized power in East Asia.[64]

Sakatani and Nishimura worked together to promote ethics education in Japan, founding the Tokyo Society of Scholars for Ethics Education (Tōkyō shūshin gakkai) in 1876. Although Sakatani died soon after in 1881, Nishimura subsequently centered his career on ethics instruction. He reorganized the Tokyo Society as the Japanese Society for Expanding Morality (Nihon kōdō kai) in 1887—an organization that remains in existence today—and served as its president until his death in 1902.[65] Through his textbooks on moral instruction and his work with the Japanese Society for Expanding Morality, Nishimura articulated ethical principles that would supplement Western learning in the effort to mold a good people and nation. His *Elementary Instruction in Ethics* (1880), which was officially adopted by the Ministry of Education for use in public schools, synthesized an eclectic range of precepts— excerpted from Chinese, Western, and Japanese texts—on scholarship, livelihood, the will to succeed, cultivating virtue, nurturing wisdom, managing affairs, family ethics, and social interactions. The section on cultivating virtue, for example, includes Chinese classics like the Confucian *Analects* and *Mencius*; Western texts like the Wisdom of Solomon and Samuel Smiles' *Self-Help*; and Japanese ethics texts from the Tokugawa period such as the

Great Learning for Women and the *Yamato zokkun* (Instruction in Japanese Custom).[66]

During the 1880s, moral instruction became the site in which Chinese learning regained respectability by mediating Japan's complex traditions and the widespread westernization under way in the Meiji period. To put the point of this chapter another way: in the face of two profound destabilizations—on the one hand, the displacement of many Tokugawa institutions and traditional technologies with Western alternatives; on the other hand, the political and social assumptions questioned by the shift in institutions and technologies—Chinese language and learning mediated between Japan and the West. In retrospect, it becomes especially clear why the Meirokusha scholars were so dismayed by Fukuzawa's attempt to redefine a scholar's duty in a way that eliminated government service. From the perspectives of both the enlightenment model of civilization and the Confucian theory of behavioral modeling, it was entirely appropriate that the intellectually, morally, and socially superior members of society undertake the education of the masses. If *bunmeikaika* civilization ultimately encouraged individual autonomy among the people—and the Meirokusha generally supported that program—it became all the more important that they were tutored as thoroughly as possible, especially since a segment of the former samurai was already stirring up trouble and setting a bad example. Hence it only made sense that government undertake the effort to build character and prepare the people for political participation, since it occupied the most influential position among the people. As we shall see in subsequent chapters, the terms by which this tutelage proceeded—liberty, rights, and society—became sites of debate over the meanings of these new concepts and the actions they represented. The received notion of duty—loyalty to one's superior in fulfilling one's allotted task—could not be jettisoned when so much was at stake. Before Fukuzawa's vision could be actualized, where an individual's self-interest defined a common good, the political situation and the course of civilization demanded stability among the people.

3

Translation Techniques and Language Transformations

The project to import Western civilization into Japan made a necessity of managing differences of language, for westernization confronted the Japanese with the problem of engaging foreign things and ideas signified in different codes of language. As we have seen in Chapter 2, the Meiji Restoration made Western civilization an official goal, and soon the enlightenment model of civilization had located a series of problems in popularizing westernization for the Japanese public: first the issue of educating the people in preparation for intelligent participation, then the question of how best to encode Western knowledge into the Japanese language, and finally the uncertain facility of the Japanese language to transcode Western terminology into a Japanese idiom. This chapter turns to the actual practices implicit in the second and third of these problems: how Western knowledge was in fact translated into Japanese. This raises a related question: how did the Japanese language change as Japanese scholars and educators began to write and translate materials on westernization in the 1860s and 1870s?

Two critical processes were under way by the 1870s among aspiring westernizers. In the first place, many scholars were involved in translating Western texts and ideas into Japanese—work that necessarily involved the creation and dissemination of new terminology. This work had been given official urgency by the Tokugawa shogunate's need for information on international law after the signing of treaties with the United States, Holland, and other Western powers in 1858. In addition to a Chinese translation of Henry Wheaton's *Elements of International Law*, which was imported in 1865 and reworked into several Japanese translations over the next decade, the shogunate encouraged several works on international law, natural law, and constitutional law, which were undertaken at the official foreign studies institute, the Bansho shirabesho. Translators then focused on the political economy and political administration of the West—especially England and the United States—to glean information about the origins of its wealth and power. Fukuzawa Yukichi's *Seiyō jijō* (Conditions in the West), which included both his firsthand descriptions of the West and his translation of a large part of William and Robert Chambers' *Political Economy*, was widely read and reprinted from 1866; Nakamura Keiu followed his celebrated translation of Samuel Smiles' *Self-Help* in 1870 with J. S. Mill's *On Liberty* in 1871. As I show in this chapter, translation techniques developed quickly in the 1870s before settling into a rather routine practice in the 1880s.

In the second place, certain scholars imagined transforming the Japanese language in order to incorporate Western words and ideas more efficiently and thereby more readily enlighten the Japanese people. Nishi Amane advocated replacing the Japanese script with the Latin alphabet, a step that would allegedly allow European concepts to be incorporated directly into the Japanese language. Others like Shimizu Usaburō imagined reducing the complexity of written Japanese through the exclusive use of the cursive *hiragana* syllabary. Still others called for modifying the written Japanese language in order to make writing accord with spoken Japanese. Such interest in transformation culminated in the Genbunitchi (vernacular) movement of the late 1880s and 1890s—which, as Yamamoto Masahide and Nanette Twine have thoroughly documented, was most successful among newspaper journalists and practitioners of the Western-style novel.[1] Although the early translators and educators under review here were largely uninvolved in "vernacularized writing"—Fukuzawa Yukichi was a prominent exception—their habits of translation nonetheless began to transform the written Japanese language in the 1870s.

It is in the context of these two processes, translation and transformation, that we can begin to understand key decisions through which the Japanese language began to assume its present written form. First, the vast majority of translation words were created in Chinese characters, and in the early 1880s, largely through the efforts of Inoue Tetsujirō and Kikuchi Dairoku at Tokyo Imperial University, scholars began to standardize translation words for Western concepts. Second, although the typescript used in works related to civilization was initially the mixed form of Chinese and *katakana*, during the 1880s Japanese began to print these works in the cursive *hiragana* script rather than in the square *katakana* as had been standard during the 1870s. And third, Ōtsuki Fumihiko introduced in 1884 the category of loanwords (*gairaigo*) and *katakana* was reserved for encoding these non-Japanese terms. Gradually, Japanese translators came to prefer transliterated loanwords instead of Chinese-character translation words. In certain respects, the development of a unified language and standardized printing for westernization can be interpreted as one of many effects of the centralization undertaken by the Meiji government.

But let us pause to reconsider the problem of translating Western knowledge into Japanese. Translation is best understood as a referential operation whereby words, phrases, and statements of one language are used to refer to those of another language. Simply put: translation is an effort to produce an adequate set of correspondences between two (or more) languages.[2] I stress "adequate" because a language is not a simple code like the Morse code—a list of equivalences insofar as a given array of dots and dashes is held to correspond, element to element, to a given series of alphabetic letters. As I argued earlier in my critique of semantic transparency, meaning is not fixed in words once and forever; rather, the meaning of words can both change and be contested.[3] Hence when Japanese undertook to translate a Western concept, they had to evaluate the possible meanings in one or several European languages and then figure out a way to convey that meaning in Japanese. To recall an example from Chapter 2: if Fukuzawa Yukichi first translated "civilisation" as *bunmei* and later as *bunmeikaika*, and others in turn used *kaimei*, *kaika*, or *bunka,* the process by which these all came to be equated with "civilisation" was haphazard. Only through reuse can an instance of word usage become a general meaning for a word.

To put the point in the technical terms of linguistics: the individual usage or instance of a term—called the sign token (such as Fukuzawa's use of "*bunmei*" in the first volume of *Seiyō jijō*)—is a usage of language different from the general use of *bunmei* at the time—the sign type—to mean "Chinese civilization." Because signs signify, Fukuzawa could make use of *bunmei*, which existed in the general vocabulary as "universal civilization" (especially the Chinese variety). But signs also interpret. Thus his specific usage of *bunmei* (as a sign token) exploited the interpretive capacity of (the sign type) *bunmei* and began to shift its meaning from "universal Chinese civilization" to "universal Western civilization." It is this capacity of signs to double as types and tokens that makes them amenable to metaphoric shifts and changes in meaning. Hence repeated use of sign tokens contributes to the modification of a sign type; as Japanese reused Fukuzawa's example of *bunmei*, it assumed the new general meaning of Western civilization.[4]

Because there are no ready equivalents for such translations of concepts, Japanese translators were often faced with a serious incompatibility between Japanese and European conceptions. Take, as an extended example, a concept that motivated the Perry expedition and subsequent U.S. treaty with Japan: "international law," which was translated first in China and then Japan as *bankoku kōhō* (C: *wanguo gongfa*), the "public law of all countries," where *hō* (C: *fa*) can mean "law" in the sense of common standards of behavior—those regulations, orders, and penal reprisals established and upheld through the power and authority of the absolute ruler (corresponding somewhat to "positive law" in Europe). To many Japanese, international behavior was neither so consistent nor so subject to a sovereign power as to warrant the designation of "law" in Japanese. Although they understood that *kōhō* did attempt to refer to principle in order to preclude a simple reliance on arbitrary force, the divergence of behavior from normative expectations begged the question of the status of "law."

To make sense of this largely incompatible European notion of "law," translators initially engaged certain Confucian habits of thought. The first scholars translated into Japanese, Henry Wheaton and Simon Vissering, followed Hugo Grotius in grounding international law in natural law. International law was not a body of positive law but the operation of natural law among the natural community of nations. As a branch of natural law, its orderliness was an emanation of God's creation ("natural order"), which humankind could grasp through the power of human reason granted by God ("natural reason"). W. A. P. Martin and Nishi Amane, the translators of Wheaton and Vissering, respectively, translated divine agency into Confucian idioms: "heaven-actualized" (C: *tianran*/J: *tennen*) and "naturally so" (C: *ziran*/J: *shizen*). But the dominant conception of law common to China and Japan—regulations, orders, and punishments—contradicted such a representation of "natural law" as a pattern of human behavior inferred from a hypothetical and prior state of nature, from which humankind had necessarily departed in order to come under the sovereign rule of positive law. Chinese philosophers in antiquity had grounded human morality in human nature and were content to describe universal habits of civilized behavior in terms of cultivating human nature (*xing*); these ideas remained central to Confucian philosophy in both China and Japan; and accordingly, the translation of "natural law" in Wheaton and Vissering, *xingfa* (J: *seihō*), was a peculiar oxymoron. Martin and Nishi turned to the neo-Confucian concept of "natural principle" (C: *xingli*/J: *seiri*) to explain the regularity accorded to natural law; in effect, "law" could be interpreted as "principle"—the principle that informed the regularity of the seasons and the ideal behavior of human society.[5]

Nonetheless, some Japanese objected immediately to the representation of international law as *kōhō*, public or official law, on a number of grounds. In the first place, such an appellation suggested that the community of nations constituted a public entity. Given that one thread of political rhetoric during the Tokugawa period had attempted to establish the public interest in the Tokugawa shogun's rule, when Martin and his Japanese interpreters asserted that international law is based on the public authority of "justice," which Martin translated as *gongyi* (J: *kōgi*)—a satisfactory term in Chinese meaning "honorable by official standards"—one Japanese connotation of *kōgi* was the attempt to justify the collective nature of the Tokugawa shogunate's personal rule. Even as nativists and other anti-shogun factions were protesting the illegitimacy of the shogunate and demanding a return to imperial rule, the suggestion that a set of alliances with and among barbarians constituted a new official political order was simply obnoxious.[6] In the second place, based on their experience with Americans and Europeans in the 1850s and 1860s, many Japanese statesmen concluded that the international law of the West was a set of proposals bearing little relation to actual practice. They objected to the characterization of Western principles of action as "law"—models of behavior—because Western practices seemed instead to reflect the more obvious value of "might."[7] And in the third place, a nativist scholar like Ōkuni Takamasa objected to the Western origins of international law; his response to Wheaton, titled *The New, True Law of Nations*, protested that this new, Western international law was no more valid than the imperial Chinese arrangement forced on Japan centuries earlier. Both of these barbarian efforts to dominate Japan were doomed to failure because both failed to take into account Japan's superior position among the peoples of the earth. Neither the Confucianism of Chinese pretensions nor the Christianity of Western conceits offered true ethical principles by which the nations of the world could be ranked; only Japan's divine creation and the principles thus available in Japanese Shintō promised a just order for humankind.[8] The analogy between law and *hō* could not hold: no ruling power or authority existed that could enforce such a public set of laws—and to describe the principles asserted in books of *kōhō* as law was to beg the question of what authority could possibly guarantee that all nations would uniformly maintain these "laws." The Western imperialism by which Japan was coerced into the family of nations convinced some Japanese that international law was merely a capricious subterfuge masking the fact of Western force.

But these Japanese were not alone in objecting to the putative authority of international law. European scholars too had voiced some doubt about the wisdom of calling such divergent behavior the "law of nations," but these objections had been forgotten by the time Japan encountered the new science of international law. J. M. Gerard de Rayneval, Jeremy Bentham, and John Austin had admitted that in the absence of a sovereign power which could make and enforce laws, the "general opinions current among nations" did not deserve the name of law. To Rayneval, the law of nations was simply "rules of conduct"; Austin argued that it was more properly called "international morality"; Bentham proposed doing away with the law of nations and creating instead a new science, called "international law," which would empirically describe rules of international behavior as they are observed. For his part, Henry Wheaton followed both Bentham's suggestion, as he systematized his learned observations of international practice as the "elements of international law," and the lead of Rayneval and Austin, when he parted from the earlier tradition, established by Grotius, of discussing the laws of war and peace and instead categorized his observations as the "rights of nations" in war and in peace.[9] What is "right" in international relations if not an attempt to assert power on the authority of a principle based on questionable precedent?

The Japanese were not the first, in other words, to point out the ambiguity surrounding the authority and status of so-called international law. It was a concept contested in Europe, and the work of Japanese translation necessarily engaged this contestation of meaning. Not until 1874, with the publication of his *Hyakuichi shinron*, did Nishi Amane differentiate Confucian notions of rule by ritual pattern and morality from Western notions of governing by law, freeing *hō* from its initial connotations.[10]

Authenticity and Accessibility

Hence when Japanese undertook the work of translation, they were faced with the difficulties of shifting or incompatible meanings of words, which they of course had to address in the texts in which these words were embedded. My understanding of the solutions produced by translators relies on a pair of analytical constructs—authenticity and accessibility—which relate the three components in the act of translation: first, the translator, who has some grasp of the languages of the source text and the languages of his new text; second, the pair of texts, the text being translated (called the original or "source" text) and the new ("target") text, the translated text as a new version of the original; and third, the audience of the new, target text—the imagined readership on whose behalf the translator produces the target text. (There is also the audience of the original text, but this audience is largely irrelevant to the act of translation.)

Authenticity and accessibility are overlapping criteria that evaluate the translator's emphasis in the work of translation: does the source text, the target text, or the target audience take priority? Authenticity draws attention to the fact that Japanese translators approached their problem as one of successfully reproducing a text for the Japanese reader that seemed genuinely to correspond to the original. One could privilege the source text and try to produce an accurate or ideally equivalent text—thereby giving one's readers access to the source text. In this case, the authenticity of the new text follows from the prestige of the source text and the perceived fidelity of the new text to the source text. Certain medieval European translators, for example, attempted to reproduce the grammatical word order of the original; hence Jerome's Latin translation of the Bible (the Vulgate) mimics with peculiar effect the word order of the Greek Septuagint.[11] By contrast, one could privilege the target audience and produce a variant or "interpretive" text, which may be imaginably more suited to target readers and thereby make the original more accessible to the target reader but at the risk of being less exacting a version of the original. In such a case, the target audience receives the more accessible new text with the experience of an authentic fit between the text and their world.

Accessibility, by comparison, refers to how the translator approaches the problem of producing a new, target text that can be read by target readers. If authenticity compares the source and target texts and their imagined worlds, accessibility evaluates the new text in its relationship to the source text and the target audience: is the source text or the target audience the primary point of access? The translator may try to make the source text accessible by rendering a new version that exhibits fidelity to the original; one could also privilege the target audience and adjust one's fidelity to the original accordingly. Translations do not so much attempt only one or the other approach as they combine both alternatives. But the interpretive translation that privileges the target audience is more likely to be expressed in familiar or "reader-friendly" language that simplifies or otherwise interprets the original. In acts of translation, authenticity and accessibility interact in varying combinations to inform the translator's negotiations between text and imagined audience.[12]

A specific example will help to explain the significance of these interpretive criteria: the series of translations based on a British primer titled in English *Graduated Reading; Comprising a Circle of Knowledge in 200 Lessons* and, in Chinese, *Zhihui qimeng shuke*. Published in Hong Kong in 1856 and 1864 by the London Missionary Society, the primer was largely the work of James Legge, who hoped to teach Chinese lads the English language and the ordinary branches of an English education in progressive steps: from simple facts in noun form, to information in sentence form, to, finally, the exertion of the reasoning powers.[13] Because *Graduated Reading* is bilingual—the top half of the page is in English, the bottom in literary Chinese—it emphasizes the practice of language transcoding, for the presence of two languages accentuates the fact of two comparable constructions. (See Figure 1.) A second pedagogical goal, reflecting a Victorian missionary ideology traceable to an alliance of utilitarianism and the evangelical movement in Britain, is the understanding that the diffusion of useful knowledge benefits not only individuals but society as a whole. The primer asserts the dependent relationship of man to God, the usefulness of God's creation to man, and the duty of each individual to improve himself—to make himself useful to society. Great Britain persistently serves as the point of reference and the example of an enlightened and superior society.[14]

As one of many Chinese books about Western civilization imported to Japan in the mid-nineteenth century, Legge's primer especially appealed for its overview of enlightened civilization and its stress on the utility of both Western knowledge and the individual to the nation. A second edition was reprinted in Edo (Tokyo) in 1866, and in the course of the next decade at least eight versions of the text were produced, several with multiple editions, so that

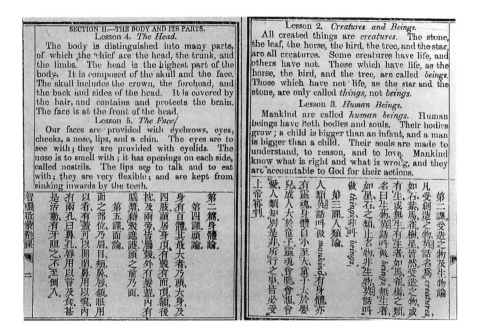

Figure 1. Lesson 4 ("The Head") in James Legge, *Graduated Reading.*

one scholar has identified a total of fifteen printings between 1866 and 1876. Because the reorganization of local government in 1871 and the Education Law (Gakusei) of 1872 encouraged the development of educational materials, the majority of these texts were published between 1872 and 1876.[15]

The most frequently and widely reprinted of these Japanese versions was that made by Uryū Tora, with Chō Sanshū, titled in the edition at my disposal *Keimō chie no kan*, or *A Circle of Knowledge for Childhood Instruction.*[16] Uryū and Chō were officials in the Ministry of Education when they published their version of Legge's primer, and it was likely because of their contacts through the ministry and their location in the new capital, Tokyo, that their text circulated more widely than any other. Their version of the primer strikingly shifts the point of reference to Japan and the Japanese state, which strengthens a nationalistic Japanese point of view in the text. Correspondingly, it is printed in a cursive *hiragana* script, a written Japanese style that emphasizes its Japanese aspects over Chinese, verging on what Japanese at the time would have called *wakan konkōbun* (mixed writing of Japanese [*hiragana*] and Chinese). (See Figure 2.)

By contrast, a much rarer and more regional version of Legge's primer was

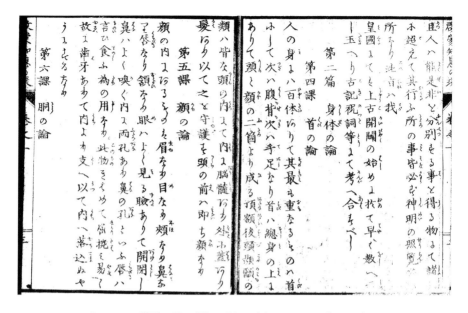

Figure 2. Lesson 4 ("The Head") in Uryū Tora, *Keimō chie no kan.*

that prepared with the authority of the Ishikawa prefectural schools by a pair of teachers in Kanazawa, Hirose Wataru and Nagata Tomoyoshi. Titled *Chikan keimō wakai*, or *A Circle of Knowledge for Childhood Instruction, Reworked into Japanese*—by which they meant that they had reordered the literary Chinese of Legge's text into the syntax of Japanese (a practice to which literary Chinese was routinely submitted)—Hirose and Nagata's text is a rather verbatim translation of Legge's primer. They typically reproduce the actual language of Legge's Chinese interspersed with verb endings and syntactic connections printed in the *katakana* or "square" syllabary of Japanese; this manner of printed text is known as *kanamajiribun* ([Chinese] writing mixed with *katakana*), the style typically used during early Meiji in texts concerned with westernization.[17] (See Figure 3.) Such *kanamajiribun* texts bear an awkward formality because they stress the Chinese aspects of written Japanese and the foreign references of the things and ideas in question. Keenly aware of the potential difficulty of foreign references, Hirose acknowledged in his preface that he and Nagata had for that reason supplemented Legge's original text with illustrations borrowed from *Webster's Dictionary* and elsewhere. Perhaps it was for this reason that Uryū too supplied his readers with illustrations, although the illustrations differ, a point to which I return.[18]

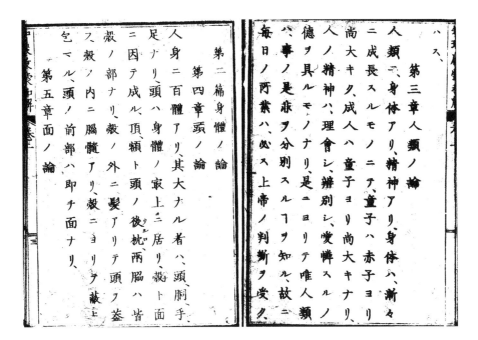

Figure 3. Lesson 4 ("The Head") in Hirose Wataru and Nagata Tomoyoshi, *Chikan keimō wakai.*

What we find upon close examination of these two Japanese versions of *Graduated Reading* are different approaches to authenticity and accessibility. Hirose and Nagata's *Circle of Knowledge . . . Reworked into Japanese* privileges Legge's original in producing an authentic version, while Uryū's *Circle of Knowledge* privileges the target audience in creating a "Japanese" text that is accessible to readers. Take, as a first example, Legge's initial goal of presenting "simple facts," which abound in nouns and for which he is careful to make the English and Chinese texts parallel in giving lists of the names of objects such as parts of the body, animals used for food, and so on. His overall conception of the body—"The body is distinguished into many parts, of which the chief are the head, the trunk, and the limbs"—is parallel in Chinese, and we duly note Legge's choice of terminology: the *tou* or "head" (J: *tō*), the *dashen* or "larger body" (J: *taishin*), and the *sizhi* or "four limbs" (J: *shishi*). (See Figures 1–3.) Hirose and Nagata reproduce the Chinese for "head," substitute *dō* for *dashen*, which is merely a more archaic Chinese character for "torso," and substitute a Japanese metaphoric expression, *teashi* (hands and feet), for "four limbs." Uryū goes further by substituting another Japanese usage for *tou* and indicating that it be read in a colloquial Japanese manner as *kubi*; this is followed by two Japanese words, *hara* and *se* (belly and back), instead of "trunk," and the same metaphoric expression used by Hirose, "hands and feet," for "limbs." Where Hirose and Nagata typically leave their readers to use the approximate Chinese pronunciation of the Chinese characters, Uryū indicates with *furigana*—small *kana* that appear alongside a character to indicate pronunciation—that his readers are to read these characters with colloquial Japanese expressions.

In other words, Hirose and Nagata attempt to translate Legge's Chinese exactly. Although they occasionally substitute Japanese usages of Chinese characters for Legge's Chinese, they usually keep Legge's characters, even if they are strange to Japanese, and indicate their meaning with a Japanese reading to the side—this practice of *furigana*. For example, Legge's metaphoric Chinese for "back of the head" (*houzhen*)—literally, "the back pillow" and nonsensical in Japanese—is reproduced by Hirose and Nagata, who indicate that it should be read *ushiro*, or "back [of head]." Uryū, by contrast, typically substitutes Japanese expressions for Legge's Chinese and freely adds or subtracts items—changes indicating that he is intent to provide a Japanese environment for the primer. For example, he augments Legge's and Hirose's list of "parts of the trunk"—shoulders, chest, ribs, belly, and back—with *koshi*, the buttocks, a word and anatomical part of frequent metaphoric significance in Japanese. Or again: his list of "fish used for food" is nearly twice as long as that of Legge or Hirose, a realistic extension of Legge's list for a readership that gathers a great variety of food from the sea.[19] In other words, at the level of the "simple facts" of nouns, Hirose and Nagata consistently try to reproduce Legge's language, while Uryū modifies it in order to encode Japanese references and hence establish a Japanese context. For Hirose and Nagata, authenticity is directed at making Legge's original accessible; for Uryū, authenticity is directed at the target audience and creating a "Japanese" text that is accessible to readers.

Illustrations serve an analogous purpose in the two Japanese texts. (See Figures 4 and 5.) Compare the first two illustrations in each of the texts—that illustrating "creatures" in Lesson 2 and that illustrating the "bones" in Lesson 10. Hirose's are diagrams; he names an image and thereby ties it to concrete words in the text. Uryū's, by contrast, are less pedagogical diagrams than artistic illustrations; they are available images whose association with the text must be established by the reader. Moreover, because his bird is reminiscent of Chinese bird-and-flower painting, and his skull and bones evoke

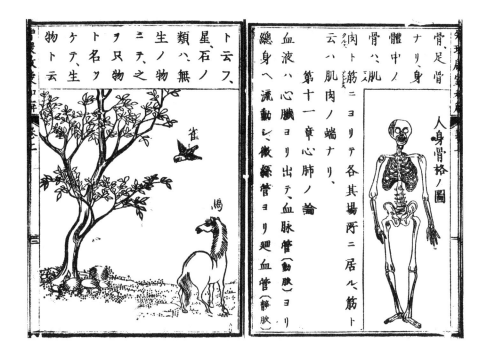

骨ハ足骨
ナリ、身
體ハ骨
骨ハ肌
筋ニヨリテ各其場所ニ居ル筋ト
肉ハ肌肉ノ端ナリ、
云フ
第十一章　心肺ノ論
血液ハ心臓ヨリ出テ、血脉管（動脉）ヨリ
總身へ流動シ、微絲管ヨリ廻血管（静脉）

人身骨格ノ図

ト云フ、
星、石ノ
類ハ無
生ノ物
ケトテ、生
物トハ
物ト云

雀

馬

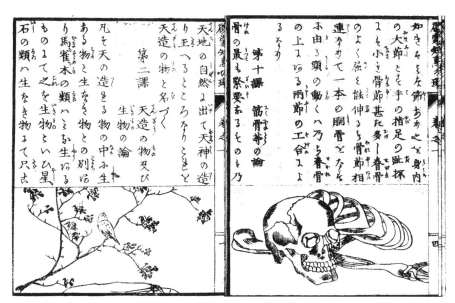

第十課　筋骨等ノ論
骨ノ最モ緊要ナルモノ

第二課　生物ノ論
天造ノ物及ビ
生物ノ論
天地ノ自然ニ出テ天神ノ造
レル王へルトコロナリ、天
造ノ物ト名づく
凡ソ天ノ造レル物ノ中ニ生
アル物ト生ナキ物トノ別ハ
リ馬雀木ノ類ハ皆生アル
ものにて之ヲ生物トいひ、星、
石ノ類ハ生ナキ物ニテ只ス

Figure 4 (top). Illustrations for Lessons 2 ("Creatures") and 10 ("The Bones") from Hirose Wataru and Nagata Tomoyoshi, *Chikan keimō wakai*.

Figure 5 (bottom). Illustrations for Lessons 2 ("Creatures") and 10 ("The Bones") from Uryū Tora, *Keimō chie no kan*.

illustrations in Tokugawa ghost stories, his images recall other familiar images from Japanese texts.[20]

It is striking, then, that a near reversal of this pattern takes place at the syntactic level in conjunction with certain kinds of information and reasoning (Legge's second and third goals). Here I will limit myself to the persistent theme of utility, for Uryū reproduces Legge's emphasis on utility whereas Hirose and Nagata minimize it. In the long series of Lessons 43 through 109, which emphasize the usefulness of animals, plants, and minerals to humankind, Uryū demonstrates a much greater fidelity to Legge's syntax and word choice, particularly in the way that utility is encoded. Where Legge typically writes in English "the part of animal X *supplies us with* Y thing," or "animal X *affords us* Y," or the "Y thing of animal X *is made into* Z product," Legge's Chinese and Uryū's Japanese repeat the Chinese character *yong* (J: *yō*), which serves as the kernel of verb expressions "to use something for" or "to be used as" and noun or adjective expressions like "has a use for" or "is useful to someone for." By contrast, there is a conspicuous avoidance of this Chinese character for "use" in Hirose and Nagata's text. They encode utility most often with *to nari*, which we might translate as "become," or *to su(ru)*, which means something between "to regard as" and "to act on so as to result in." In other words: animal X or part Y of animal X "becomes," "turns into," or "is turned into" Z thing.[21]

Such techniques in translating Legge's primer modify the relationship of authenticity and accessibility in the two translations. While Hirose and Nagata do not particularly stress Legge's theme of utility—the active appropriation of the world for the benefit of humankind—it appeals greatly to Uryū, who went on from his work in various branches of government to become a significant figure in the railroad and shipping industries. That this was an appropriate goal for Meiji students is Uryū's point in his formulation of Lesson 150 on "Property." Legge writes: "Persons who have money to spare often employ a part of it in promoting useful or benevolent undertakings." Uryū restates this with specific emphasis: "People today with money to spare will take a part of their resources and invest it in enterprises useful to the nation." (Like hospitals and railroads, both of them add.)[22] Uryū's translation of Legge's text is an opportunity to promote, not simply Legge's brand of utilitarianism, but one that expresses a syntactic connection between man and nation; he intended that his readers infer a practical connection between the two. His is indeed a nationalistic text, a point made obvious by his alterations of Legge's text: he adds a new Lesson 144, "On Japan," and replaces most of Legge's descriptions of society in Britain with corresponding descriptions of Japan.

Moreover, he dispenses entirely with the foundation of Legge's universe: Section XXIV, "Attributes of God." In Uryū's primer, nature creates man, and in death man returns to nature, completing the circle. While alive, man strives to benefit the Japanese nation.

Hirose and Nagata, by contrast, prefer more logically to equate creatures and things. As with the "simple facts" of nouns, they are concerned to establish strict correspondences between codes—between nature and culture, between English, Chinese, and Japanese. Theirs is an effort to produce a Japanese text that best reproduces the language of Legge's text. In this respect, their primer advocates no activity particular to the Japanese student and at best affirms two of Legge's goals: to convey information and encourage a certain way of reasoning. Unlike Uryū, Hirose and Nagata plainly reproduce much of the Victorian ideology native to Legge: God, in his absolute wisdom, created the world for use by humankind. They intend that their reader understand the world in this light.

These two Japanese versions of Legge's primer, then, reveal how authenticity and accessibility inform the work of the translator. Hirose and Nagata have produced a target text that largely mimics the original in order to grant their readers access to the source text. In this case, the authenticity of the new text follows from the value of the source text and the perceived fidelity of the new text to the source text. As a strategy of translation, this exacting attempt to reproduce the original makes a particular demand on the imagined reader, who must share the translator's familiarity with the source text and its languages. Simply put: Hirose and Nagata's text demands a capacity to understand literary Chinese equal to that of Legge's original. Readers who do not qualify will experience their ignorance as a difficulty in understanding. Uryū, by contrast, has produced a target text that interprets the original; his version privileges target readers and makes the original more accessible to them; but unlike Hirose and Nagata, he has deliberately made changes to the language of the original. In Uryū's case, authenticity follows from the imagined familiarity of the new text upon its reception. It "feels" Japanese in its use of *wakan kankōbun* and more "natural" terminology. As a strategy of translation, such a version that interprets the original for the benefit of the target reader promises to unite translator and reader in an imagined reality where the text seems to reflect the world around it. The seeming naturalness of this form of translation is certainly more appealing, and likely more effective, in the case of textbooks like these.

Let me close this section with some examples that figure in the subsequent chapters of this book. Both Nakamura Keiu's translation of Smiles' *Self-Help* (*Saikoku risshi hen*) and Fukuzawa Yukichi's translation of the Chambers brothers' *Political Economy*, included in *Seiyō jijō*, were the sort of interpretive translation that defines authenticity in terms of target audience response by making the original accessible in familiar language. By contrast, Nakamura's translation of J. S. Mill's *On Liberty (Jiyū no ri)* is a remarkably exacting translation that reproduces an authentic version of the original text and is thus very demanding of its readers. Where the former translations rarely introduce transliterations of English words (which require some knowledge of English to read), *Jiyū no ri* includes many such transliterations and the complicated signs I call analogs. Although all three of these texts were widely read and profoundly influential, Japanese readers were more persistently engaged by accessible translations whose authenticity was defined less by fidelity to the original than by a shared vision of a familiar world: Fukuzawa's *Seiyō jijō* was the most often pirated publication in early Meiji, and Nakamura's *Saikoku risshi hen* stayed in print until the 1930s.

Analogs and Their Resolution

In turning from a consideration of texts to an examination of words in translation, we can see a similar range of attention to authenticity and accessibility. Of the three main forms I examine in this chapter—analogs, translation words, and loanwords—the most authentic form of translation was the analog: a juxtaposition of words (or signs) in a compound form that attempted great fidelity to the original words of Western texts. Analogs retained the Western-language word—either in the foreign script or preserved as sound in a phonic transliteration—in juxtaposition to a Japanese word, most often in Chinese characters. But if analogs were particularly authentic, they were relatively inaccessible, for they ideally conveyed their meaning to a reader familiar with the Western-language words included in the analog. It quickly became clear to Japanese translators that accessibility was best defined from the perspective of the target audience rather than the source language, for comprehension proved much easier when one coined a new word and used it consistently than when one attempted to maintain an exacting fidelity to the words of a source language.

An instructive example is the case of Nishi Amane, familiar for his proposal to write Japanese with the Western alphabet. As a translator of Western learning in his early work *Hyakugaku renkan*—to which he also gave the English

Figure 6. Nishi Amane's analogs.

title *Encyclopedia*—he undertook a translation practice with analogs that was open-ended and deliberately avoided the fixity of meaning that necessarily affords stable and predictable translation habits. If Nishi's *Encyclopedia* is idiosyncratic, it is still valuable because its spectrum of translation techniques concentrates on a given page what others' texts feature less frequently. In confronting the text of Nishi's *Encyclopedia*, the reader's eye is roused by the variety of scripts scattered over the printed page. Nishi wrote in Chinese characters, in Japanese *hiragana* and *katakana*, and with English, French, Greek, and Latin words as well.[23] Generally the text is in Chinese characters and *hiragana*, the usual handwritten style. *Katakana* are exceptional—used primarily to indicate syntactic connections between Chinese characters or pronunciation, either as *furigana*, the traditional pronunciation notation written in a smaller script to the right of a Chinese character, or as phonic transcriptions of foreign words. In introducing European-language words, Nishi made extensive use of what I call compound signs, or analogs. (See Figure 6.)

Of the total number of European-language words used in Nishi's *Encyclopedia*, roughly two-thirds appear in the form exemplified in Figure 6(a): the European word is placed askew in the vertical text, and juxtaposed to it in subscript on the left is a Chinese-character translation. Here we are to understand Figure 6(a) as an equivalence between "philology" and 語原學 (*gogengaku*). (Note that for simplicity, I frequently substitute an "English" transliteration of the Japanese signs.) Nevertheless, there is no correlation between initial and subsequent appearances of words in analog form. These European-language words appear alone in Nishi's text or in the form of an analog—and randomly so. That is: Nishi does not consistently introduce European-language words in analog form, nor does he "translate" all words in this manner, nor does he limit himself to one such "translation" per European-language word.

There are, however, a number of frequent variations. The subscript may include *katakana* that provide syntactic links between Chinese-character items, as in Figure 6(b), where *aru* (having) in *katakana* joins two sets of Chinese characters, *kuhō* (meter) and *kekkō* (composition), to produce the phrase "composition-having-meter." This is most common in Nishi's word-for-word renderings of English or Latin phrases and sentences. The subscript may also indicate the language to which the word belongs—as in 6(c), where *futsu* (French) indicates that *père* is a French word. Or it may provide information concerning the class of the word—as in 6(d), where *Gijin* (Greek person) informs us that "Dionysius" is the proper name of a Greek person. Or fourth, the subscript may provide pronunciation information—a transliteration or phonic transcription—in *katakana*, as in 6(e) (*akkorudo* for "accord"), or in Chinese characters as in 6(f) (*hirippu* for "Philippic"). Although this latter phenomenon, called *ateji* ("pointing" or "phonetic" characters) in Japanese, is rare in Nishi's *Encyclopedia*, it is common in the contemporary works of his peers for proper names of countries and persons—as in Nakamura Keiu's translation of Samuel Smiles' *Self-Help*.

There is a second general form for analogs in Nishi's text, as indicated in Figure 6(g). This is quite simply an extension of the long-established convention of supplying *furigana* superscript on the right as pronunciation notation for obscure or unusual readings of Chinese characters. In effect, this is a rewriting of the Chinese character. Thus, by way of example, the word for the nocturnal animal "bat" in 6(g) could be read *henpuku* according to a Chinese (*kun*) reading, but the *furigana* superscript indicates that we are to read it with the Japanese (*on*) reading: *kawahori* (now read *kōmori*). Figure 6(h), which would usually be read *kokugo*, meaning (Japanese) national language, is to be read here as *kunikotoba*, meaning native or local parlance. A frequent variation on these traditional usages, however, is exemplified in Figure 6(i), where the *furigana* superscript is a *katakana* transliteration of the English word "philology"; we are to read as *hiroroji* what might otherwise be read as *gogengaku*. A very uncommon modification of this form is the addition of a *katakana* transliteration for a word in European print—as in Figure 6(j), where we are to read "Nirvana" as *nivena*.

Combining the foregoing examples yields one general form for the analog—as in Figure 6(k), where: (1) is a word, or "main sign," in a column of print; (2) is a superscript sign sequence in *katakana*, identified as either traditional *furigana* or a phonic transcription of a foreign word; and (3) is a subscript sign sequence either in Chinese characters or *katakana*, identified as a translation word, a footnote, or a phonic transcription. And indeed, we do find analogs including both superscript and subscript in precisely this form—as exemplified in Figure 6(l), where we are told to read "eternal repose" as *iterunaru repāsu* and to understand it as *eikyū kyūsoku*. Nonetheless, there are exceptions to such a general form. In Figure 6(m), for example, the superscript indicates that the word "Belles lettres" is from the French language, and the subscript provides a word-for-word translation of the two terms—"*kō* [fine] *moji* [letters]."[24] Although it should be clear from Figure 6 that the analog in Nishi's *Encyclopedia* has two primary functions—translation and phonic transcription—the analog is not restricted to these two functions. It is a form available for a number of transcoding practices, and its utility is limited only by Nishi's imaginative extension of the recognized convention of *furigana*. The superscript and subscript are supplementary (sets of) signs, and the juxtaposed scripts refer to each other, presumably qualifying or enhancing the individual meanings of the separate parts. Hence I think of these compound signs as analogs in order to emphasize this fundamental juxtaposition of two or more (sets of) signs.[25]

But in using analogs for purposes of translation, Nishi juxtaposes signs in a temporary fashion. *Bunshō*, for example, is paired with "literature," "belles lettres," and "rhetoric" at various places in the text; likewise, "Sanskrit" is paired with "the grammar of ancient India," "the language of ancient India," and "the Holy Texts of the Brahmins." These analogs are not signs in and of themselves—independent units of language, or sign types—nor can we definitively state "what they mean" as the result of an act of translation. Rather the fact of temporary juxtaposition demands that the reader make sense of the analog through one of two processes of resolution. One process, a cumulative resolution, occurs when the signifier of the sign in superscript or subscript is understood to be the signifier of the sign in the main text. In effect, the first sign *indicates* the second. Take, for example, the subscript アッコルド (*akkorudo*) in Figure 6(e). The signifier (a set of phonic signs) is an element of sound; it signifies the phonic aspect of an item in the English language: "accord." Collectively the subscript sign denotes the main sign. In turn, the signifier of the main sign, the physical word "accord," signifies the meaning of "accord." Clearly no new meaning is produced in this denotation; the sign in subscript supplements the main sign—the subscript points directly to the main sign. We might say that meaning is unidirectional in this type of analog, and accordingly I term this a "cumulative resolution." This sort of resolution occurs as well in those examples I cited as instances of "footnoting." In Figure 6(c), 佛 (*futsu*) supplements the main sign, *père*; it signifies "French word," denoting the fact that the main sign *père* is a French word. In effect, there is a rule operating in these cumulative resolutions, a rule based on the traditional practice of *furigana*, such that the superscript or subscript means the sign in the main text.

And in fact, to introduce another technical term, in the case of phonic transcriptions, these cumulative resolutions produce what are commonly called loanwords—the direct borrowing of the phonic form of a foreign word into the Japanese language. Among European languages, a loanword is a word borrowed directly from one language into another, like the German auto manufacturer's name, Volkswagen, which is now a word in English referring to autos made by that company. Because of the differences between European and Japanese writing systems, however, loanwords between these languages necessitate the coordination of different phonetic spelling systems. So, for example, English today includes Japanese loanwords like sushi, tatami, and Toyota, which we obviously write not with a Japanese syllabary but with our own alphabet. As we shall see, Japanese during the early Meiji period introduced many such loanwords: *raito* for "right," *riberuchi* for "liberty," and so on.[26]

The second process of resolution, which I term substitutive, occurs when an equivalence between the signifiers is suggested by virtue of the convention of juxtaposition but neither of the two signifieds indicates the other signifier. Figure 6(a), for example, consists of the main sign "philology" and the subscript 語原學 (*gogengaku*). Neither of these signifies a phonic item in Japanese; both of them, presumably, signify some meaningful content. The signifier "philology" signifies whatever it is that "philology" means—the study of words, to the reader of English. By contrast, the signifier 語原學 signifies, to the reader of Chinese characters, the study of word (or language) origins. This denotation effectively exploits the differences and similarities among the content and expression of signs, but in isolation there is no rule for preferring one sign over the other (as with cumulative resolution). Neither sign supplements the other directly; because both signs refer to each other, we might say that meaning is multidirectional in this type of analog. Here the analog is resolved by separating the signifiers and thereafter using only one of the two signs, which nevertheless remains "contaminated" by the other sign. The two signs are in effect mutually substitutive, and typically the signifier of one is simply substituted for the signified of the other. One sign is held to mean the other.

From Figure 6(a) we understand that "*gogengaku*" and "philology" are mutually substitutive, or equivalent signs. This is precisely the kind of correspondence between languages that produces translation words and informs acts of translation generally.

Typically, then, Nishi "translates" foreign-language words by introducing an analog that he resolves by directly substituting the analog subscript (or a portion thereof) into the main line of text. In other words, the analog introduces a Western word, and thereafter the Japanese subscript slips out from under the Western word to stand on its own in the text while the Western word is abandoned. In the preceding example, after introducing the analog "philology/*gogengaku*," Nishi subsequently uses *gogengaku* on its own, assuming the reader will recall that it means "philology." Take Figure 6(m) as a complex example: the superscript 佛語 (*futsugo*) denotes the main sign, "belles lettres," as a "French word." This is a case of cumulative resolution. The subscript 好文字 (*kō moji*), by contrast, signifies something akin to "fine letters." Subsequent to the appearance of this analog in Nishi's text, we would see 好文字 standing on its own, having been substituted for the analog and the main sign. By way of a substitutive resolution, Nishi has temporarily translated "belles lettres" as 好文字. But recall that he is free to translate "belles lettres" as *bunshō* (literature) elsewhere.

These two processes of resolving analogs were long-established pedagogic methods by 1870. *Furigana* juxtaposed to Chinese characters had long been used as a tool for reading Chinese characters, and with popular literature during the Tokugawa era it became a rich source of verbal play.[27] The practice of juxtaposing foreign-language signs and *katakana* transliterations (or Chinese character and *katakana* transliterations) was an established method for learning Dutch during the Tokugawa era and persisted well into the Meiji period. Properly resolving, or understanding, these analogs, then, has been both a goal and method of education in Japan for centuries. Indeed, "learning" itself has been often managed as the problem of "learning to read," a fact true of Nishi Amane's instruction and a wide range of Japanese courses of instruction still today. English-language learning in Japan, for example, continues to be faulted for its focus on grammar and the written word at the expense of some comprehension of the spoken language.

Nonetheless, the two processes of cumulative and substitutive resolution are the standard operations in early Meiji translation activity—and in all efforts to specify meaning. As Roman Jakobson rightly observed, "the meaning of any linguistic sign is its translation into some further, alternative sign, especially a sign 'in which it is more fully developed.' "[28] (Readers will note that in the foregoing paragraphs I too have supplied translations of signs in order to get at their meanings.) We understand signs, especially those of a foreign language, by translating them into more familiar signs. The simplest form of this process, phonic transcription, produces loanwords like *akkorudo* (Figure 6(e): "accord") or *hiroroji* (Figure 6(i): "philology"), and such loanwords depend on some familiarity with the source-language sign. The more complex form, translation words, depends on imagining or otherwise creating a new meaning available through Chinese characters, which offer more meaning than the mere sounds of a phonetic syllabary.

Translation Words and Loanwords

Analogs remained a common technique by which to introduce foreign terms and substitute translation words and loanwords within Japanese texts—the most common form of analog in the 1870s was that in Figure 6(i), which combines a Chinese-character translation word (*gogengaku*) with a foreign-language loanword in superscript (*hiroroji*). Admittedly it is a demanding form to read and resolve, and overly complicates writing and printing. To use the language introduced earlier in this chapter, Nishi's analogs translated source language with a preference for authenticity defined by the original text rather than accessibility defined by the reader and, as I have indicated, a reader more often appreciates the latter. Moreover, Nishi's chain of substitutions, while making a virtue of unfixed meaning, tended to reduce clarity for the reader, whose expectations commonly gravitate toward repetition and consistency. Hence analog usage declined in the last two decades of the nineteenth century—although, I hasten to add, the surprising example still appears in publications today.[29]

But this separation of translations from their original words meant that the meaning of a translation word, particularly a neologism, was at risk for ambiguity or obscurity. What was a reader to do when confronting a new expression or one used in a novel way? Nishi Amane expressed this concern in his preface to his first major work of translation, Joseph Haven's *Mental Philosophy*:

> In our country, translations of European books on the "fundamental principles of human nature," or "psychology," have hitherto been extremely rare. So I do not know what to appropriately follow in

the matter of translation characters. Even if I tried to match my terms to those which the Chinese learning scholars and Confucians expound, the problem is not simply that their distinctions of "nature of mind" are tremendously minute; but because the names indicated by their terms naturally have other significances, I have necessarily and expressly selected alternative characters and created my own words. Accordingly, although certain terms conform to those that existed previously—such as "perception," "memory," "consciousness," and "imagination"—other items are primarily new constructions, and the reader may very well have a difficult time formulating the meaning of those terms—such as "reason," "sensibility," "sense," and "understanding." . . .

Nevertheless, in all these terms, the most important character, along with the most important characters concerning the main point of a section, together employ a single, fixed character for making sense of the section. If, according to the context, the section still lacks all sense of obligatory force [of meaning] and the reader cannot translate it for himself by daring perhaps to arbitrarily exchange one word for a different word and thereby assume some intended meaning, then the reader should guess at the context and try to illuminate that which precedes and follows the section in question, pondering it energetically; it should not be at all difficult to comprehend the main point. That is what this translator earnestly hopes.[30]

In departing from his use of analogs, Nishi was clearly aware that he disengaged the translation from the original and exposed the newly translated text to the potential problem of reader misinterpretation. Received "Confucian" words may have multiple significances. Even if Nishi provided keys to understanding in the form of repeated and hence dominant characters, when the reader had to resort to daring, arbitrary substituting, and guessing, Western knowledge and enlightenment might be compromised. Nishi quickly recognized, in other words, the key problem of translation projects: how to produce an adequate set of correspondences between two languages. In making translations and writing about the new enlightenment knowledge from the West, he and his fellows pursued that adequacy—in effect a clarity of translation—through a joint effort to increase specificity and decrease ambiguity. Three major processes describe Japanese strategies in the 1870s and 1880s: first, a simplification of translation techniques to largely two forms, the (phonic) loanword and the translation word; second, developments in printing techniques to mark the new loanwords borrowed from European languages; and third, a gradual process of standardizing terminology, which began in the 1880s.

As I stated earlier, Japanese writers and educators settled quickly on a pair of translation techniques that became standard in the 1880s: translation words and loanwords. Translation words, those Chinese-character compounds used to translate foreign words, derived either from existing words, to which were added new meanings (such as *bunmei* for "Western civilization"), or from neologisms (newly coined words like *jiyū* for "freedom" or *kenri* for "right"). Loanwords were phonic transcriptions of foreign words (such as *furīdomu* for "freedom" or *raito* for "right").[31] Each type of translation word, as Nishi Amane noted, raised a respective difficulty. On the one hand, a translator could recirculate an established word by giving it a new meaning—as with *bunmei*, which shifted from Chinese to Western "universal civilization." This type of translation word depended on the principle of metaphorical extension and the expectation that the reader would make sense of a word used in a new context and to a new purpose. As we have seen in Chapter 2, *bunmei* seems to have had an easy passage in becoming a translation word for "(Western) civilization." But the case of *jiyū* in Chapter 4 demonstrates the opposite: as a translation word for "liberty," *jiyū* did not entirely escape its extant meaning of "as you will" or "willful."

On the other hand, a translator could create an entirely new word. Such a neologism depended on the leap of meaning that so troubled Nishi—the reader's ability to create new sense from a novel combination of Chinese characters. But the length of this leap varied a great deal depending on the abstractness of the reference of the neologism. Concrete things, once identified, could be clearly named; neologisms like *shashin* for "photograph" or *tetsudō* for "railroad" were as clear as one's perception of the object so named. Other new "things" in the world such as political institutions—*kokkai* for "national assembly" or *daitōryō* for "president"—could likewise be clearly named and identified in discussions of government. The case that so demanded a leap of meaning was the abstract terminology cited by Nishi—words such as "reason" or "sensibility." In Chapter 5, I discuss the host of translation words associated with *ken*, a Chinese character that figures in translation words for "right," "power," "authority," "sovereignty," "privilege," and more. It was a slow process by which the meanings of these terms were fixed in translation words, a process accompanied by much political debate. By comparison, the neologism *shakai*, a translation word for the new abstraction "society," seems to have required less of a leap of meaning—not simply because it was not very controversial politically, but because it fulfilled the need for a new identification. As I relate in Chapter 6, the word "society" facilitated the inclusive identification of everyone—from government officials and samurai to common people—as a new entity: "Japanese society."[32]

Hence in proposing Chinese-character translation words for the new things and ideas from the West, Japanese translators were more often than not aided by widespread familiarity with Chinese script and writing in Japan. The eminent linguist Hida Yoshifumi attributes the prevalence of Chinese-character translation words through the Meiji period to the tradition of Chinese learning and the widespread use of literary Chinese during the Tokugawa period; he quotes the Meiji philologist Ōtsuki Fumihiko's impression that many young government officials and teachers were former samurai who were proud of their intellectual traditions and their facility with literary Chinese.[33] Certainly another factor in the prevalence of Chinese translation words during Meiji was the extensive importing of Chinese books about the West and Chinese translations of Western books during the nineteenth century; translations of legal terminology—including "right" and so on—were especially informed by Chinese books. Similarly, a great many *ateji* terms—phonic transcriptions in Chinese characters for mainly place and personal names (see Figure 6(f))—were borrowed from Chinese sources.[34]

In other words, the availability of Chinese language and learning in nineteenth-century Japan meant that translators could assume a familiarity with Chinese characters on the part of their target readers and build upon that in constructing their translations. But again, translators' choices regarding translation words were determined by different relations of authenticity and accessibility informing the translation at the level of the text. Fukuzawa Yukichi's *Seiyō jijō*, for example, included largely paraphrastic translations that defined authenticity more in terms of target reader accessibility than in terms of fidelity to source texts. Fukuzawa rarely used analogs, more often than not used familiar and common words rather than introduce a specific translation word, and on the rare occasion that he created a new translation word, such as *jiyū* for "liberty" or *tsūgi* for "right," he provided extensive explanation for the new idea. Although Fukuzawa's work was accessible and widely read in early Meiji, he chose familiar words rather than produce translation words more authentic to the originals. Hence nearly none of his translation words survived into general usage—a fact he noted with regret at the end of his long career. As Mazaki Masato pointed out decades ago, of the many new Western things and ideas introduced by Fukuzawa in *Seiyō jijō*, only *bunmei* for "civilization" and *jiyū* for "liberty" persisted in the Japanese vocabulary. We would have to agree with Nishi Amane that, whatever initial difficulties it might present, a measure of technical distinction is necessary.[35]

By comparison, Nakamura Keiu's rather paraphrastic translation of *Self-Help* and his exacting translation of *On Liberty* include many examples of analogs and innumerable specific translation words for elements of Western civilization—including progress, independence, liberty, will, individual, and self—many of which became standard translation words in the course of the 1870s.[36] Given the long-term popularity of Nakamura's *Self-Help*, it would seem that the difficulty presented by specific and hence authentic translation words recedes in the face of an accessible translated text—Nishi Amane's hope that readers would be able to ponder and comprehend was apparently well founded. In fact, if we compare Nakamura's *Self-Help* and *On Liberty* on the point of translation words for "liberty," there is a far greater range of analogs and translation words in *Self-Help*. Whereas *On Liberty* makes a point of consistently using *jiyū*, *Self-Help* employs *jishu* (self-mastery), *jiyū* (self-directed), *jiritsu* (self-established), and others.[37] As we shall see in Chapters 4 and 5, many early Meiji translations made a virtue of reader familiarity with Chinese characters and, like Nishi Amane's use of analogs in his *Encyclopedia*, translated a foreign word in a variety of ways, establishing a range of translations from which fixed meaning might be condensed, rather than fixing meaning in one term at the outset.

In fact, the evidence presented in this book would indicate that a wide range of translation words was initially established by translated texts and, moreover, that this range was soon sorted out into a compatible set of terms that was in turn reduced to one or two standard usages. Starting from reader familiarity with Chinese characters, in other words, both facilitated and restricted the authenticity of translation. Take the case of *ken* translation words—power, privilege, right, and sovereignty. On the one hand, a simple equation between a foreign concept and a familiar word might not persuade readers. Nishi Amane's definition of *ken* (right) as "duty" (*gi*) did not endure, nor did Fukuzawa Yukichi's definition of "right" as "status" (*bun*)—particularly at a time when the public had begun discussing "the people's right" (*not* duty or status) to constitute a government.[38] On the other hand, the capacity of *ken* to translate power, privilege, authority, right, and sovereignty necessitated a slow process of differentiation. Phonic transcriptions from European languages in analog form helped to link translation words to their originals, and such denotations might assert that *kenri* means right, that *kensei* or *kenryoku* means power, legal power, or legitimate power, or that *shuken* means sovereignty—but *ken* was still available for whatever related meaning a translator might intend. As I show in Chapter 5, the newspaper debate on sovereignty in 1882–1883 introduced a great many terms and distinctions among ways of conceiving sovereignty, but ultimately these were irrelevant, since *shuken* as a translation word for "sovereignty" was firmly authenticated by virtue of an exact parallel construction: English "sovereign" is to "sovereignty" as Japanese *shu* is to *shuken*.

In comparison to the great range of clarity in producing translation words, the second primary translation technique—the loanword—was much more reliably specific and unambiguous. But the condition placed on the reader in making sense of a loanword was an absolute familiarity with the reference denotated by the loanword—in the language I used earlier, cumulative resolution depended on knowledge of the original reference. A loanword was always a neologism. And since, unlike Chinese characters, it conveyed no initially meaningful content but only the sound of a European word, the loanword made a virtue of specificity. As a matter of usage, loanwords came to be used in ways different from what we have seen earlier in Nishi Amane's construction of analogs (Figure 6(e), 6(j), and 6(l)). Nishi used phonic transcriptions for a wide variety of words; his contemporaries too used phonic transcriptions in analog form to denote new references for names of things and abstract ideas. But early Meiji writers preferred loanwords proper—*katakana* phonic transcriptions on their own in a line of text—for proper nouns (place-names and personal names) and the names of concrete things. Some examples of the latter from 1870s newspapers include *tonneru* (tunnel), *semento* (cement), *bisuketto* (biscuit), and *hankachi* (handkerchief)—new consumer goods and things related to new construction projects.[39] Probably the most common personal-name loanword in 1870s newspapers was *Guranto*, for Ulysses S. Grant, the former U.S. president whose visit to Japan in 1879 was a remarkable media event.[40] It stands to reason that loanwords became preferred for proper nouns, since each loanword replaced multiple *ateji* for the same country or personal name. (Multiple ways to write proper nouns in Chinese characters was a result of the multiple Chinese and Japanese sources for such transcriptions, which were often the personal creation of the writer or translator.) Abstract ideas, by contrast, were rarely translated with loanwords—an example in Chapter 5 is Katō Hiroyuki's use of *suberēnitēto no ken* (right of sovereignty). Instead, translation words were preferred.

Japanese linguists have noted a small but significant growth of loanwords by 1886. My own survey of newspaper article titles, comparing 1879 and 1887, produced a ratio of nearly 1:3—a tripling of loanwords between those years. But according to Hida Yoshifumi, in a survey of the modern composition of Japanese vocabulary, the increase in loanwords noted in 1886 was a shift from merely one-tenth to two-tenths of a percent of all Japanese words used in newspapers.[41] To underline the growing presence of loanwords in Japanese vocabulary during the 1880s, loanwords were reified as a category of word in the 1880s. The term *gairaigo* or loanword appears to have been the invention of Ōtsuki Fumihiko, scion of one of the most prestigious Tokugawa-period Dutch studies families and the first "modern" scholar of language in Japan, famous both for his construction of Japanese grammar and for his dictionary, *Genkai*, still in print today. In 1884, Ōtsuki published a list of 432 loanwords with an introduction that explained his wish to collect these words so that future Japanese users would know their origins. Ōtsuki's motive was in part purity: he pointed out that since the medieval period, Chinese, Koreans, Ryūkyūans (Okinawans), and Ezo (Ainu) had lived among and intermarried with Japanese, mixing races and languages. Accordingly, foreign words were commonly incorporated into daily use and eventually the Japanese people lost its own native language; Ōtsuki wanted to maintain the identity of Japanese as "one kind" of language. Hence his list specifies words borrowed from Ezo, Ryūkyū, Portugal, Spain, Holland, England, France, and so on but, curiously, not words derived from China. Chinese words were exceptional; because their sound had been domesticated in Japan, they were best treated as elements of Japanese language. Thus Ōtsuki's category of loanword normalized and domesticated translation words in Chinese characters and henceforth marked foreign words as non-Japanese language.[42]

As the Meiji period continued, loanwords were increasingly used for introducing new words and ideas from the West. The domestication of Chinese-character translation words gave way to a strict marking of foreign words as loanwords written in *katakana*.[43] Hida Yoshifumi surmises that the tide of translation words ebbed in favor of loanwords during the Taishō reign (1912–1926) on account of two developments: one was the absolute growth of literacy through the school system, which encouraged the prominence of a modern Tokyo dialect at the expense of regional mannerisms and education in literary Chinese; the other was the expansion of the Genbunitchi movement ("to unite speaking and writing") in the 1890s, which substituted spoken Japanese words and loanwords for Chinese-character translation words in newspaper writing, the reading of which expanded hand in hand with literacy.[44]

But the practice of marking loanwords had begun already in the transition from Tokugawa to Meiji. If we recall that the texts of enlightenment civilization were printed in *kanamajiribun*, which combined Chinese characters and *katakana* words, syntax, and loanwords, it is understandable that a technique would develop to distinguish new linguistic material—especially phonic transcriptions of European names and words—from what was presumably familiar, including newly domesticated translation words in Chinese characters. Readers could profit from a printing technique that differentiated phonic transcriptions from "normal" linguistic material. This technique was the use of underlining—or, given the vertical layout of Chinese and Japanese prose, what is best called "sidelining." This new practice of sidelining appeared in the 1860s in texts printed at the Tokugawa institute for Dutch learning. The 1866 reprint of Legge's *Graduated Reading* and many of the law texts published in 1868 use sidelining to distinguish *ateji*, denoting proper names, from Chinese characters used in their conventional meaningful forms. The habit of extending sidelining to *katakana* loanwords seems to have begun with Fukuzawa Yukichi's *Seiyō jijō*, in which all *katakana* names and loanwords have a line to the left. It is clear that by 1870 or 1871, sidelining was used systematically. Nakamura Keiu's translation of *Self-Help*, for example, published in 1870, has extensive use of *ateji* and pronunciations in *furigana* superscript and subscript but no sidelining; *Jiyū no ri*, however, his translation of *On Liberty* published in 1871, exhibits a pattern repeated in most "civilization" books and journals of the 1870s. Although a great deal of variation exists with sidelining to the right and left of characters in print, double sidelining was used for place-names and single sidelining for personal names and general loanwords. In the case of *ateji*, spatial constraints routinely forced pronunciation indicators to the side opposite the sidelining. Given the tradition of *furigana* pronunciations in superscript to the right of Chinese characters, sidelining gravitated toward the left. Simply put: this marking of loanwords made it possible to look at a printed page and distinguish linguistic material conveying phonic transcriptions from the otherwise meaningful use of linguistic signs.

Creating Uniformity: Standardization and Formalization

In addition to the combined use of translation words and loanwords as well as the invention of sidelining to mark loanwords in print, the third development in the effort to clearly translate the West was the work of coordinating, systematizing, and authorizing translation practices. In a word: the need to produce adequate correspondences between Japanese and European languages required standardization, for in the absence of centralized control over foreign books and their translation, private scholars translated Western terminology in idiosyncratic ways. By the 1880s, a number of educators were interested in stabilizing meaning—first by standardizing translation words and second by transforming written Japanese in the interests of westernization. These decisions grew out of the cumulative interaction of popular and academic journals, private educators and their institutions, and public educators at Tokyo Imperial University and the Ministry of Education. Professors at Tokyo Imperial University played a particularly central role. As the only national university between 1877 and 1897, Tokyo Imperial University and its professors served as the link between government, education policy, and scholarly activity.[45]

The first, albeit minor, efforts to create standard translation words were government regulations and laws. There was, in effect, a public and legal interest at stake for certain sets of words. In January 1872, for example, the Ministry of Education issued Book and Press Regulations that decreed standard terms for country names. According to Article XIV, all printed material was henceforth to use *Eikoku* for England, *Fukkoku* for France, *Pukoku* for Prussia, *Rokoku* for Russia, and *Beikoku* for the United States—and, it added, the preferred translation word for "foreign countries" generally was *gaikoku*.[46] Similarly, certain laws provided definitions of terms in order to specify rights and liabilities under the law—a commonplace activity in European and American societies. For example, Article II of the 1875 Press Law defined *hanken* (copyright) as the exclusive license to sell in published form written material authored or translated. Likewise, the 1887 Publication Regulations began with legal definitions for "publication" as well as the three main parties to the activity—author, publisher, and printer—each of whom was liable for penalties in case of infractions of the law.[47] Ideally such legal definitions produce standards that inform effective law enforcement.

By comparison, scholarly efforts at standardizing translation words were concerned to encourage the growth of a research community and a common vocabulary for the advancement of learning. If everyone worked with the same set of terms, intellectual exchange would proceed smoothly. The first person to undertake such an effort at Tokyo Imperial University, philosophy graduate Inoue Tetsujirō, compiled an English-Japanese *Dictionary of Philosophy* (*Tetsugaku jii*) in 1881 for the vocabulary of the human sciences. As he indicated in a later edition of the work, he was motivated to establish exact equivalents for English words in Japanese (and later editions included French and

German equivalents). Presumably readers and translators would benefit from a set of common translation words and a uniform understanding. Hence his dictionary offered a handy word list of Japanese translation words for English originals.[48] Subsequently, as one of the founders of the *Tōyō gakugei zasshi* (Far Eastern Journal of Arts and Sciences), he encouraged mathematics professor Kikuchi Dairoku to provide the same set of standard terminology for the natural and applied sciences. Between July 1883 and March 1885, a series of lists appeared in the pages of the *Tōyō gakugei zasshi* encouraging standard translation words for mathematics, physics, engineering, chemistry, optics, and algebra. These lists included the appropriate English, French, and German terms as well as the Chinese-character translation words for Japanese to use.[49]

Kikuchi had explained his reasons for undertaking this project in May 1882. He proposed standardizing translation words because all of the applied sciences relied on the vocabulary of chemistry, mathematics, and physics. Because it was the nature of science to be incomplete and thus perpetually progressing, Kikuchi reasoned that multiple translation words among the different branches of science created obscurity and hence it would be better to have one name for each "thing." Rather than try to incorporate foreign words into Japanese, either in foreign scripts or in *kana* transliteration—both of which Kikuchi dismissed as awkward to pronounce and hard to remember—he argued for the continued use of Chinese-character translation words as Japan had been doing since the medieval period. Specialists and professional organizations were in a position to standardize and publicize their key terms, and in the event of disagreement the Ministry of Education could arbitrate or refer the matter to some professional organization. And indeed, the lists commissioned by Inoue and Kikuchi were provided by translation committees of the corresponding professional societies.[50]

In addition to these preliminary attempts to standardize translation words, the printing of written Japanese began to change in the 1880s to better accommodate westernization. Ultimately what would evolve was the written form of Japanese we see today: what is often called *kakikudashibun* (written-down writing), which mixes Chinese characters and *hiragana*, the cursive syllabary, and punctuates it with commas, full stops (periods), and other such marks. Contemporary Japanese also reserves *katakana*, the square syllabary, for foreign loanwords in order to mark them as non-Japanese language. The slow process of evolution began in the 1880s, a decade during which the European study of language began to take hold in Japan. As I have indicated, most westernization books were printed in the mixture of Chinese characters and *katakana* called *kanamajiribun*. Journals, however, combined a variety of printing techniques for the various styles of Japanese writing—including westernization articles in *kanamajiribun*, literary essays and an occasional westernization piece in literary Chinese (*kanbun*), both Chinese-style poetry in literary Chinese and Japanese poetry in *hiragana*, and an occasional piece of Japanese belles lettres in *hiragana*.

Two points bear emphasizing. First, the *Meiroku zasshi* was exceptional among journals for its nearly exclusive use of *kanamajiribun*, a sign perhaps of the commitment of these westernization scholars to that written form. Second, *kakikudashibun* was rare in the 1870s; the few examples I have seen in my reading of westernization journals are literary essays printed in Nakamura Keiu's journal, the *Dōjinsha bungaku zasshi* (Dōjinsha Journal of Literature), and economic reports printed in Taguchi Ukichi's *Tōkyō keizai zasshi* (Tokyo Economic Journal), beginning from 1877 and 1879 respectively. Taguchi's reports on market prices were the important innovation, for they occasionally interjected a loanword in *katakana*; this style was taken up by the *Tōyō gakugei zasshi* for its "Notes" and "Reports" in 1882. The first employment of such a pattern of printing for a westernization article was, to my knowledge, the work of the educator Toyama Shōichi in an 1883 issue of *Tōyō gakugei zasshi*; three years later, Katō Hiroyuki repeated the pattern in the journal of the Tokyo Academy, *Tōkyō gakushi kaiin zasshi*, and in 1888 that journal changed its format to favor this form of *kakikudashibun*.[51]

The trend, in other words, was to eliminate sidelining by printing loanwords in *katakana*—thus freeing the line of print for punctuation, which some journals had begun to introduce early in the 1880s. The impetus for punctuation was an article by the botanist Itō Keisuke in 1881, who took his cue from his own study of foreign languages. Punctuation clarified the structure of grammar, which would benefit the progress of civilization because it helped Japanese scholars to translate foreign languages into Japanese. Conversely, if written Japanese were punctuated, foreigners might translate Japanese into their own languages more easily—and Japanese students might learn to read more readily.[52]

The point to be gleaned from these changes in printing techniques is that Japanese scholars and educators continued to strive to make the Japanese language mimic the form of European languages as explained by the European study of language. The 1880s witnessed a surge of interest in the linguistic study of Japanese: Ōtsuki Fumihiko began creating a grammar for contemporary Japanese; Fukuba Yoshizu (Bisei) did the same for classical Japanese; Hori Hidenari, Watanabe Makaji, Mori Mitani, and several other scholars began to study the evolution of spoken Japanese and to differentiate correct forms from dialect forms in order to standardize the spoken language.[53] Moreover, scholars debated the form of written Japanese thoughout the 1880s. Should Japanese continue to use Chinese characters? Should everyone the world over learn English in order to unify all languages? Should the Latin alphabet be substituted for Chinese and Japanese script so that Japanese would be written in *Rōmaji*?[54]

It is not my intention to pursue these questions here, as Yamamoto Masahide, Nanette Twine, and others have already done so. I would, however, emphasize that Japan's engagement with the West and the many efforts on the part of Japanese scholars to translate Western learning induced a slow process of reconstructing the Japanese language in the image of the West. Both vocabulary and the written representation of that vocabulary were subject to transformation in the last half of the nineteenth century. To repeat: it was a slow process of change—Inoue's and Kikuchi's projects to standardize translation words, for example, had limited success. Certainly in the case of Inoue's *Dictionary*, some of his equivalent translation words survived, others did not.[55] As I noted earlier, dictionaries provide case examples of words (sign tokens); thus Inoue's effort was at least like any other work of translation: an attempt to provide adequate correspondences between languages. At best it was a resource that many students of Western learning put into practice. As an alternative approach to the history of translation, the subsequent chapters of this book examine a few specific words—"liberty," "right," and "society"—to grasp the history of word usage and standardization.

Yet the fact remains that the scholars cited here did have an impact on the processes they began and the ends they envisioned. Many of them—Inoue Testujirō, Kikuchi Dairoku, Toyama Shōichi, Katō Hiroyuki, and Itō Keisuke—achieved preeminent status in their fields, and many of them served terms as president of Tokyo Imperial University. It was, I believe, their leading positions in education that had perhaps a greater impact than their efforts to standardize and normalize language use and printing in the 1880s. For in their positions as professors and bureaucrats, they wrote textbooks and determined curricula for the national school system that made use of the very terminology and language habits they urged their fellows to adopt. Hence the changes they advocated and initiated depended on the instruction of subsequent generations of students.[56]

4

Constructing Liberty

Liberty is not necessarily the central element of nineteenth-century political theory. As Katō Hiroyuki demonstrated in his startling typology of political administrations in 1861, *Tonarigusa* (The Grass Next Door), one can describe the range of despotic, monarchical, republican, and democratic forms of government without any reference to liberty. Japanese political theory, as it developed from Tokugawa Dutch studies and engaged Anglo-American and French theory after 1853, was, like its counterpart in Europe, grounded in a dialectic of despotism and people. To account for the limitations on monarchy and the foundations of constitutionalism requires the intervention of a second dialectic, that of arbitrary powers and law. Law limits the sovereign's privileges and transforms them into the people's rights, thereby shifting the polity's center of gravity from sovereign toward people and initiating a constitutional monarchy. As described in the work of political theorists like Thomas Hobbes and Benjamin Constant, law becomes the new sovereign, replacing the arbitrary will of the monarch and protecting the people's rights, and all become subjects of the law.

To contemplate the introduction of a European

concept of liberty to Japan in the nineteenth century, then, requires two theoretical precautions. First, we must retreat from our contemporary preference for "negative freedom," that sphere of noninterference surrounding the individual and his political rights, in order to appreciate "positive freedom," that political education of man in active self-rule, pursued through the collective enactment of law—described by Constant as "ancient liberty" and by seventeenth-century English republicans as "civil liberty."[1] Mainly because of the alleged excesses of such positive freedom perceived in the French Revolution, the Anglo-American liberal tradition, in the century and a half since the publication of John Stuart Mill's *On Liberty*, has preferred negative freedom.[2] One consequence is that Mill, Herbert Spencer, and other liberal defenders of negative freedom have jealously guarded the positive freedom of participation as a privilege, not a right, which the ruling class in its tutelary capacity judiciously grants to deserving compatriots.[3]

A second theoretical precaution is the difference between civil liberty and the tradition of civil rights (informed by negative freedom). As Blandine Kriegel has pointed out in her provocative study of royal jurisprudence in early modern Europe, the dominance of liberal arguments about civil rights since the nineteenth century has tended to obscure the older tradition of civil or "human" liberty. Defended by Hobbes, Jean Bodin, and other contemporaries in England and France, human liberty encompasses that personal security, personal liberty, and personal property upheld by the sovereign state through the rule of law. In opposition to the feudal tyranny of force, the sovereign state requires a division of powers in order to pursue justice—particularly the goals of peace and personal security.[4] If this earlier tradition, which stressed the rule of law to safeguard people from despotic lords, is now perceived as "conservative," and the later tradition, which stressed civil rights to safeguard individuals from the tyranny of the majority, is now a "liberal" position, we must remember that both were reactions to monarchical despotism in Europe—and, for that reason, both appealed to Japanese intellectuals when they were introduced to Japan in the mid-nineteenth century as justifications for constitutional government.

Given Katō Hiroyuki's precedent, liberty must be understood as a problematic element of the Western political discourse imported to Japan in the nineteenth century. In comparison to other political vocabulary such as "society," the term "liberty" and its synonym "freedom" quickly achieved a stable translation form. By 1875, *jiyū* was generally accepted among Japanese readers and writers, largely on the basis of two widely read books: Fukuzawa

Yukichi's *Seiyō jijō* (Conditions in the West), which appeared in three volumes between 1866 and 1870, and Nakamura Keiu's *Jiyū no ri* (The Principle of Liberty), a careful translation of John Stuart Mill's *On Liberty*, published in 1871. But the link between *jiyū* and liberty was no simple equation at a time when the political value of liberty as "self-determination" was repeatedly compromised by the negative denotation of liberty as "selfishness" (as in "libertine"). Although Fukuzawa and Nakamura worked to contain this tension by reiterating that liberty had to do with cooperation, mutual respect, and the rewarding of talent, they were allegedly so unsuccessful that some Japanese philologists argue today that this powerful tension is still present in *jiyū*, which, accordingly, does not mean the equivalent of "liberty" in contemporary Japanese.[5]

But this is surely an overstatement, for the development of "liberty" in Japan corresponds in great measure to that of "liberty" and the related "liberal" in English. While the earliest use of the term was "liberal arts," the mark of a free man and a generous mind (ca. 1375), liberty soon followed in the context of permission or privilege—as in "liberties of the subject," which referred to those rights granted within an unquestionable subjection to a particular sovereignty. The other word for such a formal right was "license," and in tandem with the negative form, "licentious," the negative sense of liberty as "unrestrained" developed in the sixteenth century, as we read in Shakespeare's *Much Ado About Nothing*, "like a liberall villaine," or John Knox's *First Blast*, "beheaded for the libertie of his tonge." The strong political sense of liberty as freedom dates from the fifteenth century, and like the development of the Latin term *libertas* in the free cities of medieval Italy, liberty proclaimed freedom from feudal constraints and celebrated self-rule. In England, liberty became attached to the political position of "liberal" as being open-minded or reforming in the late eighteenth century. But the persistent negative sense of liberal as "improper" or "unorthodox" allowed defenders of the status quo to castigate their rivals as "liberal," which questioned their beliefs as "foreign" or "unorthodox." Both liberal and liberty, and free and freedom, have oscillated between these positive and negative denotations from the fifteenth century on.[6]

What distinguishes Japanese interpretations of liberty in the early Meiji period is less an unbridgeable gap between *jiyū* and liberty than the fact that Japanese intellectuals encountered the centuries-long history of the English concept in the two decades spanning 1855 and 1875. Generally, the majority of Japanese leaders remained unconvinced that *jiyū* or "liberty" was the beneficent force praised by English theorists like J. S. Mill or Albany de Fonblanque. They noted its dynamism but remained suspicious that it undermined the virtues more appropriate to the people and to the maintenance of order within local and national communities—duty to others and loyalty to one's superiors, particularly the government administration that rightly protected public peace by repressing public unrest. As we shall see, the Japanese construction of liberty faced two problems. On the one hand, there was a tension of values—between liberty as an absolute endowment of individuals and liberty as a means to some greater good. On the other hand, there was a question of causation: did liberty produce—or was it an effect of— constitutional government and civilization? Ultimately, early Meiji intellectuals were more interested in liberty as a means to civilization than as a necessary right of the individual. In a surprising set of reversals in 1874 and 1875, just at the moment that "liberty" entered the public sphere of the newspaper debate over freedom of the press, Meiji intellectuals retracted the liberal interpretation of personal liberty in favor of the earlier tradition of civil (human) liberty introduced in the 1860s. The state's claim to safeguarding the well-being of the people under the rule of law outweighed the liberal claim to individual freedom from state interference.

Autonomy and Personal Discretion

Japanese philologists agree that, by 1870, Japanese lexicographers were translating the English word "liberty" and its close relations—French *liberté*, Dutch *vrijheid*, German *Freiheit*, and English freedom—with four main expressions. All four of these were Chinese-character expressions available to educated Chinese or Japanese of the time: (1) *jishu*, self-mastery, or acting on one's own authority; (2) *jiyū*, following one's intentions without restriction; (3) *jizai*, also meaning following one's intentions unrestrictedly but with a nuance not so much directional (*yū*) as stative (*zai*); and (4) *fuki*, a metaphor drawing on the image of a horse "without reins," connoting unfettered or free. In addition, these terms were used in two emphatic combinations: *jishujiyū* (self-determining and free) and *jiyūjizai* (utterly free to do whatever one likes). But in the key legal and political texts of the 1860s—and not in the dictionaries on which philologists base their work—we rarely find either the metaphor *fuki* or *jiyū*, the future standard translation word. Instead we find both *jishu* and *jizai*, but only the latter expression can be confidently called a translation for "liberty."[7]

These key texts, composed during the 1860s, were all based on Dutch sources and written by Tokugawa Dutch studies officials who in time joined the Meiji government. Katō Hiroyuki's *Tonarigusa* (1861) and *Rikken seitai ryaku* (An Outline of Constitutional Political Forms; 1868), which were derived from unspecified holdings at the Dutch studies institute, described the main types of European "bodies politic": monarchies and republics. Tsuda Mamichi's *Taisei kokuhō ron* (On State Law of the West; 1868) and Nishi Amane's *Fisuserinku-shi bankoku kōhō* (Vissering's International Law; 1868) were based on the lectures of the Dutch political economist Simon Vissering, which they attended in Leiden during 1863–1865. Tsuda reviewed the division of state powers, civil and penal law, rights and duties of citizens, and so on; Nishi reviewed state rights of war and peace and included a detailed chapter on diplomatic protocol. Moreover, Nishi's *Hyakugaku renkan/Encyclopedia* (1870–1871) broadly outlined Western learning, and his summary of Vissering's lectures on natural law also provided the basis for their colleague Kanda Takahira's *Seihō ryaku* (An Outline of Natural Law; 1871), which explicated the theory of individual natural rights.[8]

These texts survey the political systems discussed in European political theory and employed in Europe and North America at the time. For the purposes of this chapter and the next, they are especially important introductions of the key concepts of liberty and right. Collectively they offer three important discussions of politics. Katō, Nishi, and Tsuda all identify five basic systems: despotism, absolute monarchy, constitutional (or limited) monarchy, aristocratic republic, and democratic republic. Katō and Nishi describe the tripartite division of power at the heart of constitutional systems: the legislative, executive, and judicial branches of administration. And Kanda, Katō, and Tsuda discuss the common rights of citizens—Kanda in the context of natural law and Katō and Tsuda under the two varieties of constitutional government: the constitutional monarchy and the democratic republic. It is in this third discussion of common rights that liberty appears, as *jizai*.[9]

Katō, for example, discusses liberty toward the end of *Rikken seitai ryaku*, where he enumerates the eight private rights of the people in a constitutional system: (1) a right to life, (2) a right to bodily autonomy, (3) a right to liberty of action, (4) a right to assemble and form associations, (5) a right to liberty of thought, speech, and writing, and (6) a right to liberty of faith. Seventh is a "right to the identicality of the people," about which Katō explains: granted the identicality (equality) of the laws that protect the rights of all people, one has a right to absolute impartiality regardless of family or official position. And eighth is the "right of each person to freely hold property."[10]

Rights (3), (4), (5), and (6) clearly interpret what to us are fundamental civil liberties; we can be confident that Katō's and Tsuda's term, *jizai*, is indeed their translation word for "liberty." But if we compare Katō's list to that of Tsuda, there are two apparent tensions in such a rendition of liberties. First, as Tsuda makes clear with his different phrasing of the liberty of faith, one need not couch liberty in the abstract language of a "right to liberty." Whereas Katō specifies a right to liberty of faith and goes on to explain the priority of one's own discretion in matters of faith, Tsuda makes the point more directly: one has a "right to one's own discretion in believing a sectarian doctrine or engaging in sectarian ceremony."[11] Liberty is implicit in the personal discretion of believing. This difference between Katō and Tsuda is a tension between abstracting liberty as a specific right and describing liberty as a general mode of action—relying on one's discretion. Both conceptions are present, and neither Katō nor Tsuda unequivocally favors one over the other. The difference between the two approaches to liberty lies in an implied moral agent at work in the notion of discretion. Where the abstract right to liberty seems to set no subjective conditions, discreet action depends on the moral responsibility of the agent.

This contrast is even more pronounced in a second tension in these enumerations of rights, raised by the expression *jishu* (self-mastery or autonomy), which figures in both Katō's and Tsuda's right to bodily autonomy ("one should not be arbitrarily bound or thrown into jail"). Although Katō and Tsuda are referring to what in English is usually called a "right to personal liberty," and although some texts, notably dictionaries, use *jishu* as a translation word for liberty, *jishu* does not entirely mean "liberty" here. Rather, given Tsuda's extensive deployment of *jishu* in his historical discussion of "self-governing peoples" and "non-self-governing peoples," it is clear that "self-governing" refers to the status of a person as independent of external political force—in a word, autonomous. Or, as Kanda employs the term, our rights in making contracts are all based on our "right to self determination."[12]

In sum, these texts propose two related conceptions of liberty: on the one hand, the autonomy of the self (*jishu*); on the other hand, following one's own mind in specified activities (*jizai*). This difference is not yet articulated in terms of what the Anglo-American tradition has described as two forms of liberty: positive liberty (self-realization enacted politically through self-government) and negative liberty (freedom from external interference).[13] Rather the issue seems to be one simpler and more fundamental to all republican or democratic societies now and in the past—namely, the degree of individual freedom acceptable to others in the community. The fact that the two expressions, autonomy and liberty, are related in the common character signifying self-reflexivity, *ji*, underlines the Japanese concern with the role of the self or person in European constitutional thought. The autonomous self is free to use his discretion, as is every other such autonomous self. Clearly this Japanese use of *ji* is not a simple correspondence to the Latin reference in our word liberty: *liber*, the free man who, in distinction to the slaves, self-governs with other free men. Rather Katō and Tsuda implicitly question the autonomy of the individual within the polity. To what degree can and should an individual "entrust his own discretion" as he pursues his interests within the constitutional state?

Most often Katō concludes that "the restrictions of supreme law" are a reasonable external limitation on the activities of individuals. In a commentary on liberty of thought, speech, and writing, he explains that arbitrary behavior cannot be tolerated:

> The liberty of thought cannot be prohibited in the manner of "ancient and infamous tyranny." Rather, it is usual in a despotism or monarchy to prohibit the act of freely writing, printing, or speaking what is thought. Only the two forms of constitutional systems [democratic republics and constitutional monarchies] permit such liberty. . . . But this right to liberty does not permit arbitrary writing. If writing gravely corrupts the heart or damages peaceful rule, it is certainly appropriate that the writer receive his due punishment. Hence the law entrusts the responsibility for justification to the writer.[14]

This is very much in the spirit of John Locke's comment in his *Second Treatise on Government:* "Where there is no law, there is no freedom."[15] Freedom is not the liberty to do what one wants but the liberty to order one's person, actions, and property within the limits of the law. In Katō's formulation of private rights and liberty, when tyranny and monarchy no longer provide external limits on the autonomy of the individual, law must fill the breach; public peace and morality justify legal restrictions upon the liberties. The language of moral agency, implicit in words like "arbitrary" and "responsibility," assumes a prevailing counterpoint to liberty. As Tsuda Mamichi put it: "Even in daily interactions among common people, the law demands limits and standards; two people are free to say whatever they like in conversation, but there is a clear prohibition on something like their harming a third party."[16]

Comparable comments appear in all of these texts. What we do not find in general use is an abstract term, "liberty," standing on its own as a motive for action or principle of political organization.[17] The appearance of the principle of liberty must be credited to Fukuzawa Yukichi and Nakamura Keiu, with their turn to Anglo-American liberalism and its grounding of the general concept of liberty in the individual.

Independence and Selfishness

Fukuzawa's *Conditions in the West* and Nakamura's *Principle of Liberty* advanced the Japanese conception of liberty beyond the Dutch-based texts in three important ways. First of all, by casting historical narratives of political revolution and change in terms of liberty, they established a connection between liberty and the creation of constitutional political forms. Second, by posing these conflicts among individuals and groups both in concrete, historical terms and in the abstract, they domesticated the passage from "liberties," those specific principles of action enumerated by Katō and colleagues, to "liberty," a general, abstract principle. And third, by struggling to overcome others' misconceptions about liberty, they both publicized and contributed to the persistence of a fundamental conflict within the Japanese conception of liberty—that between independent action and selfishness. To address this third issue, both Fukuzawa and Nakamura ultimately imposed moral limitations on liberty in order to keep individuals from giving themselves over to objectionably selfish behavior.[18]

In the first volume of *Seiyō jijō,* Fukuzawa observes that "all civilized states" in Europe are constitutional monarchies; first of the attributes of these civilized administrations is *jishu nin'i* (self-determination and personal discretion), an expression he equates with both liberty and *jiyū*. Because Nakamura Keiu later quotes this discussion of liberty as the premier precedent for his use of *jiyū* in translating Mill, I retranslate it in full:

When the country's traditions are relaxed and people no longer restricted, each can do what pleases himself. Those who take pleasure in official life can become officials; those who enjoy farming become farmers. Not the least discrimination is established among the [four classes of] officials, farmers, artisans, and merchants. Of course, there is no discussion of lineage, no slighting of persons according to their status at court; among the high and low, the noble and mean, each obtains what is due him, without any interference into the "liberty" of others, which is the aim of extending the talent granted by heaven. Nonetheless, the difference between noble and mean is appropriate in the arena of public service, where positions at court alone are revered. Except for this, there are no differences among the four classes. Literacy, reasoned discussion, and ambitious effort make the superior man, who is respected; illiteracy makes the small man, who performs manual labor. *Note:* In this text, the expressions *jishu nin'i* and *jiyū* do not mean selfishness, dissoluteness, or contempt for the country's traditions. In general, the people of the land interact without anxiety or formality, with the aim of expanding each one's personal ability as each sees fit. In English, this is called *furīdomu* [freedom] or *riberuchi* [liberty]. There is still no appropriate translation word.[19]

Fukuzawa thus introduces liberty as a clear alternative to the status discriminations instituted by the Tokugawa regime. He duly notes the exceptional nobility of the imperial court and the fact—dear to those of his contemporaries advocating revolution—that Western regimes value talent and reward ability. If Fukuzawa presents this notion somewhat quaintly in the classical Confucian language of the superior man and the small-minded laborer, his point is clear in the note: a new model of social relations is available in the West that will serve the cause of fostering ability.

In addition to communicating this possibility, Fukuzawa and Nakamura felt the need to safeguard this new concept, "liberty," from popular misconceptions. One source for confusion in the 1860s, the less direct, lay in the pragmatic history of the word in Chinese texts. Like Katō's and Tsuda's preference (*jizai*), *jiyū* was a long-standing expression in the Chinese lexicon with an equally wide range of meanings borrowed by the Japanese and centered on "following one's inclinations" or "having one's way"—activities that emphasized the individual at the expense of the community.[20] The second and direct source of misunderstandings lay in the history of *jiyū* as a translation word in Japan. From the mid-1500s it had been used to translate expressions akin to liberty: first in Portuguese Christian texts as a translation for the Latin *libertas*; later in Edo-period Dutch studies texts as a translation for the Dutch *vrijheid*; and then in Anglo-American missionary histories and geographies of the 1850s, imported from China, as a Chinese translation for the English "freedom" and "liberty." *Jiyū* took a peculiar turn in the early nineteenth century, however, when it became associated with *wagamama* (selfish) and *katte* (willful) as a result of a surprising translation of *vrijheid* by the shogun's official interpreters in Nagasaki. Whether through the error of inexperience or the intention of value judgment, an unnamed Nagasaki interpreter is credited with producing the memorable "Dutch" remark that "the world situation tends toward greater selfishness every year," in which the original term, *vrijheid*, is rendered *wagamama*. The association of *wagamama* and *katte* with *jiyū* persisted in Dutch-Japanese dictionaries and was transferred to official uses of English. Where the U.S.-Japan treaty signed by Commodore Matthew Perry in 1854 demands that shipwrecked sailors and American citizens be "free to go where they please," the Japanese version translates this with *kanyū* (openly) and *katte ni* (willfully). The Harris Treaty of 1858 substitutes *jiyū* for identical instances of "free," thus reproducing the same association of *jiyū* and selfish with the English word "free" that had earlier occurred in Japanese understandings of *vrijheid*.[21]

In the face of this potential confusion, Fukuzawa and Nakamura worked to ground liberty in a positive light through a history of political reform and revolution. Both emphasize the expression *fuki dokuritsu* (unfettered and independent) or, reversed, *dokuritsu fuki*. At the start of *The Principle of Liberty*, for example, Nakamura explains the right to liberty as the limit placed on a master's privileges. Following Mill he reiterates the general problem, seen in the histories of Greece, Rome, and England, of the people's struggle against the ruler's privilege and power of "freedom and independence" (*fuki dokuritsu*), which threatened always to turn into tyranny. To protect themselves, the people invoked their "liberty" and placed a limit on the power of the ruler through the imposition of laws. What is striking about Nakamura's characterization of liberty is that he equates *jiyū* and *jishu:* freedom from tyranny is the autonomy of self-rule, a state that graces the people with "freedom and independence" as they displace their former and despotic king.[22]

In Fukuzawa's narrative of the American revolt, the transformation is both more subtle and more thorough. Liberty is the Americans' goal: the creation of a federation (*gasshūkoku*) that is likewise "free and independent." In his translation of the Declaration of Independence, a comprehensive but deliberately colloquial version of the English, Fukuzawa repeats the character for "all" (*shū*) as he shifts from "all the people" (*shūmin*) to the idea of "collective independence" (*gasshū dokuritsu*) to the "independence of the federation" (*gasshūkoku no dokuritsu*).[23] The fact that all the people replace the one king (*doku*) when they have combined as a federation, becoming a new collective "one," is signified in the term "independent" (*dokuritsu*). Fukuzawa symbolizes in language that the new collective unit has incorporated the oneness—and independence—of the former ruler.[24]

Liberty, in the Anglo-American tradition presented here, thus commands attention as a means to the establishment of independent constitutional systems. Moreover, as Nakamura makes clear, because these polities are animated by individuals pursuing their own interests, the greater collective utility of the liberties is served. Following Mill, Nakamura introduces the personal liberties of judgment, of taste and occupation, of friendly assembly, of thought, of speech or discussion, of publishing, of religion, and of action. These are all good and useful because they encourage the progressive sequence of exploratory debate, the discovery of truth, the application of knowledge, and the advancement of humankind. But Mill and Nakamura are not blind to a common consequence of constitutionalism—that, in the absence of a common understanding of good and evil, the population may divide into larger and smaller factions. Of course, Nakamura states, people will turn to the government for direction, but at the same time they still want to guard against the unfair interference of government. Mill and Nakamura seek to persuade their readers that in this absence of moral unanimity, it is far better that everyone acknowledge a general "principle of liberty" than not, for liberty grants far more benefits than it harms public well-being. Where Katō and Tsuda saw liberties as structural propositions of constitutionalism, Nakamura and Fukuzawa propose a new form of social dynamism animating the talents of each individual for what promises to be a progressive collective whole.[25]

Two changes thus occur with the introduction of the liberal interpretation of liberty. First, in demonstrating its utility in multiple situations, liberty is reified as a general concept. Liberty of discussion works to advance humankind; liberty of occupation grants us the well-being of suitable work; liberty of assembly serves us well for support in times of need; and so on. Nakamura sensibly translates Mill's title as "the principle of liberty" because his central argument concerns the general applicability and utility of an abstract notion of liberty.[26] Second, liberty is grounded in the individual, acquiring a much more internalized point of reference than Katō and Tsuda's principle of "discretion." Whereas they treated liberty of thought, for example, in terms of the objectified act of "thinking," akin to comparable acts such as speaking and writing, all of which are tempered by an external standard of discretion, Nakamura locates liberty within the individual. He follows Mill's point that the first appropriate region of liberty is the inward domain of consciousness—and hence we must have freedom of thought.[27] Whereas Katō and Tsuda juxtaposed a person's free actions to the laws of the domain, the people, or some collective understanding of discretion, Nakamura sees the individual agent in juxtaposition to other such individual selves, against whose propensity to combine in a tyrannous majority one must always be on guard.

What is potentially disturbing about this interpretation of liberty is that its typically negative presentation—that one is free from the interference of others—never returns logically to the original creation of a free polity grounded in law. As Blandine Kriegel has argued, the liberal version of liberties abandons the state protection of those human liberties that were the reason for establishing a constitutional system in the first place.[28] The rights to life, home, and personal security, which Katō and Tsuda included in their enumerations of rights, no longer matter per se. Instead we are to imagine a self-interested people whose autonomy is defined less by self-rule and more by the exclusion of external interference. The government's only justification for interfering with people, as Nakamura renders Mill's point regarding the self-protection of society, is to protect them from the harm that others might perpetrate. Nakamura follows Mill in opposing the individual to the majority—the government, that vague external "society" which has the power to oppress the individual—but he does not solve the Meiji problem of the government versus the people. If anything, he previews the conflict essential to the later "freedom and popular rights" movement: the close rhetorical association between liberty and descriptions of the state as a despotic authority.

This conundrum is acute in the third volume of *Seiyō jijō,* where Fukuzawa turns to the history of France and is flummoxed by the French Revolution. France follows the precedents of England and the United States: the winds of freedom blow across the country in the face of tyranny, and the National Assembly proclaims independence. Although a republic is established, vulgarity and violence grow, with the surprising result of "freedom in name, but not at all in reality."[29] The confusion generated by the reigns of Napoleon and Charles X redirects Fukuzawa's narrative from liberty back to the question of rights—establishing the rights of participatory government through law. Clearly the fact that "true" liberty is in danger of being undermined by selfish or willful behavior compels Fukuzawa to add a second set of clarifications regarding liberty in his prefatory remarks to volume three. He points out that liberty is a matter much more serious than granting a child who has finished his homework the permission to go outside and play; it has nothing to do with polite requests or likes and dislikes. Rather, quoting the American proclamation "give me liberty or give me death," he concludes that liberty is a principle devoted to saving the people from misery, a case of not interfering with the rights of the inhabitants of the country: "simply put—to invigorate the work of mind and body, to work together without interfering, to aim for the prosperity of each person."[30]

The way out of this impasse, for both Fukuzawa and Nakamura, follows the path taken by Katō and Tsuda: to impose external limits on liberty. For Fukuzawa, the samurai conception of duty (*shoku*) provides a solution. He makes clear that freedom comes with the body, and since both are granted by heaven they cannot be taken away by another man or the nation. In this regard he admits that we are most free in the state of nature—a condition of barbarism, to be sure—but contends that this "freedom" is the freedom to starve, the freedom to be destroyed by force, not a true freedom at all. Hence we must remember that people are members of families and belong to nations; these associations impose upon us "natural" limits to liberty, which Fukuzawa calls "duty." These begin naturally: each man's effort to preserve his own person—the most fundamental right of liberty—is extended to his family. From this follows the general duties to prevent trouble for others and obey the law. Because it forces us to consider other people in human interaction, duty keeps the free individual from utterly selfish behavior.[31] In fact, it is duty that holds the human community together. Fukuzawa declares:

> The great fundamental of human interaction is that free and independent people assemble, employing strength and laboring minds, attaining goals and achieving rewards, in an effort to preserve an order and to plan for the general benefit of all. . . . Our wish for human interaction must be to cultivate moral behavior and to maintain law. . . . Those who harm customs, who are lazy, and who steal the accomplishments of others deserve punishment. Whether public criticism or a legal judgment, it is our duty to uphold such judgments.[32]

Nakamura, by contrast, in a surprising set of additions to Mill's essay, enlists a Christian perspective on liberty. Where Mill supports freedom of religion but is markedly ambivalent about middle-class Christianity in England, Nakamura strongly recommends Christianity as a corrective for the human propensity to err on the side of selfishness. At issue for Nakamura, much as in Fukuzawa's history of France, is the difference between "true" and "false" freedom. True freedom is limited. As Nakamura's friend and spiritual counselor

Edward Warren Clark stated in a preface to *The Principle of Liberty:* "Liberty in its highest sense must have limitations; though men are less apt to respect its bounds than to accept its freedom. In some, there is a certain restless spirit which brooks no restraint, either from civil code or from individual conscience, & which feigns itself free in proportion as it is independent of rightful rule." In fact, this false freedom is a "pitiable form of bondage," the licentious delusion of "total independence," which can only be corrected by heeding the example of the "true liberator" of mankind, the Messiah who came to "unchain the captive, not from a temporal, but from a spiritual despotism."[33] Key to this true freedom is the capacity to love. Whereas Mill's text concerns the limits of government, the problem for humankind, Nakamura adds, is to emulate God's limitless love for man. The difference between God's limitless love for man and mankind's limited institutions, Nakamura implies, highlights the rightful limitations on man's control over others, for liberty ultimately refers to Christian promise and responsibility—self-development to the glory of God.[34] Both Fukuzawa and Nakamura, in other words, understand that liberty grounded in the individual imparts a progressive dynamism to the community; but both recast the independence of the individual as a bounded autonomy by linking him to family and others through duty and love. Neither condones the licentious delusion of unrestricted, false freedom.[35]

Religious Liberty: Personal Faith and Collective Worship

In addition to providing the momentum for standardizing *jiyū* as the translation word for freedom and liberty, the liberal interpretation of freedom introduced by Fukuzawa and Nakamura is crucial for a second reason. It defined freedom of conscience as a right internal to the individual, out of reach of political authorities, and, as such, freedom of conscience immediately became the reference for religious liberty, defined as the freedom of personal faith. Nakamura in particular is to be credited with linking this internal freedom of conscience to religious liberty. Although Nakamura's additions to Mill stressed the value of Christian belief for liberty and civilization, Mill himself judged religious belief a prominent site of social tyranny—especially because of the close relation between religion and (to him oppressive) middle-class morality. As a consequence, Mill found most praiseworthy the great religious leaders' assertions of freedom of conscience. Suppressing the freedom of religion, like the suppression of any liberty, harms human development; and religion, like so many aspects of social life in Mill's world, can only benefit from the liberty of thought and discussion, which, for the Christian, tests belief and thus forges a living belief.[36]

But no Japanese, to my knowledge, in the early Meiji period was willing to accept Mill's scenario of an actively inquiring citizenry taking the lead as the minimal state observed from the sidelines. Nor did anyone imagine organized religions in a position to infringe on the freedom of individuals. Rather, writers in the 1870s largely accepted as valid the role of the state in supervising religion. Given the presence of Christianity in the Shimabara Uprising defeated in 1638 and the several riotous cults affiliated with popular forms of Buddhism during the Tokugawa period, the shogun's use of legal ban to suppress socially objectionable forms of religion was a normative precedent.[37] Accordingly, discussions of religious liberty in the early Meiji period developed along the lines first suggested by Katō Hiroyuki's translation of Johann Kaspar Bluntschli's *Allgemeines Staatsrecht*, the first installment of which appeared in 1872. On the one hand, each individual had a personal right to faith; on the other hand, groups had a right to worship the religion of their collective choice. Because these two rights overlapped in the space of public worship, the state too had a right to involve itself in religious matters, if only to protect public order.[38] What a majority of scholars objected to was the state's attempt to prescribe one religion above others as suitable for all Japanese people.

Debates over religious liberty were precipitated by the new Meiji government's official policy toward religion on two fronts. First, the policy of "uniting politics and religion," decreed in April 1868 and reinforced with the subsequent promulgation of the Three Standards of Instruction in April 1872, attempted to establish a newly constructed Shintō as the national religion of Japan and put Buddhist sects under the domination of a Shintō hierarchy. Second, the reiteration of the official Tokugawa ban on Christianity in April 1868 generated controversy by the continuing arrest and deportation of Christians from southern Japan between 1867 and 1870. Although the two series were independent developments, they provoked a common set of arguments whose outcome provisionally affirmed a principle of religious freedom.

The first set of events draws us immediately into the problem of naming "religion" in the early Meiji period. Variously described as *saisei itto* (one road of ceremony and administration) or *seikyō itchi* (union of administration and instruction), this policy of uniting politics and religion consistently points to political administration as one half of the combination while the other half vacillates between the expression of religious practices and the content of religious teachings. For "religion" during the first fifteen years of Meiji was translated with multiple combinations of Chinese characters referring to Buddhist sects, terms for worship or ceremony, expressions for faith or belief, terms for religious or philosophical doctrines or schools, and terms for religious or philosophical law or principles. Although these words covered a range of faiths and programs of instruction, from Buddhist sects to Chinese philosophical schools, from Christianity to Shintō, they all share the notion of a set of beliefs or instructions that presumably inform a code of behavior. As James Ketelaar has observed, the key term *kyō* shifts gradually from "doctrine" to "religion" during these early years of Meiji.[39] As an official policy, uniting politics and religion meant that Shintō priests and advocates of Japanese nativism advised the oligarchy and the Meiji emperor to return to the model of imperial rule established by ancestral Emperor Jimmu, articulated as *matsurigoto*, when "politics and religion were one and the same."[40] Practically this meant creating an Office of Shintō within the Meiji government (replaced with the Ministry of Doctrine in 1872), on the model of Jimmu's ancient administration, and indoctrinating the people with the new Shintō teachings, the official goals of which were to revere the spirits (*kami*) of the land, to illuminate human morality, to rectify the hearts of the people, and to fulfill duty, all of which would instill service to the imperial court.[41] Four years later, the Three Standards of Instruction reiterated similar goals. The "union of politics and religion," in sum, was an attempt by the new government to unify talk of morality, the cult of Shintō, and loyalty to the emperor as a project for mobilizing the new citizenry. What was once nameable as one, *matsurigoto*, had become the duality of politics and religion that had to be rejoined—a bureaucratic measure that provoked talk of liberty.[42]

The second set of events prompting calls for religious freedom was the ban on Christianity. The reintroduction of foreigners to Japanese ports, after the establishment of a treaty-port system beginning in 1858, allowed American, English, and French religious personnel to serve their countrymen in Yokohama, Nagasaki, and elsewhere. Although traveling in the countryside and proselytizing among the Japanese people was forbidden, French Catholic priests in the Nagasaki area defied Japanese law by making contact with and encouraging local "hidden Christian" groups to practice their faith publicly after a hiatus of two and a half centuries (following the shogun's ban in 1614). The shogun's representative in Nagasaki arrested sixty-some villagers in July 1867 and, as the numbers increased to some four thousand in the course of a year, the new Meiji government inherited the problem. It quickly became an international diplomatic issue as the Meiji oligarchy tried, on the one hand, to placate southern lords opposed to Christianity and Western intrusions and, on the other hand, to secure the support of the Western powers as the oligarchy commenced the work of state building. The Western powers, of course, would be satisfied with nothing less than a repeal of all laws prohibiting Christianity.[43] But like the union of politics and religion simultaneously under way, the ban on Christianity, in addition to its rationale of preventing such corrupting foreign influences, was publicly justified by the need to respect the *kami* of the land, illuminate the moral relations between lord and subject, and protect the state in order to preserve loyalty and affection.[44]

In other words, both sets of religious policy indicate that the new government hoped to enlist the support of the Shintō cult and traditional forms of morality in the effort to foster obedience to the emperor and the new administration. Reactions to this religious policy came accordingly from two directions and prominently in 1872: Japanese Buddhists objected to government interference with their practice of religion and to the relegation of Buddhism to a secondary status in relation to official Shintō; the intelligentsia associated with the Meirokusha objected to the government's religious policy as a matter of principle. The debate returned to three main arguments: that politics and religion comprise two different spheres of activity; that choice of doctrine or religious faith is a matter for the individual to determine; and that freedom of religion is but one element of the progress of civilization, to which Japanese leaders must be committed. Implicit in these three arguments was a set of negotiations over the boundaries of religion in a civilized domain: What is the appropriate unit of religious faith—individual, community, or nation? And what is the appropriate sphere of religious faith—private or public?

In opposing the union of doctrine and administration, Shimaji Mokurai, a charismatic leader of the Jōdo Shin sect, offered the first extended differentiation of *sei* and *kyō* in his Memorial Opposed to the Three Standards of Instruction. The former, political administration, has to do with ordering the form of human affairs—such as departmentalizing countries, domains, and areas—and as a particularizing effort its practical goal is to urge people to study hard and improve themselves. The latter, doctrine (or religion), has to do with divine affairs—the ordering of the internal heart and the connecting of all domains—a universalizing effort inclining people to the good.[45] Nishi Amane, in an address to the Meirokusha, reiterated the point that politics and religion comprise two different spheres of activity; but he added, as if to reassure the ruling oligarchy, that religion cannot interfere with Japan's body politic since the latter is properly the sphere of secular law and obedience thereto.

Hence Nishi made specific recommendations for the Meiji government: the Ministry of Doctrine should have no control over religion other than to prevent disturbances; should take no notice of what is in people's hearts, since rulers are not gods; and should establish prohibitions on arguments between sects. Controlling religion, in other words, should be limited to licensing shrines and temples and restricting outdoor services; it should not intervene in people's choice of religion or ecclesiastic ranking.[46] In a similar response to the Meirokusha, Katō Hiroyuki added warnings that historical cases such as the Reformation in Europe demonstrate that the union of politics and religion is a bad policy: it oppresses human knowledge and brings disorder to the world. Religious worship and freedom of conscience concern the individual, who believes what is in his heart, while the government's appropriate sphere of action is external—to use law to protect morality and duty and to look after public benefit and collective advantage. In this regard, Katō pointed out, the government has the right to prohibit religious practices that harm public order—polygamy among the Mormons, for example, or suicide among Indian widows. But one should follow the example of the U.S. Constitution and those of the individual states, which typically prohibit laws interfering with religious liberty.[47]

Mori Arinori and Nakamura Keiu, both of whom were favorably impressed with Christianity during their periods of study abroad (Nakamura was eventually baptised on Christmas Day, 1874), reiterated this differentiation between politics and religion and went further in attempting to justify religion itself on utilitarian grounds.[48] Mori began his *Religious Freedom in Japan* with the audacious observation that the attempt to combine Buddhism and Shintōism had failed. And he went on to note that religion is a person's duty as a rational being—hence governments let individuals judge the value of religion for themselves. It is false that religion promotes social discord; rather, it promises to bring improvement; thus those who say banning Christianity is a necessary precaution against disturbances are in error. Current policy, as Mori saw it, actually neglected religion where it might have instead fostered progress.[49] Nakamura, in his infamous memorial urging the emperor to convert to Christianity, declared that Christianity is in fact the basis of European wealth and power and hence deserves much more than a lifting of the ban. He argued that since Japan was about to become the most wealthy and powerful country in Asia—the Europe of Asia—the emperor would do well not to repeat the mistake made by the former Tokugawa regime in its policy of seclusion—which everyone knows did not contribute to the enlightenment of human intelligence—but to realize that European wealth and power depend on the bold activities of Europeans who base their acts on faith in Christianity. In the same way that Japanese had tried everything else in Western civilization and found it good—railroads, telegraphs, steamships, cannon, short hair, beef and mutton—so too they must not simple-mindedly dismiss Christianity as evil but must try its benefits.[50] If Tsuda Mamichi was perhaps alone in agreeing publicly with the idea that Christianity seemed to be the religion most conducive to progess and enlightenment, the repeated discussion about civilized or "scientific" religion among the Meirokusha would indicate that many members equated, if not Christianity, certainly a monotheistic religion like Christianity with the progressive civilization of the West.[51]

Religion, in other words, had its properly personal and internalized domain of action that, whether directly or indirectly, contributed to progress and civilization. Religious freedom, then, was both acceptable and necessary as an individual choice and internal practice. But what if the government wanted to create a state religion? Was it, as a matter of principle, forbidden to do so? On the one hand, this intelligentsia agreed that religious liberty was one of the fundamental freedoms. A frequent explanation for this position, aside from the perfunctory justification that it was a mark of civilized government, was that because human nature is such that some people are good and some bad, belief cannot be forced on everyone with uniform results. What is good and true to one will not necessarily appear so to another.[52] And the same could be said of the state's preferences. As the compilers of a survey of "religious laws" undertaken by the Translation Bureau of the Dajōkan (Supreme Executive Council) concluded, countries too have their preferred religions and teachings about one's duty to God, all of which may differ. Therefore, the best policy was that of the United States, which did not attempt to produce correct personal behavior in religion.[53]

On the other hand, acknowledging an individual's religious freedom did not preclude the government's right to establish a national religion. At best, the debate in 1874 concluded in a draw, for the two sides took the debate about religious freedom into the matter of the government's duty to protect public peace and morality. In libertarian fashion, Nakamura argued against any government involvement in religion—even, as some of his fellows had suggested, to encourage public morality. In an essay determined to allay concerns over a conflict of interest between Christianity and Japanese sovereignty, Nakamura observed that the English pray daily for the prosperity of their lords and fathers and raise their glasses to the prosperity of the queen. Because the people share in the responsibility of national administration, the joint rights of sovereign and people encourage the ruler to cherish the people and the people to appreciate the law. To assume that the people are stupid and must be ordered from above is to encourage the people to think of rebellion. Rather, Nakamura cautioned, religion is food for the spirit and must be left to people's discretion.[54]

Mori Arinori, playing devil's advocate for the opposing view, enlisted Emeric Vattell and Robert Phillimore on international law to directly relate the issue of a national religion to that of religious liberty. The crux of Mori's argument depends on differentiating the two fundamental forms of religion: religion in the heart of the individual and religion expressed externally in a publicly established form. According to Vattell, the individual's right to freedom of religion pertains only to resisting official orders to worship and revere a particular religion; one cannot be forced to believe what one does not approve. At the same time, however, one does not have the right to harm social interaction by doing as one likes in public. Hence when all the people worship one deity or honor one religion, the government can rightly support such a national religion. In the absence of such unanimity, the ruler nonetheless has both a duty to plan for the people's well-being and a right to select a national religion according to what he personally finds most true and good. But he does not have the right to order or oppress the people. In light of Vattell, in other words, Mori's version of "national religion" is at best a description of majority habits and not a prescription for national behavior.[55]

One conclusion to be drawn from this discussion of the proper spheres of religion and government is that as Meiji intellectuals began to determine the appropriate activities of government and the respective duties proper to individuals and government, they differentiated a domain of personal freedom, as a private, interior space, from the public domain of law and order. That is, they absolutized the individual's right to faith but invoked the government's duty to maintain public order as a way to justify its interference with a group's collective right to public worship. As we have seen, Fukuzawa and Nakamura's earlier, liberal interpretation of freedom minimized government and restrained the individual through his duties to others. Ultimately, however, the earlier tradition of civil liberty, represented by the Dutch-based texts on law, proved most compelling for Japanese considerations of liberty: when individual discretion lapsed and personal behavior threatened public well-being, law was the appropriate measure for restraining individuals.

Two points merit emphasis. First, we see among Meirokusha intellectuals a new approach to the political problem inherited from Tokugawa political discourse—the opposition between people and government. As a consequence of the liberal interpretation of liberty introduced by Fukuzawa and Nakamura, the people have become a set of individuals. Second, the general consensus on religious freedom failed to serve as a precedent for the subsequent debate over the liberty of the press. Indeed, the separation between an absolute right to freedom of conscience or faith, defined as internal, and the external manifestation of that faith as a qualified right to freedom of religion proved irrelevant in the debate over publicizing opinions, which is necessarily a public activity and largely meaningless when confined to the internal domain of thought or conscience. What united the Meiji leadership and intellectuals in the debate over religion was the general commitment—however variable in intensity—to the goal of constitutional government and the government's duty to maintain peace. The liberal valorization of the individual's personal freedom proved to be the easily dispensable aspect of a theory of liberty. It was a fine line between not oppressing the people in matters of religion, by forcing them to believe, and oppressing the people in public discussion, by restricting the expression of their opinions.

Liberty of the Press: Natural Progress and Temporary Panic

The freedom of the press began to distress members of the Meiji oligarchy in 1873 when a budget squabble among the ministers of finance, education, and justice was publicized in the newspapers—a previously unthinkable breach of the propriety of rulership. Although the oligarchy and the press had collaborated at the start of the new regime—officials and journalists shared a common samurai background and interests—the events of 1874 and 1875 began to differentiate the government's interests from certain constituents of the press.[56] Oligarch Kido Takayoshi, for example, who established the *Shinbun zasshi* (News Journal) in 1871 with the intent to communicate Japan's reforms to the people, began privately lamenting in 1873 the appalling lapses of propriety among local officials, soldiers, and all manner of malcontents who wrongly intruded into the affairs of the central government. As he saw it, the hierarchy, law, and discipline required for the security of the new state was breaking down, and he came to the conclusion that he must assist in protecting the government from those who would destroy it.[57] While Kido's concerns were those of a man besieged in high office, they do reflect the crisis situation portrayed in the news from late 1873 through 1875—what Mill had called "temporary panic." Japan was beset by destructive fighting among the oligarchy over whether or not to launch a punitive invasion of Korea, the threat of war with China over the Taiwan Incident, the first samurai rebellions in opposition to the oligarchy, and the growing demands for an elected national assembly.

It was in this last set of events, initiated by Itagaki Taisuke's January 1874 memorial, that the press figured most prominently as a public forum. Because the discussion necessarily criticized the ruling oligarchy and the political status quo, it drew great ire and most justified the government's stringent Newspaper Law of 1875, which censored a range of political topics from the media and provided heavily punitive measures to silence newspaper owners, editors, and journalists.[58] Public response was less a debate than a massive protest, for the government did little more than decree the 1875 law and enforce it with a vengeance. On repeated occasions, groups of journalists representing Tokyo's major newspapers requested from the Home Ministry clarification of the new restrictions on political content. The government responded with silence, presumably attempting to use fear of reprisal to intimidate the press into self-censorship.[59]

The idea of liberty of the press had been introduced in the 1860s. Katō and Tsuda included "freedom of writing" among their enumerations of rights, but the preferred expression was "freedom to publish," which combined the translation word *jiyū* with a variety of expressions for publishing, all of which referred to the traditional East Asian practice of woodblock printing. A liberal rationale for *shuppan jiyū* (liberty of publishing) was developed in Fukuzawa's *Seiyō jijō* and Nakamura's translation of Mill, as well as in two influential translations from European authors: Albany de Fonblanque's then popular but now forgotten textbook on the British government, *How We Are Governed,* and the chapter "Liberty of the Press in the United States" from Alexis de Tocqueville's *Democracy in America.*[60] Moreover, Tsuda and Nakamura addressed the Meirokusha on the issue in 1874. This early Meiji rationale for liberty of the press follows logically from the earlier discussion of liberal freedom. Books and newspapers play a central role in a constitutional polity because they disperse news and information that encourage an exchange of ideas and the public discussion of laws, customs, and government decisions. Generally, they promote intellectual progress; specifically, they are a politically important source of public power to check or support public affairs.[61]

But this seeming unanimity over the value of freedom of the press was compromised by a widespread acceptance of the government's right to regulate publishing. There were two sources for this acquiescence. In the first place, as in the case of government control of religion, there were long-standing precedents in Tokugawa censorship of the press and a measure of continuity from the shogunate to the Meiji regime.[62] The first Meiji press laws reasserted Tokugawa decrees, and some intellectuals reiterated traditional justifications for censoring certain content in the press. The persistence of lewd and vulgar customs among the ignorant people, evident in the popularity of traditional novels and broadsides of the Tokugawa age, only enouraged the people to read the trash of scandal, which it only made sense to censor.[63] In the second place, the example of Western nations was equivocal: where England and the United States tolerated an outspoken press, France and Prussia were restrictive. As secondary scholarship has surmised and recently available documents from the Translation Bureau of the Dajōkan would indicate, the 1852 press law issued by Napoleon III of France provided the model for Japan's 1875 Newspaper Law.[64] France licensed newspapers, required prior official approval of content, prohibited slander and incitement to riot, and outlined sanctions for suspending or forbidding publication and fining or imprisoning lawless authors and editors. As Nishimura Shigeki would later argue in support of the government's position, even civilized countries restrained the press. Ultimately, like control of religion, censorship of the press was justified on the grounds of preserving public peace and order.[65]

Few indeed were arguments to the contrary. Only Mill and Fukuzawa declared unequivocally that there was no justification for any restriction on public discussion and publication, although Nakamura and Fukuzawa both, we recall, tempered liberty by pairing it with duty. Mill asserted that only temporary panic could "drive ministers and judges from their propriety." Only fear of insurrection and public disorder—precisely the fear observed in Kido's *Diary*—would force officials to revive dormant statutes and curtail freedom of the press.[66] But the dangers in such a reaction, both the sober Tsuda and Tocqueville in translation pointed out, were several. Apart from giving the country a reputation for despotism, legal recourse to censorship laws ensured, ironically, that objectionable material received a second and potentially wider hearing. Moreover, as Tsuda concluded from his examination of French history, restricting public discussion and publications did not necessarily accomplish the goal of public peace: Napoleon III was overthrown in spite of—perhaps because of—government repression of the press. And was it not impractical, if not futile, for the government to try to read and censor beforehand every word that every individual wished to publish?[67]

But when the Newspaper Law was promulgated in June 1875, the protest in defense of liberty of the press did not measure up to the defense of freedom of religion undertaken by Fukuzawa, Nakamura, and their fellows. There was no discussion of liberty of the press or its correlate, freedom of speech, as a natural endowment of the individual. In fact, there was no mention in this context of the individual and his rights at all—which is all the more surprising since some writers, following Tocqueville, acknowledged that to restrict the press is necessarily to restrict both speech and popular sovereignty.[68] Instead of treating liberty as an absolute endowment of individuals, liberty was valued most in terms of its utility toward some greater end.

Spokesmen for the press and a few Meirokusha intellectuals foregrounded what they understood to be a causal relationship between freedom of the press and the progress of civilization. Tsuda and Nakamura reiterated the point that freedom of public discussion in the press refines understanding and encourages mental progress; they cautioned the government not to interfere with the momentum of Japan's progress toward civilization. Press dissidents like Narushima Ryūhoku, Yokose Fumihiko, and Minoura Katsundo, by contrast, declared repeatedly that the Newspaper Law was the work of barbarian despots; no civilized nation would enact such a law, which threatens to undermine Japan's progress and jeopardizes future generations. Minoura, moreover, explained that by prohibiting free speech the law produces hypocrisy because it disengages speech from truth when it forces writers to evade the truth in committing their opinions to paper.[69] As an ironic editorial pointed out: "We will never know whether this law is good or bad, unless we lawlessly discuss its advantages and disadvantages."[70] Much as Fukuzawa and Nakamura presented liberty as a means to mental enlightenment and a constitutional state, support for freedom of the press in 1875 rested on liberty as a means to civilization. Such a position was not very convincing, however, since many had already acknowledged that even civilized nations restrict the press.

The most prominent defense of the government's law came from Nishimura Shigeki in November 1875. Nishimura began with the obvious tactic of challenging the causal relationship between freedom and civilization: if self-governing peoples in civilized countries enact such laws, they must be excellent laws. He refused to believe that the absence of a national assembly in Japan somehow disqualified the government's restrictions on freedom of expression. The problem, he asserted, was that opponents of the Newspaper Law were not acknowledging the fact of different levels of development in Japan and the West. What was already a forest in the West was but a sprouting field in

Japan—but in either place, "to treat the good as evil or to treat the empty as full must be called libel." Nonetheless, Nishimura's discussion is rather disingenuous. By focusing on the Libel Law (also enacted in 1875), he implies that libel and misrepresentation are the main issues regarding the government's Newspaper Law. He never directly addresses the law's suppression of discussion concerning government policy. Instead he turns to the problem of truthful representations—these laws are only an effort to contain outrageous talk. In time, he concedes, a legislative assembly will be established and then there will be occasion for plenty of discussion. In other words, Nishimura uses the protest over the 1875 Newspaper Law to reiterate the government's gradualist approach to popular government. The entire package—a constitution, a national assembly, and civil liberties—will come in due course if only the people will be patient and obedient.[71]

Apart from witnessing an important moment at which the fledgling popular rights movement intersects with the discussion of freedom of the press, we also see here the displacement of liberty by the dominant ideological project of "civilization." Liberty has been pushed back into the context in which Katō Hiroyuki, Tsuda Mamichi, and Kanda Takahira first mentioned it in the preceding decade. Liberty follows from a constitutional government, which is the mark of a civilized state. Only when a state has a constitution can there be a lawful consideration of liberty. Hence the first order of business is not liberty but preparing the groundwork for civilization and a constitution.

Tocqueville had questioned the possibility of finding an intermediate position between the utter freedom and the utter baseness of the press, and typical of the healthy skepticism with which he regarded liberty in America, he answered indirectly. He did not worry about an unregulated press—most people either did not pay attention once the novelty had faded or did not have the intellectual requirements to formulate defensible opinions anyway. Thus he believed that "to enjoy the inestimable benefits that the liberty of the press ensures, it is necessary to submit to the inevitable evils that it creates."[72] Tsuda Mamichi approached the spirit of Tocqueville's ambivalence in what is perhaps the last liberal enunciation of an ideal conception of liberty among the early Meiji intelligentsia. He noted:

> The right of liberty is one of man's inherent and proper rights held most honored by civilized countries. But one must not use one's own rights in any way that harms the liberty of others—a misuse of liberty called arbitrariness. We Easterners have long taken liberty to be a perverse virtue;

we see the harm of liberty without recognizing its benefit. Hence we destroy the true nature of liberty, and slavish and mean customs emerge among the people.[73]

Three conclusions can be drawn from this analysis of the Japanese construction of liberty in the years prior to 1875. First, the passage from freedom of religion to freedom of the press exposes a practical disjunction between the individual and the people on questions of liberty. By couching the debate on freedom of the press in terms of the level of development of the people, the individual's right to free speech dropped out of the discussion. The liberal concept of liberty as an unconditional endowment from heaven was confined to the individual's pursuit of liberty in the realm of religion—an interior realm of conscience and faith.[74] Public worship, like all public activities related to civil liberties, concerns the people and their external actions. These could no longer be justified on the basis of a natural endowment but were henceforth linked to the movement for a constitutional government that would uphold liberties through law.

Second, the now standard translation word *jiyū* has escaped the tutelage of the transitional intellectuals—those men associated with Tokugawa Dutch studies and the Meirokusha—and entered the public domain. In the midst of the 1875 protest over the Newspaper Law, we see the first of many terms to be circulated in the newspapers: *jiyū hatsuron* (free discussion).[75] With *jiyū* in general circulation, the self-appointed educators no longer have a monopoly on its value. Before the end of the decade, "liberty" will invade popular consciousness with a plethora of amusing fads and ridiculous products for mass consumption—"freedom pills," "freedom candy," "freedom water," "freedom walks," and "free marriage"—and at the height of the popular rights movement in the early 1880s "liberty" will figure in the popular novelty of political fiction.[76] As I describe in the next chapter, "liberty" became abstracted as an ideal principle freed from its grounding in concrete freedoms—a development that accompanied the public discussion of people's rights.[77]

And third, just at this point when *jiyū* entered the public domain, it became a target of revision by members of the Meiji Six Society—including Nakamura Keiu, who had helped to standardize *jiyū* in his translation of Mill. One is initially baffled to read Nakamura declaring in an 1874 address to the Meirokusha that there is no suitable translation word in Chinese or Japanese for "liberty" or Nishimura Shigeki asserting on the eve of the promulgation of the 1875 Newspaper Law that the translation for "liberty" is *jishujiyū*. To be sure, this is the period in which *jiyū* stabilizes as the standard translation word and we should not be surprised by alternative expressions. But this is also the point at which *jiyū* begins to be advocated by journalists representing the people, and I believe that Nakamura and Nishimura were attempting a last-minute revision to forestall the possibility of the people embracing *jiyū* and actively asserting their freedom to do whatever they wanted. Nakamura, remember, had anticipated the promise of Christianity to restrain the selfish mob; in 1874, he was surely aware that discussions of liberty received a greater public hearing than the message of the church. Accordingly, when he tried to reopen the matter of defining liberty, he specifically criticized terms like *jishu* (autonomy) and *nin'i* (discretion) that implied "the right and power of people to act according to their wishes."[78]

Nishimura, by contrast, undertook to justify political gradualism by rejecting the liberal conception of liberty. In a manner recalling Katō Hiroyuki's *Rikken seitai ryaku* (1868), Nishimura identified, on the one hand, "natural" or "personal liberty," which comes from God, is granted by heaven at birth, and is that by which people satisfy their desires as individuals. Nishimura reminded his listeners that people are not solitary and independent creatures within the social world; rather, they must interact—and the conditions of that interaction force us to acknowledge the fact that others, like ourselves, possess liberty, so we must give up a part of our liberty to fulfill "the way of social interaction." On the other hand, he identified "social" or "political liberty," which is provisionally identical with natural liberty but which, in the interests of the prosperity and peace of the whole society, is a limitation on the liberty of the individual—controlling and confining personal liberty to its appropriate area. Nishimura's best example was the use of law to control the unreasonableness of the one who interferes with the liberty of others—in fact, the law increases the one's social liberty. Hence this social liberty is also political liberty; it opposes political bondage and the tyranny of lords or ministers in order to protect one's body and property.[79]

We have here a return to the human liberties enumerated by Katō, Tsuda, and Kanda in the 1860s in the social environment recalling Thomas Hobbes' description of perpetual war. Nishimura specifically mentions the three main rights demanded by this rule of law: self-protection; personal liberty except where prohibited by law; and personal property. The liberal version of liberty—what Nishimura calls natural or personal liberty—serves only to stress our social nature and the need to restrain ourselves. For the most part, Nishimura's focus on the earlier tradition of human liberties allows him to reiterate the government's gradualist approach to the question of popular participation. He declares that people acquire liberty as more and more of them acquire scholarship and knowledge; in time, the situation of a few officials governing the many will shift to the general right of the majority to participate in political administration.[80] Implicitly, in this diminishing of personal liberties, Nishimura rejects liberalism's utilitarian justification for liberty. Liberty does not produce or cause anything; it grows with knowledge and is manifest under conditions of political constitutionalism.

5

Differentiating
Right and
Sovereignty

M odern European political theory defines privilege as a particular power, granted to some and not others, and right as a universal endowment that has been secured historically through law. While privilege is characteristic of the arbitrary power of absolutist states, right is characteristic of republican or otherwise "free" states in which the law empowers the citizens with their rights. The power to make law is the power of sovereignty—once monopolized by the monarch but wrested from him in the revolutionary struggles that established constitutions, republics, or democracies. Constitutions have located sovereignty in the people and transformed the king's privileges into the people's rights, giving legal form to the bourgeois state. Although it simplifies one version of a Western tradition, this description of the relations among privilege, right, sovereignty, and law clarifies a truism concerning political practice: the struggles between king and people or among factions within the people over control of law are essentially a question of power.

While such a reduction of political traditions to struggle for power is not a particularly sophisticated point of departure for an analysis of right and sovereignty, the perspective does strongly resonate with

Japan's efforts to import these Western political concepts in the nineteenth century. For in Japan, these terms were all translated with the Chinese character *ken*, an ancient word for "balance" or "scale" and hence to balance or weigh, to judge, the power to judge, or simply the power and authority of judgment. One Tokugawa historian, Rai San'yō, used *ken* to mean the authority a sovereign rightfully possesses in ruling the country properly and peacefully.[1] That is to say: the effort to translate power, privilege, right, and sovereignty into Japanese was largely the effort both to understand and to invent distinctions among these terms in order to adequately differentiate them in Japanese translation into expressions more complex than their common denominator, *ken*. Although distinctions are now comfortably in place—*tokken* for privilege, *kenri* for right, *shuken* for sovereignty, and *kensei* for power—this was not the case in 1880. Unlike the original English terms, the range of Japanese translation words philologically resonates with this expression for power—and particularly the human agency that commands power.

Because these key terms can all be signified with *ken*, early Meiji translations of right and sovereignty present a more complex problem than that of liberty. Several translation words signify multiple meanings: *kokken* can be construed as "state sovereignty," "state right," and "state power"; *minken* doubles as "people's rights" and "popular sovereignty"; and *shuken* as "sovereignty" and "royal privilege." Such polysemy follows from the fact that preliminary Japanese efforts to make sense of Western concepts proceeded largely by trial and error—the experimenting with analogs described in Chapter 3, in which Chinese translation words were supplemented with European-language pronunciations in *furigana* to mark a translation word as such. And, of course, the possibilities for experimentation were increased because the conceptual fields of European languages differed among themselves, particularly with regard to the vocabulary of "law," "power," and "right": where English strongly differentiates all three terms, Dutch *regt*, French *droit*, and German *Recht* conflate the three. This chapter demonstrates that as usage of *ken* evolved in the course of the movements for a national assembly and for people's rights (1874–1884), these political debates not only differentiated right, power, and sovereignty but guided *ken* away from people's rights in favor of the state's right and sovereign power.

One key to this process was of course the Western threat of military force. Many Japanese argued that in the face of Japan's international insecurity, the state's right took precedence over the people's right—which only begged the question of who constitutes the state: the government or the people? Another key was the fracturing of the close association between freedom and rights introduced in the legal translations of the 1860s and confirmed by early Meirokusha pronouncements. Mitsukuri Rinshō declared: "The meaning of liberty . . . is that people can freely enact their rights without the interference of others." Fukuzawa Yukichi noted, after the example of early modern European jurists such as Hobbes, that the natural freedom of humankind is reconstructed as a set of civil liberties encoded through the structure of law as the set of personal rights.[2] In the absence of this specific context of law, the language characteristic of the 1860s texts—*jiyū no ken* (right to liberty)— became redundant, and we see such usage decline in the 1870s. As I show in this chapter, after a vociferous public debate over the people's civil rights and the people's right to constitute a government, right was gradually replaced by an abstracted and idealized notion of freedom.

Translating Western Law and Political Institutions

As early as 1841, the shogunate ordered some of its Dutch studies scholars to translate Dutch texts on law. But not until the first unequal treaties were signed in 1858 did scholars at the Tokugawa institute of foreign studies undertake systematic translations of the terminology of European law and political institutions.[3] These 1860s texts broke with the earlier work of the 1840s and began to establish what would become the standard translation of legal and political terminology.[4] In addition to the works by Katō Hiroyuki, Tsuda Mamichi, Nishi Amane, and Kanda Takahira introduced in Chapter 4—all based on Dutch works, particularly the lectures of Simon Vissering—another key text was Henry Wheaton's *Elements of International Law*, translated into literary Chinese by W.A.P. Martin and Chinese assistants in 1864 and imported into Japan in 1865, where it was reproduced in various editions for the next decade as *Bankoku kōhō* (The Public Law of All Domains).[5] Martin's translation was the main precedent for using *ken* to translate right and sovereignty; it was also a problematic point of departure, however, because Martin used *ken* to cover a field of political and legal terminology that included right, power, authority, sovereignty, force, jurisdiction, status, and legitimacy. From this plethora of meaning surrounding *ken* can be traced two significant developments of the 1870s: the evolution of the standard translation word for right, *kenri,* and the fundamental opposition between state right and personal right that informed the debate over the people's rights.

Although we often read that W.A.P Martin first coined the translation word *kenri* for the English term "right," this account is not so straightforward as we might believe.[6] In fact, Martin initially used *kenri* as his translation word for an ambassador's "privileges"; it also served to translate "powers," "rights," and even "rights and privileges."[7] By itself, *ken* is most often Martin's translation word for: (1) power, as in the legislative, executive, and judicial powers of state, the unlimited power of the monarch, or treaty-making powers; (2) authority, as in superior authority, state authority, or acting on one's own authority; and (3) rights, as in equal rights among states, the right of self-protection, rights of self-preservation and independence, fishing rights, rights of war, and so on.[8] *Ken* is also an occasional translation word for status, force, and jurisdiction, and Martin combines it with other Chinese characters (as in *kenri*) to form translation words for sovereignty, neutrality, rights, privileges, and eminent domain.[9] Such seemingly inexact use of *ken* in translating Wheaton is an indication, I believe, that Martin was guided less by distinctions among the English terms power, right, and authority, and more by the conceptualization in continental European languages—Dutch *regt*, French *droit*, and German *Recht*—that we might characterize as a rightful use of the power of law and hence law and right as a just use of force.[10]

This overlap of meaning characterizes the development of political language in the early Meiji period and invites an examination of how *ken* came to differentiate several European concepts in Japan. In the Dutch studies texts of the 1860s, five general patterns of the usage of *ken* are readily observable. The first is unique to *Tonarigusa*, the earliest of these texts, where Katō used *ken* to translate what might be called the "power of state" (or Dutch *regt*) at the basis of every political form. He translated "monarchy" as the "holding of *ken* by the monarch," constitutional monarchy as the "division of *ken* between high and low," aristocratic republic as "domination of *ken* by illustrious families," and democratic republic as the "*ken* shared by all the people." His second book, *Rikken seitai ryaku*, however, established the pattern repeated in Nishi's and Tsuda's works; instead of *ken*, Katō used *ji*, an abbreviation for *seiji*, political administration, so that monarchy became "the political administration of the monarch" and so on. *Ken* by itself quickly ceased to be used to refer to the power animating government structures.[11]

The second usage of *ken* translates the tripartite division of powers within a state: the legislative, executive, and judicial powers—what we often refer to as the three branches of government, which ideally manifest a balance of power. Nishi and Tsuda used *ken* alone to translate each of these powers; Katō, by comparison, expanded this to *kenpei* (controlling power). This usage persisted during the Meiji period as writers repeatedly referred to the "three great powers" (*san dai ken*)—still in the Japanese language today.[12]

A third and related usage is the set of translation expressions for "sovereign power" or "sovereignty," which we find in Martin, Nishi, and Tsuda. These can be understood as progressive abbreviations: from *jiritsu jishu no ken* (the power of self-establishment and self-mastery), to *jishu no ken* (power of autonomy), to simply *shuken* (sovereign power). Wheaton explicitly mentioned the European habit of identifying the sovereign with the state, and Chinese-character constructions of sovereignty repeat this identification of sovereignty with the sovereign's power. Given the claim in international and state law that states are autonomous and sovereign powers, a related usage of *ken* is the expression *kokken*, meaning "state authority," "state power," "state right," and "state sovereignty."[13]

In addition to these three usages of *ken* to refer to aspects of state power, *ken* is also used in contexts that refer to individuals—particularly the power, authority, and right that accrue to legally appointed officials of the state. This is a somewhat amorphous category, for these usages are often compound expressions that add distinctive dimensions to *ken*. Hence we find several expressions that emphasize the power of right, *kenpei*, *kensei*, and *kenryoku*; an expression that emphasizes *ken* as authority, *ken'i*; the term marked as "privilege" above, *kenri*, which stresses the advantages of right; and finally the expression *tokken*, "special powers" or "privileges." Nishi's translation of Vissering, for example, demonstrates the variation of this usage; Nishi's summary of "customary usage in diplomacy" includes the *tokken* of consuls, the *kenri* of special envoys, and the *ken* of ambassadors—all of which could be acceptably translated as rights, powers, special rights, or privileges.[14] And in fact, contrary to our usage of terms today, one sees in contemporary English-language newspapers in Japan the occasional editorial that equates right, advantage, and privilege.[15]

Fifth and finally, *ken* was used as the translation word for the English concept of rights. In his work on constitutional forms, Katō used *ken* alone to translate the set of private and public rights, such as the rights to life, to personal autonomy, and to liberty of action. Although Katō used *kenri* in one instance (for "rights to liberty of thought, speech, and writing"), he implied that these constitutional rights (*ken*) have replaced the "power and privilege" (*kenri*) of king and aristocracy. We see here an initial tension over the appropriateness of *kenri* as a translation for "rights," for *ri* suggests advantages more in keeping with shogunal or royal privilege than the kind of equality and general applicability implied by theories of constitutional and natural rights.[16]

Before discussing the stabilization of *kenri* for "right," I want to emphasize the fact that *ken* in these 1860s texts is most often an attribute of states and individuals. This disposition was marked in the translations of Wheaton and Vissering by a powerful analogy derived from natural law: a nation is like an individual and hence both international and human society are grounded in fundamental "rights" to self-preservation and self-determination. In Nishi Amane's work, the rights of states are patterned after the rights of individuals. Because sovereign states are "self-established" and "independent," like individuals, states have a personal right to mutually interact, a right to autonomy, rights of property, and rights of making contracts (treaties in the case of states).[17] By comparison, Tsuda (and Martin) started with the idea of sovereignty modeled on the autonomy of an individual person and then moved to an analysis of state sovereignty (*shuken* or *kokken*) as a tripartite division of powers.[18]

These texts of the 1860s thus present us with a powerful but undeveloped opposition: on the one hand, state's rights and powers; on the other hand, personal rights. Wheaton's and Vissering's texts of international law defined a state's *ken* fairly clearly. As Nishi put it, a state has rights to equality vis-à-vis other states, to intercourse with other states, and to independence in its internal affairs; and from these three arise its rights in peace, in war, and in diplomacy. This right is equivalent to power in that a state has rights to the degree it has the power to enforce or defend these rights; in the context of international society, in other words, *ken* is equivalent to *regt*, *droit*, or *Recht*.[19] Such a usage of *kokken* had already entered official deliberations by 1869, where it figured pragmatically as a factor in Meiji government decisions regarding international relations.[20]

Personal rights, however, were neither so clearly understood nor so readily defensible. The rights to freedom of speech, of thought, and so on were collectively translated most often as *shiken*, personal or private rights, and had to do with individuals in an apparently nonpublic capacity, much like liberty in the preceding chapter. Accordingly, we find Katō's fellows working toward a more appropriate nuance. Fukuzawa Yukichi asserted that "right" in English has a dual connotation: it is related both to moral honesty and to rightness, which means having the authority and power to do something and thus fulfilling one's duty to do it. Fukuzawa made a point of translating "right" as *tsūgi* (general principle or common justice).[21] Tsuda too noted that the word "right" conflated both *ken*, a principle under the law, and "moral uprightness"; both he and Nishi accordingly translated right as *kengi* (the rightness of power), a word they treated occasionally as a compound to stress that it means both *ken* and *gi*, the power and justice of right. Tsuda then enumerated the people's rights as "common rights" (*tsūken*) or "public rights" (*kōken*) held by all subjects of the state—the equal rights of all, meant to replace the privileges (*tokken*) of ruling classes in societies of the past.[22]

The difficult novelty of the concept of rights necessitated learned explanations. Where Katō simply noted that rights are a consequence of constitutional political forms and Tsuda explained that rights are established by the statutes of civil law, Fukuzawa understood the connection between the creation of republican political forms through constitutions which, at the same time, proclaimed through law the existence and protection of certain rights for the citizens of the republic. Only Kanda Takahira matched Fukuzawa's sophistication. Given the Meiji government's effort to make the archaic values of Shintō the doctrinaire teaching of the land, Kanda specifically differentiated natural law from moral teaching. Moral teaching attempts to regulate the speech and conduct of people who vary widely in terms of human nature. Natural law, by contrast, concerns human natural rights, which include those "innate" rights with which we are born—our rights to life, to speech and action, and so on—and those "acquired" rights that arise from our labor, including rights regarding property and rights of contract.[23]

But these scholarly distinctions in defining rights gave way, in the 1870s, to the stabilization of the translation word *kenri*, the term introduced in Martin's translation of Wheaton for "right" and "privilege." Despite Katō's and Tsuda's misgivings about the nuance of "privilege" in the term, a majority of writers came to use *kenri* for "right" because of widespread exposure to that usage both in Nakamura Keiu's 1871 translation of J. S. Mill's *On Liberty* and in Katō's own 1872 translations from Bluntschli's *Allgemeines Staatsrecht* as well as his two prominent attempts to synthesize Western constitutionalism with Japan's particular traditions: *Shinsei taigi* (Fundamental Principles of the New Administration) of 1870 and *Kokutai shinron* (New Theory of the Body Politic) of 1875.[24] Nonetheless, if *kenri* was becoming standard in the early 1870s, a number of writers instead used a homonym, *kenri*, meaning "authority and principle" or "authoritative right." Certainly Nishi Amane, in his effort to retrieve "principle" from its Confucian background and rehabilitate it in the contemporary context of civilization, wanted to emphasize that "principle" contributed to a system of law; in his works, this second *kenri* suggests a "right" more principled than mere power.[25] But some texts employed both forms of *kenri* with no obvious distinction, including the *Meiji Six Journal*, Fukumoto Nichinan's *Futsū minken ron* (On the People's Common Rights), and even Nishi on occasion.[26] Only after rights had come under the attack of government censorship in the late 1870s did the expression "natural human rights" (*tenpu no jinken, tennen no jinken*) become pointedly and commonly used. Otherwise this concept of rights was routinely referred to as "human" or "people's rights": from *hito no kenri, jinmin no kenri,* and *jinrui no kenri* to simply *jinken*.[27]

A related effort to contain the nuance of advantage or privilege in the translation of right as *kenri* was to pair it with duty—as in the case of liberty. Although Fukuzawa Yukichi had introduced the pairing of right and duty, his translation words (respectively *tsūgi* and *shokubun*) were replaced by the still standard terms *kenri* and *gimu*, which figured prominently in the works of Katō Hiroyuki, Kido Takayoshi, and Nishi Amane in the early 1870s. Like Fukuzawa, who had borrowed the analysis from William Blackstone and Robert Chambers, Kido and Katō were reassured by the jurisprudential theory that an individual's personal rights were contained by corresponding duties. As Fukuzawa noted, the law protects our rights, and we have a duty to obey the law. Given the oligarchy's interest in maintaining social order, this was a promising method for incorporating rights into a Japanese constitution.[28] But when activists like Itagaki Taisuke and Ueki Emori began to pair right and duty in advocating people's rights—asserting, for example, that the people fulfill their duty to pay taxes and hence deserve their right to political participation "right and duty" declined as a central point in discussions of rights by those advocating a gradualist approach to the introduction of representative government. Draft constitutions eventually revived right and duty, and ultimately the pair was instituted in the Meiji Constitution of 1889. While earlier distinctions such as innate and acquired, or private and public, may have disappeared because they were largely irrelevant in a political debate that still had to establish the legitimacy of rights generally, the pairing of right and duty eventually complemented the gradualist approach to the institutional grounding of rights.[29] Unlike the international society into which Japan was forced and in which Japanese officials immediately learned to refer to Japan's state rights, domestic society in Japan would have to adjust its laws and political structures in order to actualize the idea of personal rights—precisely the issue dominating Japanese politics between 1874 and 1890.

Minken: People's Rights and the People's Right

Let us turn from these formal descriptions of state right and personal rights to the ways in which concepts were deployed in political argument. In general, the debates that engaged the concepts associated with *ken* encompassed four sets of issues. One was the constitutional form of the new state; this was raised early in the 1870s by some of the oligarchs, and it reached a public forum with the newspaper debate on sovereignty in 1881 and 1882. What type of constitution should Japan have, given Japan's unique body politic? And who would hold sovereign power in a constitutional Japan? A second and related issue concerned the participation of the people in the new state; this debate, called the "movement to establish a national assembly," began in 1874, when a faction of the oligarchy left the government in protest and demanded a national assembly of "the people," and continued to 1881 when the emperor decreed that a constitution would be promulgated in 1889 and an assembly convened in 1890. A third issue was the question of the people's rights or liberties in the new state: did they not have rights of free speech, free assembly, a free press, even the right to participate in politics? Apart from a rather academic debate over the equal rights of men and women, the better-known debate was the widespread protest against government censorship and restrictions on political discussions and meetings during the early 1880s—voiced increasingly in local communities and newspapers and encouraged by the establishment of local branches of Itagaki Taisuke's national Liberty Party (Jiyūtō). At the time this protest was called the "people's rights and freedom argument," but it is now routinely treated as the "freedom and popular rights movement."[30] This "freedom and people's rights argument" intersected with a scholarly debate over the nature of rights provoked by the publication in late 1882 of Katō Hiroyuki's *Jinken shinsetsu* (A New Theory of Human Rights), which rejected the theory of natural rights in favor of an evolutionary theory of acquired rights. And a fourth issue engaging *ken* was Japan's insecure international position, remedies for which were envisioned in treaty revision to eliminate extraterritoriality and restrictions on Japan's import and export duties. This issue was phrased in terms of *kokken*, or state's right, which integrated the earlier discussions of state sovereignty with Japan's international sovereignty. Rather than treat this set of issues chronologically, I will focus on sovereignty and state's right in the following section and concentrate here on the people's right and personal rights.

The immediate political problem in early Meiji was how to situate the people and their rights institutionally. As most activists would insist, the people's rights were included in the blueprint for the Meiji state, the Charter Oath, which inspired the goal of public discussion in some form of assembly for the administration of the new state in which both samurai and commoner would participate.[31] However one defined the nature of the assembly, public discussion, and participation, as the oligarchy began to consider the political forms and divisions of powers brought to their attention in the texts of the 1860s, their memorials on Japan's constitution (and draft constitutions) recognized two tensions central to the institutional project: on the one hand, the need to balance the monarch's right (*kunken*) and the people's right (*minken*); on the other hand, the need to establish a constitutional government that specified the rights (and duties) of all parties in the state.

Some focused on the former issue, others the latter. Ōkubo Toshimichi, for example, reacting to accounts of the violence of the French Revolution, advocated the "joint rule of sovereign and people" and called for a system that would somehow balance *kunken* and *minken*; this minimal position persisted among the oligarchy, reiterated during the political crisis of 1881 by Yamagata Aritomo (and eventually informing the Meiji Constitution).[32] By contrast, Kido Takayoshi and members of the Sa'in and Genrōin (senate-like elite assemblies that imitated bureaucratic agencies) emphasized the need to establish a constitutional government that would create a national assembly as the vehicle for *minken* and protect the people's liberties. Ōkuma Shigenobu reiterated this position in 1881, only to be forced out of office—an indication of the increasingly besieged outlook of the oligarchy. A majority of oligarchs, in other words, were committed to constitutional government provided that popular participation proceeded gradually. What divided them was the degree to which the people's rights would be institutionally guaranteed.[33]

Accordingly, a common thread running through all the discussion of constitutional law and the place of rights was a paradigmatic opposition between government and people. Western political theory, as Katō showed in his 1868 survey of constitutional forms, identified monarchy and democracy as the extremes of a fundamental opposition between monarch and people, whose respective powers could be modified through republican and constitutional variations. But in Japanese practice, "the people" found themselves in a struggle with the institutional powers that momentum had left in place when the former despotism of Tokugawa rule had been overthrown. Hence the opposition between government and people resonated powerfully in several contexts for Japanese readers—from its cooperative expression in the 1860s texts, where government administration upholds the law that protects our personal rights, to the explicit hostility in the 1870s translations of liberal classics like Mill's *On Liberty* and Herbert Spencer's *Social Statics*, where government is the power intent on depriving the people of their rights and thus the people must be vigilant in limiting the power of government. After 1874, many writers turned to the ideological promise of harmony between monarch and people and phrased the conflict more explicitly as that between the ruling officials and the people. As Itagaki and his allies asserted in their memorial of 1874, the emperor and the people—the primary constituents of Japan—found themselves in a dangerous position because political right had been usurped by government officials. Hence a people's elected assembly must be established in order to restrict the officials' power and restore the unity of high and low proposed in the Charter Oath.[34] In the course of the 1870s, it was precisely the oligarchy's willingness to delay the creation of people's institutions and to suspend the people's rights of free speech and a free press that fueled the opposition between government and people and encouraged the movement to establish a national assembly. The people's project under the new Meiji regime came to be seen as the need to establish both their right to constitute a government, in cooperation with the emperor, and their individual and collective rights as the people of Japan.

After 1874, the term *minken* would comprehend both halves of this project—and to indicate this duality I formally translate *minken* as "the people's right(s)." Surprisingly, in light of his subsequent opposition, it was Katō Hiroyuki, in his rejoinder to Itagaki, who synthesized *minken* as people's rights and the people's right in government. Katō acknowledged that *minken* arose in situations of absolute monarchy, like Russia and Prussia, where the people were given no opportunity for education and advancement, and hence *minken* became an appropriate counterpoint to the monarch's absolute right. Katō conceded that a popularly elected national assembly would likely be established in the future, and he acknowledged the truth that "government is made for people, not people for government." Hence he would support extending private rights and promoting education in order to hasten Japan's becoming a civilized state, a prerequisite to popular participation.[35] In the wake of this inauguration of the movement for a national assembly, Nagamine Hideki's translation of Mill's *Considerations on Representative Government* further promoted this comprehensive notion of *minken*. Like Katō, Nagamine juxtaposed absolute right and *minken;* but he also translated "democracy" as *minkensei* and equated it with "free government." A free government was the people's government, and even though Mill, in keeping with his gradualist preferences, advocated not democracy but "representative democracy," the connection between the people's liberty and a people's government was established.[36]

The construction of this concept of *minken*—which I consider a transition from the more general and abstract concept of human natural rights, *jinken*, to a more specific and pragmatic concept of the people's right(s)—combined two very different notions of right: one, the term introduced through international law and best considered as Dutch *regt*, that conflation of law and right as the rightful application of power and authority under law; the other, the term introduced in English constitutional theory and most often plural, "rights," those liberties or privileges enjoyed by all persons and protected by law. While the process of disentangling these English and Continental meanings in order to differentiate rights from law had begun in the 1860s with Martin's translations of "law" as *hō* and "right" as *ken*, Japanese conceptualizations of *ken* in the 1870s had to instead integrate the English and Contintental meanings in order to collectively ground, in the concept of *minken*, the people's personal rights and the people's right to rule through the creation of law.[37]

Given the usage of *ken* in the 1860s texts and the context of opposition between government and people, one of the most signficant shifts in meaning in the 1870s was to differentiate *ken* as mere power from *ken* as the legitimate power of right. Fukuzawa had already introduced in 1869 the pointed narrative of the English, American, and French revolutions, in which the people revolted against the injustice of royal power and established constitutional law both to assert their right to self-rule and to protect their rights. In the 1870s, translations of Mill's *On Liberty* and *Considerations on Representative Government*, Rousseau's *Social Contract*, and a number of Japanese commentaries on rights reiterated the narrative of the people's assertion of their rights against the power of the monarch, and these later texts made a point of consistently translating "rights" with *kenri* and "power" with terms more reflective of "force" such as *kensei* and *seiryoku*. Only constitutional forms of power were legitimately the ground of rights. Until the oligarchy produced a constitution, their *ken*—which some critics called pointedly *kanken* (officials' right)—was mere power to rule, not any legitimate right to govern. In the writings of *minken* advocates, the legitimacy of the people's action followed a trajectory of meaning stabilized in the persisting usage of *ken* to signify the three main powers of government into which state right (*staatsregt* or constitutional law) is divided: the legislative, executive, and judicial. The legislative power of government was defined as the legislative right of the people, which was actualized through the right to elect the people's representatives and manifested in a people's national assembly (*minkai* or *kokkai*). Hence some advocates of a national assembly and the people's right(s), such as Fukumoto Nichinan and Toyama Shōichi, began to emphasize the right to participate in government (*sansei kenri*), for only the enactment of the people's right, through participation, could guarantee the people's rights. Both Fukumoto and Toyama introduced the term *kengen*, or "right's limit" (now a word meaning authority or jurisdiction), as the parallel shift in government: the government's right was limited as the people's right(s) expanded.[38]

A related development during the decade was the discussion of *dōken* (equal rights), which had a wide hearing in the context of husbands and wives. In 1867, Tsuda Mamichi first mentioned the "equal rights" of everyone before the law, and Nakamura Keiu's 1871 translation of *On Liberty* asserted that wives and husbands have the same rights before the law. But the issue was elaborated in 1874 and 1875 when Fukuzawa Yukichi and Mori Arinori criticized injustices in the traditional family institution.[39] Both protested the unfairness of a husband's right to take multiple wives, and both advocated monogamy as a solution appropriate to the parity of wife and husband in the family. But in the wake of Mori's contract marriage in February 1875, a surprise to his fellows in the Meirokusha, the society roundly critiqued this idea of the equal rights of husbands and wives and men and women. Spurred by his utter dismay at the deference that Western men exhibited toward women, Katō irately denounced such a preposterous notion; Tsuda reminded his audience of the appropriate differences between men and women regarding political rights—a principle shared by Western societies.[40] As the decade developed, "equal rights" was enlisted by advocates of a national assembly and people's rights, particularly as an assertion of the equal rights of all the people of Japan against the privileges of former samurai and government officials.[41]

By the late 1870s, some advocates had taken the concept of *minken* in decidedly populist directions. Ueki Emori, for example, followed Rousseau in asserting that people are born free, that the people are the basis of the state, and that the government manages state affairs on their behalf—a comment not unlike that of Katō's 1874 response to Itagaki. Ueki went beyond what Katō could tolerate when he pointed out the problems that monarchs and unjust governments had created for states in the past; he contended that the best, if only, way to advance the state, to benefit the people, and to protect the state internationally was to expand the people's rights and freedoms. In fact, given that the body of the people is like a family, so that the state is in fact a "state-family" or "nation," the free state is that state which most extends the autonomy and freedom of each individual.[42] As Itagaki Taisuke insisted as leader of the Liberty Party in 1881, the state's affairs involve both private and public benefits, and the only way to integrate the two is through the people's participation in government. The solution for Japan that Ueki and then the Liberty Party advocated was to establish a constitution that guaranteed the people's liberty, actualized the people's political right, and specified the rights and duties of both emperor and people.[43]

This need to maintain public loyalty to the emperor restricted the degree to which activists might extend populism into pure democracy. In other words: a subversive connotation lurking in *minken* was the specter of popular sovereignty, for it would have been unseemly to advocate a constitution that omitted the emperor. Kojima Shōji, who was committed to integrating Japan's traditional body politic and a national assembly, early on attempted to dispel fears that *minken* implied popular sovereignty. Although Rousseau's assertion, that the people are the state, arguably equated *minken* and sovereignty, the power and right of the people were typically harnessed by their leaders—Napoleon, for example—so that constitutions established the people's right in a national assembly, the seat of legislative power, and the monarch, as in France, managed executive power. Like later advocates of "Taishō democracy" in the 1910s and 1920s, Kojima was especially concerned to demonstrate that *minken* did not challenge the imperial house.[44]

A related and patriotic development in the writings of *minken* advocates was the linking of the people's right(s) to the state's right (*kokken*). The year 1878 witnessed Japan's first apparent success at treaty revision—a commitment from the U.S. government to restore Japan's tariff autonomy (ratification of which, because of the most-favored-nation clause, depended on the agreement of other Western states, which was not forthcoming)—and newspapers were full of discussions of *kokken*. From 1879, *minken* advocates such as Ueki and Fukumoto began asserting a causal relationship between the expansion of the people's right(s) and national stability, strength, and reputation. Ueki and several local and national groups, such as the Kokkai kisei dōmeikai (Alliance to Establish a National Assembly), argued that the establishment of the people's right(s) would safeguard both the people's and the state's independence; with independence jointly secured, the state's right can expand. A local group in Okayama prefecture went further in asserting that only with the creation of a national assembly could the people's right(s) be secured, which would in turn secure the state's right.[45]

The final and most significant conceptual development within *minken* arguments in the second decade of Meiji—that is, as the movement to establish a national assembly gave way to the freedom and people's rights argument in the 1880s—was that assertions of *minken* and attentiveness to rights receded in the face of an emphasis on freedom. The equation between rights and liberty was known to Japanese through Hobbes, Mill, and other writers; by the late 1870s, advocates of a national assembly, such as Kojima, Fukumoto, and Toyama, were using right and freedom somewhat interchangeably. We find in their works "natural freedom" along with "natural right" as well as the coupling of right and freedom in expressions like the "right of free speech" and the "right of freedom of religion"—expressions that were simplified to "freedom of religion" and "freedom of speech."[46] Apart from the logical ease of simplifying a perhaps cumbersome expression—"a right to freedom of" to "freedom"—this simplification occurred as advocates of a national assembly and people's rights began to substitute liberty for rights in their political arguments. Toyama, Ueki, and Itagaki had coupled right and liberty when they asserted that the people's right(s) and liberty grew together; as one expanded, so did the other. But in discussing the opposite case—that the growth of absolute government impaired the people's right(s) and liberty, as many advocates were witnessing from 1875–it was easier to frame the problem more simply as absolute power versus liberty. Increasingly in the 1880s, local groups spoke of an opposition between, on the one hand, government power and official privilege and, on the other, the people's liberty.[47] Liberty became abstracted and essentialized as the "principle of liberty" (*jiyū no shugi*) or the "spirit of liberty" (*jiyū no seishin*); activists described their work as the "liberty movement" or on behalf of a "free government" or "free society." In time, if the people were successful in "raising the lantern of liberty," the "winds of freedom" would blow and the "flowers of freedom" would blossom profusely. The meaning of freedom gradually shifted from a reference to specific rights—freedom of speech, freedom of the press, and so on—to a general concept denoting an ideal human condition.[48]

In the midst of this enthusiasm for *minken* and liberty, Katō Hiroyuki fired a broadside at the theoretical grounds of natural rights. Katō's *Jinken shinsetsu* (1882) was an effort to expose the idealistic chimera of natural rights and to ground a theory of rights in scientific principle, and Katō turned to the newly disovered law of evolution, animated by Darwin's discovery of natural selection, which Katō phrased as "the survival of the fittest." Katō applied the law of evolution to social forms and nations in order to explain the rise of civilization as the rise of the state, which proceeds from a chieftain and his followers to progressively more integrated forms of community with an acknowledged leader. Inevitably the leader of the state sees that it is in his interest to prevent arbitrary treatment among his people by granting certain rights and obligations to all. Katō utterly ignored the term *minken* and returned instead to *jinken*, human rights, which he redefined as "acquired rights" (*tokuyū kenri*). This was perhaps Katō's most important point, for he thus rephrased the gradualist approach to people's rights as a scientific and evolutionary proposition. The joint development of the state and civilization required that the intelligence and ability of the people reach levels comparable to those of Japan's competitors; only then could the Japanese state advance by granting the people's rights.[49]

Katō's argument was shocking to contemporaries and roundly criticized on a number of grounds. Yano Fumio, for one, was dismayed that Katō ignored morality in his description. Yano insisted that both morality and law arise from the conversion of human strength into legal right. Yes, one can say that rights arise from force, but not in the way Katō described: moral principle participates in the conversion of force into legal right.[50] Others faulted Katō's description of evolutionary process. Survival of the fittest is not the motive in the establishment of rights, and it is wrong to suggest it as the rationale for a sovereign's granting rights to his people; rather, constitutional systems are the origin of rights and liberties.[51] To underline this point, Baba Tatsui provided a history of the evolution of natural right from its first articulation in Justinian's *Code* to its establishment in law among the various European countries.[52] Toyama Shōichi and Ueki Emori insisted that Katō had misconstrued Darwin's principle of natural selection: it was not "survival of the fittest" as Katō would have it—the stronger consumes the weaker—but *shizen tōta hō*, a natural principle of "weeding out" the less productive, that is, an unmotivated and unconscious process at work in the plant and animal kingdoms that involves no actual struggle.[53] In fact, Toyama added, Katō misrepresents a host of writers who have nothing to say about Katō's version of evolution, including Darwin, Spencer, and Mill—he is relying on Carneri and Scheffle instead.[54]

Despite the scholarly doubt cast on Katō's theory, it made a significant impact. Given the standoff between the oligarchy and *minken* advocates, Katō offered a new justification for the status quo. The *minken* position did little more than insist on the people's natural rights and urge the government to be forthcoming. One could read of the development of republics and constitutional monarchies in Europe, but Japanese experience could not simply follow any of these received histories as if scripts. On the one hand, the oligarchy and its supporting officials and intellectuals agreed that some space for the people would be made in due course, once the latter had demonstrated their attainment of the prerequisite degree of civilization; on the other hand, their impatient fellows and, worse, their rural compatriots, angry over ever higher levels of taxation, all wanted their right to participation acknowledged and their personal rights guaranteed. Ueki Emori most clearly outlined the theoretical passage from the people's right to constitute a government to the establishment of a constitution that protected the people's rights. But unless the oligarchy voluntarily relinquished their command, the abstract and theoretical claim to people's rights could not be actualized according to a Euro-American precedent. Katō explained why the people should wait until their leaders took the initiative.

To my mind, the greater value of Katō's argument was its conceptual force. One important aspect of *Jinken shinsetsu*, as we shall see in Chapter 6, is Katō's contribution to the grounding of evolution in the new concept "society." Here I would point out that his use of "acquired right" shifted the discussion from "natural right" to "legal right." Katō had argued that rights are not natural but man-made, not something we are born with but something granted by the leader; in time, these acquired rights were written into law. In their criticisms of Katō, both Yano Fumio and Baba Tatsui insisted that these legal rights were in fact natural rights—implying, as Toyama Shōichi specifically stated, that acquired rights was a misrepresentation. The correct way of thinking, in their view, was that natural rights were at some point written into law, becoming in fact legal rights.[55] Legal rights thus became the common ground of argument between Katō and his most persistent critic, Toyama. Toyama had earlier (in *Minken benwaku*) commited himself to an alternative historical model of the development of rights, one based on the institutional securing of rights in England that did not need to take into account the concept of natural rights. Toyama and Katō, in other words, could agree that natural rights was an unnecessary concept; but where Katō argued that legal rights were granted when the ruler saw fit, Toyama insisted that people's legal rights were achieved through demand and struggle, historically constructed but nonetheless legitimate as personal legal rights. Hence the fact remained: however one might oppose the oligarchy's policy or Katō's questionable defense of it, the oligarchy was in charge, with their focus not on *minken* but *kokken*, the state's right, in order to secure a constitution that would locate sovereignty in their emperor and government in themselves.

The Newspaper Debate on Sovereignty

Although the term *shuken* (sovereignty) was included in the 1860s translations from Wheaton and Vissering, it was a relative latecomer to common usage. Prior to the public discussions in 1881 about the form that a Japanese constitution might assume, political debate focused on rights and liberties, which did not directly engage the idea of sovereignty. Katō Hiroyuki's translation from Bluntschli's *Allgemeines Staatsrecht* in 1872 was the first sustained discussion of the concept. Katō noted that Tsuda Mamichi had translated sovereignty as *shuken* in his *Taisei kokuhō ron*, but Katō objected to the connotation of lord or master (*shu*) and thus formed a cumbersome compound with a loanword: *suberēnitēto no ken*. Following Bluntschli, Katō's concern was to describe sovereignty in terms of state right (*kokken*) and did not want the concept colored by its origins in monarchy. In detailing the meaning of sovereignty, Katō described it as the highest power in the state, unfettered right, and the right to freedom in public affairs, including the autonomy of one's own country with respect to foreign countries. Sovereignty was a term representing a country's esteem and prosperity, its unlimited powers, its unrestricted *kokken*—in short, a plenitude of power. This was certainly more than the autonomy or independence suggested by *shuken* in Wheaton and Vissering. In supplying a context for the meaning of sovereignty as political action, Katō noted that sovereignty enabled a country to establish law, to create and alter a constitution, and to maintain its existence and conduct reforms. This interest in the fact that sovereignty encompassed change was related to Bluntschli's close attention to recent developments in Europe—particularly the 1848 revolutions—which helped Katō explain the continuity in France as it shifted back and forth from a people's state (*minshukoku*) to a monarchy (*kunshukoku*) yet remained the sovereign state of France.[56]

This possibility—that sovereignty could be located in the people—was the second context in which *shuken* was discussed prior to 1881. Apart from a minor reference to "sovereignty of the people" in Obata Tokujirō's translation of a section of Tocqueville's *Democracy in America*, popular sovereignty came to the attention of a wider Japanese public with Hattori Toku's 1877 translation of Rousseau's *Social Contract*, which popular-rights activist Ueki Emori and other intellectuals acknowledged reading in 1878 and 1879.[57] But as I noted above, advocates of a national assembly or people's rights did not argue for popular sovereignty; they were more concerned to put *minken*, the people's right(s), in a necessary and supportive relationship with *kokken*, the state's right. Hence the debate on sovereignty that began in 1881 concerned an issue narrowly related to the creation of a national assembly or the guarantee of people's rights: since a constitution would be the legal form that the people's right(s) would assume, did the sovereign power to create and uphold that constitution lie with the people, through their national assembly, or elsewhere in the state?

The debate on sovereignty was conducted in major Japanese newspapers largely between October 1881 and May 1882.[58] The chief contributors to the debate were the *Tokyo-Yokohama mainichi shinbun* (or *Mainichi*), edited by Numa Morikazu, and the *Tokyo nichinichi shinbun* (or *Nichinichi*), edited by Fukuchi Gen'ichirō: the *Mainichi* argued that sovereignty lies with the national legislature while the *Nichinichi* advocated the sovereignty of the emperor. Historians Inada Masatsugu and Joseph Pittau have noted at least three antecedents in the political developments of autumn 1881 that prompted this debate over the locus of sovereignty in a constitutional polity. In the first place, the formation of the Shimeikai in September 1881—a political society of Kumamoto samurai whose most prominent member was imperial adviser Inoue Kowashi, remembered as the architect of the Meiji Constitution—included a public denunciation of Rousseau's theory of social contract and the corollary belief that sovereignty resides in the people; they insisted instead that the emperor was the basis of Japan's body politic and holder of sovereignty.[59] Second, the emperor made the startling announcement on October 12, 1881, that he would convene a national assembly in 1890; key to the imperial action was the comment that his officials would determine the "organization and jurisdiction" of the assembly vis-à-vis the imperial house, a general phrasing that begged the question of who ultimately held sovereign power.[60] And third, this imperial action added new encouragement to the writing of draft constitutions—an exercise that had begun with restoration leaders like Kido Takayoshi, Ōkubo Toshimichi, and the Genrōin in the 1870s but had spread to private persons and organizations by 1880. Significantly, the earlier draft constitutions do not include clauses about sovereignty whereas the flurry of draft constitutions in 1881 and 1882 make a point of designating sovereignty to one or another constitutent of the Japanese state—the people, the national assembly, or the emperor.[61]

Like the movement to establish a national assembly, the debate on sovereignty was instigated by the elite in Japanese society, but unlike the earlier movement, which acquired a layman's idiom and reached local audiences, the sovereignty debate was primarily an erudite exercise in European political theory. An editorial in the *Mainichi* posed the main issue in question form: "Where does sovereignty reside?" In addition to offering several possibilities—in the people, in the monarch, in the legislature, in a principle of justice—the *Mainichi* editorial provoked a set of questions, including the nature of sovereignty and its relation to monarchical privilege, the types of government and political systems, the reality of the social contract, and the nature of man and rulership. As positions on these questions repeatedly referred to England's constitutional monarchy, legal and constitutional authorities like John Austin, William Blackstone, and J. K. Bluntschli were invoked to confer greater credibility for one or another position. Ultimately, of course, the question of Japanese sovereignty would be decided by the Meiji Constitution of 1889—sovereignty lies with the imperial house and the incumbent emperor who bestows the constitution—so the debate was largely moot, as its issues were incidental to the oligarchy's de facto command of sovereignty in the name of the emperor. But the debate nonetheless served an eminently practical purpose for the development of political reason in Japan: it raised and debated the issue of sovereignty and thus laid the groundwork for a resolution of the issue.[62]

As an analysis of sovereignty, the debate developed through linguistic distinctions. For central to *Mainichi* writers' tactics was their attempt to secure the independence of sovereignty from the sovereign by introducing alternative concepts and translation words that might mediate the direct conceptual and philological connection between the two. Analagous to the relation between "sovereignty" and "sovereign" in English is the relation between *shuken* and *kunshu* in Japanese—literally, the "master's power" is that of the "lord and master."[63] In the same way that European political theory in the early modern period elevated the sovereign as an embodiment of the sovereign state (and as a solution to the feudal militarization of politics), the Japanese choice of translation vocabulary reproduced the identification of sovereignty with the sovereign as head of state. One has only to compare Hegel's dismissal of "popular sovereignty" as an implausible oxymoron with Tocqueville's insightful defense of the new political structure to see that the burden of argument lay with those who advocated an alternative to the sovereign king. This is also the case in the Japanese debate.[64] But where the *Mainichi* introduced new terms and translation words, particularly transliterations of European terms either as loanwords or in analog form, the *Nichinichi* emphasized a different order of distinctions by asserting the exceptionalism of Japan's body politic and hence the fact that its imperial system defined a unique constitutional system. I begin with the former.

After acknowledging that sovereignty could not reside in an abstract principle such as justice or in the unmediated mass of people (for both alternatives promoted an unworkable surplus of mediations and positions), the *Mainichi* settled on defining sovereignty as the power to determine laws, which properly resided in a national assembly. This put the burden on the *Mainichi* writers to disengage sovereignty from the sovereign, which they attempted in several ways. First introduced was a distinction between sovereignty (*shuken*, glossed as *soberenchī)* and "royal privilege" or "prerogative" (*tokken*, glossed as *puribirijji* and *purerogechību*). According to the *Mainichi*, the *Nichinichi* had confused the two, mistaking royal prerogatives such as declaring war, negotiating peace, and opening or dismissing Parliament for aspects of sovereignty. Indeed, both the upper and lower houses of Parliament had such prerogatives, and if one were to call the monarch's prerogatives "sovereignty," then consistency urged one to call Parliament's prerogatives "sovereignty," too. The implicit and sensible alternative, however, was to recognize prerogatives as such and not to confuse them with sovereignty.[65]

In support of this interpretation of England's body politic, the *Mainichi* introduced two further distinctions based on the scholarship of Josef Hormayr zu Hortenburg and Johann Bluntschli. From Hormayr's work on the relation between the throne of Hanover and the German Confederation, *Mainichi* writers took the distinction between *Souveränität* (*shuken*) and monarchical right or privilege (*kunken*)—a distinction that strategically exploited the two different Chinese characters composing the word for sovereign (*kunshu*): *kun* and *shu* were made to refer to different powers, one of which, sovereignty, was superior to the other, monarchical right. A similar distinction was borrowed in the name of Bluntschli, who distinguished the "powers of the ruler" or "highest sovereignty" (*shuken, kunshu no ken,* or *Fürsten Souveränität*—the "prince's sovereignty") from "state sovereignty" (*ikkoku no shuken, zen kokka no ken,* or *Staats Souveränität*). The former referred to internal power and authority over departments, offices, and people of the state; the latter referred to external power and authority, encompassing all departments and branches of the nation. The *Mainichi* urged its readers to understand the two as complementary aspects of what was generally called sovereignty (*shuken*), but it emphasized that constitutions designate state sovereignty superior to the ruler's power.[66] Given that sovereignty was by definition the power to establish law, the national assembly was in a position superior to that of the king. Positive law was drafted by parliament and ceremonially endorsed by the king, who thus participated in the establishing of law as a "constitutive member" of parliament and was equally responsible to the law. To emphasize that the national assembly was sovereign, and not the king, the *Mainichi* introduced yet another distinction—a new term for "sovereign," *shukensha* (a nominalization meaning "holder of sovereignty")—to differentiate that from the common word for ruler or sovereign, *kunshu*.[67] "Sovereign" and "ruler" should be understood as different agents.

This effort to analyze sovereignty into multiple powers and thereby minimize both royal privilege and the monarch's claims upon sovereignty reached its zenith in a contribution by the *Hōchi shinbun*. Taking his authority from the legal scholar Alpheus Todd, the *Hōchi* writer distinguished supreme legislative power from supreme executive power, which combine into what is called "supreme political power of state" (*isei no saijōken*) or sovereignty proper (*shuken*).[68] The *Hōchi* writer candidly observed that sovereignty is a contested concept and that in a constitutional monarchy like that of England, or what was ostensibly promised in Japan, sovereignty was divided. Legislative power is held by the national assembly; executive power is held by the monarch. Thus the supreme political power of state is not united and can only be wielded through processes of "representation" by the assembly that represents the people and by the government and state that can represent the monarch.[69]

That sovereignty resides in a national assembly of several hundred representatives or is to be divided among an assembly and the monarch was anathema to the *Nichinichi* and supporters of monarchical sovereignty, who saw in such arguments promises of internal division and external weakness. The nation is a body politic, a unit in which the head represents sovereignty; sovereignty is thus not only the right foundation of state law (the *Mainichi* position) but also the most supreme power of the state, the purpose of which is to maintain the state's autonomy and independence. Only Japan's emperor could serve as head and holder of the sovereignty of Japan. *Nichinichi* editorials took the position that the *Mainichi* and supporters of the sovereignty of the legislative body mistook Japan for a republic. Rather, Japan was a unique form novel to political theory—a constitutional empire different from England's constitutional monarchy. Key to the structure of a constitutional empire, *Nichinichi* authors asserted, was the principle that "the emperor establishes and the people cultivate"; central to the emperor's creative capacities are sovereignty and imperial virtue. To underscore their position that sovereignty could not possibly be held by people or officials, the *Nichinichi* reiterated the uniqueness of Japan's imperial line—its unbroken 2,500-year history and the fact that the Japanese emperor has commanded sovereignty since the beginning of heaven and earth. Even the sovereignty said to abide in the emperor by the authority of a constitution would be but a portion of the emperor's actual sovereignty. To add extra emphasis to their arguments, the *Nichinichi* referred to the emperor as

"Our ＿＿ Majestic Son of Heaven," with an honorific blank space before naming the emperor, and referred to Japan as the "divine land"—a practice noticeably absent in other newspapers.[70]

Corollary to this emphasis on the Japanese emperor's defining position in Japan's body politic was a set of translation terminology intended to combat any insinuation that the *Nichinichi* position advocated despotism or autocracy. Japan's constitutional empire was neither a truly despotic "unlimited empire" like Russia and China nor a woefully compromised "limited empire"— what the *Mainichi* believed England to be. And it was neither an absolute monarchy nor what the *Mainichi* implicitly advocated, a "parliamentarian despotism." Japan's constitutional empire was different from other polities because it was not a popularly contracted constitution (*minyaku kenpō*) but a state-contracted constitution (*kokuyaku kenpō*) determined and granted for the land at the pleasure of imperial virtue.[71] Unlike a monarchy, Japan would have a constitution that provided for institutional bodies with whom the emperor jointly ruled. Unlike a popular form of government in which the assembly was sovereign—which, *Nichinichi* writers feared, promised to destroy the ruler, eliminate the differences between lord and subject, overthrow the order of society and morality, and return everything to a primordial chaos— the "great way" of Japan's constitutional empire encompassed the three principles that sovereignty is truly the command of the emperor, that the great powers of the state are in the hand of the emperor, and that the support of the peace and prosperity of the state is the work of the emperor through his greatness of heart which acts on the people's hearts.[72]

In support of their respective arguments, both the *Mainichi* and *Nichinichi* emphasized temporal shifts experienced with the Meiji Restoration. Repeated references to "the change of era" introduced mythohistorical formulations that grounded the political content of the debate within larger ideological oppositions dividing Japanese society. Although historians have routinely cast these differences as simply liberal versus conservative, the central issue was the meaning of the emperor and the political consequences which followed from that meaning. *Mainichi* editorials enlisted Japan's joining "the contemporary world of civilization" as an effort to differentiate the sovereign of barbarous antiquity from the civilized sovereign of the present age. They stressed that changes in historical context imply changes in meaning: a word like "father" or "mother" continues to designate fathers or mothers, but their power and authority change with the introduction of civilization. Likewise, the barbarian sovereign of the past would have ruled by force and decree, but the civilized sovereign of today rules jointly with the people; that is to say, despite the continuity of the sovereign, the political principle of antiquity has been replaced with an alternative in the civilized present. By contrast, *Nichinichi* editorials referred to the *Kojiki*, an early history of Japan (with much mythology and legend), to prove that in the Age of the Gods, sovereignty had passed from Amaterasu, the sun goddess, to the imperial line, her human descendants; hence the emperors have continued to command sovereignty in our present Age of Man. Although the samurai class usurped imperial sovereignty during Japan's feudal age of shogunate rule, the restoration returned the Age of Man to its proper order.[73] In other words, the political aspirations to which civilization logically led were countered by an opposition intent on asserting hierarchical order and paternal authority. The debate on sovereignty was ultimately an effort to appropriate the emperor: were he civilized, he would know to assume his ceremonial role in support of the national assembly; were he majestic, he would graciously commend the oligarchy's rule by force and decree.

The formation of the Constitutional Imperial Party (Rikken teiseitō) in March 1882, in preparation for the opening of the legislative assembly, expanded participation in the sovereignty debate during the spring of 1882. In part because the leadership of the Imperial Party included Fukuchi Gen'ichirō, chief editor of the *Nichinichi* newspaper, the party's statement reiterated the newspaper's position; similarly, the critiques and defenses of the party echoed points already made in the debate. But the terminology used in forming arguments for and against the Imperial Party was simplified—gone were the many distinctions introduced by *Mainichi* and *Nichinichi* editorials; now participants discussed only *shuken*, "sovereignty."[74] Among the opinions of the so-called populists—Ōishi Masami, Nakae Chōmin, Ueki Emori, and Ono Azusa—that appeared in smaller newspapers, only Nakae agreed with the *Mainichi* that sovereignty was in fact the power to establish law. He based his argument on the authority of philology: the Latin *res publica* implied the public creation of law and hence sovereignty could only reside in the entire people of the nation.[75] Ōishi, Ueki, and Ono, however, defined sovereignty as the highest or total power of the nation, recasting sovereignty as state right (*kokken*) and linking it to social order, peace, and independence—national phenomena of equal concern to each citizen. Hence, they concluded, this "highest power" of sovereignty must lie with the people, who are ultimately responsible for national peace and independence. As Ueki put the matter, a truly independent and sovereign state could be founded only on republican institutions.[76]

Such a linkage of sovereignty and state right, occurring at a time, recall, when popular-rights activists were turning from personal rights to an idealized liberty, further diminished the stature of *minken* in political argument. Attention turned elsewhere—on the domestic front, to the national assembly, now planned for 1890, which would actualize the people's right to participate in government, and the constitution, planned for 1889, which would presumably guarantee the people's rights. On the international front, concern mounted for the state right of Japan, as publicists agitated for the restoration of Japan's judicial rights and tariff autonomy as well as an end to extraterritoriality.[77] Documents from the late 1880s continue to criticize the authoritarian central government and to assert specific freedoms like freedom of speech and freedom of the press, but they also urge discussion of the rights of the national assembly and the assertion of Japan's state right against foreign privileges.[78] Although sovereignty remained a technical concern of political theorists, the newspaper debate brought *shuken* and sovereignty to the attention of a wider public and fixed the term as an element in both the Japanese lexicon and Meiji political debate.

Fukuzawa Yukichi on State Right

If the populists' contributions to the debate on sovereignty recall the issues animating the 1870s *minken* arguments, Fukuzawa Yukichi's responses to the sovereignty debate assume a self-consciously moderate position. His work is valuable on several accounts: he has an idiosyncratic but consistently clear set of terms to discuss the issues of power, right, and sovereignty; he candidly notes the ulterior agendas operating in his contemporaries' arguments; and nonetheless his conclusions shift from a more populist stance to the imperial stand of the *Nichinichi* during the 1880s. It was largely his accomplishment to provide an analysis of state right that might pacify both the oligarchy and people's rights advocates. Although one does not read contemporary praise of his disposition of popular right and national right, it remains as a general assumption in works of the late Meiji period—and, perhaps more important, in the actions of the government after 1890. Like other participants to the debate, Fukuzawa presented his thoughts on sovereignty as an analysis of the contemporary situation, which, in the early 1880s, he persistently saw as an opposition between a government of former domain officials, committed to their own advantage and control of political power, and the Japanese people, committed to securing their personal and political rights. In the interests of unity, the emperor offered a solution.

To explicate Fukuzawa's reasoning, let us examine two bodies of his work in the late 1870s—his writings in response to the agitation for a national assembly and people's rights and then his work on *kokken*, the state's right—that explain his pressing interest in national unity and his willingness to embrace an imperial constitution.[79]

To begin with, Fukuzawa's responses to the agitation for a national assembly and people's rights exhibit a representation of *minken* quite unlike those of his contemporaries. Fukuzawa rarely mentioned the people's personal rights; in fact, neither *kenri* nor *jiyū* figures prominently in any of his three major contributions to the political movement of the day: *Bunken ron* (On a Division of Right) of 1876–1878, *Tsūzoku minken ron* (On a Common Understanding of Popular Rights) of 1878, and *Kokkai ron* (On a National Assembly) of 1879. Rather, Fukuzawa conceived *ken* as the conflation of right and legal power, as in Dutch *regt*. Indeed his most common usages of *ken* in these three texts are respectively *kenryoku* (power or force), *minken* (the people's right), and *seiken* (political right or power). I believe that this idiosyncratic usage is meant to present the issues in terms of historical continuity with the past and, in a manner compatible with the goals of Katō Hiroyuki, to defend the unity and power of the central government.

In *Bunken ron*, Fukuzawa sought to explain why former samurai might be agitating for people's rights, and he focused on the reconstruction of power with the Meiji Restoration. Recalling the division between the Tokugawa central government and the many local domains, he advocated for the Meiji state a division of right between, on the one hand, the central government, whose proper domain was governance (*seiken*)—creating law, managing taxation and foreign affairs, overseeing the army and navy, and so on—and, on the other hand, local governments, who could more appropriately manage administration (*chiken*)—domestic matters of local concern such as police, roads, bridges, schools, temples, public gardens, and sanitation. Although both spheres of power comprised the totality of state right (*kokken*), Fukuzawa privileged the governance of the central government, which represented both a concentration of right and the power of the entire state. The people's right (*minken*) was best expressed in local administration.[80]

By 1878, however, Fukuzawa had reconceived *minken* as the domestic complement of an international *kokken*: *minken* deserved as much commitment at home as *kokken* deserved abroad. In *Tsūzoku minken ron*, while reiterating his distinction between central government and local administration, Fukuzawa asserted that the best means for integrating the two would be a national assembly, for that body would harmonize the concerns and duties of all parties to the state. This recommendation followed from his general explanation of his concept of *ken*, which he compared to *bun* or status (a reference to the status system of the Tokugawa regime) and understood to extend from individuals to villages, wards, and prefectures. Thus he arrived at the two main expressions of right in the state: people's right (*minken*) and state's right (*kokken*). Although this linkage of right to status and duty is highly reminiscent of the Tokugawa habits that Fukuzawa had earlier deplored, he now began to side with the people against the government oligarchy. His recommendations were long-term and paternalistic—to expand the people's intelligence, to increase the wealth of families, to improve the character and physical health of individuals—but he nonetheless saw evidence that these improvements were under way and strongly took exception to the government's delaying the establishment of a national assembly on the grounds that the people were ignorant. Fukuzawa noted that the relationship between government and people is a contract of law and that, after all, a government is a people's government— if the people are too stupid, it follows that the officials too are too stupid.[81] *Kokkai ron* in 1879 reemphasized this position: the contract of law was in fact a constitution; the success of the local assemblies demonstrated that a national assembly was possible; and—Fukuzawa's only commitment to any of the people's rights per se—the people had a right to participate in government. Their recent transformation through reading, public speaking groups, and formal education showed that they were ready for participation. A national assembly was now necessary for the peace and well-being of Japan, and the people's growing independence would contribute to the expansion of Japan's state right.[82]

As Fukuzawa proceeded to explicate state right in an international context, his appreciation for *minken* altered—in large measure around the goal of independence. Already in 1875, with the publication of *An Outline of a Theory of Civilization*, Fukuzawa had announced the reversal of his earlier idealism about world civilization. Where he had once echoed a Western theoretical position on the equality of nations under a system of international law, he became convinced that the fact of national divisions among humankind undermined the universality of such ideals. National governments produce national goals of wealth and power; hence nations encourage patriotism and partisanship and make a virtue of competition for both profit in trade and victory in military affairs. As he succinctly stated: "The present world is a world of commerce and warfare." There were no equal rights among nations; one had to strive to be dominant in both trade and war.[83] From this analysis, Fukuzawa drew two conclusions that would animate his major works for the next decade. First, he insisted that foreign relations was Japan's major concern and difficulty, for Europeans invariably prevented foreign lands from developing their rights, making the most of their natural advantages, and preserving their independence. Second, therefore, Japan should focus on national independence as the goal of its engagement with world civilization. Fukuzawa went so far as to consider civilization and independence equivalent—in fact, you could not have one without the other.[84]

This goal of national independence informs Fukuzawa's linkage of the people's right and the state's right. To some extent this connection was implicit in his earlier thought on civilization, when he stressed that the wealth and power of the nation is based on the wealth and power of its people and that a nation's degree of civilization reflects the degree of civilization of its people. But his work of 1878 on state's right, *Tsūzoku kokken ron* (On a Common Understanding of State's Right), placed that concept securely in an international setting. *Kokken*, he asserted, concerned the state's ability to act freely at its own convenience, just as Perry and the other foreigners had done with Japan in the 1850s. He glossed *kokken* as "nationality" and curiously defined it as the development of national power, which requires that all people participate—including women and children—taking as their guide the great principle of independence. Japan's ability to maintain its international independence, particularly in treaty negotiations, depended on one key factor that linked state and people, *kokken* and *minken*: the strength of national assets, determined by resources, production, and the ability to conduct self-determined trade.[85]

Fukuzawa's worries about Japan's international position led him to disengage this structural connection between people and state. I see this development first in his 1881 analysis of international relations, *Jiji shogen* (A Short Discussion of Current Affairs), a book he began by asserting a distinction between, on the one hand, natural freedom and popular rights and, on the other, artificial state rights. People might be born with heaven-granted rights, but because peoples were distributed naturally around the world into their own homelands, the environments of which varied in size and resources, each people's making the most of their natural advantages and building their own laws and government produced a situation in which wealth and rights among peoples could not be equal. Hence, Fukuzawa concluded, each people inevitably trades what they have for what they need, and accordingly, the European attempt to link all peoples through international law and collective progress relies on treaties as a mechanism for such integration. The main purpose of treaties, he believed, was to safeguard trade—but whether treaties were honored or broken depended precisely on the artifice of state right.[86]

In declaring state right "man-made," Fukuzawa disengaged his proposals for domestic Japanese society from those concerning Japan in an international context. The establishment and protection of the natural rights of the Japanese people would be best served through the gradual introduction of a national assembly, which would potentially contribute to national wealth and power. But Fukuzawa subordinated the debate over a national assembly to what seemed to him the more urgent problem of foreign relations. The man-made fact of state right meant that a country had to take deliberate action to create, secure, and extend its state right, for a country's ability to rely on international law and to seek international justice depended on its ability to uphold its state right. Fukuzawa urged Japan to assert itself immediately in foreign relations— to assert its state interest in times of crisis with military force and pursue its state interest in international trade—because the international setting was the arena in which Japan could extend its state right and safeguard state independence.[87]

Given this background of Fukuzawa's analysis of *minken* and *kokken*, one can see that *kokken* was Fukuzawa's idiosyncratic way of understanding the issue of national sovereignty construed internationally. Hence the newspaper debate on sovereignty seemed a distraction.[88] As he understood the issues, the power to govern runs through human society and political forms. The protection of "personal rights"—the rights to life, security, and livelihood— is the cause for which government is instituted, giving rise to men's "political rights," foremost of which in 1882 is the right to participate in a constitutional system. Fukuzawa represented "people's rights" as an unexpected intrusion into these basic personal and political rights: as education expanded and people learned about the West, they became aware of their political rights and banded together in the name of people's rights, which Fukuzawa saw as an appropriate response to the officials' usurpation of political power, particularly in light of the constitutional government that was planned for Japan. Hence people's rights came to oppose both the government and especially officials' rights (*kanken*)—which began as the legitimate power of men to manage national affairs in their capacity as officials of a formal government but which became distorted through their misuse of power in suppressing views contrary to their own interests. It was in this context that Fukuzawa mentioned sovereignty (*shuken*), for he read the newspaper debate as a diversionary tactic, an attempt by a conservative wing of officials to put the emperor in a cage and use him to oppose people's rights. Fukuzawa feared the creation of an "Officials' Rights Party" that would dominate the emperor.[89]

But even as he distanced himself from the ruling officialdom, Fukuzawa also expressed his disapproval of those people's rights advocates who criticized the imperial house. Rather, he recommended the people's reverence for the emperor, noting that even people's rights advocates respond to the emperor's innate capacity to harmonize and bring peace to the land. In a formulation that would in time become commonplace, Fukuzawa praised the spiritual influence of the imperial house: it concentrates the people's hearts, harmonizes the people and the administration, calms society and pacifies the realm, encourages learning and the arts, and so on. Most important, it puts the emperor above politics. The emperor may have "special powers" (*tokken*)— like the right to pardon—and a ceremonial role in state institutions, but he is above politics, which is the proper sphere of the government administration and national assembly. The emperor's "great power" is best described as a moral leadership that the government could not possibly undertake.[90]

Like the *Mainichi* and certain populist writers, Fukuzawa thus located political action (if not sovereignty) in some mediated form of the people—a national assembly. Like the populist writers and the *Nichinichi*, Fukuzawa understood the goal of political action as the maintenance of state right—the peace and independence of the nation-state—which could only be achieved by the united efforts of all. But ultimately Fukuzawa's position is most like that of the *Nichinichi* endorsement of the emperor. If we look at the trajectory of solutions for political conflict that Fukuzawa imagined in his writings of the 1880s, it becomes clear, as Ishida Takeshi once intimated, that Fukuzawa moved from institutional structures as enactments of principle to national character as emotional response.[91] Fukuzawa was always concerned with unity, insisting that everyone in Japan join together and act as one family in the face of hostile, external powers. Although the path to that unity in 1882 was to be provided by political parties defending the political rights of their members under a constitutional system, by 1888 the emperor had become the solution for Fukuzawa on the grounds that the Japanese people know naturally to revere their majestic emperor. By emphasizing this Japanese dependence on the dignity and sacredness of their emperor, Fukuzawa imagined that the innate Japanese responsiveness to "great men" would heal the divisions within Japanese society and extend the central principle of state right.[92] Although Fukuzawa did not generally apologize for the oligarchy, it is uncanny how his position parallels the government's policies. Ultimately this most celebrated Meiji educator and enlightener proved to be the man most able to make a principle of *raison d'état*.

In conclusion, I must stress the continuity of Japan's international insecurity as a persisting context for the development of the terminology discussed in this chapter. The Western threat had initially provided the venue for a discussion of *ken*, the dominant forms of which—state right and sovereignty—emphasized the need to maintain Japan's autonomy in an international situation where the Western powers were demonstrating their own willful autonomy in colonial actions against the less civilized. The domestic consequences of that international threat were considerable and unmasked the internal contradictions of the liberal theory that accompanied "right" and "sovereignty" to Japan. If the Meiji Restoration promised public discussion in a national assembly, as well as collective participation of high and low in administration of the new state, some Japanese emphasized the promise of both personal rights and the people's right to establish a state constitution that would protect their rights. Others emphasized the right of elite tutelage: the gradual education of the people in preparation for their participation in these activities. Liberalism in practice, both in Europe and in Japan, was an ideology of potentially contradictory values. And it generated a vocabulary that remained a powerful point of reference for future debates.

6

Representing
the People,
Imagining Society

concept of society was indispensable to Japanese
efforts to translate the West. As declared in the
inaugural Charter Oath of 1868, the Meiji oligarchy
intended to reconstruct the administration of state
affairs, which meant eliminating the exclusive rule of
lordly and hereditary privilege and installing a new
principle of administration: political decisions would
be made by public discussion in the setting of a broadly
constituted assembly. While assemblies had long been
part of decision making during the Tokugawa and earlier medieval periods—by clans, villages, and samurai retainers—the revolutionary aspect of the breadth
of the proposed new assemblies was the reinterpreta-
tion of "lordly" (*kō*) as "public."[1] Key to this new public was the proposed unity of high and low, which
necessitated some means of integrating the samurai
above and the common people below. Simply put: a
new concept was needed to represent all the people
of Japan.

This chapter examines the ways in which "the
people" were represented in the transition from Tokugawa to Meiji. As we shall see, as these representations
shifted from samurai self-representations to the abstract
and general notion of society, two significant changes

occurred. First, the enlightenment theory of progress was replaced by an evolutionary theory of progress informed by Herbert Spencer's writings on social evolution. And second, as advocates for an elected national assembly successfully challenged the oligarchy's policy of gradualism, they introduced new terms that conceptualized the unity of the Japanese people. Prominent among these terms was the critical Western concept of society, standardized as *shakai* in the 1880s.

Japanese motives in finding new conceptions for the people were not unlike those accounting for the rise of the English concept of society in the seventeenth century, when philosophers like Thomas Hobbes and John Locke sought new grounds for political legitimacy in the wake of regicide and revolution. We are habituated today to think of society as the "other" of the individual, or the site of mediation between the individual and the state, or an organic and cultural system of interdependent functions.[2] But when the word entered Japan in its nineteenth-century English idiom, society referred primarily to the first of these meanings: the social milieu of the individual. More salient was the political significance of society, "civil society," a meaning established in the wake of the English Revolution and recalled by the English writers whose works informed initial Japanese translations of society—William and Robert Chambers, Samuel Smiles, and J. S. Mill. "Society" had entered the English language in the sixteenth century as a conception for human association or fellowship, especially among the aristocracy, as in "the pleasure of one's society," but it quickly became a synonym for community, particularly a political community, as deliberately suggested by the widespread seventeenth- and eighteenth-century usage, "civil society," a community of citizens.[3] Unlike current usage, civil (or political) society in the formative works of Hobbes and Locke was equated with "body politic" and "commonwealth"—precursors of the state. Both philosophers imagined that men in a state of nature sought to avoid endemic warfare and therefore joined together to form a civil society, uniting their several wills as one and consenting to live according to a common code of law.[4]

The Scottish enlightenment philosopher Adam Ferguson reworked this conjectural history into the form Japanese readers found in the Chambers brothers, Smiles, and Mill. Ferguson, who was motivated to explain the human progress he observed in the expansion of manufactures, trade, and colonization by the 1760s, dispensed with the mythical state of nature and insisted that the basic form of mankind is society. Ferguson held that so-called civilized societies are marked by an initial recognition of property and social rank;

they proceed to establish patterns of subordination and basic forms of government; and they progress by enacting legislation that more comprehensively represents the consent of the people. Astutely he noted that the division of labor (or "separation of arts and professions") extended human progress but produced new "distempers" calling for new remedies.[5] In sum, then, the concept of society introduced to Japan in the 1860s was embedded in an explanation of dynamic development and civilizing change. The liberal interest in personal freedom and initiative evinced by Mill and his contemporaries recast this progressive society as the background for the individual agent of progress, who acted within key institutions that organize the people and integrate society with the state: civic and economic "corporations," legislative assemblies, and public opinion. Before proceeding with the discussion of translations for society, however, I want to clarify the Tokugawa paradigm inherited by Meiji representations of the people.

Tokugawa Social Status: The Four Divisions of the People

In the course of Tokugawa rule, the most prominent marker of a person's social existence was *mibun*, which refers to the circumstances of one's birth, one's family's rank among the noble or the common, and hence one's station in life or position in society: an appropriate translation is social status. *Mibun* grew in importance in Japan during the late sixteenth century, a period of great social change and mobility brought on by new commercial opportunities and warfare, both of which tend to promote new individuals and groups to higher positions in society. In this regard, *mibun* represents a conservative wish to reduce social fluidity and fix social status. This point has long been established by Takikawa Masajirō: alarmed at the ease with which rural inhabitants of sixteenth-century Japan undertook both farming and fighting, the hegemon Toyotomi Hideyoshi moved to differentiate warriors and farmers in the interests of peace and stability—to define a man's status as one or the other and thus contain both groups.[6]

Scholarship continues to explain this act of imposing status distinctions upon Japanese society in the 1580s and its full elaboration under the Tokugawa shoguns as two related constructions. Status defines, first, a series of occupations serviceable to society and, second, a moral system of orderly social relations. By the 1700s, both the occupational and the moral approaches to status were explained in terms of *shimin*, the "four divisions of the people," a theoretical construct based on ancient Chinese and largely Confucian pronouncements.[7] Whether translated as the "four peoples," the "four classes," or the "four orders," the concept of *shimin* clearly defines a division of labor: the officials (or samurai), peasants, artisans, and merchants. As the mid-Tokugawa scholar and official Ogyū Sorai explained, in the likely point of reference for modern Japanese scholarship on *shimin*, the ancient sages created the four peoples as a division of labor when they separated the human community from nature. At the same time, the sages naturalized a moral hierarchy, dividing the people into their proper order, from high to low.[8] This overlap of a division of labor and a moral hierarchy is implicit in the point established by ancient Confucian philosophers and many of their rivals: the natural distribution of talent and ability justifies the social division of labor.[9] Key to the moral significance of labor is its productive value: the samurai are morally highest because they assist the sovereign in ruling; the peasants second, because they work the earth to produce the food that sustains humankind; the artisans third, because they transform the products of earth into tools useful to humankind; and the merchants last, because, unproductive, they merely take advantage of human need in moving goods from one market to another.

Nonetheless, the perennial problem for all who consider status from the perspective of the four divisions is the gap between the theoretical and the real. Scholars in the eighteenth century noted that officials in China, defined by their learning and expertise, were different from the samurai in Japan, defined by their military service.[10] Sorai himself pointed out that Japanese in his day typically referred to the four orders as three: samurai, peasants, and townspeople (combining artisans and merchants). To bridge the bookishness of the model and the reality of Tokugawa society, scholars have taken a number of routes, each of which emphasizes a more refined manifestation of status and thereby grounds *mibun* concretely in social life. One approach is to invoke additional determinants of status—to specify, for example, the requirements of "service," which more fully define the status divisions as a labor system, or the criterion of "privilege," which individualizes status in social practice.[11] A second approach is the perspective of Tokugawa law, for legal descriptions of status specified the more diverse division of the people into which law enforcement structured social practice from high to low: the daimyo (feudal lords), the imperial court aristocracy, the samurai, the priests (with whom are often grouped doctors and teachers), peasants, townsmen, outcastes (*eta*), and nonpersons (prostitutes, the ostracized, other itinerants).[12] And a third and more sociological approach is simply to describe status differences, for at its most concrete, status attempted to regulate daily life down to its basic details in Tokugawa Japan: social position, domicile, clothing, travel, housing, food, marriage, social interactions, occupation, expenditures, consumption, rituals, the employment of others, and samurai privileges such as possessing a surname or the wearing of swords.[13]

Status, however, cannot explain the startling economic development that realigned status groups from the late seventeenth century on. As a description of an ideal and static social order, status fails to take into account systemic socioeconomic changes. A critical example here is the fact that the lowest samurai, by the 1800s, was often worse off than most commoners. What had become of his superior status? Likewise, the theoretically lowest status group, the merchants, amassed great wealth in Osaka and Edo during the 1700s—indeed, Osaka moneylenders increasingly managed the fiscal affairs of the daimyo.[14] A second weakness of status as a description of society is that it begins to look like a simplistic standard in the face of wide variation. The exception was the twin of the rule in that special privileges could always be granted to one or another individual, raising his status incrementally above that of his fellows. The peasant who was granted the privilege of using a surname or wearing swords encroached upon the samurai's status; so too did the merchant granted the privilege of raising his roofbeam to the height of a domainal retainer. Clearly we must heed Fukaya Katsumi's precaution against reifying status as a system and remember that status changed persistently during the Tokugawa period. Should we not, he asks, consider status as the development of power relations instead?[15]

With the Meiji Restoration, an attempt was made to undo the status system precisely at the point of privilege and power relations. The slogan "equality of the four peoples" served oligarchs like Kido Takayoshi and Ōkubo Toshimichi as a principle for transforming the Japanese people so that all would participate in the goal of a civilized nation.[16] Sonoda Hidehiro has argued that early Meiji interpretations of the "equality of the four peoples" were grounded in the overlap between the concepts of samurai "duty" (*shokubun*) and commoner "occupation" (*shoku*)—which share the Chinese-character word for office or function. From a samurai perspective, one could hold that duty was not limited to the samurai class but should be extended to the commoners; the samurai thus became the basis for the new Japan—as some of the oligarchy maintained.[17] From a commoner perspective, by contrast, one could choose to fulfill the samurai office in the interests of reforming the samurai and creating a new society as the basis for the new Japan. A mediation of the two perspectives was eventually provided as duty was redefined as talent or ability—

with the understanding that as subjects of the emperor and members of the nation, all people should study and develop their talents in order to serve emperor and nation. The Education Law of September 1872 and the Conscription Law of January 1873 actualized the principle of equality of the four peoples by eliminating status as a consideration for military service or higher school admission. As a consequence, the new army, navy, and "university" became sites of social reconstruction.[18]

This is not to say that the Meiji oligarchy set off at once to unify the people and did so successfully. As Fukaya Hakuji has pointed out, efforts like those in the new military and education systems did indeed undertake to create a new people for Japan by raising all groups to a new and common level, but occasionally reactionary samurai desires influenced political developments. Although the Tokugawa status groups were nullified, privileges remained. Those at the top of Tokugawa society—the aristocracy, lords, and samurai—were officially reorganized into the privileged ranks of peers (*kazoku*), former samurai (*shizoku*), and samurai-soldiers (*sotsuzoku*) in 1869 and 1870. In 1871, a new status law redefined the four peoples as the imperial family, the aristocracy, former samurai, and commoners. And although there was upward and downward movement among the lower two of these new ranks, the majority of officials, teachers, students, newspaper editors, and political leaders during the first decades of Meiji rule were from the Tokugawa samurai class.[19] The more pessimistic Fukaya and the more positive Sonoda agree that the actualization of the equality of the four peoples was a slow process—due ultimately to the mingling of stations as commoners undertook duties formerly the privilege of samurai and samurai undertook the commercial occupations formerly restricted to commoners. The moral and occupational hierarchy conceived in the "four peoples" gave way to "society" (*shakai*) in the 1890s; and the unity of the people became the unity of a modern class system that developed in tandem with industrial capitalism.

Bourgeois and Samurai Self-Representations as Society

In addition to the theory of the four peoples, a second paradigm for social relations in early Meiji was the simple and persisting opposition between government and people discussed in preceding chapters. In many documents, this paradigm overlaps with the Tokugawa notion of four peoples in that the government is identified as the preserve of the former samurai class and the people are understood to be the lower three status groups (peasants, artisans, and merchants)—an anachronistic usage in view of legal reality but a view persisting in language and conceptual representations.[20] In reality, of course, the paradigms were not identical; former samurai, in the company of farmers and merchants, led the antigovernment opposition in the movement for a national assembly; and eventually the social and political reconstruction of Japan envisioned by the Meiji Restoration did substitute a new set of economic privileges for the political, educational, and social privileges of the Tokugawa samurai. Here I want to emphasize, as in Chapter 2, that in speaking on behalf of government, many former samurai continued to identify themselves as a social elite. Hence in their initial forays into translating "society," this largely samurai intelligentsia relied on terms representing samurai conceptions of sociality. The Tokugawa regime had made the samurai class both the dominant social agent and the intellectual spokesman for social agency itself; and the "four divisions of the people" and the opposition between government and people were convenient and meaningful points of reference.[21]

Fukuzawa Yukichi's and Nakamura Keiu's early translations of what they took to be contemporary monuments of English thought—William and Robert Chambers' *Political Economy*, Samuel Smiles' *Self-Help*, and John Stuart Mill's *On Liberty*—reveal key tensions in liberal thought on the relations among society, government, and people. In the Chambers brothers' and Smiles' view of political economy, individuals compete as free citizens, contribute to the betterment of the whole, enjoy their rights protected by society, and fulfill their duties in return, primary of which is to uphold the rule of law. As in Ferguson, this improvement of the whole is the progress of civilization. And the Chambers brothers, Smiles, and Mill all endorse what I have called the enlightenment theory of progress: the basis of individual development lies in education—the most important provision that parents and society can undertake for their children and that individuals can pursue for themselves.

In these texts "society" is largely undifferentiated from "body politic." Both the Chambers brothers and Smiles begin with the easy equation between society and political community. But when they turn to an explanation of human progress in forms of government, society per se falls out of the discussion. Instead, as in the legal translations of the 1860s, the Chambers brothers stress government and people and Smiles foregrounds a related pair, nation and individual. In the former, the people animate the various systems within political economy—manufacturing, commerce, banking—and the government oversees and facilitates on behalf of the people. In the latter—and Smiles' purpose, of course, is to emphasize self-improvement and self-advancement—

individuals compete and collectively advance the nation. Mill, by contrast, provocatively reconsiders the sociopolitical conditions of that political economy by foregrounding the individual's free and independent standing in the face of society and government. He too uses society and government interchangeably, although less so than the other English philosophers I have mentioned; in his work the two terms have begun to refer to different objects. Only with the work of Herbert Spencer are government and society fully distinguished as conceptually separate reifications of social reality.

The degree to which the work of translation encouraged Fukuzawa and Nakamura to creatively rethink their terminology for "society" is clear from a comparison of the first and second volumes of Fukuzawa's *Seiyō jijō*.[22] In his account of Western institutions and political history in the first volume, Fukuzawa employs descriptions of the people familiar in received Tokugawa usage: he makes repeated references to the "people" as *jinmin*, *hitobito*, and *tami*; the "people of the domain" or "nation's people" as *kokumin* and *kokujin*; and only rarely "the human world" (*seken*) or "humankind" (*ningen*). Since he is intent on negating the Tokugawa status divisions, he rarely employs terms like the "four divisions of the people," "high and low," and "noble and base."[23] His translation of Chambers' *Political Economy* in the second volume, by contrast, in which both "society" and "civil society" figure prominently, employs a great many terms for society that move beyond simple references to the people: he uses *seken*, *sekai*, *sejō*, and *sejin* (or *yo no hito*), the meanings of which range from "the world," "humankind," and "the people" to "everyone"; *jinrui*, or "humankind"; and his best-known translation word for society, *kōsai*, literally "association" or "interaction," which he used widely in the constructions *ningen kōsai* and *hitobito kōsai*, or "human society," and *gaikoku kōsai*, "international society."[24]

Two observations regarding this work of translation are pertinent. In the first place, this terminology reflects a compatibility between the language of Tokugawa social thought and the universal aspirations of English political economy.[25] "Man" and *"ningen"* were comfortable equivalents, likewise "world" and *"sekai."* The oppositions of government and people as well as individuals and nation—from the Chambers brothers and Smiles, respectively—are readily translated into the familiar terms of *seifu* and *jinmin* and certain individuals and *kuni* (the term for "domain," now shifting to mean "nation").[26] Samurai and English bourgeoisie could speak these general terms with one voice; to this degree, English political economy was familiar to Japanese translators.[27]

But in the second place, both Fukuzawa's translation of Chambers and

Nakamura's translation of Smiles alert the reader to profound differences in social organization in the West—most obvious of which is a different hierarchy of groups. Both address the phenomenon of a working class, who merit special concern because their condition deserves reform, and identify this group as a lower segment in society by using familiar Japanese terms for largely unskilled workers. Fukuzawa translates "working class" with *kamin* (or *shimo no tami*), the "lower people," and *ekifu-shokunin*, an aggregation of "laborers and artisans"; Nakamura uses *karyū* (or *shimo no nagare*), the "downstream" group, and *kōjin*, "artisans" or "workmen."[28] By contrast, the merchants, *shōnin* or *shōmin*, are elevated as a higher group by virtue of their privileged relationship to the key unit of Western society: the corporation or professional society. To be sure, foregrounding the merchants is to turn upside-down the "four divisions of the people," a possibility familiar from Tokugawa history, but more important, it acknowledges the prominent position of merchants within the political structure of Western society.

Fukuzawa follows the Chambers brothers in noting the development of parliamentary government from municipal corporations under the leadership of independent burgesses or citizens. His translation for "municipal corporation" is *shimin kaidō* (an assembly of townsmen), employing the term that eventually became the standard translation word for "citizen" (*shimin*), but here it is interchangeable with "merchant." His translation for "assembly," *kaidō*, refers to the companies and societies of townsmen that assemble. Fukuzawa's emphatic expression for "each company and society" (*maisha maikai*) underscores the neologism he uses extensively in *Seiyō jijō* to translate "company," "corporation," or "society": *kaisha*. Apart from providing a means of translating the names of commercial institutions (such as the East India Company or the English Wool Society) and various learned societies, *kaisha* also underscores the close relation between corporation and civil society. In the same way that "society" in English at the time was both a synonym for government and a name for a professional organization or corporation (the English Wool Society), so too *kaisha* is an inversion of the Japanese term that would become the standard translation word for "society": *shakai*. In the Japanese language, the connection between the corporation and civil society remains closer than in contemporary English. And in fact Fukuzawa, Nakamura, and other contemporaries occasionally used *kaisha* as a translation word for (civil) society. To Fukuzawa, these municipal corporations are significant because they take action on their own and fund their assembly from their own pockets; as a civil society, their purpose is to regulate membership and safeguard law and order.

In other words: both Fukuzawa and Nakamura successfully represented the way in which political economy at midcentury depended on the self-representation of the bourgeoisie as civil society.[29]

Nakamura's subsequent translation of Mill's *On Liberty* is, by comparison, a vastly more complex linguistic act. Unlike the consistency with which he translated "liberty" as *jiyū*, his translations for society are diverse. Instead of a preferred translation word for society—that abstract and general "association of free men" implied most often in Mill's use of "society"—we find a field of terms that disclose three main conceptualizations of social relations reflecting samurai sensibilities. One is marked by the active interaction of people we call "associating" or "fraternizing" (*kōsai* or *tsukiai*) and by concrete associations, as in a band, a club, a company, a guild, or a society (*kaisho, kaisha, kumiai, nakama, renchū*).[30] These usages refer to face-to-face encounters among individual peers and share with the English word "society" the meaning of "company"—one's own society, the individuals with whom one interacts.[31] Like the merchants' guild, samurai too had established peer group ties in horizontally organized groups and academies that afforded associations outside the usual vertical hierarchy of Tokugawa society and bureaucracy. A second set of translation terms refers to conceptions of "the people" that circulated among intellectuals involved in reform efforts of the eighteenth and nineteenth centuries. These include not only terms akin to the public (*kō, ōyake,* and *kōshū*) or "everyone" (*sōtai,* literally "the whole body") but also, quite simply, the people (*jinmin*), including domainal or national people (*kokumin* or *kuni no tami*), common people (*heimin*), and all the people (*shūmin* or *minshū*). As aspiring reformers and restorationists judged Tokugawa social ills in the context of a Confucian exhortation to safeguard the well-being of the people, they elevated their paternal concern for the people as members of the ruling samurai class.[32] And a third set of terms even more pointedly reflect samurai superiority as a ruling class, for they assume the moral function of the samurai as a superior group fit to guide the lower orders through their good example. These terms include the Confucian abstraction *jinrin* (humanity)—which refers to the moral principle differentiating the hierarchy of human relations—and expressions for the Tokugawa class divisions discussed earlier: the Confucian conception of the four divisions, high and low, rich and poor, noble and base, aristocrat and commoner.[33] Nakamura's translations for "society," then, reflect his position as a self-conscious member of the ruling elite—defined on the one hand by a Confucian moral sensibility and paternal concern for the people constituting society and, on the other hand, the academies and samurai associations that constituted the rudimentary institutions of civil society so essential to constitutional theory.

Nonetheless, this list is striking for the remarkable absence of certain Tokugawa terms we might expect. Unlike his translation of Smiles and unlike Fukuzawa's translation of the Chambers, Nakamura's translation of Mill appears deliberately to avoid familiar terms of Tokugawa times: *yo*, *yo no naka*, and *seken*, all of which can cover a range of meanings—from the world, the age, or the times to humankind, the social world, or the people.[34] Clearly Nakamura has taken a proactive approach to translating "society" in Mill: he shuns familiar language and instead creates new associations for the new Meiji age.[35]

At the same time, Nakamura complicates an understanding of Mill by conflating "society" and "government" to an extent beyond that of Mill himself. The host of terms for sociality, the public, and the people (and even related terms like majority, bureaucracy, and nation) are largely interchangeable with *seifu*—"government." Most are equated with *seifu* at one point or another through the analog form I described in Chapter 3.[36] To be sure, in *On Liberty*, Mill himself does not consistently name the force that so threatens the freedom of the individual; although he most often writes "society," he occasionally uses "mankind," the "public," "public opinion," the "government," and the "State." But from Mill's diagnosis of the social danger confronting the individual, it is clear that the middle class who define "society" are responsible for the erosion of individual liberty, for it is they who authorize the government—by means of representative institutions—to interfere with an individual's liberty.[37] That Nakamura does not differentiate between society and government certainly follows from the lack of a standard conceptualization for "society" in 1871. But in repeatedly conflating society and government, he demonstrates that he conceives the problem of the human exercise of authority over one's fellows as essentially the problem of governmental exercise of authority over its subjects. To paraphrase Hegel: Nakamura is like the eighteenth-century burgher who experiences the externality of the state as a subject of the prince, but who has not yet arrived at the political consciousness of a citizen, where universal and particular interests are synthesized.[38] To Nakamura, interference with individual freedom is necessarily governmental interference. And consequently, I believe, much of the permutability we detect in Nakamura's translations for society expresses his attempt to explicate what Mill might mean when he writes that society interferes with individual freedom.

This indifference to distinguishing between society and government becomes a problem precisely when Nakamura attempts to describe the theoretical conception of the lawmaking community—when the people rise up against their lord and master and demand a code of law that will defend the rights of all. Because he locates this political community in an ideal village— under the conditions theorized by Hobbes, Locke, and Ferguson, where society and government are one—Nakamura succeeds in negating social hierarchy but confines himself to a pure democracy in which all citizens are simultaneously subjects and masters, lawmakers and law-enforcers. Nakamura implies that the power to rule is the freedom to make laws that both coerce the ruled and restrict the rulers. He rests confident that such a lawmaking community will choose a self-imposed limit on its power because the well-being of all is both the condition and the goal of political action. But in the absence of representative institutions and a systematic constitutionalism (which it is not Mill's purpose to explicate here), he eliminates all means of opposing the tyranny of the majority and protecting individual liberty—precisely undermining Mill's concern in *On Liberty*.[39]

In general, then, these early translations of English thought alerted Japanese readers to the phenomenon of society and the process by which political communities were constructed from the civil society of commercial and civic organizations. And indeed, social historians report that in keeping with this model, large landowners and commercial interests quickly asserted their leadership in local Japanese communities.[40] But aside from Fukuzawa's idiosyncratic *kōsai*, these early translations produced no lasting and significant transcoding of "society." *Kōsai* was one of Nakamura's translations for society in Mill, but even on the strength of Fukuzawa's popular precedent, Nakamura did not grant *kōsai* greater weight than his many other terms. Nonetheless, Fukuzawa deserves credit for this initial attempt to translate "society." Like the term in its English setting, Fukuzawa created an abstract and general translation word in that its multiple applications—human society and international society in his translation of the Chambers—succeeded in generalizing society as the site of political mediation of status and power differences.[41]

Representing the People in the Movement for a National Assembly

It is striking, then, that the first prolonged political debate of the Meiji era— the movement to establish a national assembly—makes little reference to any of this language developed by Fukuzawa and Nakamura. To some extent this can be explained by the gap between English theory and Japanese oligarchic practice, for only tangentially does the English category of civil society point to a reality of early Meiji social relations. In the same way that civil society was the self-representation of European entrepreneurs and intellectuals, so too the former samurai, a similarly elite minority within Japan, represented themselves as leaders of universal human progress in Japan. That is, their role as progressive vanguard paralleled that of their European counterpart. But unlike civil society in Europe, the samurai hold on political power was not matched by the economic power responsible for the development of industrial capitalism. Hence the arguments made in the course of the movement to establish a national assembly begin by straightforwardly reiterating the enlightenment theory of progress under samurai political tutelage—largely in terms inherited from Tokugawa language.

Before proceeding, however, I must reemphasize two key conditions under which the debate over a national assembly ensued. In the first place, Meiji leaders, including the ruling oligarchy, activists, and intellectuals, shared from the start a commitment to some form of constitutional system. This was, on the whole, phrased in terms of Tokugawa hierarchy—as the "joint rule of sovereign and people" or the "joint rule of high and low"—and often included a national assembly of high and low or some other phrasing.[42] That this "constitutional system" was described as enlightened or as guiding Japan to a civilized state underscored the official policy of gradualism. As the ruling elite, former samurai like Kido Takayoshi and Ōkubo Toshimichi and court aristocrats like Iwakura Tomomi were in a position to oversee the people. As the people were educated and able to think rationally and independently, they would be ready to take their place in representative institutions. Both Kido and Ōkubo urged in 1873 that the introduction of the common people into political participation should proceed cautiously according to domestic conditions and the national level of enlightenment.[43] The enlightenment theory of progress informed this official policy of political gradualism—a connection that would be reiterated in 1880 and 1881 by the successors to the first set of oligarchs: Yamagata Aritomo, Itō Hirobumi, Inoue Kaoru, and their fellow councillors.

In the second place, the movement to establish a national assembly was the first political debate conducted in the new popular press, and it coincided with the Meiji oligarchy's first efforts to insist upon gradualism by arresting the development of the institutions of a European civil society in Japan. Meiji laws restricted freedom of the press, public assembly and discussion, the formation of groups, and the attendance of such group activities. The oligarchy tried to undo participation in a public sphere at every turn by attempting to compel all institutions of the public sphere—the print media, private clubs and societies, and political organizations—to keep silent on matters concerning government decisions and actions. That is, the oligarchy attempted to reinforce the division between government and people. And the Meirokusha intellectuals largely agreed that these measures, if temporary, were appropriate.

Thus the issue of representing the people in Meiji Japan, as reflected by the movement for a national assembly, was a series of negotiations among the Meiji elite—primarily composed of former samurai but gradually including wealthy farmers, merchants, and manufacturers—which required locating the former samurai vis-à-vis not only the people but also the ruling oligarchy. When we look at the memorials, proposals, commentaries, and draft constitutions written in the course of the movement, terminology concerning the people points to two general groups of texts. First are what I call "stratifying" proposals: the initial set of 1874 and 1875 statements precipitating the event as well as the subsequent memorials and commentaries supporting the status quo. These were written not only by government leaders, Meirokusha intellectuals, and editors of national newspapers in Tokyo and Osaka but also by the original group of former samurai dissidents led by Itagaki Taisuke and Soejima Taneomi. These samurai dissidents and government supporters shared common representations of "the people" as groups lower in the social hierarchy. Second are what I consider "unifying" proposals: statements written by national and local leaders of the new political societies and national parties and then circulated to local newspapers and national centers. I date these from the revival of the Aikokusha (Patriotic Association) in 1878 and the subsequent establishment of political organizations like the Kokkai kisei dōmeikai (Alliance to Establish a National Assembly) and the Jiyūtō (Liberty Party). This second set of proposals is informed by Herbert Spencer's work on sociology and coincides with the critiques and defenses of natural rights surrounding Katō Hiroyuki's *Jinken shinsetsu* (New Theory of Human Rights) in 1882—developments that introduced the theory of social evolution and an entirely new way of identifying the people as society.

The "stratifying" set of documents builds on the status language of the Tokugawa period. Prominent are the expressions "high and low" and the "four divisions of the people." Moreover, the "people" are typically referred to as those orders below the samurai class: the *sanmin* or "three groups of the people" (farmers, artisans, and merchants, also rendered *nō-kō-shō*) and the *jinmin* or *kokumin* (people of the domain). Another expression that reiterates hierarchy is the pairing of *shizoku* and *heimin*, former samurai and common people, often condensed to *shimin* (a homonym different from "four peoples"). One also finds in this literature direct representations of samurai paternalism toward the people—as when the latter are referred to as "our people" (*waga jinmin* or *waga tami*).[44] Perhaps the most striking document in this vein is the younger councillors' collective memorial of October 1881 on establishing a national assembly. This memorial largely reproduces the status system of the Tokugawa age by assigning the peers, selected from the aristocracy and former samurai, to an upper house and relegating lower samurai and select elements of the common people—wealthy farmers and merchants—to a lower house.[45]

The initial trio of positions encapsulates the range of arguments raised in these "stratifying" proposals: the January 17, 1874, memorial by Soejima Taneomi and Itagaki Taisuke (and their allies) to establish a popularly elected assembly; Katō Hiroyuki's rebuttal (January 26, 1874); and the response by Soejima and Itagaki (February 20, 1874). Soejima and Itagaki began by pointing out that the people have their rights and responsibilities: to extend their rights, the government must protect their freedom; to fulfill their responsibilities, the people must cooperate in the public affairs of a country. Because they pay taxes, they have a right to informed approval or disapproval of government measures.[46] In rebuttal, Katō agreed with this basic justification, invoking the principle that "government is made for the people, not people for the government." But he added that current conditions do not encourage the immediate establishment of an assembly, given the people's ignorance and the promise of foolish discussion, which only bodes ill for the nation. Instead, Katō urged, establish schools and educate the people's talents.[47]

In response, Soejima and Itagaki criticized the linkage between the enlightenment model of civilization and the gradualist policy on popular participation. They denied the implicit theory of causation which held that education produced the enlightenment that qualified one for participation. To the contrary, they maintained, education takes place *with* participation and the two lead jointly to enlightenment and progress; rather than dismiss the people as stupid, the government should work to enlighten them by granting their right to participate. Moreover, they stressed the formative role of the samurai in this development: the impetus for the Meiji Restoration had come from the lower samurai (and masterless samurai), so a deliberative assembly would be in keeping with the spirit of the restoration as it developed from below. They accused the government of acting as an exclusive oligarchy and urged it instead, invoking the authority of J. S. Mill's *Considerations on Representative Government*, to actively enlighten the people. They maintained that "human nature is such that a man becomes conscious of his shortcomings and defers to those more able." Hence the samurai would lead the people, who would naturally defer to their expertise.[48] Subsequent memorials would extend this argument about samurai virtue and leadership, condemning the governing oligarchy for ruining the greatest asset of the nation by bringing the samurai down to the level of the common people. Instead—organizations like the early Risshisha argued—the government should raise the common people to the level of the samurai.[49] It is striking that, except for the issue of when to inaugurate the national assembly, this opposition stance matched that of the oligarchy in terms of representing the people as the inferior masses below.[50]

By 1878, with the revival of the Aikokusha and ongoing political debate in the new local assemblies, followed in 1880 by the creation of major national political organizations with numerous local branches like the Kokkai kisei dōmeikai and the Jiyūtō, the second set of "unifying" proposals for a national assembly had asserted new unities and given expression to a new fraternal language.[51] Given the production of this second set of materials among local elite and their fellows newly operating on the national stage, who included samurai of varying ranks as well as farmers and merchants, these representations of the people abandon the status language of the Tokugawa age. There is a marked use of plural possessives in these documents: "our party," "our government," "our people," "our country," and even "our emperor." This range of terms suggests the unity to which the movement for a national assembly began to appeal—a unity indicated not only by new and common markers of national identity, "the Japanese people" (*Nihonjin*) and "we the people" (*wagahai jinmin*), but also with the introduction of fraternal references like "brothers" (*kyōdai*) and "compatriots" (*dōbō*). These proposals assert claims to the land, the people, Japan, and its history, insisting that earlier imperial oaths, beginning with the Charter Oath, promised the establishment of a national assembly, which it was now the government's duty to undertake. By invoking the government's duty to the people—and including everyone but the emperor within the people—local activists made a powerful appeal to compatriots and local officials that exploited growing tensions between the national and local levels of government and singled out the "great ministers" at the top of government as the unreasonable obstacle to popular participation. Like the former samurai activists on the national stage before them, local activists saw a national assembly as the best way to represent popular opinion in the national government and to dissolve tensions developing between the people and the oligarchy.

The writers of these documents typically took as a point of reference the universal human world, and they conceived the development of political society in the concrete terms of associating or interacting. The Aikokusha, for example, began with humankind and nation: in Japan, love of country should encourage persons of like intention to join their organization and plan for the public benefit of the nation. Because the human world is built from natural and mutual interaction (*kōsai*) and affection, Japan's new administration had removed the restriction that formerly limited participation to samurai so that all the people possessed the right to participate.[52] Corollary to this general claim to participation was what might be called a "bottom-up" approach to the well-being of the nation. Both the Aikokusha and the Kokkai kisei dōmeikai advocated strengthening the nation by strengthening the local structures of county and prefecture; they stressed equal and mutual interaction within the entire nation rather than centralizing rights in the national government and advocated local self-reliance rather than strengthening the national center. For in the end, as Fukuzawa and Nakamura had argued a decade earlier, the freedom and self-government of the people determine the nation's ability to become independent and to expand its state right.[53]

This second set of proposals is much less committed than the first to the enlightenment theory of progress, because their goal is to criticize the policy of gradualism. Rather than take issue with whether enlightenment prepares one for participation or whether participation produces enlightenment, these documents began to assert that the people have attained an adequate level of civilization and thus deserve to participate in a national assembly. The Tosa branch of the Risshisha, for example, observed that local strife and disaffection were interfering with Japan's progress at enlightenment; hence it seemed prudent to reconcile popular divisions by establishing a national assembly.[54] The Miyagi local assembly, by comparison, declared in 1880 that the people of Japan had in fact attained a significant level of enlightenment and independence—witness their agitation for political participation—and therefore it was time to place legislative powers in their hands by means of a national assembly.[55] In sum, then, these local materials question the legitimacy of the enlightenment theory of progress because their diverse interpretations demonstrate that the theory cannot provide an adequate guide to practical action. With local prefectural assemblies in place by 1880 and the people thus demonstrating their abilities, progress was clearly under way in Japan. The oligarchy could no longer deny the people a voice in national government, and the only solution was to begin mediating the opposition between government and people by integrating the two in a national assembly. I suspect that this realization informed the expediency with which the oligarchy acted in late 1881; as some admitted, if they promised a national assembly after an interval of ten years, activists would be pacified, which, for the most part, they were.[56]

Ultimately, however, both defenders and opponents of the status quo converged on historical argument to justify the establishment of a national assembly. The didactic force of history, everyone realized, could be invoked as a precedent for action: where opponents of gradualism found historical justifications for their demands, defenders found historical precedents for their tactics of delay. Early on, Kido Takayoshi had pointed out a pattern in universal history—the prosperity or decline of administrative standards and codes of law was ultimately responsible for the continued existence or withering away of countries. History, he maintained, demonstrates the need for change— which, in Japan's case, had been marked by the emperor's declaration of the Charter Oath in 1868. Similarly, in presenting the history of the first decade of the Meiji era, the Risshisha pointed to the Charter Oath as a pact between the emperor and his people; he had vowed to establish a national assembly and promised the equal rights of the samurai and the people. To be sure, the Meiji emperor himself had encouraged such a reading of history by citing the 1868 precedent in his 1874 decree establishing the Assembly of Local Government Officials (Chihōkan kaigi). Thus in capitulating to the opposition in October 1881, the councillors too endorsed this argument in their collective memorial: history proved that the oligarchy had all along intended to establish a national assembly. The imperial decree announcing the assembly formalized the link between the good faith of gradualism and the directedness of past events: the historical precedents of the Charter Oath, the Assembly of Local Government Officials, the House of Peers, and so on demonstrated the correct approach of proceeding without sudden or unusual changes. The emperor noted that the human heart must take in change slowly, in accord with time and condition, so as to not harm national peace.[57] Japanese history, in other words, offered one medium within which all the people of Japan could be reconciled as a political whole.[58]

But the advent of a second progressive and unifying medium is also visible in many of these "unifying" proposals—the neologism *shakai*, a translation word for "society." Unlike "the people," a general term that both collectivizes its members and enables an enumeration of them as groups or individuals, "society" is an abstraction that goes one step further in that it renames the people as a distinct unity with its own conditions of integration. In some cases, as in one anonymous draft constitution, "society" summarizes the Japanese people's rights to assemble in meetings and form associations; "political society" (*seiji shakai*) can be understood as one great organization, as with "civil society" in English liberal theory.[59] But where "the people" refers to a group integrated by what came to be understood as their necessary filiation to the nation (or "national people," *kokumin*), "society" refers to a group integrated by virtue of the moral, legal, or political conditions of the people.[60] Society serves as a new way of abstracting the people as a unit—hence it figures often in statements about "society's unity" (*shakai no itchi*) and "society's order" (*shakai no chitsujo*). Human society (*ningen shakai*), the Aikokusha announced, is animated by morality, which allows for the cohesion of the entire nation; law provides the rules for social order.[61] In the Jiyūtō statement of purpose and elsewhere, such social unity and order depend on the liberties of speech and the press; hence the goals of the Jiyūtō included defending personal liberties and working toward reviving the right to participate in administration, all of which would improve society.[62]

This is not to say that "society" effaced all the problems associated with early Meiji references to the people. One of the younger oligarchs, Yamagata Aritomo, a man remarkably skillful at combining traditional categories with new Western concepts, juxtaposed status language and "society" in a unique combination in his memorial on constitutional government. Alongside familiar references to samurai and people, and lords and people, he asserted that in all countries law is used "to maintain society" (*shakai o ijisu*) while morality and custom "discipline society" (*shakai o kōkisu*).[63] Following Yamagata's lead, the statement of intentions of the Rikken kaishintō (Constitutional Reform Party), issued in 1882 with a conservative eye to slowing down the extension of voting rights, moved from concerns about "social order" to far more innovative uses of the neologism—making "social progress" (*shakai shinpo*) and "social prosperity" (*shakai kōfuku*) rather than enlightenment the criterion for extending the franchise.[64]

"Society" in Herbert Spencer's Evolutionary Theory of Progress

By 1881, then, we see a growing conceptual unification of "the people" among political activists and, at the same time, serious doubt cast on both the enlightenment project and the policy of gradualism. One prominent sign of this new conceptual unity is the neologism *shakai*, "society," a development closely related to the introduction of translations of Herbert Spencer's social theory beginning in 1877.[65] Among the political activists familiar with Spencer's sociology, several were students of Fukuzawa Yukichi and some had studied in England in the early 1870s and returned to assume positions in the Meiji government under the patronage of Ōkuma Shigenobu. These figures included Baba Tatsui, Ono Azusa, Ozaki Yukio, and Yano Fumio, who gathered in a number of discussion societies of the late 1870s and 1880s—particularly the Kyōson dōshū (Coexistence Alliance) and the Kōjunsha (Mutual Consultation Society)—and were active in the formation of political parties in the 1880s.[66] Ono in particular played a leading role in crafting Ōkuma's speeches and public documents for the Rikken kaishintō. One important figure on the margins of this group, who also engaged Spencer's social theory, was Ueki Emori, the outspoken journalist and writer affiliated with Itagaki Taisuke and his organizations, the Risshisha and Jiyūtō; he and Baba Tatsui worked together for a time with the Jiyūtō.

As in the case of "liberty," Japanese philological research on the translation of "society" into Japanese has focused on determining a chronology for the introduction and standardization of *shakai*, the current translation word.[67] *Shakai* referred originally to an earth god cult in ancient China; by the twelfth century, it had come to mean the group organized for such a religious purpose (or an educational or commercial purpose); and in Japan of the Tokugawa period, it was used by Dutch learning scholars to refer to certain places of assembly—boys' academies, churches, and meeting halls. By 1874 or 1875, *shakai* was used to translate "society," but the question remains unsettled as to who deserves credit.[68] Certainly the efforts of Inoue Tetsujirō and Ariga Nagao at Tokyo Imperial University in the early 1880s were key to standardizing *shakai* as "society." Between the first edition of Inoue's *Dictionary of Philosophy*, which appeared in 1881, and the second in 1884 (coedited with Ariga), Inoue and Ariga asserted *shakai* as both the preferred translation word for "society" and the root of the translations for "sociology" and "social science" as well.[69] Ariga's *Study of Sociology* (*Shakai gaku*), published in 1883, was modeled on Spencer and duplicated the title of the Japanese translation of Spencer's *Study of Sociology*, which appeared the same year. Subsequently the official term for "society" at Tokyo Imperial University—*seitai,* which connotes a similarly large sphere of action, "the human world"—was phased out of "sociology" (*seitaigaku*), and in 1885 the Department of Sociology changed its name from Seitaigaku to Shakaigaku.[70] *Shakai* thus became the preferred term for the new abstraction "society," which, as a reified, organic entity amenable to scientific law and political praxis, enabled Japanese intellectuals to rethink Japanese society on a new scientific basis and to produce new interpretations of Japan's past, present, and future. As an alternative to the concept of the "people," society facilitated new forms of human agency and authorized political proposals intent on guiding the course of social development.

Spencer's social theory in translation appealed to Japanese readers in two general ways. Initially readers were most interested in his discussion of individual rights: two people's rights activists, Ozaki Yukio and Matsushima Kō, produced independent translations of the relevant portions of Spencer's *Social Statics* in respectively 1878 and 1881.[71] In *Social Statics*, Ozaki, Baba Tatsui, and Ueki Emori found a liberal justification for natural rights, which had the added advantage of doing away with uncertainties of the enlightenment theory of progress. Spencer's law of adaptation offered scientific certainty of the progress of society. And given that the people and its government formed an organic whole, Spencer's theory explained why government intrusion into the public sphere was not only contrary to the proper duty of government but destructive of optimal conditions for adaptation. Others, by contrast, including the intellectual community at Tokyo Imperial University and those opposed to popular rights, emphasized Spencer's explanation of social evolution and the development of political institutions. Spencer's theory of evolution, however, contained a contradiction that authorized two different interpretations. On the one hand, he offered a liberal interpretation of minimal government guaranteeing the natural rights of all persons so that they might contribute to the progressive development of the whole, society. On the other hand, he relied on a deterministic interpretation of society as an organism responding to its environment, and the government, like the brain of the organism, occupies the appropriately superior position to oversee the whole of systematic adaptations.[72] This dual interpretation of society faced the same ideological split among Japanese intellectuals as it did in Spencer's work: where Ozaki, Baba, and Ueki found a powerful justification for natural rights, Katō Hiroyuki took the logical step from adaptive determinism to a German theory of "state's rights," rejecting natural or popular rights in the process.

Accordingly, Spencer's works provided new strategies of argument critical to intellectuals and political activists in the 1880s. Three issues in particular were affected by Spencerian theory: the enlightenment theory of progress, the debate over natural rights, and the opposition between government and people.

In the first place, political activists had by 1878 come to doubt the veracity of the causal sequence in the enlightenment model of progress. Spencer provided an argument that undermined the theory with finality because he managed to cast doubt on the enlightenment mechanism of change—education—and to do so in a way that ratified individualism but did not make progress dependent on the rational actions of individuals. Given that the same pedagogy of education produced different effects in different individuals, demonstrating that there was no guarantee that education produced enlightened behavior, Spencer managed to reconcile the individual to the greater whole, society, without relying on education. Declaring, as a fundamental point of methodology, that one can understand society only through an examination of its constituent individuals, Spencer in *Social Statics* invoked the "law of adaptation" to explain that the random acts of individuals would in fact contribute to a more just and moral whole.[73] Contrary to the principle of tutelage at the heart of enlightenment, which depends on a superior individual guiding the novice, Spencer maintained as his first principle the "law of equal freedom" ("the moral law"): "Every man has freedom to do all that he wills, provided he infringes not the equal freedom of any other man."[74] Provided that each individual always exercises his "normal" faculties and does not inhibit such action, the beneficial and detrimental pain that we cause each other will ultimately serve the cause of social justice. For the apparent confusion between acts that are indirectly beneficial and those that are always injurious is in fact a case of the "non-adaptation of faculties to their functions"—which, in the larger context of the necessities of social life, provides evidence for the operation of the law of adaptation. In contrast to the enlightenment theory of progress, Spencer's argument has the virtue of allowing for irrational and mistaken behavior. Moreover, as J. D. Y. Peel has pointed out, the principle of adaptation to the social state allowed Spencer to treat progress not as a partial and contingent process but as an evolving process immanent within the totality of society.[75]

In Spencer's analysis, virtually all social processes exhibit such disjunction between individuals and social conditions and hence are subject to the law of adaptation. Education, the centerpiece of enlightenment progress, is a prime instance of nonadaptation. Spencer objected strongly to the authoritative and coercive habits of nineteenth-century education, which, he maintained, wrongly emphasized punishment and the correction of behavior. Instead the proper function of education was the formation of character; it should emphasize correcting character by strengthening the faculty of self-control and evoking the individual's capacity for sympathy, for sympathy is the primary mechanism by which we adapt to others in society. Spencer was certain that education was a temporary phenomenon—not an essential means of enlightening the mind or developing reason but a tool for admonishing individuals to adapt to the social state. And once it had served this function, it would die out.[76]

The second issue to which Spencer made a significant contribution was the popular rights movement as it developed in the 1880s. Spencer's explanation of the law of adaptation and the progress of human societies—or the evolution from "militant" to "industrial" forms of society—presented partisans on either side of the popular rights movement with a scientific justification for both expanding and restricting human rights and democratic institutions. In the hands of popular rights activists, Spencer's scientific explanation of social adaptation provided a powerful justification for the immediate granting of all natural rights—or, as Matsushima's Japanese translation of *Social Statics* put it, "equal rights in society" (*shakai heiken*). Given the context of the popular rights movement, where individuals and their associations protested the actions of the government, Spencer's opposition between government and individual freedom struck a powerful harmony. Ueki Emori echoed Spencer when he stated that man's purpose is happiness, the attainment of which lies in his freedom and equal rights; because these rights were granted by heaven, they take priority over all government and law; accordingly, the state was wrong to interfere with the liberty and rights of the people.[77] Spencer declared that with the advance of civilization, government necessarily decreased: its duty was limited to the maintenance of justice, which included a rightful use of police, to apprehend those who harm fellow members of society, and armed forces to fight off those who would harm society from outside—a point echoed in the Aikokusha's statement of purpose.[78] But, he added, given that all laws made by the government are subject to the law of equal freedom, each individual has a right to ignore the state if it violates that law.[79]

At the same time, Ueki and others saw in Spencer's explanation of progress that social adaptation of circumstances to conditions took the form of a fundamental conflict between morality and government. Spencer reasoned that human government arose from the immoral condition of society, which could only be corrected by the moral law of equal freedom. Hence in situations of conflict between government and the freedom of individuals, the government "must be condemned for conflicting with the moral law, and not the moral law for conflicting with it."[80] Ueki used this logic in arguing for individual rights. In two essays of the 1880s, "On the Poor" and "The Equal Rights of Men and Women," he appealed to morality in making the respective cases that current disparities of wealth and political rights in Japan reinforced conditions that were both unjust and contrary to nature's equality. In the first essay, Ueki did not advocate a socialist redistribution of property to achieve equality; instead he proposed that government do its proper duties of safeguarding freedom and guaranteeing equal rights by extending political rights to the poor.[81] The second essay, in which Ueki quoted Ozaki's translation of Spencer's chapter on "The Rights of Women," reiterated the point that the government and its laws were at fault: given that women have the same intelligence and political capacities as men, the morally appropriate course of action was to grant women equal rights and freedom so that they too could exercise their faculties and strive to attain their own happiness.[82] These appeals to morality reappeared in regional political societies like the Aishinsha (From-Regard-for-Oneself Society) of Aizu prefecture, whose statement of principles promoted Spencer's idea that we have a moral duty to use our natural faculties to produce a state that safeguards our rights.[83]

Although Ueki and his fellow popular rights activists put the government on the defensive by dominating the moral ground, their position relied primarily on the antistatist conclusions of Spencer's version of natural rights and did not make full use of his theory of the immanent process of adaptation. While the essential elements of social evolution were present in *Social Statics*— progress, necessity, adaptation, and continual modification until perfection is reached—Spencer's mature theory of evolution was fully explicated in the complete translations of *The Principles of Sociology* and *The Study of Sociology* in 1883. The scientific claims of this theory proved to be a more fruitful justification for two other significant positions—that of Katō Hiroyuki, a former member of the Meirokusha and president of Tokyo Imperial University from 1881, and that of Tokutomi Sohō, a journalist sympathetic to popular rights and peaceful solutions. Both found in the theory of social evolution the material with which to construct new arguments on a more secure footing.[84]

Largely to bolster the government's position in the wake of announcing the plan to establish a national assembly, as well as forestall a renewed call for popular elections on the basis of popular rights, Katō Hiroyuki published his *Jinken shinsetsu* in 1882. As we have seen in Chapter 5, this text was both a dramatic denunciation of theories of natural rights and a powerful endorsement of one version of the new theory of social evolution gaining ground among the younger Japanese intellectuals. Katō—and other government scholars engaged in creating a constitution for Japan—sought to replace natural rights doctrine with the theory of state's rights—the idea that rights emanate from the state—and to combine it with a theory of the evolution of the state drawn from Spencer, the German biologist Ernst Haeckel, and others. In *Jinken shinsetsu*, Katō explained that the state emerged in the natural context of "survival of the fittest." People united for mutual protection, creating a division of labor and forms of solidarity beyond that of the primitive herd; in time, leaders took charge in order to prevent arbitrary treatment among members of the group. These forms of power and privilege, called rights, evolved from the dictatorial protection of the leader and depended entirely on that superior man. It was in the interests of the leader to grant rights and obligations to the people. And Katō noted, from the historical and evolutionary record, that rulers eventually began to restrict their own actions in order to advance the security and happiness of the people. Katō's allegedly empirical exercise in evolutionary history was intended to justify the supremacy of the state, which he felt was rightfully in a position to determine the best course of action for the people, now essentialized as society.[85] Although Katō made a point of rejecting Spencer's assertion of natural rights, he acknowledged Spencer's contribution to his understanding of evolution. To Katō, the people's rights movement was premature and inappropriate; if anything, social evolution demonstrated the naturally slow pace of change.

Tokutomi Sohō, by contrast, drew quite different conclusions from Spencer's theory of evolution. In his popular work *The Future Japan* (1886), he described Japan as flooded with change—but, he reasurringly added, we can make sense of this change by correctly understanding the natural development of society. After laying out Spencer's law of adaptation and the theory that societies progress from militant to industrial types, he noted that contrary to what his enlightenment teachers had argued, the world was at present a great battleground for the survival of the fittest. Progress, however, in the form of economic distribution and communications, was shifting the militarist phase of the world toward the industrial.[86] Tokutomi did not take a stand on the volatile question of the origin of rights; instead, he stressed progress. Progress is natural and represents the will of the Creator, and as anyone could see from the historical development of the United States, the Creator's chosen people, a democratic government was the destiny for Japan and all peoples. In accord with Spencer's theory that adaptation followed from the confusion of the conventional and the necessary, Tokutomi assured his readers that Japan would overcome its lingering maladaptive customs and fall in line with the general pattern of progress.[87] The problems that Ueki and other activists raised—the inappropriate distribution of wealth in Japan, for instance—were but one example of lingering aristocratic habits, and he chastised those on both sides of the popular rights movement for their "feudal" mentality—their excessive interest in power. In a statement that seemed to fuse Japan's Confucian heritage with Spencer's comments on the duty of the state—if characterized by a degree of paternalism that Spencer would not have authored—Tokutomi urged all to remember that the purpose of the nation was to protect individuals.

Common to these three discussions of progress from Spencer's evolutionary perspective is the presumption of certitude—Spencer's primary claim to scientific practice in *Social Statics*. Reasoning from part to whole, from the nature of the individual to the future state of Japanese society, Ueki and Tokutomi used Spencer's scientific principle of progress to improve upon the earlier enlightenment model. Enlightenment educators like Fukuzawa condemned the authoritarianism of the feudal past—it corrupted social interaction and the development of genuine morality—and urged individuals both inside and outside government to improve themselves. But Ueki, Tokutomi, and other popular rights activists went one step further.[88] They too condemned the morality of the present and understood that individuals needed to change their behavior; but they also placed authoritarianism in society's evolutionary process, anticipating that it would die out. Following Spencer in faulting government for present conditions, they forced government into the position of either relenting on individual rights or fighting back with repressive laws. Katō, by contrast, found in evolution firm ground for the government's authoritarian stance. The de facto official policy of gradualism did accord with the natural progress of peoples and nations. It was appropriate, then, that the government suppress the popular rights movement; rather than an act of oppression, this was an appropriate measure of adaptation in light of Japan's specific conditions.[89] As scholars of modernity have argued, such certitude is the goal of a more rational politics, and Katō anticipated the advent of social science—the creation of more precise systems that integrate terminology and the means of repeatable measurement.

In addition to the enlightenment theory of progress and the debate over natural rights, Spencer's concept of society made a third significant contribution: it began to solve the problem that undermined the enlightenment and gradualist positions of government officials and the Meirokusha scholars—the persisting opposition between government and people. Spencer offered a new and alternative way to conceptualize the problem. Instead of pitting government against people, society had its own laws of evolution that could account for the development of the opposed pair. This argument was evident in one of his first pieces translated into Japanese, "The Rights of Women," which appeared in late 1879. Spencer explains that "as barbarians advance a step and settle, they become a society [*shakai*], with social interaction [*kōsai*] so dense as to constitute a people. Their affairs become correspondingly more diverse and thus the division of labor between men and women becomes more specialized." Spencer then generalizes two fundamental types of society—the militant and the industrial—developmental types that prove to be chronological stages in social evolution. Based on the fundamentally contrastive pair of Polynesians—the militant Fijians and the industrial Samoans—Spencer describes social evolution in terms of the progress of the rights of women: The military stage of society exhibits polygamy and fewer rights for women; the industrial stage advances to monogamy and greater rights for women. The military stage utilizes a class system so that the lower orders can provide for the ruling warriors; the industrial stage utilizes a more refined division of labor so that social relations are more equal and the society experiences greater peace.

In this description, the concept of society provides a point of mediation between people and government: the earlier, militant form of society is typically ruled by a monarchy, while societies evolving into industrial forms establish more collective and democratic forms of government.[90] Recall that in Katō's hands this history hinges on the superior man who can generate the cohesion of a strong and stable society and begin to delegate rights and duties to the people, integrating them into collective rule. For Tokutomi Sohō, current tensions between government and people were but artifacts of Japan's evolutionary position—in time, Japanese society would attain a united harmony under democratic government. For both positions, apparent conflicts among factions in society could be dissolved within the fundamental national unity of society.[91] Nonetheless, this capacity of society to mediate government and people was temporary and would soon enough be transformed when socialists took up the new cause of society against the state.

What is most striking in the 1880s is that the reification of society as a corporate body creates new possibilities for human agency. In his famous discussion of the "Right to the Use of the Earth" in *Social Statics*, Spencer offers, as an alternative to private property in land, the collective ownership by society. As the lawful owner of land, society can determine appropriate rents, and this arrangement should further the adaptation of individuals to the moral law of freedom. Spencer's model here is the joint-stock company, an institution that takes his Japanese readers well beyond the personal encounters of individuals and the opposition between people and government.[92] Individuals adapt their naturally repulsive and cohesive forces to society, thereby advancing civilization. As Ueki Emori had learned from Spencer, the benefits of recognizing the natural rights of individuals accrued to society at the expense of government. It is because of this revolutionary new conception, I am convinced, that Matsushima Kō gave *Social Statics* the Japanese title *Shakai heiken ron*, meaning "On Equal Rights in Society." Society is that mass into which we dissolve our barbarian impulse to wander, and in return for the mutual protection of our natural rights, we partake of the new organic power. Analogous to the organic individual, the new aggregate agent can act with autonomy in the world.

Apart from endowing society with such power of agency, the reification of society empowered new political activists, sociologists, and others to exercise their new forms of action in this new totality, thus stimulating adaptation and evolutionary progress. As Katō Hiroyuki declared, in a form typical of nineteenth-century sociology and revelatory of the Japanese shift from enlightenment tutelage to scientific certitude, the application of physical principles to human affairs would yield substantive discoveries which promise to clear our minds of the deceptions that currently obstruct the progress of society.[93] As an object of knowledge, society is to be studied; as a formation of the people, society is to be manipulated. Government officials, intellectuals, and popular rights activists can suggest courses of action for society because, above all, society is amenable to the guidance of others through either the promotion or the suppression of individual conduct.[94]

By the 1880s society had begun to move beyond the analysis of Herbert Spencer—an indication that lasting neologisms evade the source of their domestication. Society became the site of new divisions capable of reification for further analytical work. In "On the Poor," Ueki Emori divided human society into "higher-level society" and "lower-level society"—an incipient class analysis in which the higher are characterized by their wealth, literacy, and knowledge and the lower by their poverty, illiteracy, and dumbness. But the opposition also corresponds to the difference between the political class and the masses of the people—blame for the existence of which (like Fukuzawa a decade earlier) Ueki places on Japan's long tradition of authoritarian government and arrogance among the rulers. In addition to advocating the granting of equal political rights to the poor, as noted earlier, Ueki mentions the existence of the "socialist party" (*shakaitō*) in European countries, whose political goal was to equalize these levels of society—to reunify human society.[95] By the turn of the century, others would begin to advocate these socialist programs under the banner of the new neologism *shakaishugi* (socialism).[96]

What the translation of "society" ultimately signifies, I believe, is that in the course of the 1880s the political control of the former samurai class over the people had begun to dissolve. With the class system of the Tokugawa age dismantled and the simple equation of status, occupation, and moral standing undone, the new unit, society, became reified as a new reality. Based on a new and Western understanding of the human world, society was the site of new divisions, tendencies, and processes and required a new set of experts to explain its dynamics and a new set of approaches to manage its directions. Greater sophistication, in other words, was needed as Japan progressed to a level of civilization that coupled industry with the problems of rural tenancy and urban slums. The concept of society was central to the new work, and the scientific method that accompanied the concept of society called for an analytic approach. The earliest manifestation in Japan of the kind of science that Americans easily associate with "social" did not appear until the turn of the century with the discovery of "social problems" *(shakai mondai)* that could be quantified, charted, and acted upon.[97]

By the end of the 1880s, then, the largely liberal theory of civil society had been displaced—in part by the Japanese state and its growing commitment to an alternative theory of imperial rule, in part by the Spencerian notion of society, which promised a new conceptualization of the whole. With the qualified success of the movement to establish a national assembly, the status divisions of the Tokugawa paradigm gave way to new conceptual unities: the people of Japan, the Japanese nation, and Japanese society. And these signal that the enlightenment theory of progress under former samurai tutelage was largely abandoned as interest in evolutionary progress continued to grow. "The people" and "the nation" remained inclusive concepts to which Japanese intellectuals would return for their democratic and ethnic possibilities. "Society," by contrast, remained the abstract whole characterized by its tensions, conflicts, and adaptive developments. More than one liberal intellectual saw in society the active force of change emerging from the people below to confront the oligarchy above—an oligarchy whose existence had increasingly little political justification apart from its power and passive momentum. But to Katō Hiroyuki, this confrontation demonstrated the truth of the moral survival of the fittest.

This much was one consequence of the introduction of Herbert Spencer to Meiji Japan. In providing partisans on both sides of the popular rights movement with a scientific argument regarding human rights and the evolution of democratic institutions, as well as the abstract conception of society amenable to scientific law and political praxis, Spencer in translation points to the general conclusion that political theory is subject to the same uncertainties faced by all considerations of language and terminology. First, it is relatively easy to speak of things that are not yet realized in reality; "society" at the start of this period is equivalent to the unicorn, a thing we can all identify but have not yet seen. And second, as political debate enlists ideological positions, we are witnessing the reification of new knowledge about a new reality. As a sign of this new reality, the Rikken jiyūtō (Constitutional Liberal Party) announced in its founding prospectus of 1890 that the party would be committed to "the public benefit of society" (*shakai no kōeki*). Where the Charter Oath had been content with *kōeki* (public benefit), the new conception specified that the public was the social.[98]

7

Conclusion

I n comparison to anthropology or linguistics, which often seek to explain cultures or languages as totalities, history is always a partial account. Hence a history of Japanese translation and political thought has inherent limitations. Although we focus on one phenomenon to the exclusion of another, historical reality would indicate that the two coexist. As Talal Asad argued two decades ago, we cannot presume "structures of meaning" that hold reality in place; his point is particularly apt in the case at hand, as words, their cultural references, and multiple temporalities flow and ebb among Japan, China, Western Europe, the United States, and who knows elsewhere.[1] Because language is embedded in perpetual circulation and change, we pause to discuss meaning at the risk of reifying an ideal semantics. Yet this is the case with most philological work on translation: we identify European concepts such as liberty and society and then proceed—inadvertently anticipating some normative meaning—by examining how Japanese words came to mean "liberty" or "society." Our efforts to fix language in time in order to account fully for causes and effects are washed out by the fluidity of language. Histories remain partial. From William E. Connolly's "essentially contested concepts" to Reinhard Koselleck's *Begriffsgeschichte*, attempts to write the history of concepts compensate for this inherent partiality by assuming an adequate field of meaning as a point of departure.[2] Even the most thoughtful work on the history of ideas risks reifying semantics when it starts with "Western political discourse," identifies key terms, and investigates how these terms came to mean what they do.[3] But rigor insists on a lingering doubt: are we certain that we know what our words mean?[4]

In this study I have been deliberately partial and hence limited. I have examined three problems in the history of Japanese translations of Western political thought: in Chapter 4, "liberty," a concept readily translated but highly contested; in Chapter 5, a set of concepts—"right," "authority," "power," and "sovereignty"—initially equated as *ken* but gradually differentiated through their usage in a series of political debates; and in Chapter 6, the appearance of a neologism, *shakai*, that accompanied the revelation of "society." If these were initially embedded in a Japanese project of enlightened civilization, largely informed by Western liberal theory and practice, the Western hypocrisy that some Japanese observed in the disjunction between Western theory and practice—especially regarding international relations—compromised concepts like liberty, right, and sovereignty from the outset. And the stabilization of these concepts in the early Meiji movement to establish a national assembly simultaneously began to change the conditions of that enlightenment project. For the decline of attention to the people's right(s) and the abstraction of liberty into a nonspecific ideal corresponded to the reification of society and the location of sovereignty in the emperor.

Despite the changing contexts and meanings of terms, translation technique and political thought developed in parallel: the simplification of technique is related to a simplification of power relations in the Japanese state. To return to Koselleck's language raised in my introduction: because linguistic phenomena and political events develop at different rates, these multiple temporalities are not strictly causal but parallel developments. Where early translations, by way of analogs, allowed for multiple meanings and welcomed indeterminacy, the later practice of direct translation and standardization posited authoritative language. In a corresponding political practice, the revolutionary period of early Meiji, with its multiple authorities, gave way to the work of consolidation in the 1880s as the oligarchy asserted an authoritative center that determined the positions hierarchically lower to it. My point in this book is that the introduction of conceptual and cultural forms of English liberalism participated in the structuring of historical agency in Japan. But a liberal project, no longer called enlightened civilization and hence a different effort, persisted well after the confines of this book: the question of sovereignty in Japan, for example, would be revisited again in the 1910s in terms of the "organ theory of the emperor" and "Taishō democracy."[5] The creation of a constitutional political system generated institutional expections that Japanese continued to revisit in the twentieth century—or, as Mark Lincicome recently put the point, liberalism remained an alternative historical legacy for those opposed to the state's agenda.[6]

One phenomenon missing here is the nation. In addition to people and society, it was another contemporary concept for mediating the state and the individual. Although several scholars and activists introduced the nation in the 1870s and it surfaces occasionally in this account, its history has not yet been written—in large measure because of the problematic nature of its translation and terminology.[7] Unlike the translation words for liberty, right, and society, which were either neologisms or new meanings for older, obscure words, the term that came to mean "nation," *kokumin*, was widely and continuously used from the Tokugawa through the Meiji periods. At what point did a majority of persons use *kokumin* to mean not "subjects of the domain" but "nation"? And what is a nation?

Henry Wheaton, in *The Elements of International Law*, defined a state as a society of men united for mutual safety and advantage by combined strength and defined a sovereign state as a nation or people that governs itself independent of foreign powers.[8] W. B. Lawrence, who annotated the 1863 edition of Wheaton, pointed to nationality and ethnology as the basis of such sovereignty. Asserting that a nation is a unity of race, he concluded that Italy was the first nation-state—the first fully autonomous and self-governing race.[9]

It is clear that, between the departure of Perry in 1854 and the suppression of the Satsuma Rebellion in 1877, Japanese leaders acquired the self-perception as a state, but this process preceded an analysis of the internal structure of the state.[10] At several points in the 1870s the nation appeared in various forms: *kokka*, the nation-as-family; *kokumin*, the nation-as-people; and *minzoku*, the people-as-tribe. All of these expressions functioned less like "people" and more like "society" in that they directed attention to the state's internal constituents. Ueki Emori, for example, imagined a "national democracy" that would unify the state and individuals; Fukuzawa Yukichi pondered both "citizens" and "nation" before turning to the nation to mediate public and private interests.[11] As Ochiai Hiroki has argued regarding samurai and merchant activists committed to a national assembly, the people's right(s), and the emperor, the nation promised a medium into which all classes would dissolve, for a striking feature of modern life is that national values can be detached from class consciousness.[12] In other words, differing conceptions of the nation-state implicitly informed the debates on liberty, right, sovereignty, and the people in Chapters 4, 5, and 6. In addition to contributing to the construction of new concepts, these debates also figured as modes of integrating the individual and the new nation-state.

If the terminology and uses of the nation were diverse, Japan's national project was additionally complex in that its sources were both domestic and international. State forces like the bureaucracy and institutionalized education developed the nation from above; popular forces like the movements for a national assembly and the people's right(s) developed it from below.[13] More consistent pressure was exerted by international relations. Yamamuro Shin'ichi differentiates state construction from nation construction in order to emphasize that the former invoked tradition, modernization, and statecraft, while the latter persistently problematized the level of the people's intelligence. In the international context of national competition, which Fukuzawa so forcefully expounded, the advance of the nation depended on raising the quality of the people.[14] Hence national aspects of internal state structure—national identity and integration, for example—were in large part determined from outside.[15] The problem was always: how would the individual and the nation-state be integrated? The government, in forcing its own agenda of integration, took its cue from the international arena. But the context of international competition and conflict—which, in many minds, corrupted the integrity of Western liberal theory—had the effect in Japan of diverting self-determination and autonomy away from the domestic context to the international context of competitive capitalism and colonialism.[16] As we have seen in Chapter 5, state right took precedence over the people's right(s).

In this international context, the nation as race or tribe appeared a solution. For the theory of social evolution in an arena of international competition, understood in terms best explained by Katō Hiroyuki, began to resolve the apparent contradictions between, on the one hand, the state and the people and, on the other hand, the domestic and international arenas. That is, the "ethnic nation"—to refer to Kevin Doak's important formulation and analysis—reconciled, first, the competitive nature of the international arena and the oligarchy's need to manage the ethnic culture and, second, the state project of constitutional empire and the national project of developing loyal and capable subjects—all within the context of a developmental history.[17] The turn from a corrupt and Western universalism, defined in terms of liberalism, to a unique history and ethnic identity defined in terms of German *Kultur* made a virtue of the long-standing commitment to Japanese particularity with its emphasis on Japanese history, the Japanese race, and the Japanese emperor. In light of domestic and international demands, the shift from enlightenment to evolution produced a more fully rational, national project—which would nonetheless be contested, by populists, socialists, and more, as soon as it was constructed.

What is missing here is the category of the citizen—some way to represent the individual constituent of the state. It was easy to identify the individual as one of the people, or a member of society, but Japanese leaders had hardly begun to conceptualize the state and its integration with its constituent persons. While mobilization of the people on the part of the state and private organizations began to dissolve status and regional differences, as well as to produce dislocation and relocation, disorder and new order, the fact remains, as Carol Gluck has observed, that "the modern state makes its national demands directly on the individual."[18] In the absence of a viable concept of citizen, the state could only encourage its articulate dissidents to challenge its ways as authoritarian.

In place of citizenship, the Meiji oligarchy offered a subjecthood best defined by moral hierarchy and education. The maintenance of moral relations persisted as one of the primary expectations and responsibilities of Japanese government. From the early comments on high and low, and the natural deference of the people to their superiors, to later comments that the social change provoked by enlightened civilization would be best contained by reasserting morality among the people, who naturally revere their emperor, moral relations remained a component of the political imagination of many contributors to Meiji political debate.[19]

Hence Nishimura Shigeki's early diagnosis of the problem of educating the masses offered an eminently practical plan of action. The Ministry of Education, under the leadership of men like Nishimura and Mori Arinori, proceeded to insert itself into Japanese society, expanding its control in the last two decades of the nineteenth century. Increasing numbers of schools were established; increasing numbers of parents were persuaded to send their children to schools. Although both the corps of teachers and their student audiences were overwhelmingly composed of former samurai until the 1890s, increasing numbers of the common people were apprehended by the developing system as a new state structure was gradually imposed and new textbooks and content were introduced—stressing science, morality, patriotism, and loyalty to the emperor.[20] This was a new national people, to be educated for participation in state and national affairs, under conditions best described as the persistence of hierarchy. For it was the legacy of westernization to remake Tokugawa paternalism as enlightenment tutelage, which in turn gave way to the expertise of social scientists in the service of civilian and military bureaucracies.

Notes

Abbreviations

FYS   *Fukuzawa Yukichi senshū*, ed. Tomita Masafumi. Tokyo: Iwanami shoten, 1980–1981.

JGD   W. W. McLaren, ed. *Japanese Government Documents* (1914). Tokyo: Asiatic Society of Japan, 1979.

JJGNY   *Jiyūjiji gannen no yume*, ed. Ide Magoroku. Tokyo: Shakai hyōronsha, 1991.

JYMKH   *Meiji bunka zenshū*, vol. 5: *Jiyū minken hen*. Tokyo: Nihon hyōronsha, 1927.

JYNR   Nakamura Keiu, *Jiyū no ri* (1871). In *Meiji bunka zenshū*, vol. 5: *Jiyū minken hen*. Tokyo: Nihon hyōronsha, 1927.

MRZS   *Meiroku zasshi* (1874–1875). Tokyo: Rittaisha, 1976.

NKKS   *Nihon kensei kiso shiryō*, ed. Miyakoshi Shin'ichirō. Tokyo: Giin seijisha, 1939.

SSMHS   *Shinbun shūsei Meiji hennen shi*, ed. Nakayama Yasumasa (1934–1936). Tokyo: Honpō shoseki, 1982.

SYJJ   Fukuzawa Yukichi, *Seiyō jijō* (1866–1870). In *Fukuzawa Yukichi zenshū*, vol. 1. Tokyo: Iwanami shoten, 1958.

TKGSKIZS   *Tōkyō gakushi kaiin zasshi* (1880–1901).

TYGGZS   *Tōyō gakugei zasshi* (1881–1922).

1. Introduction

1. Norbert Elias, *The Civilizing Process: The History of Manners and State Formation and Civilization*, trans. Edmund Jephcott (Oxford: Blackwell, 1994), pp. 187 and 201–206.

2. Joseph Pittau, *Political Thought in Early Meiji Japan, 1868–1889* (Cambridge, Mass.: Harvard University Press, 1967), pp. 131–157. See also George Akita, *Foundations of Constitutional Government in Modern Japan, 1868–1900* (Cambridge, Mass.: Harvard University Press, 1967); Carmen Blacker, *The Japanese Enlightenment: A Study of the Writings of Fukuzawa Yukichi* (Cambridge: Cambridge University Press, 1964); Thomas R. H. Havens, *Nishi Amane and Modern Japanese Thought* (Princeton: Princeton University Press, 1970); and Nobutaka Ike, *The Beginnings of Political Democracy in Japan* (Baltimore: Johns Hopkins University Press, 1950). While these are excellent studies, they all engage in the oversight I call semantic transparency.

3. A persistent shortcoming of one branch of National Language philology (Kokugogaku) in Japan remains the prevalence of dictionary studies, which assume that dictionaries are the preeminent source of sign types ("general words")—instead, as I believe, that a dictionary is merely another text offering sign tokens (examples of word usage). In his early and impressive English-Japanese dictionary of 1862, for example, Hori Tatsunosuke translated "civilization" as *gyōgi tadashikusuru koto* (behavior made proper), a paraphrastic translation that is no more typical than Fukuzawa Yukichi's initial use of *bunmei*. More to the point, I have never seen *gyōgi tadashikusuru koto* used in any of the other texts examined in this book; it is not a sign type, a generally understood meaning, but a sign token, a case of word use. One might argue that Hori's purpose was, after all, merely to provide interpretations of English-language words for a Japanese readership, but such a rejoinder further marginalizes the dictionary for our understanding of language usage. Not only does a dictionary like Hori's provide merely case examples of words (sign tokens), but it offers little context for these words, since they are presented as isolated items, in parallel with the English equivalents they "translate." Most bilingual dictionaries, in other words, give us little information regarding the historical actuality of word usage. See Hori Tatsnoskay [Tatsunosuke], *A Pocket Dictionary of the English and Japanese Language/Ei-Wa taiyaku shūchin jisho* (Edo: n.p., 1862), p. 129; on the background of Hori's dictionary see Nagashima Daisuke, *Ran-Wa Ei-Wa jisho hattatsu shi* (Tokyo: Kōdansha, 1970), pp. 52–72. The Japanese literature on dictionary studies is immense; in addition to Nagashima see Yoshida Kanehiko, "Jisho no rekishi," in *Kōza: Kokugo shi*, vol. 3: *Goi shi*, by Sakakura Atsuyoshi et al. (Tokyo: Taishūkan, 1971), pp. 503–537; Matsui Toshi-

hiko, *Kindai Kango jisho no seiritsu to tenkai* (Tokyo: Kasama shoin, 1990); and Yokoyama Toshio, "*Setsuyōshū* and Japanese Civilization," in *Themes and Theories in Modern Japanese History: Essays in Memory of Richard Storry*, ed. Sue Henny and Jean-Pierre Lehmann (London: Athlone, 1988), pp. 78–98.

4. Melvin Richter, *The History of Political and Social Concepts: A Critical Introduction* (New York: Oxford University Press, 1995), p. 20; Melvin Richter, "Appreciating a Contemporary Classic: The *Geschichtliche Grundbegriffe* and Future Scholarship," in *The Meaning of Historical Terms and Concepts: New Studies on Begriffsgeschichte*, ed. Hartmut Lehmann and Melvin Richter (Washington, D.C.: German Historical Institute, 1996), p. 10. See also Reinhart Koselleck, *Futures Past: On the Semantics of Historical Time* (Cambridge, Mass.: MIT Press, 1985), pp. 73–91.

5. Koselleck, *Futures Past*, pp. 270–275 and 286–288 (quote on p. 287); see also his "Social History and *Begriffsgeschichte*," in *History of Concepts: Comparative Perspectives*, ed. Iain Hampsher-Monk, Karin Tilmans, and Frank van Vree (Amsterdam: Amsterdam University Press, 1998), p. 25. Henri Lefebvre offers a related analysis of modern space—as the production of an abstract space of modern society from the absolute space of unmediated relations (blood, family, and so on)—in *The Production of Space*, trans. Donald Nicholson-Smith (Oxford: Blackwell, 1991), pp. 48–53 and 229–291; and Matsumoto Sannosuke discusses the formation of political consciousness in the transition from Tokugawa to Meiji in a manner compatible with "abstraction"—the theorization and divergence of concepts from their circumstances—in *Kindai Nihon no chiteki jōkyō* (Tokyo: Chūōkōronsha, 1974), pp. 8–13.

6. Sakamoto Takao, independent of Koselleck's example, has discussed the new experience of time as an effect of the introduction of civilization and progress in early Meiji; see *Kindai Nihon seishinshi ron* (Tokyo: Kōdansha, 1996), pp. 20–33. For a more typical discussion of the West as a new center forcing Japan into the position of borderland see Kamei Shunsuke, "Nihon no kindai to hon'yaku," in *Kindai Nihon no hon'yaku bunka*, ed. Kamei Shunsuke (Tokyo: Chūōkōronsha, 1994), pp. 9–11.

7. The Nagasaki interpreters are also known as "Dutch interpreters" (*Oranda tsūji*) in secondary materials. For the best summaries of the background of Dutch learning and Western learning see David Abosch, "Katō Hiroyuki and the Introduction of German Political Thought: 1868–1883" (Ph.D. dissertation, University of California, 1964), pp. 63–160; Grant K. Goodman, *Japan: The Dutch Experience* (London: Athlone, 1986); Hirakawa Sukehiro, "Japan's Turn to the West," in *The Cambridge History of Japan*, vol. 5: *The Nineteenth Century*, ed. Marius Jansen (Cambridge: Cambridge University Press, 1989), pp. 432–498; Donald Keene, *The Japanese Discovery of Europe, 1720–1830*, rev. ed. (Stanford: Stanford University

Press, 1969); Numata Jirō, *Yōgaku denrai no rekishi* (Tokyo: Shibundō, 1966) and *Yōgaku* (Tokyo: Yoshikawa kōbunkan, 1989); and Sugimoto Tsutomu, *Zuroku Rangaku kotohajime* (Tokyo: Waseda Daigaku shuppanbu, 1985). See also the recent reassessment by Tetsuo Najita, "Ambiguous Encounters: Ogata Kōan and International Studies in Late Tokugawa Osaka," in *Osaka: The Merchants' Capital of Early Modern Japan,* ed. James L. McClain and Wakita Osamu (Ithaca: Cornell University Press, 1999) pp. 213–242.

8. See Timon Screech, *The Western Scientific Gaze and Popular Imagery in Later Edo Japan: The Lens Within the Heart* (Cambridge: Cambridge University Press, 1996), pp. 6–30.

9. Abosch, "Katō Hiroyuki," pp. 154–157. On Western learning in the Bakumatsu period see W. G. Beasley, *Japan Encounters the Barbarian: Japanese Travellers in America and Europe* (New Haven: Yale University Press, 1995). The Bansho (and successor Yōsho) shirabesho is often referred to as the "Western Studies Institute" (Yōgakusho or Yōgakujo), but this was not an official name; it was renamed the Kaiseijo in 1863, absorbed into the Medical Institute (Igakujo) in 1868, and thus into Tokyo Imperial University in 1877. See *Yōgakushi jiten*, ed. Nichi-Ran gakkai (Numata Jirō et al.) (Tokyo: Yūshōdō, 1984), pp. 156, 591, 727.

10. Kido Takayoshi, *The Diary of Kido Takayoshi*, trans. Sidney Devere Brown and Akiko Hirota (Tokyo: University of Tokyo Press, 1983–1986), 3:402 and 462. On Kido's role in early Meiji developments see Igarashi Akio, *Meiji ishin no shisō* (Yokohama: Seishiki shobō, 1996), pp. 11–92.

11. Kido, *Diary*, vol. 3 passim; George M. Beckmann, "Political Crises and the Crystallization of Japanese Constitutional Thought, 1871–1881," *Pacific Historical Review* 23(3) (August 1954):259–270; and Jackson H. Bailey, "Prince Saionji and the Popular Rights Movement," *Journal of Asian Studies* 21(1) (November 1961):49–63.

12. Kido, *Diary*, 2:88, 398, 407; 3:132 and 318.

13. See David Huish, "Aims and Achievement of the *Meirokusha*—Fact and Fiction," *Monumenta Nipponica* 32(4) (Winter 1977):495–514; Ivan Parker Hall, *Mori Arinori* (Cambridge, Mass.: Harvard University Press, 1973), pp. 233–245; Ōkubo Toshiaki, *Meirokusha kō* (Tokyo: Rittaisha, 1976); Tōyama Shigeki, "Meiroku zasshi," *Shisō*, no. 447 (9/1961):117–128, and "Reforms of the Meiji Restoration and the Birth of Modern Intellectuals," *Acta Asiatica* 13 (1967):55–99. Because of this focus on *bunmeikaika* after the Meiji Restoration, much of the secondary literature marks it as a qualitatively new development beyond the Western learning (*yōgaku*) of the Bakumatsu period; but Ōkubo has discussed the striking continuity of personnel from Tokugawa Western learning to the Meirokusha and Gakushi kaiin in *Meiji no shisō to bunka* (Tokyo: Yoshikawa kōbunkan, 1988), pp. 14–27 and 75–82.

14. Short discussions of the background of these two journals are included in the centenary history of Tokyo University: *Tōkyō daigaku hyakunen shi: Tsūshi* (Tokyo: Tokyo Daigaku, 1984), 1:491–500 and 614–622. On the Gakushi kaiin (Tokyo Academy) see Walter Dening, "The Gakushikaiin," *Transactions of the Asiatic Society of Japan*, ser. 1, vol. 15 (1887):58–82; and Ōkubo Toshiaki, *Meiji no shisō to bunka*, pp. 226–236 and 255–277.

15. The first major work in this vein was Hattori Shisō, *Meiji Ishin shi* (Tokyo: Taihōkaku, 1930). See also Hattori's later pronouncement, "Bunmeikaika" (1953), in *Meiji keimō shisō shū*, ed. Ōkubo Toshiaki (Tokyo: Chikuma shobō, 1967), pp. 417–424; Miyagawa Tōru, "Nihon keimō shisō no kōzō — minken giin mondai o chūshin toshite," in *Meiji keimō shisō shū*, pp. 424–436; Tōyama Shigeki, *Meiji ishin* (1951), rev. ed. (Tokyo: Iwanami shoten, 1972), pp. 293–296; E. H. Norman, *Origins of the Modern Japanese State: Selected Writings of E. H. Norman*, ed. John W. Dower (New York: Random House, 1975), pp. 457–458. My simplified account of the Marxist explanation of absolutism omits the important discussion of class relations in both Miyagawa and Tōyama; see W. G. Beasley, *The Meiji Restoration* (Stanford: Stanford University Press, 1972), pp. 7–8 and 234–235.

16. See, for example, Albert M. Craig, "Fukuzawa Yukichi: The Philosophical Foundations of Meiji Nationalism," in *Political Development in Modern Japan*, ed. Robert E. Ward (Princeton: Princeton University Press, 1968), pp. 99–148.

17. Donald H. Shively, "Nishimura Shigeki: A Confucian View of Modernization," in *Changing Japanese Attitudes Toward Modernization*, ed. Marius B. Jansen (Princeton: Princeton University Press, 1965), pp. 193–241.

18. For an excellent discussion of Japanese historiography that encompasses both Marxism and modernization theory see John W. Dower's introduction, "E. H. Norman, Japan, and the Uses of History," to Norman, *Origins of the Modern Japanese State*, pp. 3–108. Modernization theory remains an accepted paradigm today; see S. N. Eisenstadt, *Japanese Civilization: A Comparative View* (Chicago: University of Chicago Press, 1996), which mixes axial-age theory with modernization; and see Johann P. Arnason, *Social Theory and Japanese Experience: The Dual Civilization* (London: Kegan Paul International, 1997), which treats Japan's unique development as a combination of Chinese and Western (modern) bureaucracy and rationalization. Contrary to what one might anticipate from his title, Yoda Yoshiie's *The Foundations of Japan's Modernization: A Comparison with China's Path Towards Modernization*, trans. Kurt W. Radtke (Leiden: Brill, 1996), is both an analysis of what I call westernization and a valuable historicization of the introduction to Japan and China of Western ideas and institutions. For two further perspectives on modernization see the Japanese National Committee of Historical Sciences, *Recent Trends in Japanese Historiography: Bibliographical Essays: Japan at the XIIIth International Congress of Historical Sciences in Moscow* (Tokyo: Japan

Society for the Promotion of Science, 1970), 1:61–68; and Jacques Mutel, "The Modernization of Japan: Why Has Japan Succeeded in Its Modernization?," in *Europe and the Rise of Capitalism,* ed. Jean Baechler, John A. Hall, and Michael Mann (Oxford: Blackwell, 1988), pp. 136–158. See also recent comments that would redirect modernization toward the problem of state formation: Sheldon Garon, "Rethinking Modernization and Modernity in Japanese History: A Focus on State-Society Relations," *Journal of Asian Studies* 53(2) (May 1994):346–366; and Tetsuo Najita, "Presidential Address: Reflections on Modernity and Modernization," *Journal of Asian Studies* 52(4) (November 1993):845–853.

19. Blacker, *Japanese Enlightenment,* pp. xi–xii and 30–40. See also Matsumoto, *Kindai Nihon no chiteki jōkyō,* pp. 47–83, and Mori Kazutsura, *Kindai Nihon shisō shi josetsu: shizen to shakai no ronri* (Kyoto: Kōyō shobo, 1984), pp. 84–115.

20. Tetsuo Najita, *Japan: The Intellectual Foundations of Modern Japanese Politics* (Chicago: University of Chicago Press, 1974), p. 86; Carol Gluck, *Japan's Modern Myths: Ideology in the Late Meiji Period* (Princeton: Princeton University Press, 1985), p. 144; and Yamamuro Shin'ichi, *Kindai Nihon no chi to seiji: Inoue Kowashi kara taishūengei made* (Tokyo: Mokutakusha, 1985), p. 159. Recently Nishikawa Nagao has placed Meiji in a long-term pattern of cultural importing and nationalism; his historical periodization fractures the "modern" into a time of "national cultures" under the auspices of nation-states, followed by a time of mixing cultures in our contemporary period of "comparative cultures"; see *Kokkyō no koekata—hikaku bunkaron josetsu* (Tokyo: Chikuma shobō, 1992), pp. 94–115 and 289–292.

21. John Dunn, "The Identity of the History of Ideas," *Philosophy* 43(164) (April 1968):85–104; and Quentin Skinner, "Meaning and Understanding in the History of Ideas," *History and Theory* 8 (1969):3–53. Leo Spitzer had mounted this critique earlier, for very different ends, in "Geistesgeschichte vs. History of Ideas as Applied to Hitlerism," *Journal of the History of Ideas* 5 (1944):191–203.

22. Pittau, *Political Thought in Early Meiji Japan,* pp. 1 and 16.

23. Ibid., pp. 136–138 and 145. See also Mikiso Hane, "Sources of English Liberal Concepts in Early Meiji Japan," *Monumenta Nipponica* 24(3) (1969):259–272.

24. Talcott Parsons summarized his views in "A Revised Analytical Approach to the Theory of Social Stratification," in *Class, Status, and Power: A Reader in Social Stratification,* ed. Reinhard Bendix and Seymour Martin Lipset (Glencoe: Free Press, 1953), pp. 92–128; see also William Buxton, *Talcott Parsons and the Capitalist Nation-State: Political Sociology as a Strategic Vocation* (Toronto: University of Toronto Press, 1985).

25. John Whitney Hall, "Changing Conceptions of the Modernization of Japan," in *Changing Japanese Attitudes Toward Modernization,* pp. 26 and 30.

26. W. W. Rostow, *The Stages of Economic Growth: A Non-Communist Mani-*

festo (Cambridge: Cambridge University Press, 1960), pp. 16, 73, and 149; S. N. Eisenstadt, "Modernisation: Growth & Diversity," *India Quarterly* 20 (January-March 1964):17–42; Joseph J. Spengler, "Theory, Ideology, Non-Economic Values, and Politico-Economic Development," in *Tradition, Values, and Socio-Economic Development*, ed. Ralph Braibanti and Joseph J. Spengler (Durham: Duke University Press; London: Cambridge University Press, 1961), pp. 3–56; and David E. Apter, *The Politics of Modernization* (Chicago: University of Chicago Press, 1965), pp. x-xiv and 9–10.

27. On the role of functionalism in modernization theory see Apter, *Politics of Modernization*, pp. vii–x; and Dean Tipps, "Modernization Theory and the Comparative Study of Societies: A Critical Perspective," *Comparative Studies in Society and History* 15 (March 1973):199–226.

28. Robert N. Bellah, *Tokugawa Religion: The Values of Pre-Industrial Japan* (1957; Boston: Beacon, 1970); and Robert A. Scalapino, "Ideology and Modernization— The Japanese Case," in *Ideology and Discontent*, ed. David E. Apter (New York: Free Press; London: Collier-Macmillan, 1964), pp. 93–127.

29. Scalapino, "Ideology and Modernization," p. 107.

30. Ibid., p. 109.

31. Ibid., p. 126; see also pp. 93–94 and 125.

32. See Hall, "Changing Conceptions of the Modernization of Japan," p. 33; Pittau, *Political Thought in Early Meiji Japan*, pp. 31–33; and especially Robert E. Ward, "Political Modernization and Political Culture in Japan," *World Politics* 15(4) (July 1963):569–596. Another awkward point of interpretation was of course colonialism; although Japanese historians routinely mention that Japan's modernization was prompted by the Euro-American threat of invasion, modernization theorists rarely dwell on the role of Japanese colonialism in Japanese economic and political development. Generally, only Marxists (whose purpose is to critique capitalist development in all its forms) and economic historians attend to the benefits of Japan's conquest and development of Taiwan, Korea, and Manchuria. See W. G. Beasley, *Japanese Imperialism, 1894–1945* (Oxford: Clarendon, 1987); and Jon Halliday, *A Political History of Japanese Capitalism* (New York: Pantheon, 1975). On the benefits of colonialism to modernization see Apter, *Politics of Modernization*, pp. 50–56, and Rostow, *Stages of Economic Growth*, pp. 6 and 108–114.

33. Pittau, *Political Thought in Early Meiji Japan*, p. 70.

34. See Bailey, "Prince Saionji and the Popular Rights Movement"; Iyenaga Saburo [*sic*], "Problem of Accepting Foreign Ideas in the History of Japanese Thought," *Asian Cultural Studies,* no. 5 (October 1966):83–93; and, his disclaimers notwithstanding, see Ishida Takeshi, *Nihon no seiji to kotoba*, vol. 1: *Jiyū to fukushi* (Tokyo: Tokyo Daigaku shuppankai, 1989), pp. 13–14, 26–31, 39–40.

35. Graham Burchell, "Peculiar Interests: Civil Society and Governing the Sys-

tem of Natural Liberty," in *The Foucault Effect: Studies in Governmentality*, ed. Graham Burchell, Colin Gordon, and Peter Miller (Chicago: University of Chicago Press, 1991), p. 140. See also Michel Foucault, "Governmentality," in ibid., pp. 87–104, and "History of Systems of Thought, 1979," *Philosophy and Social Criticism* 8(3) (Fall 1981):353–359.

36. Uday Singh Mehta, *Liberalism and Empire: A Study in Nineteenth-Century British Liberal Thought* (Chicago: University of Chicago Press, 1999); see also Richard Koebner and Helmut Dan Schmidt, *Imperialism: The Story and Significance of a Political Word, 1840–1960* (Cambridge: Cambridge University Press, 1964), pp. 1–7, 24–25, 38–44.

37. See Mikiso Hane, "Nationalism and the Decline of Liberalism in Meiji Japan," *Studies on Asia*, no. 4 (1963):69–80, and "Early Meiji Liberalism: An Assessment," *Monumenta Nipponica* 24(4) (1969):353–371.

38. Hane, "Early Meiji Liberalism," p. 367. Ivan Hall repeated the anecdote, as an illustration of Meiji liberalism, in a public lecture at the Woodrow Wilson International Center for Scholars, Washington, D.C., on Wednesday, January 21, 1998.

39. Fukuzawa Yukichi, *The Autobiography of Fukuzawa Yukichi*, trans. Eiichi Kiyooka (Tokyo: Hokuseido, 1981), pp. 243–244.

40. See Joyce Lebra, "Yano Fumio: Meiji Intellectual, Party Leader, and Bureaucrat," *Monumenta Nipponica* 20(1–2) (1965):1–14; and Nagai Michio, "Mori Arinori: Pioneer of Modern Japan," in *Higher Education in Japan: Its Take-off and Crash*, trans. Jerry Dusenbury (Tokyo: University of Tokyo Press, 1971), pp. 166–196.

41. Hane, "Nationalism and the Decline of Liberalism." "Traditionalism" is the analogous culprit in his "Fukuzawa Yukichi and Women's Rights," in *Japan in Transition: Thought and Action in the Meiji Era, 1868–1912*, ed. Hilary Conroy, Sandra T. W. Davis, and Wayne Patterson (Rutherford: Fairleigh Dickinson University Press, 1984), pp. 96–112.

42. Germaine Hoston too treats the Meirokusha intellectuals as a set of "Meiji pioneers of Japanese liberalism" who unproblematically absorbed "Western liberalism" and then simply succumbed to the appeal for state leadership. To her credit, Hoston notes in passing that "caution must prevail" in seeking thinkers to fit her predetermined set of liberal ideas and, moreover, that it is "the liberal contents of ideas" which ultimately matter. But in her mission to contrast liberalism and illiberal notions such as loyalty to the emperor, the problem of identifying Japanese contents for Japanese ideas of liberalism is eliminated. See "The State, Modernity, and the Fate of Liberalism in Prewar Japan," *Journal of Asian Studies* 51(2) (May 1992):287–316; see pp. 291, 293, 295 for quotes.

43. Until recently the name "movement to establish a national assembly" (*kokkai*

kaisetsu undō) was rare in scholarship; it often appears in the context of the early 1880s "petition drive to establish a national assembly" (*kokkai kaisetsu seigan undō*); see Banno Junji, *Kindai Nihon no kokka kōsō, 1871–1936* (Tokyo: Iwanami shoten, 1996), pp. 55–56 and 95; Ike, *Beginnings*, pp. 87–88 and 105; Matsuo Shōichi, *Jiyū minken shisō no kenkyū*, rev. ed. (Tokyo: Nihon keizai hyōronsha, 1990), pp. 63–64, 107, 110; Ochiai Hiroki, "Meiji zenki no rikugun kashi to jiyūminken," *Jinbun gakuhō*, no. 74 (3/1994):37–65; and Osatake Takeki, *Nihon kensei shi taikō* (Tokyo: Nihon hyōronsha, 1938–1939), 2:511. In a June 1879 memorial to the emperor, one of the emperor's tutors, Motoda Eifu, referred to recent events as agitation for *kokkai minken* (national assembly and popular rights); see *Nihon kensei kiso shiryō*, ed. Miyakoshi Shin'ichirō (Tokyo: Giin seijisha, 1939), p. 262. Watanabe Ikujirō pointed out in 1939 that activists in the 1870s advocated both "freedom and popular rights" and "establishing a national assembly" and that, in time, the former was a more strategic name for the movement because it aspired to an international character; see "Rikken seiji no yurai," in ibid., pp. 11–17. This ambivalence over naming is overtly manifest in the fact that both George Akita and Sandra Davis translate *jiyū minken undō* as the "movement for parliamentary government"; see Akita, *Foundations*, p. 208, n.1; and Sandra T. W. Davis, *Intellectual Change and Political Development in Early Modern Japan: Ono Azusa, a Case Study* (Rutherford: Fairleigh Dickinson University Press, 1980), p. 319. See also Fukuzawa Yukichi's 1889 commentary on the newly promulgated Meiji constitution, "The History of the Japanese Parliament," in W. W. McLaren, ed., *Japanese Government Documents* (1914; Tokyo: Asiatic Society of Japan, 1979), pp. 577–593.

44. Hence—contrary to the example of Irokawa Daikichi and Roger Bowen— I would not be willing to characterize local movements that stressed popular *autonomy* as constituting origins of democracy, even if I agree that the high degree of autonomy or self-government among Tokugawa villages was deliberately undermined by the Meiji Restoration; see Roger W. Bowen, *Rebellion and Democracy in Meiji Japan: A Study of Commoners in the Popular Rights Movement* (Berkeley: University of California Press, 1980), pp. 201 and 303–310, which quotes Irokawa Daikichi, Ei Hideo, and Arai Katsuhiro, *Minshū kempō no sōzō: uzumoreta kusa no ne no ninmyaku* (Tokyo: Hyōronsha, 1970), pp. 159–162. See also Hiroshi Tanaka, "The Development of Liberalism in Modern Japan: Continuity of an Idea— From Taguchi and Kuga to Hasegawa," *Hitotsubashi Journal of Social Studies* 21 (1989):259–268; and Rikki Kersten's insightful contextualization of autonomy as a theme in modern Japanese history: *Democracy in Postwar Japan: Maruyama Masao and the Search for Autonomy* (London: Routledge, 1996), especially pp. 109–136.

45. "Constitutional Government in Japan," *Japan Weekly Mail* (September 10, 1881), pp. 1046–1048.

46. Dipesh Chakrabarty, "Afterword: Revisiting the Tradition/Modernity Binary," in *Mirror of Modernity: Invented Traditions of Modern Japan*, ed. Stephen Vlastos (Berkeley: University of California Press, 1998), p. 287.

47. Kido, *Diary*, 1:128–129.

48. William J. Bouwsma, "Intellectual History in the 1980s," *Journal of Interdisciplinary History* 12(2) (Autumn 1981):279–291. See also John E. Toews, "Intellectual History After the Linguistic Turn: The Autonomy of Meaning and the Irreducibility of Experience," *American Historical Review* 92(4) (October 1987): 879–907; and Donald R. Kelley, "Horizons of Intellectual History: Retrospect, Circumspect, Prospect," *Journal of the History of Ideas* 49(1) (1987):143–169.

49. See, for example, H. D. Harootunian, *Things Seen and Unseen: Discourse and Ideology in Tokugawa Nativism* (Chicago: University of Chicago Press, 1988); *Japanese Thought in the Tokugawa Period: Methods and Metaphors*, ed. Tetsuo Najita and Irwin Scheiner (Chicago: University of Chicago Press, 1978); Tetsuo Najita, *Visions of Virtue in Tokugawa Japan: The Kaitokudō Merchant Academy of Osaka* (Chicago: University of Chicago Press, 1987); Gluck, *Japan's Modern Myths*; and Stefan Tanaka, *Japan's Orient: Reordering Pasts into History* (Berkeley: University of California Press, 1993). See also Samuel Hideo Yamashita, "Reading the New Tokugawa Intellectual Histories," *Journal of Japanese Studies* 22(1) (Winter 1996):1–48.

50. See Helen Hardacre, "Introduction," in *New Directions in the Study of Meiji Japan*, ed. Helen Hardacre, with Adam L. Kern (Leiden: Brill, 1997), pp. xiii–xlii.

51. Ishida Takeshi, *Kindai Nihon no seiji bunka to gengo shōchō* (Tokyo: Tokyo Daigaku shuppankai, 1983), pp. 3–31 and 49. For a contextualization of Ishida's work see Yamamuro, *Kindai Nihon no chi to seiji*, pp. 191–205.

52. Quentin Skinner, *The Foundations of Modern Political Thought: Volume One: The Renaissance* (Cambridge: Cambridge University Press, 1978), p. xiii.

53. Toews, "Intellectual History After the Linguistic Turn," pp. 880 and 906. I say "in theory" because Skinner has been criticized for his pursuit of "intentions"; see Lotte Mulligan, Judith Richards, and John Graham, "Intentions and Conventions: A Critique of Quentin Skinner's Method for the Study of the History of Ideas," *Political Studies* 27(1) (March 1979):84–98. See also James H. Tully's defense of Skinner, "Review Article: The Pen Is a Mighty Sword: Quentin Skinner's Analysis of Politics," *British Journal of Political Science* 13(4) (October 1983):489–509; and Skinner's "A Reply to My Critics," in *Meaning and Context: Quentin Skinner and His Critics*, ed. James Tully (Princeton: Princeton University Press, 1988), pp. 260–281.

54. Richter, "Appreciating a Contemporary Classic," p. 13. See also his *History of Political and Social Concepts*, pp. 124–142, and his earlier statement, "Conceptual History (*Begriffsgeschichte*) and Political Theory," *Political Theory* 14(4) (November 1986):604–637.

55. Koselleck, *Futures Past*, pp. 80 and 84. Koselleck's interpreters too make a virtue of the distinction between words and concepts; see Hans Erich Bödeker, "Concept-Meaning-Discourse: *Begriffsgeschichte* Reconsidered," in *History of Concepts*, p. 53; Terence Ball, "Conceptual History and the History of Political Thought," ibid., p. 81; and Bernhard F. Scholz, "Conceptual History in Context," ibid., pp. 88–89.

56. Koselleck, as quoted by Bödeker, "Concept-Meaning-Discourse," p. 54.

57. Ibid., pp. 57–59. See Koselleck, *Futures Past*, p. 87.

58. Richter, *History of Political and Social Concepts*, p. 9. James Farr, an associate of Quentin Skinner, has made this claim about his own work; see James Farr, "Understanding Conceptual Change Politically," in *Political Innovation and Conceptual Change*, ed. Terence Ball, James Farr, and Russell L. Hanson (Cambridge: Cambridge University Press, 1989), p. 27n2.

59. Bödeker, "Concept-Meaning-Discourse," p. 54.

60. V. N. Voloshinov, *Marxism and the Philosophy of Language*, trans. Ladislav Matejka and I. R. Titunik (New York: Academic Press, 1973), pp. 99–106; Quentin Skinner, "'Social Meaning' and the Explanation of Social Actions," in *The Philosophy of History*, ed. Patrick Gardiner (Oxford: Oxford University Press, 1974), pp. 111–112, and "Language and Political Change," in *Political Innovation and Conceptual Change*, pp. 8–11 (printed as "Language and Social Change" in *Meaning and Context*). See also Terence Ball and J.G.A. Pocock, eds., "Introduction," in *Conceptual Change and the Constitution* (Lawrence: University Press of Kansas, 1988), p. 8.

61. Koselleck, *Futures Past*, pp. 80–84.

62. Reinhart Koselleck, "Linguistic Change and the History of Events," *Journal of Modern History* 61(4) (December 1989):648–666.

63. Koselleck, "Social History and *Begriffsgeschichte*," pp. 30–31.

64. Ibid., p. 31.

65. See the editors' "Introduction" to *History of Concepts*, p. 2; and Richter, *History of Political and Social Concepts*, pp. 44–47. On the study of semantic fields see especially Suzanne Öhman, "Theories of the 'Linguistic Field,' " *Word* 9 (1953):123–134; N.C.W. Spence, "Linguistic Fields, Conceptual Systems, and the *Weltbild*," *Transactions of the Philological Society* (1961):87–106; and Adrienne Lehrer, *Semantic Fields and Lexical Structures* (Amsterdam: North-Holland, 1974).

66. "Introduction" to *History of Concepts*, p. 7; Bödeker, "Concept-Meaning-Discourse," p. 55; and Hans-Jürgen Lüsebrink, "Conceptual History and Conceptual Transfer," in *History of Concepts*, pp. 115–129.

67. Koselleck explains his grounding in semantics in "Some Reflections on the Temporal Structure of Conceptual Change," in *Main Trends in Cultural History: Ten Essays*, ed. Willem Melching and Wyger Velema (Amsterdam: Rodopi, 1994),

pp. 7–16; see also Scholz, "Conceptual History in Context," p. 89. Two succinct discussions of semantic theory are Oswald Ducrot and Tzvetan Todorov, *Encyclopedic Dictionary of the Sciences of Language*, trans. Catherine Porter (Oxford: Blackwell, 1981), pp. 264–272; and William F. Hanks, *Language and Communicative Practices* (Boulder: Westview, 1996), pp. 66–86, 118–122, 214–223.

68. Iain Hampsher-Monk, "Speech Acts, Languages, or Conceptual History?," in *History of Concepts*, pp. 44 and 49.

69. J.G.A. Pocock, "Concepts and Discourses: A Difference in Culture?," in *Meaning of Historical Terms and Concepts*, pp. 51 and 53. Koselleck's associate Rolf Reichardt has apparently pursued such a revisionist approach within *Begriffsgeschichte*; see Melvin Richter, "*Begriffsgeschichte* in Theory and Practice," in *Main Trends in Cultural History*, pp. 126–129; and "*Begriffsgeschichte* and the History of Ideas," *Journal of the History of Ideas* 48(2) (1987):247–263.

70. Willem Frijhoff, "Conceptual History, Social History, and Cultural History," in *History of Concepts*, p. 113. See also Farr, "Understanding Conceptual Change Politically," p. 34, who describes these changes as "dialectical."

71. Lüsebrink, "Conceptual History and Conceptual Transfer," pp. 115–117.

72. Koselleck, "Linguistic Change and the History of Events," p. 659.

73. Richter, "Appreciating a Contemporary Classic," p. 10; Ball, "Conceptual History and the History of Political Thought," pp. 83–86; and Gabriel Motzkin, "On Koselleck's Intuition of Time in History," in *Meaning of Historical Terms and Concepts*, p. 41.

74. Koselleck, "A Response to Comments on the *Geschichtliche Grundbegriffe*," in *Meaning of Historical Terms and Concepts*, p. 68. See also James Van Horn Melton's account of the background of *Begriffsgeschichte* in a National Socialist critique of liberalism, "Otto Brunner and the Ideological Origins of *Begriffsgeschichte*," in *Meaning of Historical Terms and Concepts*, pp. 21–33.

2. The Project of Enlightened Civilization

1. Nativist scholars in the nineteenth century also sought to recover a pure Japanese language and culture from centuries of Chinese influence; see H. D. Harootunian, "The Functions of China in Tokugawa Thought," in *The Chinese and the Japanese: Essays in Political and Cultural Interactions*, ed. Akira Iriye (Princeton: Princeton University Press, 1980), pp. 9–36; Harootunian, *Things Seen and Unseen*, pp. 23–75; Naoki Sakai, *Voices of the Past: The Status of Language in Eighteenth-Century Japanese Discourse* (Ithaca: Cornell University Press, 1991), pp. 211–239 and 255–277; and David Pollack, *The Fracture of Meaning: Japan's Synthesis of China from the Eighth Through the Eighteenth Centuries* (Princeton: Princeton University Press, 1986), pp. 15–54.

2. To my knowledge, Nishimura Shigeki first referred to *bunmeikaika* as a his-

torical period that followed the earlier *sonnō-jōi* period; see "Tenkan setsu," *Meiroku zasshi,* no. 43 (11/1875):1b (hereafter *MRZS*). The best general discussions of *bunmeikaika* are Asukai Masamichi, *Bunmeikaika* (Tokyo: Iwanami shoten, 1985), pp. 1–27 and 109–163; Maeda Ai, *Bakumatsu-ishinki no bungaku* (Tokyo: Hōsei Daigaku shuppankyoku, 1972), pp. 290–324; Nishikawa, *Kokkyō no koekata*, pp. 172–181; Ōkubo Toshiaki, *Meiji no shisō to bunka*, pp. 107–146; and Suzuki Shūji, *Bunmei no kotoba* (Hiroshima: Bunka hyōron, 1981), pp. 5–68.

3. Thomas Henry Buckle, *The History of Civilization in England* (1857–1861), translated into Japanese by Ōshima Sadanori (?) as *Eikoku kaika shi sōron* (1875); and François-Pierre Guizot, *A History of Civilization in Europe*, English translation of 1873 translated into Japanese by Nagamine Hideki as *Yōroppa bunmei shi* (1874). Excerpts from both of these works, with parallel passages and commentary, are available in *Nihon kindai shisō taikei*, vol. 15: *Hon'yaku no shisō*, ed. Katō Shūichi and Maruyama Masao (Tokyo: Iwanami shoten, 1991), pp. 91–157 and 416–427. On the relation of Buckle and Guizot to Meiji ideas of historical progress see Matsuzawa Hiroaki, "Varieties of *Bunmei Ron* (Theories of Civilization)," in *Japan in Transition: Thought and Action in the Meiji Era, 1868–1912*, ed. Hilary Conroy, Sandra T. W. Davis, and Wayne Patterson (Rutherford: Fairleigh Dickinson University Press, 1984), pp. 209–223; and Stefan Tanaka, *Japan's Orient*, pp. 36–40.

4. Elias, *Civilizing Process*, pp. 3–5 and 29–33. See also Emile Benveniste, "Civilization: A Contribution to the History of the Word," in *Problems in General Linguistics*, trans. Mary Elizabeth Meek (Coral Gables: University of Miami Press, 1971), pp. 289–296; and Raymond Williams, *Keywords: A Vocabulary of Culture and Society* (New York: Oxford University Press, 1976), pp. 48–50.

5. Fukuzawa Yukichi, *Seiyō jijō* (1866–1870), in *Fukuzawa Yukichi zenshū* (Tokyo: Iwanami shoten, 1958), 1:290–291 and 395–397 (hereafter *SYJJ*). Mori Arinori too offered an early outline of progress in "Kaika daiichi hanashi," *MRZS*, no. 3 [4/1874]:1.

6. D. R. Howland, *Borders of Chinese Civilization: Geography and History at Empire's End* (Durham: Duke University Press, 1996), pp. 13–14, 211–213, and 294, n. 34. The constituent terms of *bunmeikaika* had been used earlier in Japanese history for imperial reign names: the ninth Emperor Kaika (r. 158–198), and segments of the reigns of emperors Go-Tsuchimikado (r. 1465–1500) and Kōkaku (r. 1780–1817), respectively titled Bunmei (1469–1486) and Bunka (1804–1817).

7. On the Iwakura Mission see the official diary by Kume Kunitake, *Tokumei zenken taishi Bei-Ō kairan jikki* (1878; Tokyo: Munetaka shobō, 1975); Marlene J. Mayo: "The Iwakura Mission to the United States and Europe, 1871–1873," in *Researches in the Social Sciences on Japan: Volume Two*, ed. Stanleigh H. Jones Jr. and John E. Lane (New York: Columbia University, East Asian Institute, 1959), pp. 28–47; Marlene J. Mayo, "The Western Education of Kume Kunitake,

1871–76," *Monumenta Nipponica* 28(1) (1973):3–67; Eugene Soviak, "On the Nature of Western Progress: The Journal of the Iwakura Embassy," in *Tradition and Modernization in Japanese Culture*, ed. Donald H. Shively (Princeton: Princeton University Press, 1971), pp. 7–34; and Yamamuro Shin'ichi, *Hōsei kanryō no jidai: kokka no sekkei to chi no rekitei* (Tokyo: Mokutakusha, 1984), pp. 5–22 and 41–62.

8. Watanabe Shūjirō, *Meiji kaika shi* (Tokyo: Matsui suji, 1880), pp. 189–207.

9. Neil Pedlar, *The Imported Pioneers: Westerners Who Helped Build Modern Japan* (New York: St. Martin's Press, 1990), p. 23.

10. "Zareuta kaika shindai," *Chōya shinbun* (1875.11.30), in *Shinbun shūsei Meiji hennen shi*, ed. Nakayama Yasumasa (1934–1936; Tokyo: Honpō shoseki, 1982), 2:440 (hereafter *SSMHS*). The Tomioka silk filature, the first government-sponsored silk factory in Japan, was established in Gumma prefecture north of Tokyo where water power was available. For yet another list, the "twelve pillars" of civilization, see *SSMHS*, 1:263.

11. *SSMHS*, 1:431; 2:51; 3:229, 293. See also Katō Yūichi, *Bunmeikaika* (1873), in *Meiji bunka zenshū*, vol. 24: *Bunmeikaika hen* (Tokyo: Nihon hyōronsha, 1967), p. 5. For an amusing selection of early Meiji poems on things Western, including steak houses, haircuts, telegraphs, post offices, and horse-drawn carriages, see Kinoshita Hyō, *Meiji shika* (Tokyo: Bunchūtō, 1943), pp. 190–233 passim.

12. Katō, *Bunmeikaika*, pp. 33–35. For a discussion of this literature see Hattori Shisō, "Bunmeikaika," p. 419.

13. Kimura Ki, *Bunmeikaika* (Tokyo: Shibundō, 1954), pp. 1–2, 10–11, 15–18, 25–33. In his fascinating study Kimura argues that the greatest changes in the period arose from trade and the demise of the old government. For most people, it was things and customs that changed most significantly, induced through technology and social habits—especially steam engines, schools, the solar calendar, and the railroad. Kimura concludes that *bunmeikaika* meant primarily four things for the majority of Japanese: eating beef; cutting one's topknot in favor of a short haircut; riding rickshas; and constructing brick buildings. For a long-term perspective of "civilization" among the common people see Mukihara Norio, "Bunmeikaika ron," in *Iwanami kōza—Nihon tsūshi*, vol. 16: *Kindai*, pt. 1 (Tokyo: Iwanami shoten, 1994), pp. 251–290; and Susan B. Hanley, *Everyday Things in Premodern Japan: The Hidden Legacy of Material Culture* (Berkeley: University of California Press, 1997), pp. 155–175.

14. Kimura, *Bunmeikaika*, pp. 18–24. Contemporary traveler Isabella Bird commented on Japanese government efforts to control public bathing and prohibit Ainu tatooing; see *Unbeaten Tracks in Japan* (1880; Boston: Beacon, 1987), pp. 210 and 265.

15. Kido, *Diary*, 1:148. Sanjō Sanetomi reiterated the point in 1871; see Mayo, "Iwakura Mission," p. 30.

16. Elias, *Civilizing Process*, pp. 4–10 and 22–25. In addition to being a translation word for "civilization," *bunka* could be used as a modifier meaning "civilized" or "Western," as in the occasional expression *bunka jūtaku* (Western-style home). On the rise of *bunka* in opposition to *bunmeikaika* see Suzuki, *Bunmei no kotoba*, pp. 53–56, and Nishikawa, *Kokkyō no koekata*, pp. 195–205. Suzuki isolates the years 1898–1911 as the period during which *bunka* became influential; Nishikawa challenges the accepted fact that Miyake Setsurei was first to use *bunka* to mean "culture" (*Kultur*) in 1891, with a significant discussion of Kuga Katsunan's theory of "national culture" (*kokumin bunka*) ca. 1888. Recent work by Takagi Hiroshi, however, reveals that *bunka* was enlisted in the 1880s to designate "cultural assets" (*bunkazai*) in Nara prefecture, as the preservation of ancient Yamato sites commenced in the effort to recover indigenous Japanese civilization; see *Kindai tennōsei no bunkashi-teki kenkyū: tennō shūnin girei, nenchūgyōji, bunkazai* (Tokyo: Azekura shobō, 1997), pp. 17–18 and 264–283. The best discussion in English of the Japanese reaction to Meiji civilization, which includes the issue of treaty revision, is still Kenneth B. Pyle, *The New Generation in Meiji Japan: Problems of Cultural Identity, 1885–1895* (Stanford: Stanford University Press, 1969), pp. 76–117.

17. Iwakura Tomomi, quoted in Kimura, *Bunmeikaika*, p. 6 ("enlightened civilization" is apparently in English in the original); and Mori Arinori, *Religious Freedom in Japan: A Memorial and Draft of Charter* ([Washington, D.C.]: privately printed, [1872]), pp. 3 and 10.

18. Even Nishi Amane, in his systematic exposition of Western learning in 1871, does not mention the Enlightenment but refers to "enlightened" in the same context of Buddhism as Inoue Testujirō; see *Hyakugaku renkan/Encyclopedia*, in *Nishi Amane zenshū*, ed. Ōkubo Toshiaki (Tokyo: Munetaka shobō, 1981), 4:123.

19. The series of four sets of articles, titled "Keimō undō no rekishi to kyōkun," appeared in *Shisō*, nos. 363–366 (September-December 1954). The most revealing discussion of the utility of *keimō* for Japanese intellectual history is Miyagawa Tōru, "Nihon no keimō shisō," in *Kōza: Kindai shisō shi*, vol. 9: *Nihon ni okeru seiyō kindai shisō no jūyō*, ed. Kaneko Masashi and Ōtsuka Hisao (Tokyo: Kōbundō, 1959), pp. 115–119.

20. A number of these translations are reprinted in W. W. McLaren, ed., *Japanese Government Documents* (1914; Tokyo: Asiatic Society of Japan, 1979)—for examples see pp. 428, 436–437, 449, 457, 459, 474–476, 586–587 (hereafter *JGD*). A contemporary Yokohama trader, Francis Hall, exhibits the same interchangeability of civilization and enlightenment in his diary: *Japan Through American Eyes: The Journal of Francis Hall, Kanagawa and Yokohama, 1859–1866*, ed. F. G. Notehelfer (Princeton: Princeton University Press, 1992), p. 401.

21. On Honda Toshiaki see Keene, *Japanese Discovery of Europe*, pp. 91–122

and 175–226, and Satō Shōsuke, *Yōgaku shi no kenkyū* (Tokyo: Chūōkōronsha, 1980), pp. 130–137.

22. See, for example, Nishimura Shigeki, "Chingen issoku," *MRZS*, no. 3 [4/1974]:1b-2a.

23. On the continuity of personnel from Tokugawa to Meiji institutions see Ōkubo Toshiaki, *Meiji no shisō to bunka*, pp. 14–27 and 75–82. For a classic statement of the intelligentsia's role in early Meiji see Maruyama Masao, "Meiji jidai no shisō" (1953), in his *Senchū to sengo no aida* (Tokyo: Misuzu shobō, 1976), pp. 567–576.

24. This enlightenment model of civilization is implicit in several works: Fukuzawa Yukichi, *An Encouragement of Learning*, trans. David A. Dilworth and Umeyo Hirano (Tokyo: Sophia University, 1969), pp. 1–7 and 15–20; and *An Outline of a Theory of Civilization*, trans. David A. Dilworth and G. Cameron Hurst (Tokyo: Sophia University, 1973), pp. 35–45 and 125–134. See also Nakamura Keiu's translation of Samuel Smiles' *Self-Help*, *Saikoku risshi hen*, the first three volumes of which are reprinted in *Nihon kyōkasho taikei: kindai hen:* vol. 1, *Shūshin—[Part] 1* (Tokyo: Kodansha, 1961).

25. For a very different interpretation of the debate, which reads into it each participant's lifework, see Motoyama Yukihiko, "Bunmeikaika ki ni okeru shin chishikijin no shisō—Meirokusha no hitobito o chūshin toshite," *Jinbun gakuhō* 4 (1954):45–84; an abridged translation is included in Motoyama Yukihiko, *Proliferating Talent: Essays on Politics, Thought, and Education in the Meiji Era*, ed. J. S. A. Elisonas and Richard Rubinger (Honolulu: University of Hawai'i Press, 1997), pp. 238–273. The debate is also summarized in Toriumi Yasushi, *Meiroku zasshi to kindai Nihon* (Tokyo: Nihon hōsō shuppan kyōkai, 1994–1995), 1:77–120.

26. Howland, *Borders of Chinese Civilization*, p. 212. Hayashiya Tatsusaburō has expressed a similar conclusion in "Bunmeikaika no rekishi-teki zentei," in *Bunmeikaika no kenkyū*, ed. Hayashiya Tatsusaburō (Tokyo: Iwanami shoten, 1979), pp. 3–4; and Asukai Masamichi wonders if *kaika* was not implicit in Bakumatsu calls for *kaikoku*, as the rigid Tokugawa placing of people had begun to deteriorate—see *Bunmeikaika*, pp. 18–20. See also Mori Arinori, "Kaika daiichi hanashi," *MRZS*, no. 3 [4/1874]:1; and Suzuki Shūji's comments on Mori in *Bunmei no kotoba*, p. 154. Fukuzawa himself used *kaika* to mean "development" in *Bunmei ron no gairyaku*, in *Fukuzawa Yukichi senshū*, ed. Tomita Masafumi (Tokyo: Iwanami shoten, 1980–1981), 4:242; see also *Outline of a Theory of Civilization*, p. 189. (Hereafter *Fukuzawa Yukichi senshū* is abbreviated *FYS*.)

27. Fukuzawa's speech was printed as chapter 4 of *Gakumon no susume*, in *FYS*, 3:76–83. The English translation by Dilworth and Hirano elides many of these points; see *Encouragement of Learning*, pp. 21–28.

28. Matsuda Kōichirō comes to a similar conclusion in his analysis of Fukuzawa's understanding of "public" and "private"; see "Fukuzawa Yukichi to *kō-shi-bun* no saihakken," *Rikkyō hōgaku,* no. 43 (1996):76–140.

29. The set of rebuttals was printed in *MRZS,* no. 2 [4/1874]. The English translation of the journal, however, does not bring out many of the points I raise; see *Meiroku Zasshi: Journal of the Japanese Enlightenment,* trans. William R. Braisted (Cambridge: Harvard University Press, 1976), pp. 21–29.

30. Fukuzawa, *Gakumon no susume,* pp. 83–85; Mitsukuri Rinshō, "Bakkurushi no Eikoku kaikashi yori shōyaku," *MRZS,* no. 7 (5/1874):4a-6a. Sakatani Shiroshi later criticized Mitsukuri and defended government tutelage of the uncivilized people; see "Shitsugi issoku," *MRZS,* no. 11 (6/1874):7–9.

31. For a comprehensive narrative of language reforms in Japan see Nanette Twine, *Language and the Modern State: The Reform of Written Japanese* (London: Routledge, 1991); and Nanette Gottlieb, *Kanji Politics: Language Policy and Japanese Script* (London: Kegan Paul International, 1995).

32. *Katakana* was at the time the standard typescript form for public writing; by 1888, *hiragana* had become generally acceptable as typescript in newspapers, journals, and books. See Chapter 3.

33. Nishi Amane, "Yōji o motte kokugo o shosuru no ron," *MRZS,* no. 1 [3/1874]:1–10a; see also Nishimura Shigeki's rebuttal in the same issue, pp. 10b-12. The content of their disagreement is summarized in Toriumi, *Meiroku zasshi to kindai Nihon,* 1:35–76.

34. I have relied on Yaeko Sato Habein, *The History of the Japanese Written Language* (Tokyo: University of Tokyo Press, 1984).

35. See Sugimoto Tsutomu, *Kokugogaku to Rangogaku/Japanese Linguistics and Dutch Linguistics* (Tokyo: Musashiya shoin, 1991), pp. 8–55 and 315–331.

36. Douglas Howland, "Nishi Amane's Efforts to Translate Western Knowledge: Sound, Mark, and Meaning," *Semiotica* 83(3–4) (1991):283–310; see also Takao Suzuki, "Writing Is Not Language, or Is It?," *Journal of Pragmatics* 1(4) (1977):407–420; and J. Marshall Unger, "The Very Idea: The Notion of Ideogram in China and Japan," *Monumenta Nipponica* 45(4) (1990):391–411.

37. Nishi, "Yōji o motte kokugo o shosuru no ron," pp. 1b-2; Yatabe Ryōkichi, "Rōmaji o motte Nihongo o tsuzuru no setsu," *Tōyō gakugei zasshi,* no. 7 (4/1882): 127–130 and no. 8 (5/1882):151–152; and Okabe Keigorō, *Bunmeikaika hyōrin* (1875), in *Meiji bunka zenshū,* vol. 24: *Bunmeikaika hen* (Tokyo: Nihon hyōronsha, 1967), pp. 239–240. (Hereafter I abbreviate *Tōyō gakugei zasshi* as *TYGGZS.*)

38. Nishi," Yōji o motte kokugo o shosuru no ron," pp. 4b-5; Yatabe, "Rōmaji o motte Nihongo o tsuzuru no setsu," p. 129; Toyama Shōichi, "Kanji o haishi Eigo o shi ni okosu wa kyō no kyūmu nari," *TYGGZS* no. 33 (1884.6.25):72; and "Rōmaji o shuchōsuru mono ni tsugu," *TYGGZS* no. 34 (1884.7.25):104–106. Kido

Takayoshi and Mori Arinori also voiced this idea informally; see Kido, *Diary*, 2:295; and Hall, *Mori Arinori*, pp. 189–195.

39. Shimizu Usaburō, "Hiragana no setsu," *MRZS*, no. 7 (5/1874):8–10; and Toyama Shōichi, "Kanji o haisubeshi," *TYGGZS*, no. 30 (3/25/1884):307–312 and no. 31 (4/25/1884):7–12. Maejima Hisoka had first proposed this plan in 1867 and continued to work with Shimizu, Toyama, and others until his death in 1919; see "Kanji o kaishi no gi," in *Maejima Hisoka jijo den* (Hayama: Maejima Hisoka denki kankōkai, 1955), pp. 153–159; and Janet Hunter, "Language Reform in Meiji Japan: The Views of Maejima Hisoka," in *Themes and Theories in Modern Japanese History: Essays in Memory of Richard Storry*, ed. Sue Henny and Jean-Pierre Lehmann (London: Athlone, 1988), pp. 101–120.

40. Nishimura Shigeki, "Kaika no do ni yotte kai monji o hassubeki no ron," *MRZS*, no. 1 [4/1874]:10b. A decade later, Sekiwa Masamichi invoked "society's practical utility" (*shakai no jitsuyō*) as a criterion in considering Chinese characters: "Kaika to kaika no sensō," *Chōya shinbun* (1884.9.28), in *Nihon kindai shisō taikei*, vol. 12: *Taigaihen*, ed. Shibahara Takuji et al. (Tokyo: Iwanami shoten, 1988), pp. 304–307.

41. See Earl H. Kinmonth, *The Self-Made Man in Meiji Japanese Thought: From Samurai to Salary Man* (Berkeley: University of California Press, 1981), pp. 9–80; and Sanada Shinji, *Hyōjungo wa, ikani seiritsu shita ka?* (Tokyo: Sōtakusha, 1991), pp. 75–85.

42. See the discussion of Nakamura's *Saikoku risshi hen* by Okamoto Isao, *Meiji shosakka no buntai: Meiji bungo no kenkyū* (Tokyo: Kasama shoin, 1980), pp. 447–511.

43. Fukuzawa, *Encouragement of Learning*, pp. 2, 4, 9, 24, 37, 71, 98; and *Outline of a Theory of Civilization*, pp. 6, 22, 39, 56, 60, 87, 111, 179. Fukuzawa's remarks were very much in keeping with late-Tokugawa critiques of China as no longer *Chūka* (the central, civilized kingdom) but as *Shina*, an instance of decline; see Harootunian, "Functions of China in Tokugawa Thought," pp. 29–36. Kanda Takahira wrote a particularly malicious account of the Chinese as barbarian cannibals; see "Shinajin jinniku o kuu no setsu," *Tōkyō gakushi kaiin zasshi* 3(8) [1881]:1–9 (hereafter *TKGSKIZS*).

44. Nakamura Keiu, "Shina fukabu ron," *MRZS*, no. 35 (4/1875):1–3a. In 1874, Japan invaded Taiwan to punish Taiwanese fishermen for attacking Ryūkyū (Liuqiu) islanders who had been fishing in Taiwanese waters. The Taiwanese were clearly under the jurisdiction of China, but both China and Japan had claims over the Ryūkyūs.

45. Okabe, *Bunmeikaika hyōrin*, pp. 239–240; Toyama Shōichi, "Rōmajikai o okosu no shui," *TYGGZS*, no. 39 (1884.12.25):229–230. An interesting comparison is the defense of Chinese writing by nativist and archaeologist Kurokawa Mayori, "Moji denrai kō," *TKGSKIZS* 6(2) [1/1884]:53–65; Kurokawa noted that,

like Western languages in the present, Chinese language had fulfilled a lack in Japan's past.

46. Ariga Nagao, "Shina no kaimei to seiyō no kaimei to no sabetsu," *Gakugei shirin*, vol. 12 (4/1883):356–378; Inoue Tetsujirō, "Ki Nakamura Keiu sensei sho," *TYGGZS*, no. 18 (3/1883):484–486; Okabe, *Bunmeikaika hyōrin*, pp. 239–240; Sekiwa, "Kaika to kaika no sensō," pp. 304–307; and Toyama, "Kanji o haishi Eigo o shi ni okosu wakyō no kyūmu nari," p. 71.

47. Inoue, "Ki Nakamura Keiu sensei sho," pp. 484–485. For a recent argument regarding the problematic relation between Chinese language and scientific thought see Alfred H. Bloom, *The Linguistic Shaping of Thought: A Study in the Impact of Language on Thinking in China and the West* (Hillsdale, N.J.: Lawrence Erlbaum, 1981), especially pp. 54–60.

48. Ariga is engaging in the quaint habit of reading Chinese characters literally according to their constitutive parts. For further examples of such interpretations of Chinese characters see Léon Wieger, *Chinese Characters: Their Origin, Etymology, History, Classification, and Signification. A Thorough Study from Chinese Documents*, trans. L. Davrout, 2nd ed. (New York: Dover, 1965).

49. Ariga, "Shina no kaimei to seiyō no kaimei to no sabetsu," pp. 357–364 and 368–375.

50. "Kangaku-kanbun gakkō," *Chūgai shinbun* (4/26/1869), in *SSMHS* 1:268; "Kanbun wa keikoku no yō," *Chōya shinbun* (10/10/1877), in *SSMHS* 3:321; "Kangaku saikō no kiun," *Yomiuri shinbun* (4/2/1878), in *SSMHS* 3:375; and Nakamura Keiu, "Shisho sodoku no ron," *TKGSKIZS* 3(2) [1880–1881]:12.

51. "Kanbun wa keikoku no yō," p. 321; Nakamura Keiu, "Kangaku fukahai ron," *TKGSKIZS* 9(4) (5/1887):65–66; Shigeno Yasutsugu, "Kangaku yoku seisoku ikka o mōke, shōnen shūsai o erami, Shinkoku ni ryūgaku seshimubeki ronsetsu," *TKGSKIZS*, no. 4 [1880]:77–93. See also B. F. Chamberlain, "Shinago dokuhō no kairyō o nozomu," *TYGGZS*, no. 61 (10/1886):19–21.

52. Shigeno, "Kangaku yoku seisoku ikka o mōke," pp. 87–88; see also Demin Tao, "Shigeno Yasutsugu as an Advocate of 'Practical Sinology' in Meiji Japan," in *New Directions in the Study of Meiji Japan*, ed. Helen Hardacre with Adam L. Kern (Leiden: Brill, 1997), pp. 373–386. I have discussed the problematic relation between practical and scientific learning in *Borders of Chinese Civilization*, pp. 173–177 and 288, n. 45.

53. Kawada Kō [Takeshi], "Ron kangaku gibun keiseki, ishū shin, seiji, keiritsu, kōgei, shoka senkō kigyō," *TKGSKIZS* 2(5) [1880]:4–5, with an untitled rebuttal by Shigeno Yasutsugu, pp. 9–10; and Nakamura, "Kangaku fukahai ron," pp. 52–53 and 63–68.

54. Kawada, "Ron kangaku gibun keiseki," p. 5; see also Howland, *Borders of Chinese Civilization*, pp. 202–209. Mark E. Lincicome notes that certain educa-

tional reformers in the 1880s found precedents for developmental education in ancient China and compares Wang Yangming to Herbert Spencer and Horace Mann; see *Principle, Praxis, and the Politics of Educational Reform in Meiji Japan* (Honolulu: University of Hawai'i Press, 1995), pp. 144–145.

55. Nakamura, "Kangaku fukahai ron," pp. 33–39. See also his 1883 rebuttal to Inoue, "Fuku Inoue sonkenkun sho," *TYGGZS,* no. 19 (4/1883):512–514.

56. Nakamura, "Kangaku fukahai ron," pp. 36–39, 41–49, 51–55.

57. Nishimura Shigeki, "Shūshin chikoku futamichi arazu ron," *MRZS,* no. 31 (6/1875):4a. There is an interesting contemporary translation of this piece as "Morals and Politics Not Different Things," *Japan Weekly Mail,* April 10, 1875, pp. 308–309, but Nishimura is not credited as author.

58. Matsumoto Sannosuke has suggested that moralism in Japanese political theory is a long-term development from the Tokugawa through Meiji periods, such that samurai morality and family structure were institutionalized with the Meiji Civil Code; see *Kindai Nihon no chiteki jokyō,* pp. 14–18, and *Meiji seishin no kōzō* (Tokyo: Nihon hōsō shuppan, 1981), pp. 29–32.

59. Nishimura, "Shūshin chikoku futamichi arazu ron," pp. 3b-6. Nishimura's understanding of the progress from individual cultivation to universal peace echoes *The Great Learning,* one of the Confucian "Four Books"; for a helpful discussion of Nishimura see Ienaga Saburō, *Nihon kindai shisō shi kenkyū,* 2nd ed. (Tokyo: Tokyo Daigaku shuppankai, 1980), pp. 133–168.

60. Sakatani Shiroshi, "Seikyō no utagai," *MRZS,* no. 22 (12/1874):4–5, and no. 25 (12/1874):3b-6; Nishi Amane, "Kyōmon ron," pts. 1 and 7, *MRZS,* no. 4 [4/1874]:5b-8b and no. 12 (6/1874):1–3a. See also Nishimura Shigeki, "Chingen issoku," 1b-2a. On Sakatani's relation to neo-Confucianism and Western learning see Matsumoto Sannosuke, "Atarashii gakumon no keisei to chishikijin," in *Nihon kindai shisō taikei,* vol. 10: *Gakumon to chishikijin,* ed. Matsumoto Sannosuke and Yamamuro Shin'ichi (Tokyo: Iwanami shoten, 1988), pp. 424–464; and Ōtsuki Akira, *Kinsei Nihon no jugaku to yōgaku* (Kyoto: Shibunkaku, 1988), pp. 277–347.

61. Nakamura Keiu, "Jinmin no seishitsu o kaizōsuru setsu," *MRZS,* no. 30 (2/1875):7–8; Nishi Amane, "Kokumin kifū/*Nashonaru kerekutoru* ron," *MRZS,* no. 32 (3/1875):1–3. Tsuda Mamichi maintained that human talent appears to the degree that people develop character; see "Jinsai ron," *MRZS,* no. 30 (2/1875):4–5b. Nakamura extended his discussion of the people's character specifically to women, advocating their education in order to develop their naturally affectionate dispositions into qualities making good mothers; see "Zenryō naru bo o tsukuru setsu," *MRZS,* no. 33 (3/1875):1–3.

62. Sakatani Shiroshi, "Amakudari setsu," *MRZS,* no. 35 (4/1875):3–5 and no. 36 (5/1875):1–6a.

63. Ibid., no. 36:1b-3; Fukuzawa, *Outline of a Theory of Civilization*, pp. 126–134 and 153–157.

64. Sakatani Shiroshi, "Yō seishin issetsu," *MRZS,* no. 40 (8/1875):6 and no. 41 (8/1875):6–8.

65. The Nihon kōdō kai was initially the Japanese Society for Lecturing on Morality but was quickly retitled with a homonym *(kō)* meaning "expanding." See Takahashi Masao, *Nishimura Shigeki* (Tokyo: Yoshikawa kōbunkan, 1987), pp. 143–161, as well as Nishimura's 1887 manifesto, *Nihon kōdō ron,* in *Meiji keimō shishō shū,* pp. 369–402.

66. Nishimura Shigeki, *Shōgaku shūshin kun* (1880), in *Nihon kyōkasho taikei— kindai hen,* vol. 2: *Shūshin,* pt. 2, ed. Kaigo Tokiomi (Tokyo: Kōdansha, 1962), pp. 6–37.

3. Translation Techniques and Language Transformations

1. Twine, *Language and the Modern State,* and the works of Yamamoto Masahide, including *Kindai buntai hassei no shiteki kenkyū* (Tokyo: Iwanami shoten, 1965), *Genbunitchi no rekishi ronkō,* 2 vols. (Tokyo: Ōfūsha, 1971 and 1981), and, as editor, *Kindai buntai keisei shiryō shūsei,* 2 vols. (Tokyo: Ōfūsha, 1978–1979).

2. On translation generally see Susan Bassnett-McGuire, *Translation Studies* (London: Methuen, 1980); Mary Snell-Hornby, *Translation Studies: An Integrated Approach* (Amsterdam: John Benjamins, 1988); Reuben A. Brower, ed. *On Translation* (Cambridge, Mass.: Harvard University Press, 1959); and George Steiner, *After Babel: Aspects of Language and Translation* (London: Oxford University Press, 1975). For two reliable surveys of translation work in early Meiji see Kamei Shunsuke, "Nihon no kindai to hon'yaku," and Katō Shūichi, "Meiji shoki no hon'yaku," in *Nihon kindai shisō taikei,* vol. 15: *Hon'yaku no shisō,* ed. Katō Shūichi and Maruyama Masao (Tokyo: Iwanami shoten, 1991), pp. 342–380. For two distinctly Japanese approaches to translation see Sugimoto Tsutomu, *Kokugogaku to Rangogaku,* pp. 376–390, who distinguishes "meaning (paraphrastic) translation" from "direct (word-for-word) translation" and from "phonic translation"; and Yanabu Akira, *Hon'yaku to wa nani ka?—Nihongo to hon'yaku bunka,* 2nd ed. (Tokyo: Hōsei Daigaku shuppankyoku, 1985), whose "cassette effect" proposes that words are like tapes to be rerecorded with new meaning.

3. See Volosninov, *Marxism and the Philosophy of Language*; and P. N. Medvedev, *The Formal Method in Literary Scholarship: A Critical Introduction to Sociological Poetics,* trans. Albert J. Wehrle (Baltimore: Johns Hopkins University Press, 1978).

4. See Tzvetan Todorov, "Sign," in Ducrot and Todorov, *Encyclopedic Dictionary of the Sciences of Language,* pp. 99–105; Benveniste, *Problems in General Linguistics,* pp. 17–27 and 43–48; and C. S. Peirce, *Philosophical Writings of Peirce,* ed. Justus Buchler (New York: Dover, 1955), pp. 98–119.

5. [Henry Wheaton], *Wanguo gongfa* [trans. W.A.P. Martin] (Beijing: n.p., 1864), reprinted as *Bankoku kōhō* (Edo: Kaiseijo, 1865), 1:1–3; and Nishi Amane, trans., *Fisuserinku-shi bankoku kōhō* (Edo: n.p., 1868), 1:1–7. Yoshino Sakuzō discussed *kōhō* in Wheaton in "Waga kuni kindaishi ni okeru seiji ishiki no hassei" (1927), in *Yoshino Sakuzō Hakase: Minshushugi ron shū*, vol. 8: *Meiji bunka kenkyū* (Tokyo: Shinkigensha, 1948), pp. 57–72.

6. [Wheaton], *Bankoku kōhō*, 1:1a. *Gongyi* figures in several ancient Chinese philosophers (Xunzi, Han Fei, Mozi) as the corrective to selfishness; during the Tokugawa period, it was a respectful term for the shogunate, arguably an equivalent for *seifu* (government). See Watanabe Hiroshi, "About Some Japanese Historical Terms," trans. Luke S. Roberts, *Sino-Japanese Studies* 10(2) (April 1998):32–42. On "public authority" (*kōgi*) in Tokugawa politics see the debate among Mary Elizabeth Berry, "Public Peace and Private Attachment: The Goals and Conduct of Power in Early Modern Japan," *Journal of Japanese Studies* 12(2) (1986):237–271; James W. White, "State Growth and Popular Protest in Tokugawa Japan," *Journal of Japanese Studies* 14(1) (1988):1–25; and Mark Ravina, "State-building and Political Economy in Early-modern Japan," *Journal of Asian Studies* 54(4) (November 1995):997–1022. There is a remarkable linkage of this Tokugawa "public authority" to the "public law" of international relations in an exhortation written on the advent of the Meiji Restoration; see Tokugawa Mochitsuku and Kuroda Nagatomo, "Taigai washin kokui sen'yō no fukoku" (1868.1.15), in *Nihon kindai shisō taikei*, vol. 12: *Taigai kan*, ed. Shibahara Takuji et al. (Tokyo: Iwanami shoten, 1988), p. 3.

7. Kido, *Diary*, 1:148. John Peter Stern, *The Japanese Interpretation of the "Law of Nations," 1854–1874* (Princeton: Princeton University Press, 1979), pp. 80–92, includes a revealing statement to the Iwakura Mission by Otto von Bismark (March 15, 1873) asserting that international behavior is guided by fear, force, and profit and that only national power guarantees equality (pp. 88–89).

8. Ōkuni [Nonoguchi] Takamasa, *Shinshin kōhō ron* [1867], in *Nihon shisō shi taikei*, vol. 50: *Hirata Atsutane, Ban Nobumoto, Ōkuni Takamasa*, ed. Tahara Tsuguo et al. (Tokyo: Iwanami shoten, 1973), pp. 495, 500, 503–505. For a discussion of Ōkuni's text in the context of international law see Stern, *Japan's Interpretation*, pp. 74–75; in the context of nativism see Harootunian, "Functions of China in Tokugawa Thought," pp. 26–29.

9. Henry Wheaton, *Elements of International Law*, 6th ed. (Boston: Little, Brown, 1855), pp. 16–20, and 2nd ann. ed., by William Beach Lawrence (Boston: Little, Brown, 1863), pp. 16–20; and see John Austin, *The Province of Jurisprudence Determined* (1832), ed. W. E. Rumble (Cambridge: Cambridge University Press, 1995), pp. 123–124 and 171–175.

10. Nishi Amane, *Hyakuichi shinron*, in *Nishi Amane zenshū*, ed. Ōkubo Toshi-

aki (Tokyo: Munetaka, 1981), 1:248–251, 258–261, 265–274; see also Richard H. Minear, "Nishi Amane and the Reception of Western Law in Japan," *Monumenta Nipponica* 28(2) (1973):151–175; and Watanabe Kazuyasu, *Meiji shisō shi: jukkyō teki dentō to kindai ninshiki ron*, 2nd ed. (Tokyo: Perikansha, 1985), pp. 70–92.

11. I am grateful to Karen Scott for this observation; see Rita Copeland, "The Fortunes of 'Non Verbum Pro Verbo': or, Why Jerome Is Not a Ciceronian," in *The Medieval Translator: The Theory and Practice of Translation in the Middle Ages*, ed. Roger Ellis (Wolfeboro, N.H.: Brewer, 1989), pp. 15–35.

12. My point regarding authenticity and accessibility has a striking parallel in Peter Newmark's theory of semantic versus communicative translating: whereas a semantic translation privileges the content of the source text, a communicative translation privileges the comprehension and response of the target audience. But Newmark discusses this difference only in terms of accessibility in order to offer advice for translators; his mentalist theory of language, unlike my approach, assumes that texts have effects and intentions which translators can ideally and exactly reproduce; see *Approaches to Translation* (Oxford: Pergamon Press, 1981), pp. 20, 38–56, 67. A second and closer parallel to my approach is Gideon Toury's theory of adequacy and acceptability. See Gideon Toury, *In Search of a Theory of Translation* (Tel Aviv: Tel Aviv University, Porter Institute for Poetics and Semiotics, 1980), pp. 11–13, 75–76; and Palma Zlateva, "Translation: Text and Pre-Text: 'Adequacy' and 'Acceptability' in Crosscultural Communication," in *Translation, History, and Culture,* ed. Susan Bassnett and André Lefevere (London: Pinter, 1990), pp. 29–37.

13. [James Legge], *Graduated Reading: Comprising a Circle of Knowledge in 200 Lessons* (Hong Kong: London Missionary Society, 1864; repr. Edo: Kaimushō, [1866]), [p. ii]. In his preface to the first edition, Legge stated that the English text was adapted from a Mr. Baker's lessons at the Anglo-Chinese College; Legge himself did the Chinese translation and revised both English and Chinese versions for the second edition in 1864. Incidentally, he also translated "The Chinese Classics" and held the first chair in Chinese Language at Oxford University in 1876.

14. On the link between missionaries and utilitarianism, particularly the Society for the Diffusion of Useful Knowledge in China, see Kenneth Scott Latourette, *A History of Christian Missions in China* (London: Society for Promoting Christian Knowledge in China, 1929), pp. 220–226 and 377–405.

15. Ozawa Saburō, "*Chikan keimō* to Yasokyō," in his *Bakumatsu Meiji Yasokyō shi kenkyū* (Tokyo: Nihon Kirisutokyōdan shuppankyo, 1973), pp. 123–139; see also Masuda Wataru, *Seigaku tōzen to Chūgoku jijō* (Tokyo: Iwanami shoten, 1979), pp. 16–22. Furuta Tōsaku compares Legge's original and Uryū Tora's translation regarding terminology and usage of relative pronouns in "*Chikan keimō* to *Keimō*

chie no kan," in *Kindaigo kenkyū,* vol. 2, ed. Kindaigo gakkai (Tokyo: Musashino shoin, 1968), pp. 549–578; Satō Tōru compares the vocabulary of Legge's original with W. Lobscheid's *English and Chinese Dictionary* in his *Bakumatsu-Meiji shoki goi no kenkyū* (Tokyo: Ōfūsha, 1986), pp. 26–68.

16. The copy owned by Masuda was titled *Keimō chie sunawachi tamaki,* or *Knowledge Forms a Circle for Childhood Instruction;* see *Seigaku tōzen to Chūgoku jijō,* p. 20. Uryū published his translation under a pseudonym, Oto Shigeru; to complicate matters further, he is also known as Uryū Mitora, and Chō Sanshū's surname is sometimes read Osa.

17. Scholarship is divided on the matter of classifying the Bakumatsu and Meiji prose used in Western translations and texts; as a result, distinctions between *wakan konkōbun* and *kanamajiribun* are not as clear as one might like: both mean "a mixed form of Chinese and Japanese" and date from the late Heian and Kamakura periods. One persistent point in definitions concerns the type of *kana* used; hence *wakan konkōbun* is a mixture of Chinese characters and *hiragana,* as in the medieval war tales (such as *Heiki monogatari*) that define the style, while *kanamajiribun* is a mixture of Chinese characters and *katakana,* as in the medieval tales and legends (such as *Konjaku monogatari*) that define the style. The fact that war tales appear in both styles confuses the definitions, for variations in copying or printing might alter the style of a text. Nanette Twine implies that early Meiji writings on westernization are stylistically *wakan konkōbun;* see "The Genbunitchi Movement: Its Origin, Development, and Conclusion," *Monumenta Nipponica* 33(3) (Autumn 1978):334–337. Similarly, Hayashi Ōki reifies this style as *keimō buntai* or *kaika buntai* (enlightenment style) and terms it an outgrowth of *wakan konkōbun;* see "Gendai no buntai," in *Kōza: Kokugoshi,* vol. 6: *Buntaishi-gengo seikatsu shi,* ed. Satō Kiyoji (Tokyo: Taishūkan, 1972), pp. 178–183. Other scholars, however, reserve *wakan konkōbun* for medieval styles that mix *kana* and Chinese characters; instead they describe both the rather stilted translations from European languages in early Meiji and the prose of early journals such as *Meiroku zasshi* as *kanamajiribun.* Moreover, the few self-conscious comments about written style offered by Meiji scholars that I have seen describe their own writing as *kanamajiribun*—hence I follow this line of interpretation. See Habein, *History of the Japanese Written Language,* pp. 39–42 and 48–50; Konakamura Kiyonori, "Kokubun no seishitsu narabi [ni] enkaku," *Gakugei shirin,* vol. 4 (5/1879):289–298; Nakamura, "Shisho sodoku no ron," p. 7; and Toyama Shōichi, "Kanji o haisubeshi," pp. 308–309. For a variation on this second point see Christopher Seeley, who describes all forms of Japanese that mix Chinese characters and *kana* as *kanjikanamajiribun;* see *A History of Writing in Japan* (Leiden: Brill, 1991), p. 90.

18. Hirose Wataru and Nagata Tomoyoshi, *Chikan keimō wakai* (N.p.: Ishikawa ken gakkō zōhan, [1873]), 1:[1].

19. Oto Shigeru [Uryū Tora], *Keimō chie no kan* (Tokyo: n.p., [1872]), 1:7b.

20. See also Hashizume Kan'ichi, *Chie keimō zukai* (Tokyo: Hōshūdō, [1872]); this is a highly selective abridgement of Legge's text that offers detailed anatomical drawings for the teaching of body parts.

21. See Hirose and Nagata, *Chikan keimō wakai*, 1:32b-33a.

22. [Legge], *Graduated Reading*, p. 38b; [Uryū], *Keimō chie no kan*, 3:4b-5a.

23. Because of the innumerable printing difficulties, the *Encyclopedia* remained unpublished until 1981, some 110 years after it was written; see Nishi, *Hyakugaku renkan/Encyclopedia*, in *Nishi Amane zenshū*, vol. 4.

24. Analogs present a degree of complexity well beyond the standards of postwar research into *furigana*, interpretation of which varies considerably. My position follows the classic statement by Shindō Sakiko, who treats all of these *kana* superscripts and subscripts as *furigana*—as does Hida Yoshifumi. Similarly, Chieko Ariga treats them all as *rubi*, which she asserts is but one of many different terms for *furigana* functions and positions. Recently, however, Kobayashi Masahiro has made a distinction in Meiji texts between subscripts that transcribe sound, which he calls *hidari rubi* (*rubi* on the left side), and superscripts that translate meaning, which he calls *furigana* proper. My research demonstrates that his distinction is not generally edifying. See Shindō Sakiko, "Meiji shoki no furigana," in *Kindaigo kenkyū*, ed. Kindaigo gakkai, vol. 2 (Tokyo: Musashino shoin, 1968), pp. 489–504; Chieko Ariga, "The Playful Gloss: *Rubi* in Japanese Literature," *Monumenta Nipponica* 44(3) (Autumn 1989):309–335; and Kobayashi Masahiro, "*Saikoku risshi hen* ni okeru hidari rubi no jiongo," in *Nihon kindaigo kenkyū*, vol. 1, ed. Kindaigo kenkyūkai (Kasugabe: Hitsuji shobō, 1991), pp. 93–116. For an extensive and helpful analysis of *furigana* usage in selected Meiji texts see Hida Yoshifumi, *Tōkyōgo seiritsu shi no kenkyū* (Tokyo: Tōkyōdō, 1992), pp. 782–864.

25. For an extensive discussion see Howland, "Nishi Amane's Efforts to Translate Western Knowledge."

26. On loanwords generally see Theodora Bynon, *Historical Linguistics* (Cambridge: Cambridge University Press, 1977), pp. 217–232.

27. See Ariga, "Playful Gloss."

28. Roman Jakobson, "On Linguistic Aspects of Translation," in *On Translation*, ed. Reuben Brower (Cambridge, Mass.: Harvard University Press, 1959), pp. 232–233.

29. For an example in the 1880s see Ariga Nagao, "Shina no kaimei to seiyō no kaimei to no sabetsu," pp. 358–359 and 371, where analogs exchange "individual" and "particular" as well as "general" and "abstract." For a recent example see Nishikawa Nagao, *Kokkyō no koekata*, p. 83, where analogs juxtapose *tōyō* (East) and *oriento* (orient) as well as *seiyō* (West) and *okushidento* (occident).

30. Nishi Amane, "*Shinrigaku* hon'yaku hanrei" (1878), quoted in Yamamoto, *Genbunitchi no rekishi ronkō*, 1:84.

31. Readers interested in Chinese studies should note that where Japanese distinguishes between loanwords (*gairaigo*) and translation words (*hon'yakugo*), Chinese parlance treats these as two types of *wailaici* or *jieci* (loanwords)—respectively *yiyin* (sound transfers) and *yiyi* (meaning transfers). In English, Jerry Norman refers to these sound transfers in Chinese characters (what Japanese call *ateji*) as "loanwords" and refers to translation words composed of Chinese characters as "calques" (or loan translations); see Jerry Norman, *Chinese* (Cambridge: Cambridge University Press, 1988), pp. 20–21. Recently Ping Chen has introduced more complex terminology: phonetic transcription (loanwords); loan translation (morpheme-for-morpheme or "literal translations" such as *mali* for "horsepower"); and semantic translation (neologisms that otherwise attempt to capture meaning). See Ping Chen, *Modern Chinese: History and Sociolinguistics* (Cambridge: Cambridge University Press, 1999), pp. 101–105.

32. Although I find his reliance on dictionaries a limitation, the authoritative guide to early Meiji translation words is Morioka Kenji; see his [*Kaitei*] *Kindaigo no sei ritsu: goi hen*, rev. ed. (Tokyo: Meiji shoin, 1991), and "Kaika ki hon'yaku sho no goi," in *Kindai no goi*, ed. Satō Kiyoji (Tokyo: Meiji shoin, 1982), pp. 63–82. For a useful, if popular, discussion of selected translation words see Tsuchida Mitsufumi, *Meiji-Taishō no shingo-ryūkōgo* (Tokyo: Kadokawa shoten, 1983); for a general discussion of word coinage with Chinese characters see Suzuki Shūji, *Kanji—sono tokushitsu to kanji bunmei no shōrai* (Tokyo: Kōdansha, 1978), pp. 167–200. Hinata Toshihiko examines translation words in the *Meiji Six Journal;* see "Kindai kanji no isō—*Meiroku zasshi* o chūshin to shite," *Nihon gogaku* 12(8) (7/1993):66–74.

33. Hida, *Tōkyōgo seiritsu shi no kenkyū*, pp. 443–444. On the prevalence of Chinese-character translation words see also Ishiwata Toshio, "Gendai no goi," in *Kōza: Kokugo shi*, vol. 3: *Goi shi*, by Sakakura Atsuyoshi et al. (Tokyo: Taishūkan, 1971), pp. 358–368.

34. An essential tool for the study of Meiji-period *ateji* is *Ateji gairaigo jiten*, ed. Ateji gairaigo jiten henshū iinkai (Tokyo: Kashiwa shobō, 1979).

35. Mazaki Masato, "Fukuzawa Yukichi to *Seiyō jijō*," *Shigaku* (Keiō Gijuku Daigaku) 24(2–3) (1950):89–105; see also Satō Tōru, *Bakumatsu-Meiji shoki goi no kenkyū*, pp. 394–436. Fukuzawa is also credited with coining the translation word for "public oration," *enzetsu*; he discusses his approach to translation and his regrets at being too "commonplace" in his autobiography and the preface to his collected works: *The Autobiography of Fukuzawa Yukichi, with Preface to the Collected Works of Fukuzawa*, trans. Eiichi Kiyooka (Tokyo: Hokuseido, 1981), respectively pp. 80–84 and pp. 3–13 and 33–36.

36. Morioka, [*Kaitei*] *Kindaigo no sei ritsu: goi hen*, pp. 96–106.

37. Nakamura Keiu, trans., *Saikoku risshi hen* (Tokyo: Ginkadō, 1888), pp. 38, 93, 144–145, 195–196, 228, 257. For an introduction to aspects of Nakamura's translation habits scc Nishio Mitsuo, "*Saikoku risshi hen* no furigana ni tsuite," in *Kindaigo kenkyū*, 2:473–488; for the contribution of Nakamura's translation to standard written Japanese (*futsūbun*) see Okamoto, *Meiji shosakka no buntai*, pp. 447–468. Kawanishi Susumu criticizes Nakamura's translation of *Self-Help*, particularly his representation of "individual," in "*Serufu-herupu* to *Saikoku risshi-hen*," in *Kindai Nihon no hon'yaku bunka*, pp. 79–96.

38. Nishi, *Hyakuichi shinron*, pp. 272–273; Fukuzawa Yukichi, *Tsūzoku minken ron* (1878), in *FYS*, 5:90.

39. *SSMHS*, 4:95, 123, 136.

40. Ibid., 4:58, 61, 68, 72–128 passim.

41. Hida Yoshifumi, "Kindai goi no gaisetsu," in *Kindai no goi*, p. 25; see also Hida's *Tōkyōgo seiritsu shi no kenkyū*, pp. 516–518. My own survey was based on *SSMHS*, vols. 4 (1879) and 6 (1887). The exact figures of twenty-one in 1879 and fifty-eight in 1887 include country names (from two to ten), personal names (from ten to twenty-three), and common nouns (from nine to twenty-five). Information on the growth of loanwords during the Meiji period is rare; Hida's are the only data I have seen. All experts agree that loanword usage has expanded dramatically in the postwar period. For the sake of comparison, a 1956 survey determined that loanwords comprised 10 percent of Japanese vocabulary generally, and a 1966 survey determined that loanwords comprised 12 percent of the Japanese vocabulary used in major newspapers; see Ishiwata Toshio, *Nihongo no naka no gairaigo* (Tokyo: Iwanami shoten, 1985), p. 17. On loanwords in Japanese generally see, in addition to Ishiwata, Leo J. Loveday, *Language Contact in Japan: A Socio-linguistic History* (Oxford: Clarendon Press, 1996), pp. 47–76; Roy Andrew Miller, *The Japanese Language* (Chicago: University of Chicago Press, 1967), pp. 235–267; *Eirai gairaigo no sekai*, ed. Hida Yoshifumi (Tokyo: Nagumo dō, 1981); and, for background in the medieval and Tokugawa periods, Sugimoto Tsutomu, *Sugimoto Tsutomu Nihongo kōza*, vol. 6: *Gairaigo to Nihongo* (Tokyo: Ōfūsha, 1980); and Yaguchi Shigeo, "Meiji izen ni okeru gairaigo no on'yaku," *Gairaigo kenkyū* 4(2) (1/1938):49–72.

42. Ōtsuki Fumihiko, "Gairaigo genkō," *Gakugei shirin,* vol. 17 (2/1884):122–139, (4/1884):370–384, and (6/1884):572–590. Ōtsuki has been largely ignored in English; for his biography see "Ōtsuki Fumihiko hakushi nenpu," *Kokugo to kokubungaku* 5(7) (7/1928):22–82; and Furuta Tōsaku, "Ōtsuki Fumihiko den," printed in sixteen installments in *Bunpō* between 5/1969 and 3/1971. His collected essays were published as *Fukken zassan* (Tokyo: Kōbundō shoten, 1902).

43. See Ishiwata Toshio, *Nihongo no naka no gairaigo*, pp. 138–145. During the

Tokugawa period, Dutch studies scholars typically wrote loanwords in *katakana*; according to Yaeko Sato Habein, *katakana* usage for *gairaigo* was prescribed by law in the postwar period; see *History of the Japanese Written Language*, p. 103.

44. Hida, *Tōkyōgo seiritsu shi no kenkyū*, pp. 443–444.

45. Jeffrey E. Hanes has recently argued that centralization, which many historians observe as an effect of the Meiji state, was achieved through standardization, which is hence the more important process; see "Contesting Centralization? Space, Time, and Hegemony in Meiji Japan," in *New Directions in the Study of Meiji Japan*, ed. Helen Hardacre with Adam L. Kern (Leiden: Brill, 1997), pp. 485–495.

46. "Mombushō Book and Press Regulations," in *JGD*, p. 533. I have corrected McLaren's erroneous transcription of "Fukoku" for Prussia.

47. The 1875 Press Law is reprinted in *SSMHS*, 2:391; it revised the 1872 Press Law, included in *JGD*, pp. 532–533. The 1887 Publication Regulations are reprinted in *JGD*, p. 551.

48. See Nagashima, *Ran-Wa Ei-Wa jisho hattatsu shi*, pp. 94–115; see also Hida Yoshifumi's comments in his reprint edition of the dictionary, to which he added a valuable index of the Chinese-character translation words: [Inoue Tetsujirō], *Tetsugaku jii—yakugo sōsakuin*, ed. Hida Yoshifumi (Tokyo: Kasama shoin, 1979), pp. 223–239.

49. [Kikuchi Dairoku], "Tōgen yakugo," *TYGGZS*, nos. 22–30 (7/1883–3/1884), no. 32 (5/1884), no. 38 (11/1884), and nos. 40–42 (1/1885–3/1885). On the *Tōyō gakugei zasshi* see Shimoide Junkichi, *Meiji shakai shisō kenkyū* (Tokyo: Asano shoten, 1932), pp. 270–291.

50. Kikuchi Dairoku, "Gakujutsujō no yakugo wo ittei suru ron," *TYGGZS*, no. 8 (1882.5.25):154–155.

51. See [Anon.], "Kyōkun no yakubun," *Dōjinsha bungaku zasshi*, no. 11 (1877.2.27):1a-4b; "Tōkyō sho sōba," *Tōkyō keizai zasshi*, no. 1 (1879.1.29):22–35; "Zatsuroku" and "Zappō," *TYGGZS*, no. 9 (1882.6.25):1–2; Toyama Shōichi, "*Jinken shinsetsu* no chosha ni tadashiawasete shinbun kisha no mugaku wo gasu," *TYGGZS*, no. 16 (1883.1.25):[pp. missing]; and Katō Hiroyuki, "Dansonjohi no zehi tokushitsu," *TKGSKIZS* 9(4) (1886.12.12):1–32.

52. Itō Keisuke, "Nihonjin no gazoku bunshō ni okeru, kutō danraku o hyōji-suru o motte hitsuyō to sezaru, ikketsugoto taru o benzu," *TKGSKIZS* 2(10) [late 1881]:13–18. On the development of punctuation in Japanese see Hida, *Tōkyōgo seiritsu shi no kenkyū*, pp. 865–887; and Twine, *Language and the Modern State*, pp. 250–256. Twine cites earlier examples of punctuated texts but, perplexingly, she ignores Itō's essay in favor of later advocates of punctuation.

53. Fukuba Yoshizu (Bisei), "Yōgen bengo," *TKGSKIZS*, vol. 4 (11/1882):199–221; Hori Hidenari, "Gengo no hensen," *Gakugei shirin*, vol. 9 [no. 48] (7/1881):1–9;

Watanabe Makaji, "Gengo no hensen," *Gakugei shirin,* vol. 9 [no. 48] (7/1881):9–17 and [no. 49] (8/1881):103–116; Hori Hidenari, "Gengo seika ben," *Gakugei shirin,* vol. 13 [no. 72] (7/1883):1–16; Mori Mitani, "Gengo hensen narabini seika ben," *Gakugei shirin,* vol. 13 [no. 73] (8/1883):113–142; and Watanabe Makaji, "Gengo seika ben," *Gakugei shirin,* vol. 13 [no. 73] (8/1883):143–154.

54. See Kanda Takahira, "Bankoku gengo itchi setsu," *TKGSKIZS* 4(1) (1882):211–216; and Kawada Kō, "Nihon futsū moji wa, shōrai ikan ni nari yuku ka," *TKGSKIZS* 9(1) (11/1886):1–32. On the agitation for the adoption of *Rōmaji* script see Twine, *Language and the Modern State,* pp. 214 and 240–244; and Yamamoto Masahide, *Kindai buntai hassei no shiteki kenkyū,* pp. 299–330. For a concise summary of the Meiji transformation of written Japanese see Habein, *History of the Japanese Written Language,* pp. 97–103; Hayashi Ōki, "Gendai no buntai"; and Seeley, *History of Writing in Japan,* pp. 128–151.

55. See Morioka, [*Kaitei*] *Kindaigo no sei ritsu—goi hen,* pp. 418–422.

56. There is a vast literature on the role of the educational system in producing both spoken and written forms of modern Japanese; for useful points of departure see Lincicome, *Principle, Praxis, and Politics,* pp. 204–229; and Hirasawa Akira, "Meiji nijūnendai sakubun kyōkasho no mohanbun," in *Nihon kindaigo kenkyū,* 1:139–157. The National Language Research Institute is completing a massive study of the vocabulary of school textbooks and their relation to general language; see Kokuritsu kokugo kenkyūjo, ed., *Kokutei dokuhon yōgo sōran,* vol. 1: *Daiikki (a-n)* (Tokyo: Kokuritsu kokugo kenkyūjo, 1985). On the development of what became the *hyōjungo* (standard language) based largely on Tokyo dialect see Hida, *Tōkyōgo seiritsu shi no kenkyū; Nihongo no reikishi,* vol. 6: *Atarashii kokugo e no ayumi,* ed. Shimonaka Kunihiko, 2nd ed. (Tokyo: Heibonsha, 1976); and Sanada, *Hyōjungo wa, ikani seiritsu shita ka?*

4. Constructing Liberty

1. Benjamin Constant, "The Liberty of the Ancients Compared with That of the Moderns," in *Political Writings,* ed. Biancamaria Fontana (Cambridge: Cambridge University Press, 1988), pp. 307–338; Quentin Skinner, *Liberty Before Liberalism* (Cambridge: Cambridge University Press, 1998). See also Hannah Arendt, "What Is Liberty?", in *Between Past and Future,* enl. ed. (New York: Viking, 1968), pp. 143–171; Isaiah Berlin, "Two Concepts of Liberty," in *Four Essays on Liberty* (Oxford: Oxford University Press, 1969), pp. 118–172; Hanna Fenichel Pitkin, "Are Freedom and Liberty Twins?," *Political Theory* 16(4) (November 1988):523–552; and J.G.A. Pocock, "Virtues, Rights, and Manners: A Model for Historians of Political Thought," *Political Theory* 9(3) (August 1981):353–368.

2. Richard H. King points out that Mill's ideal of self-realization is a species of positive freedom, for which negative political freedom is a prerequisite; see his

Civil Rights and the Idea of Freedom (New York: Oxford University Press, 1992), pp. 15–28.

3. Apart from the legacy of negative freedom, contemporary notions of liberty are marked by reactions to the Russian Revolution, particularly the idea of liberty as the pursuit of happiness in a free market system, but this is rare in nineteenth-century Japanese conceptions. See Harold J. Laski, *Liberty and the Modern State*, rev. ed. (New York: Viking, 1949), pp. 4–16; and Sakamoto Takao, *Shijō-dōtoku-chitsujo* (Tokyo: Sōbunsha, 1991), pp. 19–36.

4. Blandine Kriegel, *The State and the Rule of Law*, trans. Marc A. LePain and Jeffrey C. Cohen (Princeton: Princeton University Press, 1995), pp. 20–24 and 33–37. Essential to Kriegel's analysis is the separation of law and sovereignty in the early modern period, a subject also discussed by Stephen Holmes, *Passions and Constraint: On the Theory of Liberal Democracy* (Chicago: University of Chicago Press, 1995), pp. 100–133; and Franz Neumann, "The Change in the Function of Law in Modern Society," in *The Democratic and the Authoritarian State*, ed. Herbert Marcuse (Glencoe: Free Press, 1957), pp. 22–68.

5. Shindō Sakiko, *Meiji jidai go no kenkyū: goi to bunshō* (Tokyo: Meiji shoin, 1981), pp. 57–62; Yanabu Akira, *Hon'yakugo seiritsu jijō* (Tokyo: Iwanami shoten, 1982), pp. 175–176. Yanabu treats *jiyū* as an exemplary "misconstrued translation word."

6. See *The Oxford English Dictionary*, 2nd ed., prepared by J. A. Simpson and E.S.C. Weiner (Oxford: Clarendon Press, 1989), 6:157–165 and 8:881–887; Williams, *Keywords*, pp. 148–150; and the contemporary account by Mitsukuri Rinshō, "*Riboruchī* no setsu," MRZS, no. 9 (6/1874):2b-4b and no. 14 (7/1874):3a-5b. See also Werner Conze, "Freiheit," in *Geschichtliche Grundbegriffe: Historisches Lexicon zur politisch-sozialer Sprache in Deutschland*, ed. Otto Brunner, Werner Conze, and Reinhart Koselleck (Stuttgart: Klett, 1972–1989), 2:425–542; and Anna Wierzbicka, *Understanding Cultures Through Their Key Words: English, Russian, Polish, German, and Japanese* (New York: Oxford University Press, 1997), pp. 125–155.

7. Compare, for a range of contrasting examples, the 1860s English-language learning texts assembled by Sugimoto Tsutomu in *Nihon Eigo bunka shi shiryō* (Tokyo: Yasaka shobō, 1985).

8. Kanda admits in his prefatory remarks to *Seihō ryaku* that he based his work on a manuscript written by Nishi, *Seihō kōketsu*; Ōkubo Toshiaki felt so strongly about Nishi's authorship that he included *Seihō ryaku* in Nishi's collected works. See Kanda Takahira, *Seihō ryaku* (1871), in *Meiji bunka zenshū*, 2nd ed., vol. 13: *Hōritsu hen* (Tokyo: Nihon hyōron shinsha, 1957), p. 4; and Hasunuma Keisuke, *Nishi Amane ni okeru tetsugaku no seiritsu* (Tokyo: Yūhikaku, 1987), pp. 8–20. On Simon Vissering see Irene Hasenberg Butter, *Academic Economics in Holland, 1800–1870* (The Hague: Nijhoff, 1969).

9. There are several discussions of Tsuda's choice of vocabulary in *Taisei kokuhō ron* and the translation of Wheaton's *Elements of International Law*, which I discuss in Chapter 5; see Ōkubo Toshiaki, *Bakumatsu ishin no yōgaku* (Tokyo: Yoshikawa kōbunkan, 1986), pp. 119–223; Satō Tōru, *Bakumatsu-Meiji shoki goi no kenkyū*, pp. 161–197 and 356–393; and Taoka Ryōichi, "Nishi Shūsuke *Bankoku kōhō*," *Kokusaihō gaikō zasshi* 71 (5/1972):1–57.

10. Katō Hiroyuki, *Rikken seitai ryaku*, in *Nishi Amane/Katō Hiroyuki*, ed. Uete Michiari (Tokyo: Chūōkōronsha, 1984), pp. 342–343. See also Tsuda Mamichi, *Taisei kokuhō ron* (1868) (Tokyo: Tōyōsha, 1875), pp. 91–100. In place of Katō's right to life, Tsuda substitutes a right to the inviolability of one's home; in addition, Tsuda adds a right to the respect of the secrecy of one's written papers, a right to fairness of taxation according to family wealth, a right to petition, and a right to confidence in the state when making private contracts with the state. Kanda, by contrast, assumes Katō's set as "innate rights" and elaborates "acquired rights" related to property and contract; see *Seihō ryaku*, pp. 6–13. Tsuda's expanded list of rights resembles the more extensive rights granted by the Prussian Constitution, which informed Kido Takayoshi's draft constitution(s) of 1872; see Inada Masatsugu, *Meiji kenpō seiritsu shi* (Tokyo: Yūhikaku, 1960–1962), 1:213–216.

11. Tsuda, *Taisei kokuhō ron*, pp. 95–96.

12. Kanda, *Seihō ryaku*, p. 12.

13. Berlin, "Two Concepts of Liberty"; Holmes, *Passions and Constraint*, pp. 13–41; and H. J. McCloskey, "A Critique of the Ideals of Liberty," *Mind* 74 (1965):483–508.

14. Katō, *Rikken seitai ryaku*, p. 342. I have substituted "ancient and infamous tyranny" for Katō's rather hackneyed reference to two such ancient Chinese kings, Jie and Zhou.

15. John Locke, *Two Treatises on Government*, critical [rev.] ed. by Peter Laslette (New York: New American Library, 1963), p. 348.

16. Tsuda, *Taisei kokuhō ron*, p. 39.

17. I have found only one instance of liberty as an abstraction: in his discussion of executive power, Nishi Amane notes that "the concentration of executive power in France robbed the people in all provinces of their liberty *(jizai)*"—and this use of liberty exemplifies Nishi's habit of using the English word with Japanese gloss in analog form. See Nishi, *Hyakugaku renkan/Encyclopedia*, 4:226.

18. For an alternative comparison of Fukuzawa and Nakamura regarding their approaches to universals see Ishida, *Kindai Nihon no seiji bunka to gengo shōchō*, pp. 33–53. Sakamoto Takao provides a valuable discussion of Fukuzawa's liberalism that links his political and economic ideas to the background of the Scottish enlightenment; see *Shijō-dōtoku-chitsujo*, pp. 3–41.

19. Fukuzawa, *SYJJ*, p. 290. See also Nakamura Keiu, *Jiyū no ri* (1871), in *Meiji*

bunka zenshū, vol. 5: *Jiyū minken hen* (Tokyo: Nihon hyōronsha, 1927), p. 84 (hereafter *JYNR*).

20. On the background of the meaning and usage of *jiyū* see Kimura Ki's 1952 essay, "Jiyū wa itsu hajimete Nihon ni haittekita ka?," reprinted in his *Bunmeikaika*, pp. 81–122; Ishida, *Nihon no seiji to kotoba*, vol. 1: *Jiyū to fukushi*, pp. 32–37; Ōkubo Toshiaki, *Meiji no shisō to bunka*, pp. 8–14; Shindō, *Meiji jidai go no kenkyū*, pp. 32–56; Suzuki Shūji, *Nihon kango to Chūgokugo* (Tokyo: Chūōkōronsha, 1981), pp. 137–150; and Yanabu Akira, *Hon'yaku to wa nani ka?*, rev. ed., pp. 107–114.

21. See Kimura, *Bunmeikaika*, pp. 137–157. Regarding the concept of "free trade" in the 1854 and 1858 treaties, Anne Walthall offers a possible precedent in Tokugawa village life that softens the negative accusation of "willful." Peasants involved in commercialized agriculture negotiated for the privilege to sell "as one will" (*katte shidai*); similarly, some advocated unrestrained trade, or trade that was neither taxed nor regulated. See Anne Walthall, *Social Protest and Popular Culture in Eighteenth-Century Japan* (Tucson: University of Arizona Press, 1986), pp. 91 and 215.

22. Nakamura, *JYNR*, pp. 7–8.

23. Fukuzawa's colloquial preferences backfire with *gasshūkoku*, which he uses as a translation for federation or republic and in his cumbersome but thorough translation for the United States of America, *Amerika Gasshūkoku*. In sorting out this pair of terms, *Gasshūkoku* stayed as a proper name for the United States and Japanese resorted to an alternative expression, *kyōwa*, still in use today, to translate "republic." On the shift from *gasshū* to *kyōwa* as translations for "republican" see Sōgō Masaaki and Hida Yoshifumi, *Meiji no kotoba jiten* (Tokyo: Tōkyōdō, 1986), pp. 70–71, 113, 115–116.

24. Such usage of *dokuritsu* is implicit in other contemporary discussions of the rise of independent states; Katō Hiroyuki, for example, relates this independence of the United States and later, somewhat uncomfortably, describes the failed attempt of the southern states to achieve a similar independence during the American civil war. See Katō, *Tonarigusa*, pp. 317–318 and 326. Dynastic changes, by contrast, are never described in the 1860s as *dokuritsu*; Fukuzawa describes the actions of regicides and usurpers who establish new dynasties, such as William the Conqueror and Henry Bolingbroke, as *jiritsu* (self-establishing) their kingdoms. See Fukuzawa, *SYJJ*, pp. 355 and 360. On Fukuzawa's concept of *dokuritsu* generally, see Sakamoto, *Shijō-dōtoku-chitsujo*, pp. 11–17; for an alternative interpretation of Fukuzawa's translation of the "Declaration of Independence," which faults him for inaccuracies, see Tadashi Aruga, "The Declaration of Independence in Japan: Translation and Transplantation, 1854–1997," *Journal of American History* 85(4) (March 1999):1409–1431.

25. Nakamura, *JYNR*, pp. 15–17.

26. Shindō Sakiko points out in her grammatical analysis of *jiyū* that usage in

the Meiji period shifts from primarily "adjectival verb" (*keiyō dōshi*) uses to primarily noun uses; see *Meiji jidai go no kenkyū*, p. 38.

27. Nakamura, *JYNR*, pp. 16–17.

28. Kriegel, *State and the Rule of Law*, pp. 35–36.

29. Fukuzawa, *SYJJ*, p. 581.

30. Ibid., pp. 486–487.

31. Ibid., pp. 392 and 395. Fukuzawa's comments are based on William Chambers, the nineteenth-century educator, and Sir William Blackstone, the eighteenth-century legal scholar.

32. Ibid., pp. 393–394. "Human interaction" can also be construed as "society"; see Chapter 6.

33. Nakamura, *JYNR*, p. 4. There is a great deal of literature on E. W. Clark and the "Shizuoka group"; see Ōkubo Toshiaki, *Meiji no shisō to bunka*, pp. 83–106; and Ōta Aito, *Meiji Kirisutokyō no ryūiki: Shizuoka bando to bakushin tachi* (Tokyo: Tsukiji shokan, 1979).

34. Nakamura, *JYNR*, pp. 18–19.

35. Mori Arinori, in his English-language presentation of the United States, recommended virtue and education as antidotes to "the evils" that followed from the selfish freedom widespread in America; see *Life and Resources in America* ([Washington, D.C.]: privately printed, [1871]), pp. 13–14.

36. Nakamura, *JYNR*, pp. 12, 18–19, 24–30.

37. Umeda Yoshihiko, "Shūkyō hō ni tsuite—Edo bakufu kara Meiji seifu e," *Shintō shūkyō*, no. 26 (11/1961):37–55.

38. Katō Hiroyuki, trans., [J. K. Bluntschli], *Kokuhō hanron* (1872–1876), in *Meiji bunka zenshū*, supp. vol. 2 [vol. 31] (Tokyo: Nihon hyōronsha, 1971), pp. 187–201.

39. James Edward Ketelaar, *Of Heretics and Martyrs in Meiji Japan: Buddhism and Its Persecution* (Princeton: Princeton University Press, 1990), p. 125.

40. See Thomas W. Burkman, "The Urakami Incidents and the Struggle for Religious Toleration in Early Meiji Japan," *Japanese Journal of Religious Studies* 1(2–3) (1974):168–170. On *matsurigoto* see Maruyama Masao, "The Structure of *Matsurigoto*: The *Basso Ostinato* of Japanese Political Life," in *Themes and Theories in Modern Japanese History: Essays in Memory of Richard Storry*, ed. Sue Henny and Jean-Pierre Lehmann (London: Athlone, 1988), pp. 27–43; and Harootunian, *Things Seen and Unseen*, pp. 164–166.

41. "Jinshin no kisū o ichi ni subeku—Seikyōitchi no goshushi o sen'yō," *Dajōkan nisshi* (1871.7.4); in *SSMHS*, 1:383–384.

42. For the background of early Meiji religious policy see Abe Yoshiya, "From Prohibition to Toleration: Japanese Government Views Regarding Christianity, 1854–73," *Japanese Journal of Religious Studies* 5(2–3) (1978):107–138; Burkman, "Urakami Incidents"; Ketelaar, *Heretics and Martyrs*, pp. 43–135; Muraoka Tsune-

tsugu, *Studies in Shintō Thought*, trans. Delmer M. Brown and James T. Araki (1964; repr. New York: Greenwood, 1988), pp. 203–208; and Notto R. Thelle, *Buddhism and Christianity in Japan: From Conflict to Dialogue, 1854–1899* (Honolulu: University of Hawai'i Press, 1987), pp. 10–17.

43. Burkman, "Urakami Incidents"; Umeda, "Shūkyō hō ni tsuite." That key memorials opposing the government's policy—by Mori Arinori and Nakamura Keiu—were written in English suggests a degree of complicity between certain Japanese intellectuals and the foreign powers.

44. "Yasokyō yokuatsu no hōsaku," *Kyōbushō nisshi* (7/1872); in SSMHS, 1:453.

45. Shimaji Mokurai, "Sanjō kyōsoku hihan kenpakusho," in *Gendai Nihon shisō taikei*, vol. 7: *Bukkyō*, ed. Yoshida Kyūichi (Tokyo: Chikuma shobō, 1965), pp. 61–70.

46. Nishi Amane, "Kyōmon ron," pts. 1 and 2, MRZS, no. 4 [4/1874]:5b-8b and no. 5 [4/1874]:3b-6a. Nishi also treated the differentiation of *sei* and *kyō* in *Hyakuichi shinron*, p. 236.

47. Katō Hiroyuki, "Beikoku seikyō," pts. 2 and 3, MRZS, no. 6 [4/1874]:3b-6a and no. 13 (6/1874):1–4a; Nakamura Keiu, "Seigaku ippan: jūni gō no zoku," MRZS, no. 15 (8/1874):2b-4b. Katō's article summarizes the longer argument in his translation of Bluntschli; see *Kokuhō hanron*, pp. 187–225. See also Mori Arinori, "Shūkyō," MRZS, no. 6 [4/1874]:6a-12b; and "Kyōkai ritsurei," an unpublished report prepared by the Translation Bureau of the Dajōkan in 1874, in *Meiji seifu hon'yaku sōkō ruisan* (Tokyo: Yumani shobō, 1987), 12:327–381.

48. Shimaji Mokurai dismissed religion as a basis for civilization and implicitly concluded that the enlightenment achieved through scholarship should precede all reform and improvement in religion; see "Sanjō kyōsoku hihan kenpakusho," pp. 61–64; and see Ketelaar, *Heretics and Martyrs*, pp. 125–129.

49. Mori, *Religious Freedom in Japan*, pp. 4–9; see also Hayashi Takeji, "Kindai kyōiku kōsō to Mori Arinori," *Chūōkōron* 77(10) (9/1962):208–218. On Mori's memorial and his religious education among a Swedenborgian community in the United States see Ivan P. Hall, *Mori Arinori*, pp. 95–128 and 195–202.

50. Nakamura Keiu, "Gi taiseijin josho," in *Meiji keimō shisō shū*, ed. Ōkubo Toshiaki (Tokyo: Chikuma shobō, 1967), pp. 281–283. Nakamura's essay was printed first in English (May 1872) and then in erudite literary Chinese three months later; both were anonymous. The infamy of Nakamura's memorial had to do with these lines: "If the emperor wishes to establish Western religion, then he might first personally undertake baptism, make himself the head of the [Japanese Christian] Church, and then millions will shout their appreciation. If the emperor were to eliminate the ban on Christianity, from today all Western rulers would respect and love him." A subsequent revised version omits the first sentence; this version is reprinted in *Keiu bunshū* (Tokyo: Yoshikawa kōbunkan, 1903), 1:6–9. An abridged

version of the English text, also omitting the offending passage, was printed in *Japan Weekly Mail*, May 11, 1872, pp. 267–268; the unabridged version was printed the following week: May 18, 1872, pp. 285–287. An editorial response to the memorial, under the title "The Christian Question," initiated a month of editorials on the topic—see *Japan Weekly Mail*, May 18, 1872, pp. 282–284; June 1, 1872, pp. 322–324; June 8, 1872, pp. 341–342; June 15, 1872, pp. 358–359; June 29, 1872, pp. 391–392.

51. See Nishi Amane, "Kyōmon ron," pts. 3 and 5, MRZS, no. 6 [4/1874]:2a-3a and no. 8 (5/1874):6b-8a (Nishi's essay was published without a part 4); Sugi Kōji, "Jinkan kōkyo," pt. 3, MRZS, no. 19 (10/1874):6b-8b; Tsuda Mamichi, "Kaika o shinzuru hōhō o ronzu," MRZS, no. 3 [4/1874]:7a-8b.

52. Shimaji, "Sanjō kyōsoku hihan kenpakusho," pp. 65–66; Nishi, "Kyōmon ron," pts. 1 and 2; and Katō, "Beikoku seikyō," pt. 1, MRZS, no. 5 [4/1874]:10b-13.

53. "Kyōkai ritsurei," pp. 328–329. Mori Arinori and Katō Hiroyuki refer to these laws and use expressions identical to those of the Translation Bureau workers (such as "freedom of conscience" translated in the now standard form *ryōshin no jiyū*). The bureau's chief, Mitsukuri Rinshō, was a fellow member of the Meirokusha; on his role in the Translation Bureau see Ōtsuki Fumihiko, *Mitsukuri Rinshō-kun den* (Tokyo: n.p., 1907), pp. 55–59 and 70–71.

54. Nakamura Keiu, "Seikyō mu mujun no hei," in *Keiu bunshū* 13:16–17. The essay was first printed in *Tokyo shinpō*, no. 11 (9/1873).

55. Mori, "Shūkyō." Although he leaves it undeveloped, Mori does invoke the stronger version of national religion with Phillimore: in the interests of national peace, the state does have a right to enforce a national religion and proscribe other religions.

56. James L. Huffman, *Creating a Public: People and Press in Meiji Japan* (Honolulu: University of Hawai'i Press, 1997), pp. 68–69 and 76.

57. Kido, *Diary*, 1:474; 2:58, 221, 228, 238, 388–389, 394. On Kido's relationship with the *Shinbun zasshi* see Albert Altman, "*Shimbunshi*: The Early Meiji Adaptation of the Western-Style Newspaper," in *Modern Japan*, ed. W. G. Beasley (London: Allen & Unwin, 1975), pp. 52–66.

58. Many scholars have examined the Meiji newspaper and publishing laws and their shifting jurisdictions and effects, but no one has recently examined in any sustained manner the debate over freedom of the press prompted by the 1875 law. The major press laws are translated in *JGD*, pp. 529–557; see also Peter Figdor, "Newspapers and Their Regulation in Early Meiji Japan," *Papers on Japan* (East Asian Research Center, Harvard University) 6 (1972):1–44; Huffman, *Creating a Public*, pp. 76–85, 104–110, 136–142; Inada, *Meiji kenpō seiritsu shi*, 1:181–185; Nishida Taketoshi, *Meiji jidai no shinbun to zasshi* (Tokyo: Shibundō, 1961), pp. 36–38 and 85–95; Ono Hideo, "Meiji shoki ni okeru shuppan jiyū no gainen,"

Shinkyū jidai 2(4–5) (1926):83–92 (a revised version is included in *Meiji bunka zenshū*, 2nd ed., vol. 2: *Jiyūminken hen* [Tokyo: Nihon hyōronsha, 1967], pp. 16–19); and Jay Rubin, *Injurious to Public Morals: Writers and the Meiji State* (Seattle: University of Washington Press, 1984), pp. 3–31.

59. Huffman, *Creating a Public*, pp. 78–79; "Shinbun kakusha rengōshite kisai han'i o tou—Naimushō kotaezu," *Yūbin hōchi shinbun* (1875.9.25), in *SSMHS*, 2:405. For a list of two hundred journalists arrested between 1875 and 1879 see Midoro Masuichi, ed., *Meiji Taishō shi*, vol. 1: *Genron hen* (Tokyo: Kyōdō insho, 1930), pp. 73–77.

60. Fonblanque's textbook appeared in England in sixteen editions between 1858 and 1889 and was translated by Suzuki Yuichi as *Eisei ikan* (1868); in *Meiji bunka zenshū*, 2nd ed., vol. 3: *Seiji hen* (Tokyo: Nihon hyōron shinsha, 1955). Tocqueville's chapter was translated by Obata Tokujirō as *Jōboku jiyū no ron* (1873); in *Meiji bunka zenshū*, vol. 5: *Jiyūminken hen* (Tokyo: Nihon hyōronsha, 1927).

61. Fukuzawa, *SYJJ*, pp. 304–305; Nakamura, *JYNR*, pp. 17 and 19; Obata, trans., *Jōboku jiyū no ron*, pp. 130–131; and Suzuki, trans., *Eisei ikan*, p. 34. This position received editorial support in *Japan Weekly Mail*, September 6, 1873, pp. 635–636.

62. Altman, "*Shimbunshi*," pp. 59–60; Figdor, "Newspapers and Their Regulation," pp. 3–4.

63. Nishimura Shigeki, "Zanbōritsu-shinbun jōrei o hinansu," *Hyōron shinbun*, no. 45 (11/1875), in *SSMHS*, 2:444–445; Tsuda Mamichi, "Shinbunshi ron," *MRZS*, no. 20 [11/1874]:1–2b.

64. Figdor, "Newspapers and Their Regulation," pp. 8 and 16; "Fukkoku hōritsusho hon'yaku," an anonymous and unpublished report of the Translation Bureau of the Dajōkan prepared between 1872 and 1874, in *Meiji seifu hon'yaku sōkō ruisan* (Tokyo: Yumani shobō, 1987), 32:3–43.

65. Nishimura, "Zanbōritsu-shinbun jōrei o hinansu," p. 444.

66. Fukuzawa, *SYJJ*, pp. 486–487; Nakamura, *JYNR*, p. 19. See also J. S. Mill, *On Liberty*, in *Three Essays* (Oxford: Oxford University Press, 1975), p. 22.

67. Obata, trans., *Jōboku jiyū no ron*, p. 130; Tsuda Mamichi, "Shuppan jiyū naran koto o nozomu ron," *MRZS*, no. 6 [4/1874]:1–2a.

68. Obata, trans., *Jōboku jiyū no ron*, pp. 130–131; Yokose Fumihiko, "Shinbun jōrei to zanbōritsu," *Hyōron shinbun*, no. 16 (7/1875), in *SSMHS*, 2:372–373; and Minoura Katsundo, "Shinbun jōrei happu irai nikagetsu nishite—Hayakumo genron dan'atsu no kōka arawaru," *Yūbin hōchi shinbun* (1875.8.30), in *SSMHS*, 2:383–384.

69. Minoura, "Shinbun jōrei happu irai nikagetsu nishite," pp. 383–384; Narushima Ryūhoku, "Shinbun jōrei zanbōritsu wa somo izure no kuni no hōritsu zoya," *Chōya shinbun* (1875.8.15), in *SSMHS*, 2:379; and Yokose, "Shinbun jōrei to zanbōritsu," p. 372.

70. "Meiji ninen no shinbun jōrei to izure zo," *Chōya shinbun* (1875.9.8), in *SSMHS*, 2:393. Since the 1875 law prohibited criticism of government laws, this article—and many others—discussed the issue in terms of the earlier 1869 law instead.

71. Nishimura, "Zanbōritsu-shinbun jōrei o hinansu," pp. 444–445.

72. Obata, trans., *Jōboku jiyū no ron*, p. 130. See also Alexis de Tocqueville, *Democracy in America* (the Henry Reeve text as revised by Francis Bowen) (New York: Knopf, 1980), 1:184.

73. Tsuda Mamichi, "Jōyoku," *MRZS*, no. 34 (4/1875):8b–9a.

74. From 1874, newspaper reports throughout Japan attested to individuals' exercise of their freedom of religion; see *SSMHS*, 2:109; 3:381. But English-language newpapers monitored alleged abuses of religious freedom for possible revivals of official persecution of "native Christians"; see *Japan Weekly Mail*, April 3, 1875, p. 1.

75. Minoura, "Shinbun jōrei happu irai nikagetsu nishite," pp. 383–384, and "Meiji ninen no shinbun jōrei to izure zo," p. 393.

76. Ishida, *Nihon no seiji to kotoba*, 1:37; *SSMHS*, 1:403, 2:24 and 26; and the editorial comments in *Nihon kindai shisō taikei*, vol. 21: *Minshū undō*, ed. Yasumaru Yoshio and Fukaya Katsumi (Tokyo: Iwanami shoten, 1989), p. 239. On political fiction see Asai Kiyoshi, "Nihon ni okeru shimin seishin no seiritsu: Meiji shoki bungaku ni okeru 'jiyū' no juyō," *Shisō*, no. 504 (1966):61–71; Shunsuke Kamei, "The Sacred Land of Liberty: Images of America in Nineteenth-Century Japan," in *Mutual Images: Essays in American-Japanese Relations*, ed. Akira Iriye (Cambridge, Mass.: Harvard University Press, 1975), pp. 55–72; and Ike, *Beginnings of Political Democracy in Japan*, pp. 121–123.

77. Nakamura Keiu would continue to editorialize on "the true freedom of thought" through contributions to his journal. See Hosaka Yūkichi, "Jiyū ron," *Dōjinsha bungaku zasshi*, no. 8 (1876.12.23):5–7a; and Andō Katsudō, "Jiyū no heigai o ronzu," *Dōjinsha bungaku zasshi*, no. 19 (1877.12.5):2–[page missing].

78. Nakamura Keiu, "Seigaku ippan—zengō no zoku," *MRZS*, no. 12 (6/1874):9a.

79. Nishimura Shigeki, "Jishujiyū kai," *MRZS*, no. 37 (5/1875):1b–2b.

80. Ibid., p. 3a. But this argument was used by Ueki Emori in 1882 for exactly the opposite (populist) case. See *Minken jiyū ron—nihen kangō*, in *Ueki Emori shū* (Tokyo: Iwanami shoten, 1990), 1:131–133.

5. Differentiating Right and Sovereignty

1. Rai San'yō, *Nihon gaishi*, in *Rai San'yō*, ed. Rai Tsutomu (Tokyo: Chūōkō-ronsha, 1984), pp. 59–63. Rai implied that both the shogunate and the imperial court can possess such *ken*, but elsewhere he raised the issue of whether *ken* can be shared with officials; see *Nihon seiki*, in *Rai San'yō*, ed. Uete Michiari (Tokyo:

Iwanami shoten, 1977), p. 485. A study of Rai's use of Chinese words did not find *ken* a remarkable component; see Satō Kiyoji, *Kokugo goi no rekishi-teki kenkyū* (Tokyo: Meiji shoin, 1971), pp. 246–301. Compare Mark Ravina's discussion of modes of Tokugawa authority in *Land and Lordship in Early Modern Japan* (Stanford: Stanford University Press, 1999), pp. 34–45, pp. 194–196; his categories of feudal, patrimonial, and suzerain authority, however, are apparently heuristic and not grounded in Japanese conceptual terminology.

2. Mitsukuri, "*Riboruchī* no setsu," p. 2b; Fukuzawa, *SYJJ*, pp. 395 and 496–498.

3. On Dutch studies of European law and history see F. B. Verwayen, "Tokugawa Translations of Dutch Legal Texts," *Monumenta Nipponica* 53(3) (Fall 1998):335–358; Kure Shūzō, "Yōgaku no hattatsu to Meiji ishin," in *Meiji ishin shi kenkyū*, ed. Shigakkai, Tokyo Teikoku Daigaku (Tokyo: Fuzanbō, 1929), pp. 329–418 (especially pp. 404–406); and Endō Takeshi, "Bakumatsu yu'nyū no Ran-Ei hōritsusho," *Rangaku shiryō kenkyūkai kenkyū hōkoku*, no. 23 (1958.1.18):3–11.

4. Where the Dutch studies translations of the 1840s and 1850s most often translated Dutch *regt* as *seiritsu* (just statute), *shu to surubeki suji* (the reason that shall be the principal one), or simply *suji* (reason or principle), the scholars working in the 1860s instituted the widespread use of *ken* at issue in this chapter. See Verwayen, "Tokugawa Translations," pp. 353–357; and Yanabu, *Hon'yakugo seiritsu jijō*, pp. 151–152.

5. [Wheaton], *Bankoku kōhō* (Edo: Kaiseijo, 1865). Compare Shigeno Yasutsugu, *Wayaku bankoku kōhō* (Kagoshima: n.p., 1870); Takaya Tatsukuni and Nakamura Keiu, *Bankoku kōhō reikan* (n.p.: Saibi kōzō, 1876); and Tsutsumi Koshiji, *Bankoku kōhō yakugi* (n.p., 1868). On Martin's translation of Wheaton see Immanuel C. Y. Hsü, *China's Entry into the Family of Nations: The Diplomatic Phase, 1858–1880* (Cambridge, Mass.: Harvard University Press, 1960), pp. 125–131; Lydia H. Liu, "Legislating the Universal: The Circulation of International Law in the Nineteenth Century," in *Tokens of Exchange: The Problem of Translation in Global Circulations*, ed. Lydia H. Liu (Durham: Duke University Press, 1999), pp. 127–164; and Masuda Wataru, *Seigaku tōzen to Chūgoku jijō*, pp. 3–9. A useful comparison of an excerpt of Wheaton's English, Martin's Chinese, and Shigeno's Japanese in parallel, with commentary by Zhang Jianing (Jyanin Jyan), is available in *Nihon kindai shisō taikei*, vol. 15: *Hon'yaku no shisō*, ed. Katō Shūichi and Maruyama Masao (Tokyo: Iwanami shoten, 1991), pp. 3–35 and 381–405.

6. See Blacker, *Japanese Enlightenment*, pp. 104–105; Yanabu, *Hon'yaku to wa nani ka?*, 2nd ed., p. 78.

7. [Wheaton], *Bankoku kōhō*, 1:4a, 5b, 17a, 18b, 29a, 32a, 33b.

8. Ibid., 1:4b, 10a, 11b, 14a, 16a, 17a, 19, 22a, 29a, 33–35; 4:32b.

9. Ibid., 1:3a; 2:23b, 67a. *Ken* also figures in expressions where legitimate power

or authority is implied—as in "however warranted," which Martin translates as *ruhe you quan*—and in nominalized expressions like *youquanzhe* and *zhiquanzhe* (owner/holder of *quan*), which indicate that *quan* (J: *ken*) is a thing one can possess or wield—like power or authority; ibid., 1:8b, 10a, 14b. Martin's subsequent "Terms Used in Diplomatic and Official Intercourse" (1872) differs yet again: *ken* is translated as "power," *kenri* as "privilege," and "right" as *fensuo yingde* (J: *bun-sho ōtoku*)—"the share one rightly deserves." See W.A.P. Martin, "Terms Used in Diplomatic and Official Intercourse," in Justus Doolittle, *A Vocabulary and Hand-book of the Chinese Language, Romanized in the Mandarin Dialect* (Foochow: Rozario, Marcal, 1872), 2:194–200—entries for "Full Powers," "A Right," "Privilege," and "Exceed one's powers," pp. 198–199.

10. Wheaton had reproached the exceptionality of English usage distinguishing law from right; Wheaton, *Elements of International Law*, 2nd ann. ed. (1863), p. 18.

11. Katō, *Tonarigusa*, pp. 313–318; *Rikken seitai ryaku*, pp. 332–341. By itself, *ji* can also be read *chi*.

12. Nishi, *Hyakugaku renkan/Encyclopedia*, pp. 214–229; Tsuda, *Taisei kokuhō ron*, p. 33; and Katō, *Rikken seitai ryaku*, pp. 335–338. Katō also substituted the homonym *kenpei*, in which *ken* is the word for "constitution," hence "constitutional powers." For an account of the development of the idea of "division of powers" in modern China and Japan see Suzuki Shūji, *Nihon kango to Chūgokugo*, pp. 3–45.

13. [Wheaton], *Bankoku kōhō*, 1:16a, 18b, 20a, 23b, 25a, 26a, 28a; Nishi, *Fisuserinku-shi bankoku kōhō*, 1:6; 2:5a, 8a; and Tsuda, *Taisei kokuhō ron*, pp. 16, 22, 29–35.

14. Nishi, *Fisuserinku-shi bankoku kōhō*, in *Nishi Amane zenshū*, ed. Ōkubo Toshiaki (Tokyo: Munetaka, 1962), 2:84–94. By comparison, Suzuki Yuichi's translation of Albany de Fonblanque's *How We Are Governed* uses *ken* for "power" and *iken*—an idiosyncratic reversal of *ken'i*—for "power," "authority," or "jurisdiction"; *iken* reappears in Kido Takayoshi's 1872 draft constitution to mean constitutional powers. See Suzuki Yuichi, trans., *Eisei ikan*, pp. 33–36; and Inada, *Meiji kenpō seiritsu shi*, 1:217.

15. See "The Press-Laws—Natural Rights," *Japan Weekly Mail*, August 7, 1875, p. 669; the editorial relies on the authority and language of Edmund Burke.

16. Katō, *Rikken seitai ryaku*, pp. 341–343.

17. Nishi, *Fisuserinku-shi bankoku kōhō*, 2:1. Wheaton noted that the morality enforcing international behavior is comparable to that guiding private behavior in society; see the preface to the 2nd ann. ed., *Elements* (1863), p. xiv.

18. Tsuda, *Taisei kokuhō ron*, pp. 16, 21–22, 25, 33.

19. Nishi, *Fisuserinku-shi bankoku kōhō*, 2:1. I agree with Yanabu Akira's assertion that *ken* was Nishi's translation for *regt*, but I also believe that his transla-

tions were determined by the precedent of Martin's translation of Wheaton. See Yanabu, *Hon'yakugo seiritsu jijō*, p. 162.

20. Iwakura Tomomi, "Gaikō, kaikei, Ezochi kaitaku iken sho" (1869.2.28), in *Nihon kindai shisō taikei*, vol. 12: *Taigaikan*, ed. Shibahara Takuji et al. (Tokyo: Iwanami shoten, 1988), pp. 5–11.

21. Fukuzawa, *SYJJ*, pp. 392–393, 487–488, 493–498. In this text, Fukuzawa used *ken* and its compounds to refer to forms of power. For example, the feudal age in England is marked by conflict between the "privileges" (*tokken*) and "powers" (*kenpei*) of the royal government and the church; ibid., pp. 357–358, 558, 565–566, 598–600.

22. Tsuda, *Taisei kokuhō ron*, pp. 13–14, 88, 91–92; Nishi, *Fisuserinku-shi bankoku kōhō* (1962), 2:56.

23. Kanda, *Seihō ryaku*, pp. 4 and 6–7. Kanda's text includes the first usage, to my knowledge, of *waga ken*, "my (or our) right(s)"; ibid., pp. 6 and 11.

24. Kido Takayoshi's writings of the early 1870s—particularly his 1872 draft constitutions and his 1873 opinion on constitutional government—also use *kenri*, but these were not widely circulated; see Inada, 1:212–228, and *Nihon kensei kiso shiryō*, ed. Miyakoshi Shin'ichirō (Tokyo: Giin seijisha, 1939), pp. 98–104 (hereafter *NKKS*).

25. Nishi, *Hyakuichi shinron*, pp. 275–276. For an insightful discussion of the background of this text see Hasunuma, *Nishi Amane ni okeru tetsugaku no seiritsu*, pp. 21–41.

26. That the two forms of *kenri* were interchangeable is the conclusion of several Japanese scholars; see Sōgō Masaaki and Hida Yoshifumi, *Meiji no kotoba jiten*, pp. 149–150; and Yanabu, *Hon'yaku to wa nani ka?*, 2nd ed., p. 92.

27. The most rewarding text for examples of word usage in the 1870s is Fukumoto Nichinan [Tomoe], *Futsū minken ron* (1879), in *Meiji bunka zenshū*, vol. 5: *Jiyū minken hen* (Tokyo: Nihon hyōronsha, 1927), pp. 197–212. This collection is cited hereafter as *JYMKH*. For an analysis of the "natural" in "natural law" see Mori Kazutsura, *Kindai Nihon shisōshi josetsu*, pp. 116–133.

28. Fukuzawa, *SYJJ*, pp. 493–503; Katō Hiroyuki, *Shinsei taigi*, in *JYMKH*, p. 90; Katō Hiroyuki, *Kokutai shinron*, in *JYMKH*, pp. 114, 117–118, 120–121; Katō Hiroyuki, trans., [Bluntschli], *Kokuhō hanron*, p. 10; and Nishi, *Hyakuichi shinron*, pp. 272–273. See Kido Takayoshi's draft constitutions in Inada, 1:217 and 220.

29. Itagaki Taisuke et al., "Minsen giin setsuritsu no dairongi," in *SSMHS*, 2:117–118; Ueki Emori, *Minken jiyū ron* (1879), in *Jiyūjiji gannen no yume*, ed. Ide Magoroku (Tokyo: Shakai hyōronsha, 1991), pp. 14 and 23; Genrōin, *Kenpō sōkō hyōrin* (1879), in *Jiyūjiji gannen no yume*, p. 129; Nishi Amane, *Kenpō sōan* (1881–1882), in *Nishi Amane zenshū*, 2:203–208. For Kido Takayoshi's draft constitutions see note 28. Suzuki Shūji has noted that "right and duty" were most

popularly used ca. 1874–1875; see *Nihon kango to Chūgoku*, p. 54. (*Jiyūjiji gannen no yume* is hereafter abbreviated *JJGNY*.)

30. Following the appearance of Ueki Emori's book, *Minken jiyū ron*, in 1879, newspapers began to refer to both the "movement to establish a national assembly" (*kokkai kaisetsu undō*) and the "freedom and people's rights argument" (*minken jiyū setsu* or *jiyū minken ron*). See *SSMHS*, 4:139 and 472.

31. See Robert M. Spaulding, "The Intent of the Charter Oath," *Studies in Japanese History and Politics*, ed. Richard K. Beardsley (Ann Arbor: University of Michigan Press, 1967), pp. 1–36; Robert A. Wilson, *Genesis of the Meiji Government in Japan, 1868–1871* (Berkeley: University of California Press, 1957), pp. 34–39; and Sakamoto Takao, *Meiji kokka no kensetsu, 1870–1890* (Tokyo: Chūōkōronsha, 1999), pp. 28–42 and 58–62.

32. The political crisis of October 1881 developed around a difference of opinion between oligarchs Ōkuma Shigenobu and Itō Hirobumi concerning the introduction of popular participation as well as the Hokkaidō colonization assets scandal in which Itō was implicated. In opposing Itō, Ōkuma violated government unity and was forced to resign from office; in return, the government announced the establishment of a Diet in 1890.

33. Ōkubo Toshimichi, "Rikken seitai ni kansuru ikensho," in *NKKS*, pp. 106–110; Ōkubo Toshimichi, "Ōsaka sento no kenpakusho," in *Meiji shisō shū*, ed. Matsumoto Sannosuke (Tokyo: Chikuma shobō, 1976), 1:3–4; Kido Takayoshi, "Kenpō seitei no kengi," in *NKKS*, pp. 98–104; Sa'in documents in *NKKS*, pp. 83–84; Kido Takayoshi, "Rippō-Gyōsei ni kansuru kenpakusho," in *Meiji shisō shū*, 1:13–19; Genrōin, *Kenpō sōkō hyōrin*, pp. 122–126; Ōkuma Shigenobu, "Rikken seitai ni kansuru kengi," in *NKKS*, pp. 311–322; and Yamagata Aritomo, "Rikken seitai ni kansuru kengi," in *NKKS*, pp. 269–276.

34. Itagaki et al., "Minsen giin setsuritsu no dairongi," pp. 117–118. The pair—government (*seifu*) and people (*jinmin*)—is also expressed in a simplified form as *shinmin* (officials and people); but as it appears in the Meiji Constitution, *shinmin* has been translated officially as "subject."

35. Katō Hiroyuki, "Jiki shōsō to hanpaku," in *NKKS*, pp. 150–151.

36. Nagamine Hideki, trans., [John Stuart Mill], *Daigi seitai* (1875), in *Meiji bunka zenshū*, 2nd ed., vol. 3: *Seiji hen* (Tokyo: Nihon hyōron shinsha, 1955), pp. 112, 135, 144–145, 151.

37. Hence Mitsukuri Rinshō's translation of *droit civil* (civil law) as *minken*, ca. 1870, is best understood as an example of the early and superseded conflation of law and right.

38. Fukumoto, *Futsū minken ron*, pp. 205 and 208; Toyama Shōichi, *Minken benwaku* (1880), in *JYMKH*, pp. 218–219. See also Genrōin, *Kenpō sōkō hyōrin*, p. 123; Ueki Emori, "Shogen" (1877), in *Ueki Emori shū*, ed. Ienaga Saburō et al.

(Tokyo: Iwanami shoten, 1990), 3:84; and Ueki Emori, "Jinmin no kokka ni taisuru seishin o ronzu," in *Meiji shisō shū*, 1:169–178. Even Fukuzawa Yukichi, who was largely indifferent to people's rights, nonetheless stressed *minken* as the right to participate in a national assembly. See *Kokkai ron* (1879), in *FYS*, 5:122 and 135.

39. Although scholars routinely attribute such usage to them, neither Fukuzawa nor Mori used the terms "equal rights of husbands and wives" (*fūfu dōken*) or "equal rights of men and women" (*nannyo dōken*).

40. Tsuda, *Taisei kokuhō ron*, p. 16; Nakamura Keiu, *JYNR*, p. 77; Fukuzawa Yukichi, *Gakumon no susume* (1874–1876), in *FYS*, 3:110–114; Fukuzawa Yukichi, "Nannyo dōsū ron," *MRZS*, no. 31 (3/1875):8–9; Mori Arinori, "Saishō ron," *MRZS*, no. 8 (5/1874):2–3 and no. 27 (2/1875):1–3; Katō Hiroyuki, "Fūfu dōken no ryūhei ron," *MRZS*, no.31 (3/1875):1–3; and Tsuda Mamichi, "Fūfu dōken ben," *MRZS*, no. 35 (4/1875):8–9. Discussion of "equal rights of husbands and wives" was revived in political novels of the mid-1880s around the time that Mori's contract marriage ended in divorce; see Tsuchida Mitsufumi, *Meiji-Taishō shingo ryūkōgo* (Toyko: Kadokawa, 1983), pp. 52–54.

41. Fukumoto, *Futsū minken ron*, p. 201; "Jiyūtō kessei meiyaku," in *JJGNY*, p. 79; Ueki Emori, "Meirei no moji wa jiyū dōken to heikō suru mono ni arazu" (1881), in *Ueki Emori shū*, 3:238–240; Matsushima Kō, trans., *Shakai heiken ron* (1881–1883), in *JYMKH*, p. 287; Nagamine, trans., *Daigi seitai*, p. 151. In Nagamine's translation of *Representative Government*, *dōken* even figured as a translation word for "equality."

42. In this context, Ueki's use of *kokumin* as a translation for "nation" inserted a new and mediatory concept between the people and the state; see Matsumoto, *Meiji seishin no kōzō*, pp. 62–65.

43. Ueki, *Minken jiyū ron*, pp. 12–15 and 18–23; Itagaki Taisuke, "Jiyūtō soshiki no taigi," in *JJGNY*, pp. 86–88. Ueki was both a member of the Liberty Party and an adviser to Itagaki, for whom he reportedly wrote speeches and editorials; hence many of his ideas became Liberty Party proposals.

44. Kojima Shōji, *Minken mondō* (1877), in *JYMKH*, pp. 155–158 and 166–169. For a contextualization of the problem see Maruyama Masao, "Meiji kokka no shisō" (1946), in his *Senchū to sengo no aida* (Tokyo: Misuzu shobō, 1976), pp. 202–250.

45. Ueki, *Minken jiyū ron*, pp. 28–29; Fukumoto, *Futsū minken ron*, p. 201; Kokkai kisei dōmeikai, "Kokkai wo kaisetsu suru no inka o jōgan suru sho," in *NKKS*, pp. 256–257; "Jiyūtō soshiki no shuisho," in *NKKS*, p. 380; [Kōchiken jin], "San dai jiken kenpakusho," in *JJGNY*, pp. 92 and 101; [Okayamaken jin], "Dōhō kyōdai ni tsugu," in *JJGNY*, p. 77. By comparison, the gradualist political party, the Rikken kaishintō (Constitutional Reform Party), maintained that the best course of action was to reform internal administration in order to expand *kokken;* see "Rikken kaishintō shuisho," in *JJGNY*, p. 81. See also Kyu Hyun Kim, "Polit-

ical Ideologies of the Early Meiji Parties," in *New Directions in the Study of Meiji Japan*, ed. Helen Hardacre, with Adam L. Kern (Leiden: Brill, 1997), pp. 397–407.

46. Compare Kojima, *Minken mondō*, pp. 156, 161, 165, 178; Fukumoto, *Futsū minken ron*, pp. 202–203; Ono Azusa, "Kenri no zoku," in *Meiji shisō shū*, 1:181–183; Ono Azusa, "Waga seijijō no shugi," in *Meiji shisō shū*, 1:184–207; Toyama, *Minken benwaku*, pp. 217 and 221; and Ueki Emori, "Enjin kunshu" (1876), in *Ueki Emori shū*, 3:16–17; and Ueki Emori, *Minken jiyūron: nihen kangō*, 1:131–134. This interchangeability of right and liberty is especially salient in Matsushima Kō's 1881 translation of Spencer's *Social Statics* and in several of the draft constitutions of the early 1880s—for examples see Ueki Emori's draft constitution of 1881, *Nihon kuni kokken an* (1881), in *JJGNY*, pp. 110–112, which has also been printed as a Risshisha document, titled *Tōyō Dai Nihon kuni kokken an* (1881), in *Ueki Emori senshū*, ed. Ienaga Saburō (Tokyo: Iwanami shoten, 1974), pp. 93–95. See also *Nihon kuni kokken an* (1880–1881?), transcribed by Miura Kaneyuki and reprinted in *Meiji bunka zenshū*, 3rd ed., vol. 10: *Shōshi hen*, pt. 2 (Tokyo: Nihon hyōronsha, 1968), pp. 422–423; and [Kōjunsha], *Shigi kenpō an* (1881), in ibid., p. 410.

47. Toyama, *Minken benwaku*, pp. 215–224; Ueki, *Minken jiyū ron*, pp. 10, 14, 18; Ueki, "Shogen," p. 91; "Jiyūtō kessei meiyaku," p. 79; and Itagaki, "Jiyūtō soshiki no taigi," pp. 83–86. Compare the local documents from 1881 to 1884 gathered in *Nihon kindai shisō taikei*, vol. 21: *Minshū undō*, ed. Yasumaru Yoshio and Fukaya Katsumi (Tokyo: Iwanami shoten, 1989), pp. 191, 196, 202, 223, 233.

48. See the local documents in *Minshū undō*, ed. Yasumaru and Fukaya, pp. 212–219, 226, 269, 276, 284. The expression *jiyū shugi* is prominent in Toyama Shōichi's *Minken benwaku* of 1880.

49. Katō Hiroyuki, *Jinken shinsetsu* (1882), in *JYMKH*, pp. 356–357, 359–362, 372–376.

50. Yano Fumio, *Jinken shinsetsu bakuron* (1882), in *JYMKH*, pp. 394–397 and 401; and the editorial from the Tokyo-Yokohama mainichi shinbun, "*Jinken shinsetsu* o hyōsu" (1882), in ibid., p. 413.

51. Baba Tatsui, "Doku Katō Hiroyuki no kun *Jinken shinsetsu*" (1882), in *Meiji shisō shū*, 1:208–231; Tokyo-Yokohama mainichi shinbun, "*Jinken shinsetsu* o hyōsu," pp. 420–421; and Ueki Emori, *Tenpu jinken ben* (1883), in *JYMKH*, p. 477.

52. Baba Tatsui, *Tenpu jinken ron* (1883), in *JYMKH*, pp. 444–450.

53. Toyama Shōichi, "*Jinken shinsetsu* no chosha ni tadashiawasete shinbun kisha no mugaku o gasu" (1883), in *JYMKH*, pp. 428 and 434; Ueki, *Tenpu jinken ben*, pp. 476–480.

54. Toyama Shōichi, "Futatabi *Jinken shinsetsu* chosha ni tadashiawasete Supenseru-shi no tame ni en o toku," in *JYMKH*, pp. 432–434. Mori Kazutsura discusses this point in detail in *Kindai Nihon shisōshi josetsu*, pp. 134–164. Tanaka Hiroshi emphasizes that by invoking social evolution, Katō nonetheless under-

cut natural rights and natural law, which are derived from philosophical speculation; see *Kindai Nihon to "riberarizumu"* (Tokyo: Iwanami shoten, 1993), pp. 57–58.

55. Baba, *Tenpu jinken ron*, pp. 451–455; Toyama, *"Jinken shinsetsu* no chosha ni tadashiawasete shinbunkisha no mugaku o gasu,"* pp. 429–430; and Tokyo-Yokohama mainichi shinbun, *"Jinken shinsetsu* o hyōsu," p. 420.

56. Katō, trans., *Kokuhō hanron*, pp. 30–31, 33–38, 41–42. A useful comparison of an excerpt of Bluntschli's German and Katō's Japanese in parallel is available in *Nihon kindai shisō taikei*, vol. 15: *Honyaku no shisō*, pp. 34–90 and 414–415.

57. Obata, trans., *Jōboku jiyū no ron*, p. 131. Prior to the introduction of Rousseau, a more common argument was "constitutional republic versus absolute monarchy"; see, for example, Sakamoto Minao, "Katō Hiroyuki no seitairon ni taisuru ronnan" (1875.12.22), in *SSMHS*, 2:452. On Hattori's translation of Rousseau see Inada, *Meiji kenpō seiritsu shi*, 1:635. Hattori's translation was the subject of an editorial in *Chōya shinbun* (1879.12.19) protesting restrictions on freedom of public speech; see *SSMHS*, 4:139.

58. The debate is summarized in Inada, *Meiji kenpō seiritsu shi*, 1:599–644; and Pittau, *Political Thought in Early Meiji Japan*, pp. 106–114.

59. This position drew at least one editorial critique (believed to be the work of Ueki Emori), which defended Rousseau and asserted that a country was, if anything, its people; see Inada, *Meiji kenpō seiritsu shi*, 1:604. For background on the Shimeikai see Motoyama, *Proliferating Talent*, pp. 278–282.

60. The imperial announcement is included in *NKKS*, pp. 343–344. An English translation is available in *Meiji Japan through Contemporary Sources*, comp. Centre for East Asian Cultural Studies (Tokyo: Centre for East Asian Cultural Studies, 1969–1972), 3:69–70.

61. Ueki, *Nihon kuni kokken an*, pp. 110–112; *Nihon kuni kokken an*, transcribed by Miura Kaneyuki, pp. 422–423; and [Kōjunsha], *Shigi kenpō an*, p. 410. Despite Kido's commitment to constitutional government, Yamamuro Shin'ichi notes that Kido initially saw the Western principle of a division of powers (into executive, legislative, and judicial) as a threat to the revival of imperial government; see *Hōsei kanryō no jidai*, p. 27.

62. The initial two-thirds of the debate was reprinted in book form by Nagatsuka Sōtarō in May 1882 with the hope that people's rights activists would benefit; see *Minkenka hitsudoku—shuken ron san* (1882), in *JYMKH*, pp. 309–352.

63. The philological point was expressly raised in the debate; ibid., p. 328.

64. On sovereignty see Kriegel, *The State and the Rule of Law*, pp. 15–32; G. W. F. Hegel, *Elements of the Philosophy of Right*, trans. H. B. Nisbet, ed. Allen W. Wood (Cambridge: Cambridge University Press, 1991), pp. 316–321 (sec. 279); and Alexis de Tocqueville, *Democracy in America*, trans. George Lawrence, ed.

J. P. Mayer and Max Lerner (New York: Harper & Row, 1966), pp. 665–669 (vol. 2, pt. 4, chap. 6).

65. Nagatsuka, *Minkenka hitsudoku—shuken ron san*, pp. 325–326.

66. Ibid., pp. 324 and 327–328.

67. Inada, *Meiji kenpō seiritsu shi*, 1:613–615.

68. Nagatsuka, *Minkenka hitsudoku—shuken ron san*, pp. 342–347; Inada suspects that this was the work of Yano Fumio: *Meiji kenpō seiritsu shi*, 1:619. George M. Beckmann reports that a copy of Todd's *On Parliamentary Government in England* (1867–1869) was used by Prince Arisugawa and a Genrōin committee in producing a series of draft constitutions between 1876 and 1878; see *The Making of the Meiji Constitution: The Oligarchs and the Constitutional Development of Japan, 1868–1891* (Lawrence: University of Kansas Press, 1957), pp. 46–47. Several parts of Todd's work were translated into Japanese by Ozaki Yukio and published in 1882–1883; four of these have been reprinted in Ozaki's collected works: *Ozaki Yukio zenshū* (Tokyo: Heibonsha, 1926), 1:407–474 (*Ōshitsu hen*), 1:475–564 (*Naikaku kōtetsu shi*), and 1:565–714 (*Naikaku kaigi hen*); and *Ozaki Gakudō zenshū* (Tokyo: Kōronsha, 1956), 1:396–567 (*Naikaku shissei hen*).

69. Nagatsuka, *Minkenka hitsudoku—shuken ron san*, pp. 348 and 351.

70. Ibid., pp. 317, 320–321, 331–332.

71. Ibid., pp. 330–331, 333, 336.

72. Ibid., pp. 321 and 332. See also Inada, *Meiji kenpō seiritsu shi*, 1:609–612. In time the appropriate response of a subject to his rightful sovereign, duly elevated by the people in creating a political society, would develop from this 1881 debate into a national and educational issue.

73. Nagatsuka, *Minkenka hitsudoku— shuken ron san*, pp. 328 and 334–336.

74. See Inada, *Meiji kenpō seiritsu shi*, 1:621–631. The Imperial Party platform asserted the emperor's *shuken*; by comparison, the documents issued by the Liberty and Reform Parties in late 1881 never mention sovereignty; the Liberty Party commonly referred to *kokken*, state right, while the Reform Party avoided both terms; see *NKKS*, pp. 380–468 (p. 456 for the Imperial Party platform). An anonymous translation from Thomas Hobbes' *Leviathan*, published by the Ministry of Education in 1883 as *Shukenron* (On Sovereignty), reconfirmed *shuken* as sovereignty; see *Meiji bunka zenshū*, 2nd ed., vol. 3: *Seiji hen* (Tokyo: Nihon hyōronsha, 1955), pp. 235–278.

75. Inada, *Meiji kenpō seiritsu shi*, 1:636. Nakae's *kanbun* translation of Rousseau appeared from March 1882 to August 1883; curiously, his newspaper articles use *shuken* as a translation word for "sovereignty," while his translation of Rousseau uses *kunken*, an idiosyncratic usage, I believe, meant to underline Rousseau's opposition between monarch and people; see Nakae, trans., *Minyaku yakkai* (1882), in *Meiji bunka zenshū*, 2nd ed., vol. 3: *Seiji hen* (Tokyo: Nihon hyōron shinsha, 1955),

pp. 181–204. This point has been noted by Sakamoto Takao in his excellent discussion of Nakae, in *Kindai Nihon seishin shiron*, pp. 315–336; see also Sakamoto's earlier discussion of Nakae on "sovereign and freedom" in *Shijō-dōtoku-chitsujo*, pp. 104–115; and see Matsumoto, *Meiji seishin no kōzō*, pp. 77–100, some of which is available in English as "Nakae Chōmin and Confucianism," in *Confucianism and Tokugawa Culture*, ed. Peter Nosco (Princeton: Princeton University Press, 1984), pp. 251–266.

76. Inada, *Meiji kenpō seiritsu shi*, 1:632 and 639–644. For a useful discussion of Ono Azusa see Yamashita Shigekazu, "Ono Azusa to Igirisu seiji shisō," in Takeda Kiyoko et al., *Igirisu shisō to kindai Nihon* (Tokyo: Kitaki shuppan, 1992), pp. 125–161.

77. See Sandra T. W. Davis, "Treaty Revision, National Security, and Regional Cooperation: A *Mintō* Viewpoint," in *Japan in Transition: Thought and Action in the Meiji Era, 1868–1912*, ed. Hilary Conroy, Sandra T. W. Davis, and Wayne Patterson (Rutherford: Fairleigh Dickinson University Press, 1984), pp. 151–173.

78. See, for example, [Kōchiken jin], "Sandaijiken kenpakusho" (1887), in *JJGNY*, pp. 92–106; and Nakae Chōmin, "Heimin no mezamashi" (1887), in ibid., pp. 51–73.

79. Ishida Takeshi has instead abstractly analyzed "levels" of meaning in Fukuzawa's use of *seiken* (government, participation, and power); see *Kindai Nihon no seiji bunka to gengo shōchō*, pp. 55–81.

80. Fukuzawa Yukichi, *Bunken ron* (1876–1878), in *FYS*, 5:14, 19, 44–48. Fukuzawa drew on the authority of Tocqueville's *Democracy in America* for the contrast between government and administration. But he altered Tocqueville, whose point concerned centralization and contended that governmental centralization was unavoidable whereas adminstrative centralization was destined to expand and become ever more oppressive to liberty and burdensome to democratic government. For an alternative analysis of *Bunken ron*—one that pursues Fukuzawa's analysis of public governmental jurisdiction versus private corporations and the location of the "nation" therein—see Matsuda Kōichirō, "Fukuzawa Yukichi to *kō-shi-bun* no saihakken," *Rikkyō hōgaku*, no. 43 (1996):76–140.

81. Fukuzawa, *Tsūzoku minken ron*, pp. 90–94 and 97–98.

82. Fukuzawa, *Kokkai ron*, pp. 122, 127, 135, 139–143; see also *Tsūzoku minken ron*, p. 115. There is some question whether Fukuzawa wrote *Kokkai ron* himself; it was serialized in *Yūbin hōchi shinbun* by two of his students, Fujita Mokichi and Minoura Katsundo, and later reprinted with a "part 2" authored by Fukuzawa (the latter is now parts 2 and 3 of *Jiji shogen*). At some point, authorship of the original piece was attributed to Fukuzawa. See the comments of Toriumi Yasushi in *FYS*, 5:343–344; Carmen Blacker reiterates Fukuzawa's version of the "facts" in *Japanese Enlightenment*, pp. 116–118.

83. Fukuzawa, *Bunmei ron no gairyaku*, pp. 226–227 and 236–239.

84. Ibid., pp. 242–245 and 251.

85. Fukuzawa Yukichi, *Tsūzoku kokken ron*, in FYS, 7:18–19, 22–25, 29, 50–51. Fukuzawa's stress on expanding *kokken* in the international context, while preserving the people's liberties, figures among the activist army officers studied by Ochiai Hiroki, "Meiji zenki no rikugun kashi to jiyūminken."

86. Fukuzawa Yukichi, *Jiji shogen*, in FYS, 5:160–161, 164–167, 237.

87. Ibid., 5:237, 251–252, 256. Banno Junji too has observed Fukuzawa's disengagement of *minken* and *kokken* in 1881; see *Kindai Nihon no kokka kōsō*, pp. 104–107.

88. In the course of the debate on sovereignty, Fukuzawa serialized three works in his newspaper *Jiji shinpō* and subsequently published them in book form: *Jiji taisei ron* (April 1882), *Teishitsu ron* (May 1882), and *Hanbatsu kajin seifu ron* (June 1882); all three are reprinted in FYS, vol. 6. For another commentary on these works that focuses on the emperor see Pittau, *Political Thought in Early Meiji Japan*, pp. 114–118.

89. Fukuzawa, *Jiji taisei ron*, pp. 7–10 and 16–17; *Teishitsu ron*, pp. 45–54; and *Hanbatsu kajin seifu ron*, pp. 72–73.

90. Fukuzawa, *Teishitsu ron*, pp. 39, 44–47, 50, 53–60, 67. He reiterated many of these ideas in *Sonnō ron* (1888), in FYS, 6:135 and 144.

91. Ishida Takeshi, "Kaisetsu," in FYS, 6:334–340.

92. Fukuzawa, *Jiji taisei ron*, p. 26; *Teishitsu ron*, pp. 34 and 53–54; and *Sonnō ron*, pp. 140–145.

6. Representing the People, Imagining Society

1. See Hayashiya, "Bunmeikaika no rekishiteki zentei," pp. 6–7; Najita, *Japan: The Intellectual Foundations of Modern Japanese Politics*, pp. 48–50 and 72–73; Osatake, *Nihon kensei shi taikō*, 1:1–14; Pittau, *Political Thought in Early Meiji Japan*, p. 14; and Luke S. Roberts, "A Petition for a Popularly Chosen Council of Government in Tosa in 1787," *Harvard Journal of Asiatic Studies* 57(2) (December 1997):575–596.

2. For a survey of twentieth-century conceptions of society compare Talcott Parsons, "Society," in *Encyclopedia of the Social Sciences*, ed. E. R. A. Seligman (New York: Macmillan, 1934), 13:225–232, and Leon H. Mayhew, "Society," in *International Encyclopedia of the Social Sciences*, ed. David L. Sills (New York: Macmillan/Free Press, 1968), 14:577–586.

3. *Oxford English Dictionary*, 2nd ed., 3:255 and 15:913–914; Williams, *Keywords*, pp. 243–247; Eric R. Wolf, "Inventing Society," *American Ethnologist* 15(4) (November 1988):752–761; and Keith Michael Baker, "Enlightenment and the Institution of Society: Notes for a Conceptual History," in *Main Trends in Cultural History: Ten Essays*, ed. Willem Melching and Wyger Velema (Amsterdam: Rodopi, 1994), pp. 95–120.

4. Thomas Hobbes, *The Elements of Law* (Oxford: Oxford University Press, 1994), pp. 106–107, and *Leviathan* (Harmondsworth: Penguin, 1981), pp. 223–228; Locke, *Two Treatises on Government*, pp. 324 and 366–368.

5. Adam Ferguson, *An Essay on the History of Civil Society*, ed. Fania Oz-Salzberger (Cambridge: Cambridge University Press, 1995), pp. 8–10, 38, 63, 150, 159. Sakamoto Takao contextualizes the Meiji effort at progress in the context of Ferguson, Adam Smith, and the Scottish enlightenment generally in *Shijō-dōtoku-chitsujo*, pp. iii–xvii.

6. Takikawa Masajirō, *Nihon hōsei shi*, rev. ed. (Tokyo: Kadokawa shoten, 1959), p. 414.

7. The earliest reference occurs in the *Shu jing* (Classic of History), 5:20, but the original dating of this text remains uncertain. For the development of *shimin* in Japan see Asao Naohiro, "Kinsei no mibun to sono hen'yō," in *Mibun to kakushiki*, ed. Asao Naohiro (Tokyo: Chūōkōronsha, 1992), pp. 14–24. According to Banba Masatomo, *shimin* was not commonplace until the 1720s; see Herman Ooms, *Tokugawa Village Practice: Class, Status, Power, Law* (Berkeley: University of California Press, 1996), p. 298.

8. Ogyū Sorai, *Tōmonsho*, trans. J. R. McEwan, *The Political Writings of Ogyū Sorai* (Cambridge: Cambridge University Press, 1969), pp. 11, 17, 24.

9. See Hsiao Kung-chuan, *A History of Chinese Political Thought*, vol. 1: *From the Beginnings to the Sixth Century A.D.*, trans. F. W. Mote (Princeton: Princeton University Press, 1979), pp. 350–355; and Herrlee G. Creel, *Shen Pu-hai: A Chinese Political Philosopher of the Fourth Century B.C.* (Chicago: University of Chicago Press, 1974), pp. 95–100.

10. Watanabe Hiroshi reports that Korean observers in 1719 slightingly remarked that Japan had no scholar officials (*shi*) but only soldiers (*hei*); see *Kinsei Nihon shakai to sōgaku* (Tokyo: Tokyo Daigaku shuppankai, 1985), p. 61.

11. Kasaya Kazuhiko, "Bushi no mibun to kakushiki," in *Mibun to kakushiki*, ed. Asao Naohiro (Tokyo: Chūōkōronsha, 1992), pp. 207–216; Nakamura Kichiji, *Nihon shakai shi gaisetsu* (Tokyo: Usui shobō, 1947), pp. 224–227.

12. Beasley, *Meiji Restoration*, pp. 22–34; Dan Fenno Henderson, *Conciliation and Japanese Law: Tokugawa and Modern*, vol. 1 (Seattle: University of Washington Press; Tokyo: University of Tokyo Press, 1965), pp. 27 and 87–92; Minegishi Kentarō, *Kinsei mibun ron* (Tokyo: Azekura shobō, 1989), pp. 71–130; and Takikawa, *Nihon hōsei shi*, p. 415.

13. Takahashi Kamekichi, *Tokugawa hōken keizai no kenkyū* (Tokyo: Senshinsha, 1932), pp. 29–41. I discuss status in detail in "Samurai Status, Class, and Bureaucracy: A Historiographical Essay," *Journal of Asian Studies* 62(2) (May 2001):353–380.

14. Honjō Eijirō, *The Social and Economic History of Japan* (Kyoto: Nihon keizaishi kenkyūjo, 1935), pp. 195–229; Takikawa, *Nihon hōsei shi*, p. 416.

15. Fukaya Katsumi, "Kinseishi kenkyū to mibun," *Rekishi hyōron*, no. 369 (1/1981):51–52.

16. On legal equality at the start of Meiji see Aso Yoshiteru, *Kinsei Nihon tetsugaku shi* (Tokyo: Kondō shoten, 1942), pp. 152–162; Hayashiya, "Bunmeikaika no rekishiteki zentei," pp. 14–20; and Inada, *Meiji kenpō seiritsu shi*, 1:152–174.

17. On the assertion that the former samurai serve as the model for all the people see Matsuda Kōichirō, "Fukuzawa Yukichi to *kō-shi-bun* no saihakken," pp. 109–112 and 120–127; on the leadership and domination of the samurai, especially in the movements for a national assembly and people's rights, see Maruyama Masao, "Jiyū minken undō shi" (1948), in his *Senchū to sengo no aida* (Tokyo: Misuzu shobō, 1976), pp. 308–341, especially p. 311.

18. Sonoda Hidehiro, "Gun-ken no bushi—bushi mibun kaitai ni kansuru ichi kōsatsu," in *Bunmeikaika no kenkyū*, ed. Hayashiya Tatsusaburō (Tokyo: Iwanami shoten, 1979), pp. 65–76. The former shogunal academy, renamed the Daigaku in 1870, was not properly a university until it merged with the shogun's medical school and institute for foreign studies and became Tokyo University in 1877.

19. Fukaya Hakuji, [*Shintei*] *Ka-shizoku chitsuroku shobun no kenkyū*, 2nd ed. (Tokyo: Yoshikawa kōbunkan, 1973), pp. 3–15. The 1871 redefinition of the four peoples appears most often in connection with legal descriptions of the people; see Ienaga Saburō, *Nihon kindai shisō shi kenkyū*, 2nd ed., pp. 95–116; and Sakamoto Takao, *Meiji kokka no kensetsu*, p. 388. The *sotsuzoku* class was eliminated in 1872.

20. Even writers committed to equality represented the present in terms informed by their Tokugawa past—if only for critical purpose. Ono Azusa, in his 1875 indictment of the oligarchy, described society as composed of the three peoples—farmers, artisans, and merchants—confronting the aristocracy and former samurai: "Kenri no zoku," p. 183. See also [Kōchiken jin], "San dai jiken kenpakusho," pp. 92–106.

21. The debate over whether or not the Meiji government constituted a samurai autocracy (argued powerfully by Gotō Yasushi in the 1960s) persists today. See Sonoda Hidehiro, Hamana Atsushi, and Hirota Teruyuki, *Shizoku no rekishi shakaigaku-teki kenkyū* (Nagoya: Nagoya Daigaku shuppankai, 1995), pp. 1–41 and 70–83; and Sakamoto Takao, *Meiji kokka no kensetsu*, pp. 170–178. Future research must heed the issue raised by Sakamoto—that we need to find a better way to name in English the difference between (Tokugawa) samurai (*bushi*) and the former samurai (*shizoku*) of the early Meiji period.

22. Fukuzawa originally planned *Seiyō jijō* as a two-volume work that would survey Western institutions and provide the political history of the United States, Holland, England, Russia, France, Portugal, and Prussia. After completing volume one (1866), which included the United States, Holland, and England, he inserted his translation of Chambers' *Political Economy* as a *gaihen* (supplemental) volume

(1867). These two volumes were followed in 1870 by "volume two"—in actuality a third volume—that included Russia and France. He never wrote the sections on Portugal and Prussia.

23. Fukuzawa, *SYJJ*, pp. 285–382 passim; the references to status differences appear on pp. 290 and 299.

24. Ibid., pp. 385–481 passim.

25. This point is discussed by Earl H. Kinmonth in "Nakamura Keiu and Samuel Smiles: A Victorian Confucian and a Confucian Victorian," *American Historical Review* 85 (June 1980):535–556.

26. See Ravina, "State-building and Political Economy in Early-modern Japan," pp. 1003–1006.

27. The same compatibility is a feature of Kanda Takahira's 1867 translation of William Ellis' *Outlines of Social Economy* (1846), to which Fukuzawa deferred in presenting his own translation of Chambers; see Kanda Takahira, *Keizai shōgaku* (1867), in *Meiji bunka zenshū*, rev. ed., vol. 12: *Keizai hen* (Tokyo: Nihon hyōron shinsha, 1957), pp. 22–56; and see Fukuzawa, *SYJJ*, p. 385.

28. Fukuzawa, *SYJJ*, pp. 435–442; Nakamura, trans., *Saikoku risshi hen*, pp. 226–227. On the background of Nakamura's translation of Smiles see Ōkubo, *Bakumatsu ishin no yōgaku*, pp. 224–260.

29. Fukuzawa, *SYJJ*, pp. 428–429; Nakamura, trans., *Saikoku risshi hen*, p. 232. Fukuzawa drew a similar analogy in *Gakumon no susume*, where he states that "the people in a nation gather together and form a *kaisha* [company/society] called a nation, establish the company laws, and administer them . . . like a hundred townsmen forming a merchant company and establishing their laws after some discussion among the members." See *Gakumon no susume*, p. 99.

30. This usage includes a *katakana* loanword, *sosaiti*, which Nakamura equates with *nakama-kaisha* (social groups). See Nakamura, *JYNR*, pp. 47 and 72.

31. Matsumoto Sannosuke has called such personal interactions the most common understanding of society among early Meiji intellectuals: "Kuga Katsunan ni okeru *kokka* to *shakai*," *Journal of Pacific Asia*, no. 1 (1993):145–160.

32. H. D. Harootunian, *Toward Restoration: The Growth of Political Consciousness in Tokugawa Japan* (Berkeley: University of California Press, 1970), p. 408; Maruyama Masao, *Studies in the Intellectual History of Tokugawa Japan*, trans. Mikiso Hane (Princeton: Princeton University Press; Tokyo: University of Tokyo Press, 1974), pp. 274–319, 338–340, 346–349.

33. Shindō Sakiko reports a similar range of translation words for "society" in Obata Tokujirō's translation of Francis Wayland's *Political Economy* (1837): *Ei-shi keizai ron* (1871–1877); see *Meiji jidai go no kenkyū*, p. 73.

34. See Nakamura, trans., *Saikoku risshi hen*, pp. 260–261 and 324, for examples of *seken* and *sejō*.

35. *Seken* was originally a Buddhist term for "the secular world." Eiko Ikegami discusses *seken* as the Tokugawa arena of samurai honor, or the "imagined cultural community in which one's reputation is evaluated"; see *The Taming of the Samurai: Honorific Individualism and the Making of Modern Japan* (Cambridge, Mass.: Harvard University Press, 1995), pp. 18 and 90–94. Shindō Sakiko has noted that *yo* and *seken* were used during the Meiji period with reference to "general" or "common" conditions in the social world; see her *Meiji jidai go no kenkyū*, p. 28.

36. *Seifu* referred quite literally to the council chamber within Edo Castle or the imperial palace in Kyoto; by metaphorical extension, it came to mean the Council of State (who met in the chamber) and in turn the government generally.

37. Mill quite explicit endorsed the equation of humankind's naturally social state with the body politic in *Utilitarianism* (1861); see *Utilitarianism and Other Essays*, ed. Alan Ryan (Harmondsworth: Penguin, 1987), pp. 303–304. Matsuda Kōichirō has argued that Fukuzawa Yukichi too, in the first decade of Meiji, equated government and society on the basis of his reading of Francis Wayland's *Elements of Moral Science* (1836); see "Fukuzawa Yukichi to *kō-shi-bun* no saihakken," pp. 82–83.

38. G. W. F. Hegel, *Elements of the Philosophy of Right*, trans. H. B. Nisbet, ed. Allen W. Wood (Cambridge: Cambridge University Press, 1991), pp. 197–200 and 220–221.

39. Nakamura, *JYNR*, pp. 7–8.

40. See, for example, Michael Lewis, "The Meandering Meaning of Local Autonomy: Bosses, Bureaucrats, and Toyama's Rivers," in *New Directions in the Study of Meiji Japan*, ed. Helen Hardacre, with Adam L. Kern (Leiden: Brill, 1997), pp. 440–450. Mori Kazutsura has noted a precedent for "society" in Kaihō Seiryō's (1755–1817) analysis of the circulation of goods through buying and selling as a mechanism for interdomainal linkages: *Kindai Nihon shisōshi josetsu*, pp. 74–82.

41. Fukuzawa subsequently extended *kōsai* to gender relations (*danjo kōsai*) and parents and children (*oyako kōsai*); see Yanabu Akira, *Hon'yakugo no ronri* (Tokyo: Hōsei Daigaku shuppan kyoku, 1972), pp. 59–60. *Kōsai* also became Fukuzawa's vehicle for grounding morality in the project of civilization: knowledge and virtue grow in tandem through participation in the public world of human interaction (*ningen kōsai*). See *Bunmeiron no gairyaku*, pp. 98–107. Throughout his career, Fukuzawa continued to use both *kōsai* and the standard *shakai* as concepts for society.

42. The earliest discussions that include this terminology are, to my knowledge, the proposals of the Sa'in (Ministry of the Left) in 1872; see *NKKS*, pp. 80–86. See also Iwkura Tomomi, "Seitai kentei, gijiin setchi no kengi," in *NKKS*, pp. 57–60; Ōkubo Toshimichi, "Rikken seitai ni kansuru ikensho," in *NKKS*, p. 106–110; as well as contributors to the *Meiroku zasshi* such as Sakatani Shiroshi and Nishimura Shigeki, *MRZS*, no. 13 (6/1874):5a-9a and no. 28 (2/1875):4b-8a, respectively.

43. Ōkubo Toshimichi," Rikken seitai ni kansuru ikensho," in *NKKS*, pp. 106–110; Kido Takayoshi, "Kenpō seitei no kengi," in *NKKS*, pp. 98–104. An English translation and variant of Kido's proposal was published in the *Japan Weekly Mail*, November 8, 1873, pp. 796–798, and is included in *JGD*, pp. 567–577.

44. This survey is based on a review of the documents reproduced in *NKKS*, pp. 31–216; Itagaki Taisuke, *Jiyūtō shi* (Tokyo: Gosharō, 1910); and *Shinbun shūsei Meiji hennen shi*, ed. Nakayama Yasumasa (1934–1936) (Tokyo: Honpō shoseki, 1982), vols. 2–3. I have also consulted Inada, *Meiji kenpō seiritsu shi,* and Osatake, *Nihon kensei shi taikō*. Examples also exist in *Meiroku zasshi*: Sakatani Shiroshi, "Tenkan chōkō setsu," *MRZS*, no. 38 (8/1875):5–9.

45. "Shosangi rensho no rikken seitai ni kansuru kensō," in *NKKS*, pp. 339–342. This is the famous consensus of opinion to the exclusion of Ōkuma Shigenobu on October 11, 1881; an English translation is available in *Meiji Japan Through Contemporary Sources*, comp. Centre for East Asian Cultural Studies (Tokyo: Centre for East Asian Cultural Studies, 1969–1972), 3:64–69.

46. "Minsen giin setsuritsu no dairongi," in *SSMHS*, 2:117–118; it is also reprinted in *NKKS*, pp. 137–142; for an English translation see *JGD*, pp. 426–432. See also Kido Takayoshi's 1873 justification of constitutionalism in *NKKS*, pp. 101–102.

47. Katō Hiroyuki, "Jiki shōsō to hanpaku," in *SSMHS*, 2:118–120; an abridged version is reprinted in *NKKS*, pp. 145–151; for an English translation see *JGD*, pp. 433–439.

48. "Katō Hiroyuki no shoron ni hakusu," in *SSMHS*, 2:131–133; also reprinted in *NKKS*, pp. 137–142; for an English translation see *JGD*, pp. 426–432. Robert A. Scalapino erroneously attributed the Mill quotations to *On Liberty*; see *Democracy and the Party Movement in Prewar Japan: The Failure of the First Attempt* (Berkeley: University of California Press, 1953), p. 56.

49. See "Risshisha setsuritsu no shuisho," in *NKKS*, pp. 173–177; "A Reactionary Memorial," in *JGD*, pp. 448–457; and "Risshisha kenpakusho," in *NKKS*, pp. 193–216 (translation in *JGD*, pp. 457–480). This point has been developed by Fukuchi Shigetaka, *Shizoku to samurai ishiki* (Tokyo: Shunjūsha, 1956), pp. 111–123.

50. A majority of the Meirokusha too endorsed the oligarchy's gradualist policies and its justification that the people are an inferior group in need of management and tutelage, but several members urged the oligarchy to plan actively for a national assembly. Curiously, they debated the issue in terms of whether or not the government's interests and affairs were identical with those of the people. See Katō Hiroyuki, "Keikoku seifu," *MRZS*, no. 18 (10/1874):2; Nishi Amane, "Mōra giin no setsu," *MRZS,* no. 29 (2/1875):1–3; Nishimura Shigeki, "Shūshin chikoku hi nito ron," *MRZS*, no. 31 (3/1875):3b-6, and "Seifu yo jinmin i rihai ron," *MRZS*, no. 39 (6/1875):4–7a; Sakatani Shiroshi, "Shitsugi issoku," *MRZS*, no. 11 (6/1874):7–9, "Minsen giin o tateru ni wa saki seitai o sadamubeki no gimon," *MRZS*, no. 13

(6/1874):5–9, and "Minsen giin hensokuron," *MRZS*, no. 27 (2/1875):3–8 and no. 28 (2/1875):1–4a; and Tsuda Mamichi, "Seiron no mitsu," *MRZS*, no. 12 (6/1874):3–6. Mitsukuri Rinshō presented the one alternative to the general conclusion that government rightly manages the people: in "Bakkuru-shi no Eikoku kaikashi yori shōyaku," *MRZS*, no. 7 (5/1874):4a-6a, he proposes a mutual dialectic of public opinion and government action in which both contribute to the reform of common interests—in fact, the process that animates the progress of civilization.

51. On the development of Meiji political organizations see Akita, *Foundations*, pp. 15–30; Sandra Davis, *Intellectual Change and Political Development*, pp. 155–191; Itagaki, *Jiyūtō shi*, 1:151–436; and Scalapino, *Democracy and the Party Movement*, pp. 40–73.

52. "Aikokusha saikō shuisho," in *NKKS*, pp. 222–229. Its successor organization, the Kokkai kisei dōmeikai, added that the possibility for unity was being destroyed by the authoritarian policy of the oligarchy: "Kokkai kisei dōmei kiyaku shogen," in *NKKS*, pp. 247–248; Kataoka Kenkichi and Kōnō Hironaka, "Kokkai o kaisetsusuru no inka o jōgansuru sho," in *NKKS*, pp. 249–258.

53. "Aikokusha saikō shuisho," p. 227; Kataoka and Kōnō, "Kokkai o kaisetsusuru no inka o jōgansuru sho," pp. 250 and 257.

54. "Risshisha kenpakusho," pp. 203–204.

55. Miyagi Local Assembly, "Memorial Advocating the Establishment of a National Assembly," in *JGD*, pp. 480–484.

56. The editors of the *Japan Weekly Mail* noted, however, that some activists were still chafing at the delay and strategizing about how to speed up the opening date. In fact, the editors identified two sides: "the rapidly progressive and the gradually progressive"; see October 22, 1881, p. 1238.

57. Kido Takayoshi, "Kempō seitei no kengi," pp. 98–100; "Chihōkan kaigi kaikai no shō," in *NKKS*, pp. 182–183; "Risshisha kenpakusho," pp. 193–197; "Shosangi rensho no rikken seitai ni kansuru kensō," p. 339; and "Kokkai kaisetsu o tsugetamō no chokuyu," in *NKKS*, pp. 343–344, with English translation in *Meiji Japan Through Contemporary Sources*, 3:69–70. For more such uses of recent history see "Kokkai kisei dōmei kiyaku shogen," p. 254; Miyagi Local Assembly, "Memorial," pp. 482–483; and Sakatani, "Tenkan chōkō setsu," p. 6.

58. See Stefan Tanaka, *Japan's Orient*, pp. 20–21 and 181–187; and "Imaging History: Inscribing Belief in the Nation," *Journal of Asian Studies* 53(1) (February 1994):24–44.

59. *Nihon kuni kokken an* (1880–1881), transcribed by Miura Hiroyuki, pp. 418–430.

60. The development of the translation for "nation" *(kokumin)* deserves systematic study. Some oligarchs use the term in its Tokugawa meaning as the "people

of the land"; see Kido Takayoshi, "Rippō-Gyōsei ni kansuru kenpakusho" (1871), in *Meiji shisō shū*, 1:13–19; and see Genrōin, *Kenpō sōkō hyōrin* (1879), in *JJGNY*, pp. 121–146. Although Fukuzawa Yukichi mentions the nation as a point of mediation between the people and the state in his early works *Gakumon no susume* (1874–1876) and *Bunmeiron no gairyaku* (1875), he does so with a range of terms and his interest appears to have dwindled in the following decade. Ueki Emori seems to have contributed most to reinterpreting *kokumin* as "nation" in this mediatory sense in his works *Shogen* (1877), *Minken jiyū ron* (1879), *Genron jiyū ron* (1880), and *Minken jiyū ron—nihen kangō* (1882).

61. "Aikokusha saikō shuisho," p. 226.

62. "Jiyūtō soshiki no shuisho," in *NKKS*, pp. 380–382; "Jiyūtō meiyaku," in *NKKS*, pp. 385–387. See also Itagaki Taisuki, "Jiyūtō soshiki no taii," in *NKKS*, pp. 388–398 (English translation in *JGD*, pp. 605–614); and Ōkuma Shigenobu, "Rikken seitai ni kansuru kengi," in *NKKS*, pp. 318–320.

63. Yamagata Aritomo, "Rikken seitai ni kansuru kengi," in *NKKS*, pp. 269–276. On Yamagata's combining traditional and Western ideas in developing local government see Roger Hackett, *Yamagata Aritomo in the Rise of Modern Japan, 1838–1922* (Cambridge, Mass.: Harvard University Press, 1971), pp. 104–115.

64. [Ono Azusa], "Rikken kaishintō shuisho," in *NKKS*, pp. 403–405; Ono Azusa, "Waga seijijō no shugi" (6/1882), in *Meiji shisō shū*, 1:184–207; and Ōkuma Shigenobu, "Koku waga tōjin sho," in *NKKS*, pp. 406–413; see also Sandra Davis, *Intellectual Change and Political Development*, pp. 165–187.

65. I have treated these developments in "Society Reified: Herbert Spencer and Political Theory in Early Meiji Japan," *Comparative Studies in Society and History* 42(1) (January 2000):67–86.

66. For the background of these discussion societies see Helen Ballhatchet, "Baba Tatsui (1850–1888) and Victorian Britain," in *Britain and Japan, 1859–1991: Themes and Personalities*, ed. Hugh Cortazzi and Gordon Daniels (London: Routledge, 1991), pp. 107–117; Sandra Davis, *Intellectual Change and Political Development*, pp. 49–73; Eugene Soviak, "The Case of Baba Tatsui: Western Enlightenment, Social Change, and the Early Meiji Intellectual," *Monumenta Nipponica* 18 (1963):191–235; and Yamamuro, *Hōsei kanryō no jidai*, pp. 160–169 and 253–264.

67. See Hayashi Emi, "Hōyaku shakai kō," *Tōkyōjōshidaigaku fuzoku hikaku bunka kenkyū kiyō*, no. 21 (6/1966):65–112; Saitō Tsuyoshi, *Meiji no kotoba: higashi kara nishi e no kakehashi* (Tokyo: Kodansha, 1977), pp. 175–228; Satō Masayuki, "'Kojin no shūgōtai toshite no shakai' toiu kangaekata no teichaku ni hatashita shoki shakaika no yakuwari," *Shakaika kyōiku kenkyū*, no. 68 (1993):18–29; Suzuki Shūji, *Bunmei no kotoba*, pp. 69–97; and Yanabu, *Hon'yakugo seiritsu jijō*, pp. 3–22, and *Hon'yaku to wa nani ka?*, rev. ed., pp. 128–163.

68. Fukuchi Gen'ichirō, Mitsukuri Rinshō, and Nishi Amane are repeatedly

cited as originators, but Nakamura Keiu deserves a place on the list for his use of *shakai* in an 1874 explication of social order; see "Seigaku ippan" [cont.], MRZS, no. 16 [9/1874]:6a. For an excellent discussion of Nishi Amane's conceptualization of humankind and society see Nagao Ryūichi, "Nishi Amane ni okeru ningen to shakai," in his *Nihon hō shisōshi kenkyū* (Tokyo: Sōbunsha, 1981), pp. 5–34.

69. Inoue Tetsujirō, *Tetsugaku jii* (Tokyo: Tokyo Daigaku Sangakubu, 1881), pp. 82 and 85; Inoue Tetsujirō and Ariga Nagao, *Tetsugaku jii*, rev. and enlarged ed. (Tokyo: Tokyo Daigaku Sangakubu, 1884), pp. 113 and 118. On the development of *shakai* in Meiji dictionaries see Sōgō and Hida, *Meiji no kotoba jiten*, pp. 207–209. During his subsequent studies in Europe, Inoue visited Spencer in 1888, which he recounts in his diary "Kaichū zakki" (Inoue Tetsujiō Archives, Tōkyō Chūō Library); entry for Meiji 21 [1888].8.14.

70. Some scholars interpret *seitai* as an elitist term in that it connotes the highest—samurai—society in the four divisions of the people; others see it as an inclusive term in that it refers to all people. Yanabu Akira points out that as a relatively new and meaningless term, *shakai* was better able to serve as a translation for the new abstraction, "society," than a received term like *seitai* with its concrete meaning. See Saitō, *Meiji no kotoba*, pp. 181–194 and 220–225; Hayashi, "Hōyaku shakai kō," pp. 79–80 and 108–109; and Yanabu, *Hon'yakugo seiritsu jijō*, pp. 18–21. In 1882, Toyama Shōichi wrote a truly eccentric "new-style poem" on the founding principles of sociology: [Chuzan sennin], "Shakaigaku no genri o daisu," in Toyama Shōichi, Yatabe Ryōkichi, and Inoue Tetsujirō, *Shintaishi shō: shohen* (1882) (Tokyo: Sekai bunko, 1961), pp. 31–34a.

71. See Douglas H. Mendel Jr., "Ozaki Yukio: Political Conscience of Modern Japan," *Far Eastern Quarterly* 15(3) (May 1956):343–356; and Yanagida Izumi, "*Shakai heiken ron* yakusha—Matsushima Kō den," in his *Meiji shoki hon'yaku bungaku no kenkyū* (*Meiji bungaku kenkyū*, vol. 5), rev. ed. (Tokyo: Haruakisha, 1961), pp. 358–370. A useful comparison of an excerpt from Spencer's English and Matsushima's Japanese, in parallel, is available in *Nihon kindai shisō taikei*, vol. 15: *Hon'yaku no shisō*, ed. Katō Shūichi and Maruyama Masao (Tokyo: Iwanami shoten, 1991), pp. 159–183 and 424–427.

72. See J.D.Y. Peel, *Herbert Spencer: The Evolution of a Sociologist* (London: Heinemann, 1971), pp. 185–186. Spencer theorized that individuals enter a social state; this "state of society," elided to simply "the state," produces a constitution that in turn produces the collective identity of "the government." The government is thus a product of social contradictions and will dissolve with the progress of adaptation.

73. Herbert Spencer, *Social Statics: The conditions essential to human happiness specified, and the first of them developed* (1877?) (New York: Schalkenbach Foundation, 1995), p. 69; Ozaki Yukio, trans., *Kenri teikō* (1878), in *Ozaki Gakudō zen-*

shū (Tokyo: Kōronsha, 1956) 1:68; Matsushima Kō, trans., *Shakai heiken ron* (1881–1883), in *JYMKH*, p. 241.

74. Spencer, *Social Statics*, p. 95; Matsushima, *Shakai heiken ron*, p. 258; Ozaki, *Kenri teikō*, p. 88.

75. Peel, *Herbert Spencer*, p. 155.

76. Spencer, *Social Statics*, pp. 161–168 and 312–315; Matsushima, *Shakai heiken ron*, pp. 302–306; Ozaki, *Kenri teikō*, pp. 116–122.

77. Ueki Emori, "Hinmin ron," in *Ueki Emori senshū*, ed. Ienaga Saburō (Tokyo: Iwanami shoten, 1974), p. 123; Ike, *Beginnings of Political Democracy*, p. 135. Ueki reconceived civil liberties as "social liberties" (*shakai no jiyū*) in *Minken jiyū ron— nihen kangō*, p. 133.

78. "Aikokusha saikō shuisho," p. 224.

79. Spencer, *Social Statics*, pp. 185, 228, 241–242. Sakamoto Naohiro (Namio) made the same argument about the limits of government in "Honron" (On Fundamentals), quoted in Yamashita Shigekazu, *Supensā to Nihon kindai* (Tokyo: Ochanomizu shobō, 1983), pp. 90–93.

80. Spencer, *Social Statics*, pp. 170–171; Matsushima, *Shakai heiken ron*, p. 308; Ozaki, *Kenri teikō*, pp. 129–130.

81. Ueki, "Hinmin ron," pp. 122–123 and 142–146.

82. Ueki Emori, "Danjo no dōken," in *Ueki Emori senshū*, pp. 169–171 and 184–185. At several points in the essay Ueki borrows the language of Ozaki Yukio's translation of *Social Statics*; compare pp. 152, 158–159, and Ozaki, *Kenri teikō*, pp. 68 and 94–95. See also Bowen, *Rebellion and Democracy*, pp. 197–212.

83. Bowen, *Rebellion and Democracy*, pp. 224–226; Irokawa Daikichi, *Meiji seishin shi*, rev. ed. (Tokyo: Chūōkōronsha, 1973), pp. 17, 39–40, 313. Spencer's presentation of rights in *Social Statics* also served as a model for Fukumoto Nichinan's explication of people's rights in *Futsū minken ron*, pp. 197–212.

84. On the elements of Spencer's theory of evolution see Peel, *Herbert Spencer*, p. 101. The first discussion in Japan of Spencer on evolution, to my knowledge, was a set of excerpts with editorial commentary in the *Japan Weekly Mail*, September 20, 1873, pp. 664–666. Darwin's theory of evolution was introduced by Aoikawa Nobuchika in 1874, and visiting naturalist Edward S. Morse gave a popular series of lectures on Darwin in autumn 1877; see Robert S. Schwantes, "Christianity versus Science: A Conflict of Ideas in Meiji Japan," *Far Eastern Quarterly* 12(2) (February 1953):123–132; Masao Watanabe, *The Japanese and Western Science*, trans. Otto Theodor Benfey (Philadelphia: University of Pennsylvania Press, 1988), pp. 66–83; and Shimoide, *Meiji shakai shisō kenkyū*, pp. 92–96. On the introduction of Spencer's theory of evolution to Japan see Ōkubo Toshiaki, *Meiji no shisō to bunka*, pp. 53, 205, 210; and see Nagai Michio, "Supensā-shugi no ryūkō," in his *Kindaika to kyōiku* (Tokyo: Tokyo Daigaku shuppanbu, 1969), pp. 152–172.

Several scholarly articles on evolution appeared in 1882–1883: see Matsushita Jōkichi, "Jinrui no kigen," *TYGGZS*, no. 8 (1882.5.25):155–158 and no. 9 (1882.6.25):179–183; and Ariga Nagao, "Shakai to ikkojin to no kankei no shinka," *TYGGZS*, no. 19 (1883.4.25):500–509.

85. Katō Hiroyuki, *Jinken shinsetsu*, pp. 372–378. See also Abosch, "Katō Hiroyuki," pp. 430–447, and Yamamuro, *Hōsei kanryō no jidai*, pp. 128–135.

86. Tokutomi Sohō, *Shōrai no Nihon*, in *Tokutomi Sohō shū*, ed. Uete Michiari (Tokyo: Chikuma shobō, 1974), pp. 51–54, 63, 67–73.

87. Ibid., pp. 81–82 and 88–89; see also Irokawa, *Meiji seishin shi*, pp. 401–402 and 414–419; Matsumoto, *Meiji seishin no kōzō*, pp. 101–118; Sakamoto, *Shijō-dōtoku-chitsujo*, pp. 43–92; and Vinh Sinh, "Introduction," in Tokutomi Sohō, *The Future Japan*, trans. and ed. Vinh Sinh (Edmonton: University of Alberta Press, 1989), pp. xiii–xxxviii.

88. See Fukuzawa Yukichi, *Gakumon no susume*, p. 131; see also *Encouragement of Learning*, p. 74.

89. Katō, *Jinken shinsetsu*, pp. 380–382.

90. Heruberuto Supensā [Herbert Spencer], "Fujo no kenri," trans. Sakaguchi Sakichi, *Gakugei shirin*, vol. 5 (11/1879):340–354 and (12/1879):451–468; see pp. 351 and 455–457. Sakaguchi's essay is based on (but is by no means an exacting translation of) "The Status of Women" from Spencer's *Principles of Sociology*, vol. 1., pt. 3, chap. 10.

91. Katō, *Jinken shinsetsu*, p. 374; Tokutomi, *Shōrai no Nihon*, pp. 105–108. See also the responses to Katō, discussed in Chapter 5, which foreground society as the site of all human activity: Tokyo-Yokohama mainichi shinbun, "*Jinken shinsetsu o hyōsu*" (1882), in *JYMKH*, pp. 410–427; and Baba Tatsui, *Tenpu jinken ron* (1883), in *JYMKH*, pp. 439–461.

92. Spencer, *Social Statics*, pp. 107 and 111; Matsushima, *Shakai heiken ron*, pp. 267 and 270; Ozaki, *Kenri teikō*, pp. 142 and 146.

93. Katō, *Jinken shinsetsu*, p. 357. J. D. Y. Peel, incidentally, notes that Spencer's title *Social Statics* was deliberately chosen in opposition to "social science," which, at the time, had "distinctively Owenite or Saint-Simonian overtones"; *Herbert Spencer*, pp. 82–83. This latter scientific use of Spencer and evolution for liberal ends is clear in Baba Tatsui, "Shinka bunri no niryoku" (1879), in *Meiji shisō shū*, 1:232–236.

94. On the development of both sociology and statistics in Japan see Shimoide, *Meiji shakai shisō kenkyū*, pp. 50–79 and 111–153.

95. Ueki, "Hinmin ron," pp. 115–113, 125, 130–134.

96. On the beginnings of socialism in Japan see Matsumoto, *Kindai Nihon no chiteki jokyō*, pp. 159–184; Ōkubo Toshiaki, *Meiji no shisō to bunka*, pp. 27–37; and Shimoide, *Meiji shakai shisō kenkyū*, pp. 97–110.

97. Yokoyama Gennosuke, *Nihon no kasō shakai* (1899), in *Yokoyama Genno-suke zenshū*, vol. 1 (Tokyo: Meiji bunken, 1972); Gluck, *Japan's Modern Myths*, pp. 26–29. For a collection of newspaper articles see *Meiji bunka zenshū*, 3rd ed., vol. 6: *Shakai hen* (Tokyo: Nihon hyōronsha, 1968), pp. 397–571.

98. [Ōi Kentarō], "Rikken jiyūtō no shuisho," in *NKKS*, pp. 381–382

7. Conclusion

1. Talal Asad, "Anthropology and the Analysis of Ideology," *Man* (n.s.) 14 (1979):607–627; see also Ernst Gellner, "Concepts and Society," in *Rationality*, ed. Bryan R. Wilson (Oxford: Blackwell, 1979), pp. 18–49.

2. William E. Connolly, *The Terms of Political Discourse*, 2nd ed. (Princeton: Princeton University Press, 1983), pp. 10–44.

3. See, for example, the excellent collection *Political Innovation and Concep-tual Change*, ed. Terence Ball, James Farr, and Russell L. Hanson (Cambridge: Cambridge University Press, 1989).

4. See John Dunn, "Practising History and Social Science on 'Realist' Assump-tions," in his *Political Obligation in Its Historical Context: Essays in Political The-ory* (Cambridge: Cambridge University Press, 1980), pp. 81–111.

5. Frank O. Miller, *Minobe Tatsukichi: Interpreter of Constitutionalism in Japan* (Berkeley: University of California Press, 1965); Richard H. Minear, *Japanese Tradition and Western Law: Emperor, State, and Law in the Thought of Hozumi Yatsuka* (Cambridge, Mass.: Harvard University Press, 1970); Tetsuo Najita, "Some Reflections on Idealism in the Political Thought of Yoshino Sakuzō," in *Japan in Crisis: Essays on Taishō Democracy*, ed. Bernard S. Silberman and H. D. Harootunian (Princeton: Princeton University Press, 1974), pp. 29–66; and *Taishō demokurashī: kusanone to tennōsei no hazama*, ed. Imai Seiichi (Tokyo: Shakai hyōronsha, 1990).

6. Mark E. Lincicome, "Local Citizens or Loyal Subjects? Enlightenment Dis-course and Educational Reform," in *New Directions in the Study of Meiji Japan*, ed. Helen Hardacre with Adam L. Kern (Leiden: Brill, 1997), pp. 450–465.

7. See IshidaTakeshi, *Nihon no seiji to kotoba*, vol. 2: *Heiwa to kokka* (Tokyo: Tokyo Daigaku shuppankai, 1989), pp. 153–183; and Atsuko Hirai, "The State and Ideology in Meiji Japan—A Review Article," *Journal of Asian Studies* 46(1) (Feb-ruary 1987):89–103.

8. Henry Wheaton, *Elements of International Law*, 2nd ann. ed., by William Beach Lawrence (Boston: Little, Brown, 1863), pp. 31–32.

9. Ibid., pp. iii–iv and 33, n. 13. See also the work of his contemporary, Ernest Renan, "What Is a Nation?," trans. Martin Thom, in *Nation and Narration*, ed. Homi K. Bhabha (London: Routledge, 1990), pp. 8–22.

10. Hiroshi Mitani has recently argued that several features of the modern

state—territory, an imagined community, a national identity—predate the Meiji period; see "A Protonation-State and Its 'Unforgettable Other'—The Prerequisites for Meiji International Relations," in *New Directions in the Study of Meiji Japan*, pp. 293–310. On the development of the Japanese state see Yoda, *Foundations of Japan's Modernization*, pp. 70–105.

11. Matsumoto, *Meiji seishin no kōzō*, p. 66. See also Ueki, "Jinmin no kokka ni taisuru seishin o ronzu," pp. 169–178; and Matsuda, "Fukuzawa Yukichi to *kō-shi-bun* no saihakken," pp. 87–101.

12. Ochiai, "Meiji zenki no rikugun kashi to jiyūminken."

13. Matsumoto, *Meiji seishin no kōzō*, pp. 21–24.

14. Yamamuro Shin'ichi, *Kindai Nihon no chi to seiji*, pp. 147–159. See also his recent restatement emphasizing national and colonial territory, "Form and Function of the Meiji State in Modern East Asia," *Zinbun*, no. 34 (1999):179–196.

15. Where Yamamuro and other Japanese scholars have recently turned to analyze Japanese state formation in terms of differences between English, French, and German models, my work here would mitigate against such a differentiation since translation and the creation of new concepts tend to synthesize these national sources of linguistic material. See Yamamuro, *Hōsei kanryō no jidai*; Banno, *Kindai Nihon no kokka kōsō*; and Tanaka Hiroshi, *Kindai Nihon to "riberarizumu."*

16. Tanaka Hiroshi, *Kindai Nihon to "riberarizumu,"* p. 13. See also Rikki Kirsten's discussion of Maruyama Masao's interpretation of the modern development of Japanese politics as the domestic pursuit of autonomy, *Democracy in Postwar Japan*.

17. Kevin M. Doak, "What Is a Nation and Who Belongs? National Narratives and the Ethnic Imagination in Twentieth-Century Japan," *American Historical Review* 102(2) (April 1997):283–309; and "Culture, Ethnicity, and the State in Early Twentieth-Century Japan," in *Japan's Competing Modernities: Issues in Culture and Democracy, 1900–1930*, ed. Sharon A. Minichiello (Honolulu: University of Hawai'i Press, 1998), pp. 181–205.

18. Carol Gluck, "'Meiji' for Our Time," in *New Directions in the Study of Meiji Japan*, p. 17. See also the introductory comments by Helen Hardacre, Irokawa Daikichi, and Marius Jansen, ibid., pp. xiii–10.

19. See especially Sakamoto Takao's discussion of Nakae Chōmin on social contract and civil society, in *Shijō-dōtoku-chitsujo*, pp. 93–123.

20. See especially Lincicome, *Principle, Praxis, and Politics;* Ronald P. Dore, *Education in Tokugawa Japan* (Berkeley: University of California Press, 1965), pp. 291–316; Ōkubo Toshiaki, *Meiji no shisō to bunka*, pp. 43–62; and Herbert Passin, *Society and Education in Japan* (New York: Columbia University Press, 1965), pp. 76–78.

Glossary of Translation Words

ateji 宛字

bankoku kōhō 萬國公法

bun 分

bunka 文化

bunmei 文明

bunmeikaika 文明開化

bunmei no seiji 文明ノ政治

chiken 治權

daikaku 大覺

daitōryō 大統領

dōbō 同胞

dōken 同權

doku 獨

dokuritsu 獨立

ekifu-shokunin 役夫職人

fuki 不羈

fuki dokuritsu 不羈獨立

gaikoku kōsai 外國交際

gasshū dokuritsu 合衆獨立

gasshūkoku 合衆國

gasshūkoku no dokuritsu 合衆國ノ
獨立

gimu 義務

hanken 版權

heimin 平民

hitobito 人人

hito no kenri 人ノ權利

hō 法

ikkoku no shuken 一國ノ主權

isei no saijōken 為政ノ最上權

ji 自

jinken 人權

jinmin 人民

jinmin kenri 人民權利

jinrin 人倫

jinrui 人類

249

jinrui no kenri 人類ノ權利	kenri (right-and-privilege) 權利
jiritsu jishu no ken 自立自主ノ權	kenri (right-and-principle) 權理
jishu 自主	kenryoku 權力
jishujiyū 自主自由	kensei 權勢
jishu nin'i 自主任意	kō 公
jishu no ken 自主ノ權	kōgi 公義
jiyū 自由	kōhō 公法
jiyū hatsuron 自由發論	kōjin 工人
jiyūjizai 自由自在	kōken (public rights) 公權
jiyū no seishin 自由ノ精神	kokkai 國會
jiyū no shugi 自由ノ主義	kokken 國權
jizai 自在	kokujin 國人
jōge 上下	kokumin (kuni no tami) 國民
kaidō 會同	kokuyaku kenpō 國約憲法
kaika 開化	kōsai 交際
kaikabunmei 開化文明	kōshū 公衆
kaimei 開明	kumiai 組合
kaisha 會社	kuni (koku) 國 or 邦
kaisho 會所	kunken 君權
kamin (shimo no tami) 下民	kunshu 君主
kanken 官權	kunshukoku 君主國
karyū (shimo no nagare) 下流	kunshu no ken 君主ノ權
katte 勝手	kyōdai 兄弟
keimō 啓蒙	maisha maikai 每社每會
ken 權	mibun 身分
kengen 權限	minkai 民會
kengi 權義	minken 民權
ken'i 權威	minkensei 民權政
kenpei 權柄	minshū 民衆

minshukoku 民主國

minyaku kenpō 民約憲法

nakama 仲間

nakama-kaisha 仲間會社

ningen 人間

nin'i 任意

nō-kō-shō 農工商

ōyake 公

renchū 連中

saisei itto 祭政一道

san dai ken 三大權

sanmin 三民

sansei kenri 參政權利

seifu 政府

seihō 性法

seiji 政治

seiji shakai 政治社會

seiken 政權

seikyō itchi 政敎一致

seiri 性理

seiryoku 勢力

seitai 政體

seiyōka 西洋化

sejin (yo no hito) 世人

sejō 世上

sekai 世界

seken 世間

shakai 社會

shakaigaku 社會學

shakai heiken 社會平權

shakai mondai 社會問題

shakai no chitsujo 社會ノ秩序

shakai no itchi 社會ノ一致

shakai no kōeki 社會ノ公益

shakai o ijisu 社會ヲ維持ス

shakai o kōkisu 社會ヲ綱紀ス

shakai shinpo 社會進步

shakaishugi 社會主義

shakaitō 社會黨

shashin 寫真

shiken 私權

shimin (burgess/citizen) 市民

shimin (the four divisions of the
    people) 四民

shimin (samurai and common
    people) 士民

shimin kaidō 市民會同

shin 信

shizen 自然

shizen tōta hō 自然淘汰法

shizoku 士族

shoku 職

shokubun 職分

shōmin 商民

shōnin 商人

shōsha 商社

shū (all/the many) 衆

shūjin shūkai 衆人集會

shuken 主權

shukensha 主權者

shūmin 衆民

shuppan jiyū 出版自由

sōtai 總體

suberēnitēto no ken スベレーニテ
ートノ權

tami 民

tennen 天然

tennen no jinken 天然ノ人權

tenpu no jinken 天賦ノ人權

tetsudō 鐵道

tokken 特權

tokuyū kenri 得有權利

tsūgi 通義

tsūken 通權

tsukiai 交際

wagahai jinmin 我輩人民

waga jinmin 我人民

wagamama 我儘

waga tami 我民

yo 世

yōgaku 洋學

yong (J: yō) 用

yo no bunmeikaika 世ノ文明開化

yo no naka 世ノ中

zen kokka no ken 全國家ノ權

Bibliography

Abe Yoshiya. "From Prohibition to Toleration: Japanese Government Views Regarding Christianity, 1854–73." *Japanese Journal of Religious Studies* 5(2–3) (1978):107–138.

Abosch, David. "Katō Hiroyuki and the Introduction of German Political Thought: 1868–1883." Ph.D. dissertation, University of California, 1964.

Akita, George. *Foundations of Constitutional Government in Modern Japan, 1868–1900.* Cambridge, Mass.: Harvard University Press, 1967.

Altman, Albert A. "*Shimbunshi*: The Early Meiji Adaptation of the Western-Style Newspaper." In *Modern Japan*, ed. W. G. Beasley, 52–66. London: Allen & Unwin, 1975.

Andō Katsudō. "Jiyū no heigai o ronzu." *Dōjinsha bungaku zasshi*, no. 19 (1877.12.5):2.

Apter, David E. *The Politics of Modernization.* Chicago: University of Chicago Press, 1965.

Arendt, Hannah. *Between Past and Future.* Enlarged ed. New York: Viking, 1968.

Ariga, Chieko. "The Playful Gloss: *Rubi* in Japanese Literature." *Monumenta Nipponica* 44(3) (Autumn 1989):309–335.

Ariga Nagao. "Shina no kaimei to seiyō no kaimei to no sabetsu." *Gakugei shirin,* vol. 12 (4/1883):356–378.

Arnason, Johann P. *Social Theory and Japanese Experience: The Dual Civilization.* London: Kegan Paul International, 1997.

Aruga, Tadashi. "The Declaration of Independence in Japan: Translation and Transplantation, 1854–1997." *Journal of American History* 85(4) (March 1999):1409–1431.

Asad, Talal. "Anthropology and the Analysis of Ideology." *Man* (n.s.) 14 (1979):607–627.

Asai Kiyoshi. "Nihon ni okeru shimin seishin no seiritsu: Meiji shoki bungaku ni okeru 'jiyū' no juyō." *Shisō*, no. 504 (1966):61–71.

Asao Naohiro. "Kinsei no mibun to sono hen'yō." In *Mibun to kakushiki*, ed. Asao Naohiro, 7–40. Tokyo: Chūōkōronsha, 1992.

Aso Yoshiteru. *Kinsei Nihon tetsugaku shi*. Tokyo: Kondō shoten, 1942.

Asukai Masamichi. *Bunmeikaika*. Tokyo: Iwanami shoten, 1985.

Ateji gairaigo jiten henshū iinkai, ed. *Ateji gairaigo jiten*. Tokyo: Kashiwa shobō, 1979.

Austin, John. *The Province of Jurisprudence Determined* (1832). Edited by W. E. Rumble. Cambridge: Cambridge University Press, 1995.

Baba Tatsui. "Doku Katō Hiroyuki no kun *Jinken shinsetsu*." In *Meiji shisō shū*, ed. Matsumoto Sannosuke, 1:208–231. Tokyo: Chikuma shobō, 1976.

———. *Tenpu jinken ron*. In *Meiji bunka zenshū*, vol. 5: *Jiyū minken hen*, 439–461. Tokyo: Nihon hyōronsha, 1927.

Bailey, Jackson H. "Prince Saionji and the Popular Rights Movement." *Journal of Asian Studies* 21(1) (November 1961):49–63.

Baker, Keith Michael. "Enlightenment and the Institution of Society: Notes for a Conceptual History." In *Main Trends in Cultural History: Ten Essays*, ed. Willem Melching and Wyger Velema, 95–120. Amsterdam: Rodopi, 1994.

Ball, Terence, and J.G.A. Pocock, eds. *Conceptual Change and the Constitution*. Lawrence: University Press of Kansas, 1988.

Ball, Terence, James Farr, and Russell L. Hanson, eds. *Political Innovation and Conceptual Change*. Cambridge: Cambridge University Press, 1989.

Ballhatchet, Helen. "Baba Tatsui (1850–1888) and Victorian Britain." In *Britain and Japan, 1859–1991: Themes and Personalities*, ed. Hugh Cortazzi and Gordon Daniels, 107–117. London: Routledge, 1991.

Banno Junji. *Kindai Nihon no kokka kōsō, 1871–1936*. Tokyo: Iwanami shoten, 1996.

Bassnett-McGuire, Susan. *Translation Studies*. London: Methuen, 1980.

Beasley, W. G. *Japan Encounters the Barbarian: Japanese Travellers in America and Europe*. New Haven: Yale University Press, 1995.

———. *Japanese Imperialism, 1894–1945*. Oxford: Clarendon, 1987.

———. *The Meiji Restoration*. Stanford: Stanford University Press, 1972.

Beckmann, George M. *The Making of the Meiji Constitution: The Oligarchs and the Constitutional Development of Japan, 1868–1891*. Lawrence: University of Kansas Press, 1957.

———. "Political Crises and the Crystallization of Japanese Constitutional Thought, 1871–1881." *Pacific Historical Review* 23(3) (August 1954):259–270.

Bellah, Robert N. *Tokugawa Religion: The Values of Pre-Industrial Japan*. Boston: Beacon, 1970.

Benveniste, Emile. *Problems in General Linguistics.* Translated by Mary Elizabeth Meek. Coral Gables: University of Miami Press, 1971.

Berlin, Isaiah. "Two Concepts of Liberty." In *Four Essays on Liberty*, 118–172. Oxford: Oxford University Press, 1969.

Berry, Mary Elizabeth. "Public Peace and Private Attachment: The Goals and Conduct of Power in Early Modern Japan." *Journal of Japanese Studies* 12(2) (1986):237–271.

Bird, Isabella. *Unbeaten Tracks in Japan* (1880). Boston: Beacon, 1987.

Blacker, Carmen. *The Japanese Enlightenment: A Study of the Writings of Fukuzawa Yukichi.* Cambridge: Cambridge University Press, 1964.

Bloom, Alfred H. *The Linguistic Shaping of Thought: A Study in the Impact of Language on Thinking in China and the West.* Hillsdale, N.J.: Lawrence Erlbaum, 1981.

Bouwsma, William J. "Intellectual History in the 1980s." *Journal of Interdisciplinary History* 12(2) (Autumn 1981):279–291.

Bowen, Roger W. *Rebellion and Democracy in Meiji Japan: A Study of Commoners in the Popular Rights Movement.* Berkeley: University of California Press, 1980.

Brower, Reuben A., ed. *On Translation.* Cambridge, Mass.: Harvard University Press, 1959.

Burchell, Graham, Colin Gordon, and Peter Miller, eds. *The Foucault Effect: Studies in Governmentality.* Chicago: University of Chicago Press, 1991.

Burkman, Thomas W. "The Urakami Incidents and the Struggle for Religious Toleration in Early Meiji Japan." *Japanese Journal of Religious Studies* 1(2–3) (1974):143–216.

Butter, Irene Hasenberg. *Academic Economics in Holland, 1800–1870.* The Hague: M. Nijhoff, 1969.

Buxton, William. *Talcott Parsons and the Capitalist Nation-State: Political Sociology as a Strategic Vocation.* Toronto: University of Toronto Press, 1985.

Bynon, Theodora. *Historical Linguistics.* Cambridge: Cambridge University Press, 1977.

Centre for East Asian Cultural Studies, comp. *Meiji Japan Through Contemporary Sources.* 3 vols. Tokyo: Centre for East Asian Cultural Studies, 1969–1972.

Chakrabarty, Dipesh. "Afterword: Revisiting the Tradition/Modernity Binary." In *Mirror of Modernity: Invented Traditions of Modern Japan*, ed. Stephen Vlastos, 285–296. Berkeley: University of California Press, 1998.

Chamberlain, B. F. "Shinago dokuhō no kairyō o nozomu." *Tōyō gakugei zasshi*, no. 61 (10/1886):19–21.

Chen, Ping. *Modern Chinese: History and Sociolinguistics.* Cambridge: Cambridge University Press, 1999.

Connolly, William E. *The Terms of Political Discourse*. 2nd ed. Princeton: Princeton University Press, 1983.

Constant, Benjamin. *Political Writings*. Edited by Biancamaria Fontana. Cambridge: Cambridge University Press, 1988.

Conze, Werner. "Freiheit." In *Geschichtliche Grundbegriffe: Historisches Lexicon zur politisch-sozialer Sprache in Deutschland*, ed. Otto Brunner, Werner Conze, and Reinhart Koselleck, 2:425–542. Stuttgart: Klett, 1972–1989.

Craig, Albert M. "Fukuzawa Yukichi: The Philosophical Foundations of Meiji Nationalism." In *Political Development in Modern Japan*, ed. Robert E. Ward, 99–148. Princeton: Princeton University Press, 1968.

Davis, Sandra T. W. *Intellectual Change and Political Development in Early Modern Japan: Ono Azusa, a Case Study*. Rutherford: Fairleigh Dickinson University Press, 1980.

———. "Treaty Revision, National Security, and Regional Cooperation: A *Mintō* Viewpoint." In *Japan in Transition: Thought and Action in the Meiji Era, 1868–1912*, ed. Hilary Conroy, Sandra T. W. Davis, and Wayne Patterson, 151–173. Rutherford: Fairleigh Dickinson University Press, 1984.

Dening, Walter. "The Gakushikaiin." *Transactions of the Asiatic Society of Japan*, ser. 1, vol. 15 (1887):58–82.

Doak, Kevin M. "Culture, Ethnicity, and the State in Early Twentieth-Century Japan." In *Japan's Competing Modernities: Issues in Culture and Democracy, 1900–1930*, ed. Sharon A. Minichiello, 181–205. Honolulu: University of Hawai'i Press, 1998.

———. "What Is a Nation and Who Belongs? National Narratives and the Ethnic Imagination in Twentieth-Century Japan." *American Historical Review* 102(2) (April 1997):283–309.

Dore, Ronald P. *Education in Tokugawa Japan*. Berkeley: University of California Press, 1965.

Ducrot, Oswald, and Tzvetan Todorov. *Encyclopedic Dictionary of the Sciences of Language*. Translated by Catherine Porter. Oxford: Blackwell, 1981.

Dunn, John. "The Identity of the History of Ideas." *Philosophy* 43(164) (April 1968):85–104.

———. "Practising History and Social Science on 'Realist' Assumptions." In *Political Obligation in Its Historical Context: Essays in Political Theory*, 81–111. Cambridge: Cambridge University Press, 1980.

Eisenstadt, S. N. *Japanese Civilization: A Comparative View*. Chicago: University of Chicago Press, 1996.

———. "Modernisation: Growth & Diversity." *India Quarterly* 20 (January–March 1964):17–42.

Elias, Norbert. *The Civilizing Process: The History of Manners and State Forma-*

tion and Civilization. Translated by Edmund Jephcott. Oxford: Blackwell, 1994.

Endō Takeshi. "Bakumatsu yu'nyū no Ran-Ei hōritsusho." *Rangaku shiryō kenkyūkai kenkyū hōkoku*, no. 23 (1958.1.18):3–11.

Ferguson, Adam. *An Essay on the History of Civil Society.* Edited by Fania Oz-Salzberger. Cambridge: Cambridge University Press, 1995.

Figdor, Peter. "Newspapers and Their Regulation in Early Meiji Japan." *Papers on Japan* (East Asian Research Center, Harvard University) 6 (1972):1–44.

Foucault, Michel. "History of Systems of Thought, 1979." *Philosophy and Social Criticism* 8(3) (Fall 1981):353–359.

Fukaya Hakuji. [*Shintei*] *Ka-shizoku chitsuroku shobun no kenkyū.* 2nd ed. Tokyo: Yoshikawa kōbunkan, 1973.

Fukaya Katsumi. "Kinseishi kenkyū to mibun." *Rekishi hyōron*, no. 369 (1/1981): 49–54.

"Fukkoku hōritsusho hon'yaku." In *Meiji seifu hon'yaku sōkō ruisan*, vol. 32:3–43. Tokyo: Yumani shobō, 1987.

Fukuchi Shigetaka. *Shizoku to samurai ishiki.* Tokyo: Shunjūsha, 1956.

Fukumoto Nichinan. *Futsū minken ron* (1879). In *Meiji bunka zenshū*, vol. 5: *Jiyū minken hen*, 197–212. Tokyo: Nihon hyōronsha, 1927.

Fukuzawa Yukichi. *The Autobiography of Fukuzawa Yukichi.* Translated by Eiichi Kiyooka. Tokyo: Hokuseido, 1981.

———. *Bunken ron.* In *Fukuzawa Yukichi senshū*, ed. Tomita Masafumi, vol. 5:5–86. Tokyo: Iwanami shoten, 1980–1981.

———. *Bunmei ron no gairyaku.* In *Fukuzawa Yukichi senshū*, ed. Tomita Masafumi, vol. 4:5–254. Tokyo: Iwanami shoten, 1980–1981.

———. *An Encouragement of Learning.* Translated by David A. Dilworth and Umeyo Hirano. Tokyo: Sophia University, 1969.

———. *Gakumon no susume.* In *Fukuzawa Yukichi senshū*, ed. Tomita Masafumi, vol. 3:53–176. Tokyo: Iwanami shoten, 1980–1981.

———. *Hanbatsu kajin seifu ron.* In *Fukuzawa Yukichi senshū*, ed. Tomita Masafumi, vol. 6:71–131. Tokyo: Iwanami shoten, 1980–1981.

———. *Jiji shogen.* In *Fukuzawa Yukichi senshū*, ed. Tomita Masafumi, vol. 5:155–314. Tokyo: Iwanami shoten, 1980–1981.

———. *Jiji taisei ron.* In *Fukuzawa Yukichi senshū*, ed. Tomita Masafumi, vol. 6:5–29. Tokyo: Iwanami shoten, 1980–1981.

———. *Kokkai ron.* In *Fukuzawa Yukichi senshū*, ed. Tomita Masafumi, vol. 5:119–154. Tokyo: Iwanami shoten, 1980–1981.

———. "Nannyo dōsū ron." *Meiroku zasshi*, no. 31 (3/1875):8–9.

———. *An Outline of a Theory of Civilization.* Translated by David A. Dilworth and G. Cameron Hurst. Tokyo: Sophia University, 1973.

————. *Seiyō jijō*. In *Fukuzawa Yukichi zenshū*, ed. Tomita Masafumi, vol. 1:275–608. Tokyo: Iwanami shoten, 1958.

————. *Sonnō ron*. In *Fukuzawa Yukichi senshū*, ed. Tomita Masafumi, vol. 6:133–164. Tokyo: Iwanami shoten, 1980–1981.

————. *Teishitsu ron*. In *Fukuzawa Yukichi senshū*, ed. Tomita Masafumi, vol. 6:31–70. Tokyo: Iwanami shoten, 1980–1981.

————. *Tsūzoku kokken ron*. In *Fukuzawa Yukichi senshū*, ed. Tomita Masafumi, vol. 7:17–66. Tokyo: Iwanami shoten, 1980–1981.

————. *Tsūzoku minken ron*. In *Fukuzawa Yukichi senshū*, ed. Tomita Masafumi, vol. 5:87–117. Tokyo: Iwanami shoten, 1980–1981.

Furuta Tōsaku. "*Chikan keimō* to *Keimō chie no kan*." In *Kindaigo kenkyū*, ed. Kindaigo gakkai, vol. 2:549–578. Tokyo: Musashino shoin, 1968.

Garon, Sheldon. "Rethinking Modernization and Modernity in Japanese History: A Focus on State-Society Relations." *Journal of Asian Studies* 53(2) (May 1994):346–366.

Gellner, Ernst. "Concepts and Society." In *Rationality*, ed. Bryan R. Wilson, 18–49. Oxford: Blackwell, 1979.

Gluck, Carol. *Japan's Modern Myths: Ideology in the Late Meiji Period*. Princeton: Princeton University Press, 1985.

————. "'Meiji' for Our Time." In *New Directions in the Study of Meiji Japan*, ed. Helen Hardacre, with Adam L. Kern, 11–28. Leiden: Brill, 1997.

Goodman, Grant K. *Japan: The Dutch Experience*. London: Athlone, 1986.

Gottlieb, Nanette. *Kanji Politics: Language Policy and Japanese Script*. London: Kegan Paul International, 1995.

Habein, Yaeko Sato. *The History of the Japanese Written Language*. Tokyo: University of Tokyo Press, 1984.

Hackett, Roger. *Yamagata Aritomo in the Rise of Modern Japan, 1838–1922*. Cambridge, Mass.: Harvard University Press, 1971.

Hall, Francis. *Japan Through American Eyes: The Journal of Francis Hall, Kanagawa and Yokohama, 1859–1866*. Edited by F. G. Notehelfer. Princeton: Princeton University Press, 1992.

Hall, Ivan Parker. *Mori Arinori*. Cambridge, Mass.: Harvard University Press, 1973.

Hall, John Whitney. "Changing Conceptions of the Modernization of Japan." In *Changing Japanese Attitudes Toward Modernization*, ed. Marius B. Jansen, 7–41. Princeton: Princeton University Press, 1965.

Halliday, Jon. *A Political History of Japanese Capitalism*. New York: Pantheon, 1975.

Hampsher-Monk, Iain, Karin Tilmans, and Frank van Vree, eds. *History of Concepts: Comparative Perspectives*. Amsterdam: Amsterdam University Press, 1998.

Hane, Mikiso. "Early Meiji Liberalism: An Assessment." *Monumenta Nipponica* 24(4) (1969):353–371.

———. "Fukuzawa Yukichi and Women's Rights." In *Japan in Transition: Thought and Action in the Meiji Era, 1868–1912*, ed. Hilary Conroy, Sandra T. W. Davis, and Wayne Patterson, 96–112. Rutherford: Fairleigh Dickinson University Press, 1984.

———. "Nationalism and the Decline of Liberalism in Meiji Japan." *Studies on Asia*, no. 4 (1963):69–80.

———. "Sources of English Liberal Concepts in Early Meiji Japan." *Monumenta Nipponica* 24(3) (1969):259–272.

Hanes, Jeffrey E. "Contesting Centralization? Space, Time, and Hegemony in Meiji Japan." In *New Directions in the Study of Meiji Japan*, ed. Helen Hardacre, with Adam L. Kern, 485–495. Leiden: Brill, 1997.

Hanks, William F. *Language and Communicative Practices*. Boulder: Westview, 1996.

Hanley, Susan B. *Everyday Things in Premodern Japan: The Hidden Legacy of Material Culture*. Berkeley: University of California Press, 1997.

Hardacre, Helen, with Adam L. Kern, eds. *New Directions in the Study of Meiji Japan*. Leiden: Brill, 1997.

Harootunian, H. D. "The Functions of China in Tokugawa Thought." In *The Chinese and the Japanese: Essays in Political and Cultural Interactions*, ed. Akira Iriye, 9–36. Princeton: Princeton University Press, 1980.

———. *Things Seen and Unseen: Discourse and Ideology in Tokugawa Nativism*. Chicago: University of Chicago Press, 1988.

———. *Toward Restoration: The Growth of Political Consciousness in Tokugawa Japan*. Berkeley: University of California Press, 1970.

Hashizume Kan'ichi. *Chie keimō zukai*. Tokyo: Hōshūdō, [1872].

Hasunuma Keisuke. *Nishi Amane ni okeru tetsugaku no seiritsu*. Tokyo: Yūhikaku, 1987.

Hattori Shisō. "Bunmeikaika." In *Meiji keimō shisō shū*, ed. Ōkubo Toshiaki, 417–424. Tokyo: Chikuma shobō, 1967.

———. *Meiji ishin shi*. Tokyo: Taihōkaku, 1930.

Havens, Thomas R. H. *Nishi Amane and Modern Japanese Thought*. Princeton: Princeton University Press, 1970.

Hayashi Emi. "Hōyaku shakai kō." *Tōkyōjōshidaigaku fuzoku hikaku bunka kenkyū kiyō*, no. 21 (6/1966):65–112.

Hayashi Ōki. "Gendai no buntai." In *Kōza: Kokugo shi*, vol. 6: *Buntaishi-gengo seikatsu shi*, ed. Satō Kiyoji, 169–220. Tokyo: Taishūkan, 1972.

Hayashi Takeji. "Kindai kyōiku kōsō to Mori Arinori." *Chūōkōron* 77(10) (9/1962):208–218.

Hayashiya Tatsusaburō. "Bunmeikaika no rekishiteki zentei." In *Bunmeikaika no kenkyū*, ed. Hayashiya Tatsusaburō, 3–34. Tokyo: Iwanami shoten, 1979.

Hegel, G.W.F. *Elements of the Philosophy of Right.* Translated by H.B. Nisbet; edited by Allen W. Wood. Cambridge: Cambridge University Press, 1991.

Henderson, Dan Fenno. *Conciliation and Japanese Law: Tokugawa and Modern*, vol. 1. Seattle: University of Washington Press; Tokyo: University of Tokyo Press, 1965.

Hida Yoshifumi. "Kindai goi no gaisetsu." In *Kindai no goi*, ed. Satō Kiyoji, 1–38. Tokyo: Meiji shoin, 1982.

———. *Tōkyōgo seiritsu shi no kenkyū.* Tokyo: Tōkyōdō, 1992.

———, ed. *Eirai gairaigo no sekai.* Tokyo: Nagumo dō, 1981.

Hinata Toshihiko. "Kindai kanji no isō—*Meiroku zasshi* o chūshin toshite." *Nihon gogaku* 12(8) (7/1993):66–74.

Hirai, Atsuko. "The State and Ideology in Meiji Japan—A Review Article." *Journal of Asian Studies* 46(1) (February 1987):89–103.

Hirakawa Sukehiro. "Japan's Turn to the West." In *The Cambridge History of Japan*, vol. 5: *The Nineteenth Century*, ed. Marius Jansen, 432–498. Cambridge: Cambridge University Press, 1989.

Hirasawa Akira. "Meiji nijūnendai sakubun kyōkasho no mohanbun." In *Nihon kindaigo kenkyū*, ed. Kindaigo kenkyūkai, vol. 1:139–157. Kasugabe: Hitsuji shobō, 1991.

Hirose Wataru and Nagata Tomoyoshi. *Chikan keimō wakai.* N.p.: Ishikawa ken gakkō zōhan, [1873].

Hobbes, Thomas. *The Elements of Law.* Oxford: Oxford University Press, 1994.

———. *Leviathan.* Harmondsworth: Penguin, 1981.

Holmes, Stephen. *Passions and Constraint: On the Theory of Liberal Democracy.* Chicago: University of Chicago Press, 1995.

Honjō Eijirō. *The Social and Economic History of Japan.* Kyoto: Nihon keizaishi kenkyūjo, 1935.

Hori Tatsnoskay [Tatsunosuke]. *A Pocket Dictionary of the English and Japanese Language/Ei-Wa taiyaku shūchin jisho.* Edo: n.p., 1862.

Hosaka Yūkichi. "Jiyū ron." *Dōjinsha bungaku zasshi*, no. 8 (1876.12.23):5–7a.

Hoston, Germaine. "The State, Modernity, and the Fate of Liberalism in Prewar Japan." *Journal of Asian Studies* 51(2) (May 1992):287–316.

Howland, Douglas. *Borders of Chinese Civilization: Geography and History at Empire's End.* Durham: Duke University Press, 1996.

———. "Nishi Amane's Efforts to Translate Western Knowledge: Sound, Mark, and Meaning." *Semiotica* 83(3–4) (1991):283–310.

———. "Samurai Status, Class, and Bureaucracy: A Historiographical Essay." *Journal of Asian Studies* 62(2) (May 2001):353–380.

———. "Society Reified: Herbert Spencer and Political Theory in Early Meiji Japan." *Comparative Studies in Society and History* 42(1) (January 2000):67–86.

Hsü, Immanuel C. Y. *China's Entry into the Family of Nations: The Diplomatic Phase, 1858–1880*. Cambridge, Mass.: Harvard University Press, 1960.

Huffman, James L. *Creating a Public: People and Press in Meiji Japan*. Honolulu: University of Hawai'i Press, 1997.

Huish, David. "Aims and Achievement of the *Meirokusha*—Fact and Fiction." *Monumenta Nipponica* 32(4) (Winter 1977):495–514.

Hunter, Janet. "Language Reform in Meiji Japan: The Views of Maejima Hisoka." In *Themes and Theories in Modern Japanese History: Essays in Memory of Richard Storry*, ed. Sue Henny and Jean-Pierre Lehmann, 101–120. London: Athlone, 1988.

Ienaga Saburō. *Nihon kindai shisōshi kenkyū*. 2nd ed. Tokyo: Tokyo Daigaku shuppankai, 1980.

Igarashi Akio. *Meiji ishin no shisō*. Yokohama: Seishiki shobō, 1996.

Ike, Nobutaka. *The Beginnings of Political Democracy in Japan*. Baltimore: Johns Hopkins University Press, 1950.

Ikegami, Eiko. *The Taming of the Samurai: Honorific Individualism and the Making of Modern Japan*. Cambridge, Mass.: Harvard University Press, 1995.

Imai Seiichi, ed. *Taishō demokurashī: kusanone to tennōsei no hazama*. Tokyo: Shakai hyōronsha, 1990.

Inada Masatsugu. *Meiji kenpō seiritsu shi*. 2 vols. Tokyo: Yūhikaku, 1960–1962.

Inoue Tetsujirō. "Kaichū zakki." Unpublished ms. Inoue Tetsujiō Archives. Tōkyō Chūō Library.

———. "Ki Nakamura Keiu sensei sho." *Tōyō gakugei zasshi*, no. 18 (3/1883): 484–486.

———. *Tetsugaku jii*. Tokyo: Tokyo Daigaku Sangakubu, 1881.

[Inoue Tetsujirō]. *Tetsugaku jii—yakugo sōsakuin*. Edited by Hida Yoshifumi. Tokyo: Kasama shoin, 1979.

Inoue Tetsujirō and Ariga Nagao. *Tetsugaku jii*. Rev. and enlarged ed. Tokyo: Tokyo Daigaku Sangakubu, 1884.

Irokawa Daikichi. *Meiji seishin shi*. Rev. ed. Tokyo: Chūōkōronsha, 1973.

Ishida Takeshi. *Kindai Nihon no seiji bunka to gengo shōchō*. Tokyo: Tokyo Daigaku shuppankai, 1983.

———. *Nihon no seiji to kotoba*, vol. 1: *Jiyū to fukushi* and vol. 2: *Heiwa to kokka*. Tokyo: Tokyo Daigaku shuppankai, 1989.

Ishiwata Toshio. "Gendai no goi." In *Kōza: Kokugo shi*, vol. 3: *Goi shi*, by Sakakura Atsuyoshi et al., 345–411. Tokyo: Taishūkan, 1971.

———. *Nihongo no naka no gairaigo*. Tokyo: Iwanami shoten, 1985.

Itagaki Taisuke. *Jiyūtō shi*. 2 vols. Tokyo: Gosharō, 1910.

———. "Jiyūtō soshiki no taigi." In *Jiyūjijigannen no yume*, ed. Ide Magoroku, 86–88. Tokyo: Shakai hyōronsha, 1991.

Itō Keisuke. "Nihonjin no gazoku bunshō ni okeru, kutō danraku o hyōjisuru o motte hitsuyō to sezaru, ikketsu goto taru o benzu." *Tōkyō gakushi kaiin zasshi* 2(10) [late 1881]:13–18.

Iwakura Tomomi. "Gaikō, kaikei, Ezochi kaitaku iknsho" (1869.2.28). In *Nihon kindai shisō taikei*, vol. 12: *Taigaikan*, ed. Shibahara Takuji et al., 5–11. Tokyo: Iwanami shoten, 1988.

Iyenaga Saburo [*sic*]. "Problem of Accepting Foreign Ideas in the History of Japanese Thought." *Asian Cultural Studies*, no. 5 (October 1966):83–93.

Japanese National Committee of Historical Sciences. *Recent Trends in Japanese Historiography: Bibliographical Essays: Japan at the XIIIth International Congress of Historical Sciences in Moscow.* Tokyo: Japan Society for the Promotion of Science, 1970. 2 vols.

Jakobson, Roman. "On Linguistic Aspects of Translation." In *On Translation*, ed. Reuben Brower, 232–239. Cambridge, Mass.: Harvard University Press, 1959.

"Jiyūtō kessei meiyaku." In *Jiyūjiji gannen no yume*, ed. Ide Magoroku, 79. Tokyo: Shakai hyōronsha, 1991.

Kamei Shunsuke. "Nihon no kindai to hon'yaku." In *Kindai Nihon no hon'yaku bunka*, ed. Kamei Shunsuke, 7–50. Tokyo: Chūōkōronsha, 1994.

———. "The Sacred Land of Liberty: Images of America in Nineteenth Century Japan." In *Mutual Images: Essays in American-Japanese Relations*, ed. Akira Iriye, 55–72. Cambridge, Mass.: Harvard University Press, 1975.

Kanda Takahira. *Seihō ryaku* (1871). In *Meiji bunka zenshū*, 2nd ed., vol. 13: *Hōritsu hen*. Tokyo: Nihon hyōron shinsha, 1957.

———. "Shinajin jinniku o kuu no setsu." *Tōkyō gakushi kaiin zasshi* 3(8) [1881]:1–9.

Kanda Takahira, trans. [William Ellis.] *Keizai shōgaku* (1867). In *Meiji bunka zenshū*, rev. ed., vol. 12: *Keizai hen*. Tokyo: Nihon hyōron shinsha, 1957.

Kasaya Kazuhiko. "Bushi no mibun to kakushiki." In *Mibun to kakushiki*, ed. Asao Naohiro, 179–224. Tokyo: Chūōkōronsha, 1992.

Katō Hiroyuki. "Beikoku seikyō." *Meiroku zasshi*, no. 5 [4/1874]:10b-13, no. 6 [4/1874]:3b-6a, and no. 13 (6/1874):1–4a.

———. "Fūfu dōken no ryūhei ron." *Meiroku zasshi*, no. 31 (3/1875):1–3.

———. "Jiki shōsō to hanpaku." In *Shinbun shūsei Meiji hennen shi*, 2:118–120.

———. *Jinken shinsetsu.* In *Meiji bunka zenshū*, vol. 5: *Jiyū minken hen*, 353–388. Tokyo: Nihon hyōronsha, 1927.

———. *Kokutai shinron.* In *Meiji bunka zenshū*, vol. 5: *Jiyū minken hen*, 109–126. Tokyo: Nihon hyōronsha, 1927.

———. *Rikken seitai ryaku.* In *Nishi Amane/Katō Hiroyuki*, ed. Uete Michiari. Tokyo: Chūōkōronsha, 1984.

———. *Shinsei taigi.* In *Meiji bunka zenshū*, vol. 5: *Jiyū minken hen*, 85–108. Tokyo: Nihon hyōronsha, 1927.

————. *Tonarigusa*. In *Nishi Amane/Katō Hiroyuki*, ed. Uete Michiari. Tokyo: Chūōkōronsha, 1984.

Katō Hiroyuki, trans. [Johann Kaspar Bluntschli.] *Kokuhō hanron*. (1872–1876). In *Meiji bunka zenshū*, supp. vol. 2 [vol. 31]. Tokyo: Nihon hyōronsha, 1971.

Katō Shūichi. "Meiji shoki no hon'yaku." In *Nihon kindai shisō taikei*, vol. 15: *Hon'yaku no shisō*, ed. Katō Shūichi and Maruyama Masao, 342–380. Tokyo: Iwanami shoten, 1991.

Katō Yūichi. *Bunmeikaika* (1873). In *Meiji bunka zenshū*, vol. 24: *Bunmeikaika hen*. Tokyo: Nihon hyōronsha, 1967.

Kawada Kō. "Ron kangaku gibun keiseki, i shūshin, seiji, keiritsu, kōgei, shoka senkō kigyō." *Tōkyō gakushi kaiin zasshi* 2(5) [1880]:1–9.

Kawanishi Susumu. "*Serufu-herupu* to *Saikoku risshi hen*." In *Kindai Nihon no hon'yaku bunka*, ed. Kamei Shunsuke, 79–96. Tokyo: Chūōkōronsha, 1994.

Keene, Donald. *The Japanese Discovery of Europe, 1720–1830*. Rev. ed. Stanford: Stanford University Press, 1969.

Kelley, Donald R. "Horizons of Intellectual History: Retrospect, Circumspect, Prospect." *Journal of the History of Ideas* 49(1) (1987):143–169.

Kersten, Rikki. *Democracy in Postwar Japan: Maruyama Masao and the Search for Autonomy*. London: Routledge, 1996.

Ketelaar, James Edward. *Of Heretics and Martyrs in Meiji Japan: Buddhism and Its Persecution*. Princeton: Princeton University Press, 1990.

Kido Takayoshi. *The Diary of Kido Takayoshi*. Translated by Sidney Devere Brown and Akiko Hirota. Tokyo: University of Tokyo Press, 1983–1986.

Kikuchi Dairoku. "Gakujutsujō no yakugo o ittei suru ron." *Tōyō gakugei zasshi*, no. 8 (1882.5.25):154–155.

[Kikuchi Dairoku]. "Tōgen yakugo." *Tōyō gakugei zasshi*, nos. 22–30 (7/1883–3/1884), no. 32 (5/1884), no. 38 (11/1884), and nos. 40–42 (1/1885–3/1885).

Kim, Kyu Hyun. "Political Ideologies of the Early Meiji Parties." In *New Directions in the Study of Meiji Japan*, ed. Helen Hardacre, with Adam L. Kern, 397–407. Leiden: Brill, 1997.

Kimura Ki. *Bunmeikaika*. Tokyo: Shibundō, 1954.

King, Richard H. *Civil Rights and the Idea of Freedom*. New York: Oxford University Press, 1992.

Kinmonth, Earl H. "Nakamura Keiu and Samuel Smiles: A Victorian Confucian and a Confucian Victorian." *American Historical Review* 85 (June 1980):535–556.

————. *The Self-Made Man in Meiji Japanese Thought: From Samurai to Salary Man*. Berkeley: University of California Press, 1981.

Kinoshita Hyō. *Meiji shika*. Tokyo: Bunchūtō, 1943.

Kobayashi Masahiro. "*Saikoku risshi hen* ni okeru hidarirubi no jiongo." In *Nihon kindaigo kenkyū*, vol. 1, ed. Kindaigo kenkyūkai, 93–116. Kasugabe: Hitsuji shobō, 1991.

[Kōchiken jin]. "San dai jiken kenpakusho." In *Jiyūjiji gannen no yume*, ed. Ide Magoroku, 92–106. Tokyo: Shakai hyōronsha, 1991.

Koebner, Richard, and Helmut Dan Schmidt. *Imperialism: The Story and Significance of a Political Word, 1840–1960*. Cambridge: Cambridge University Press, 1964.

Kojima Shōji. *Minken mondō* (1877). In *Meiji bunka zenshū*, vol. 5: *Jiyū minken hen*. Tokyo: Nihon hyōronsha, 1927.

[Kōjunsha]. *Shigi kenpō an* (1881). In *Meiji bunka zenshū*, 3rd ed., vol. 10: *Shōshi hen*, pt. 2:377–416. Tokyo: Nihon hyōronsha, 1968.

Konakamura Kiyonori. "Kokubun no seishitsu narabi [ni] enkaku." *Gakugei shirin*, vol. 4 (5/1879):289–298.

Koselleck, Reinhart. *Futures Past: On the Semantics of Historical Time*. Cambridge, Mass.: MIT Press, 1985.

———. "Linguistic Change and the History of Events." *Journal of Modern History* 61(4) (December 1989):648–666.

Kriegel, Blandine. *The State and the Rule of Law*. Translated by Marc A. LePain and Jeffrey C. Cohen. Princeton: Princeton University Press, 1995.

Kume Kunitake. *Tokumei zenken taishi Bei-Ō kairan jikki* (1878). Tokyo: Munetaka shobō, 1975.

Kure Shūzō. "Yōgaku no hattatsu to Meiji ishin." In *Meiji ishin shi kenkyū*, ed. Shigakkai, Tokyo Teikoku Daigaku, 329–418. Tokyo: Fuzanbō, 1929.

Kurokawa Mayori. "Moji denrai kō." *Tōkyō gakushi kaiin zasshi* 6(2) [1/1884]:53–65.

"Kyōkai ritsurei" (1874). In *Meiji seifu hon'yaku sōkō ruisan*, vol. 12:327–381. Tokyo: Yumani shobō, 1987.

Laski, Harold J. *Liberty and the Modern State*. Rev. ed. New York: Viking, 1949.

Latourette, Kenneth Scott. *A History of Christian Missions in China*. London: Society for Promoting Christian Knowledge in China, 1929.

Lebra, Joyce. "Yano Fumio: Meiji Intellectual, Party Leader, and Bureaucrat." *Monumenta Nipponica* 20(1–2) (1965):1–14.

Lefebvre, Henri. *The Production of Space*. Translated by Donald Nicholson-Smith. Oxford: Blackwell, 1991.

[Legge, James]. *Graduated Reading; Comprising a Circle of Knowledge in 200 Lessons*. (1864). Edo: Kaimushō, [1866].

Lehmann, Hartmut, and Melvin Richter, eds. *The Meaning of Historical Terms and Concepts: New Studies on Begriffsgeschichte*. Washington, D.C.: German Historical Institute, 1996.

Lehrer, Adrienne. *Semantic Fields and Lexical Structures*. Amsterdam: North-Holland, 1974.

Lewis, Michael. "The Meandering Meaning of Local Autonomy: Bosses, Bureaucrats, and Toyama's Rivers." In *New Directions in the Study of Meiji Japan*, ed. Helen Hardacre, with Adam L. Kern, 440–450. Leiden: Brill, 1997.

Lincicome, Mark E. "Local Citizens or Loyal Subjects? Enlightenment Discourse and Educational Reform." In *New Directions in the Study of Meiji Japan*, ed. Helen Hardacre, with Adam L. Kern, 450–465. Leiden: Brill, 1997.

———. *Principle, Praxis, and the Politics of Educational Reform in Meiji Japan.* Honolulu: University of Hawai'i Press, 1995.

Liu, Lydia H. "Legislating the Universal: The Circulation of International Law in the Nineteenth Century." In *Tokens of Exchange: The Problem of Translation in Global Circulations*, ed. Lydia H. Liu, 127–164. Durham: Duke University Press, 1999.

Locke, John. *Two Treatises on Government.* Critical ed. by Peter Laslette. New York: New American Library, 1963.

Loveday, Leo J. *Language Contact in Japan: A Socio-linguistic History.* Oxford: Clarendon Press, 1996.

Maeda Ai. *Bakumatsu-ishinki no bungaku.* Tokyo: Hōsei Daigaku shuppankyoku, 1972.

Maejima Hisoka. "Kanji o kaishi no gi." In *Maejima Hisoka jijoden*, 153–159. Hayama: Maejima Hisoka denki kankōkai, 1955.

Martin, W. A. P. "Terms Used in Diplomatic and Official Intercourse." In Justus Doolittle, *A Vocabulary and Hand-book of the Chinese Language, Romanized in the Mandarin Dialect*, vol. 2:194–200. Foochow: Rozario, Marcal, 1872.

Maruyama Masao. *Senchū to sengo no aida.* Tokyo: Misuzu shobō, 1976.

———. "The Structure of *Matsurigoto*: The *Basso Ostinato* of Japanese Political Life." In *Themes and Theories in Modern Japanese History: Essays in Memory of Richard Storry*, ed. Sue Henny and Jean-Pierre Lehmann, 27–43. London: Athlone, 1988.

———. *Studies in the Intellectual History of Tokugawa Japan.* Translated by Mikiso Hane. Princeton: Princeton University Press; Tokyo: University of Tokyo Press, 1974.

Masuda Wataru. *Seigaku tōzen to Chūgoku jijō.* Tokyo: Iwanami shoten, 1979.

Matsuda Kōichirō. "Fukuzawa Yukichi to *kō-shi-bun* no saihakken." *Rikkyō hōgaku*, no. 43 (1996):76–140.

Matsui Toshihiko. *Kindai Kango jisho no seiritsu to tenkai.* Tokyo: Kasama shoin, 1990.

Matsumoto Sannosuke. "Atarashii gakumon no keisei to chishikijin." In *Nihon kindai shisō taikei*, vol. 10: *Gakumon to chishikijin*, ed. Matsumoto Sannosuke and Yamamuro Shin'ichi, 424–464. Tokyo: Iwanami shoten, 1988.

———. *Kindai Nihon no chiteki jōkyō.* Tokyo: Chūōkōronsha, 1974.

————. "Kuga Katsunan ni okeru *kokka* to *shakai*." *Journal of Pacific Asia*, no. 1 (1993):145–160.

————. *Meiji seishin no kōzō*. Tokyo: Nihonhōsō shuppan, 1981.

————. "Nakae Chōmin and Confucianism." In *Confucianism and Tokugawa Culture*, ed. Peter Nosco, 251–266. Princeton: Princeton University Press, 1984.

Matsuo Shōichi. *Jiyū minken shisō no kenkyū*. Rev. ed. Tokyo: Nihon keizai hyōronsha, 1990.

Matsushima Kō, trans. [Herbert Spencer.] *Shakai heiken ron*. In *Meiji bunka zenshū*, vol. 5: *Jiyū minken hen*, 231–308. Tokyo: Nihon hyōronsha, 1927.

Mayhew, Leon H. "Society." In *International Encyclopedia of the Social Sciences*, ed. David L. Sills, 14:577–586. New York: Macmillan and Free Press, 1968.

Mayo, Marlene J. "The Iwakura Mission to the United States and Europe, 1871–1873." In *Researches in the Social Sciences on Japan: Volume Two*, ed. Stanleigh H. Jones Jr. and John E. Lane, 28–47. New York: Columbia University, East Asian Institute, 1959.

————. "The Western Education of Kume Kunitake, 1871–76." *Monumenta Nipponica* 28(1) (1973):3–67.

Mazaki Masato. "Fukuzawa Yukichi to *Seiyō jijō*." *Shigaku* (Keiō Gijuku Daigaku) 24(2–3) (1950):89–105.

McCloskey, H. J. "A Critique of the Ideals of Liberty." *Mind* 74 (1965):483–508.

McLaren, W. W., ed. *Japanese Government Documents* (1914). Tokyo: Asiatic Society of Japan, 1979.

Medvedev, P. N. *The Formal Method in Literary Scholarship: A Critical Introduction to Sociological Poetics*. Translated by Albert J. Wehrle. Baltimore: Johns Hopkins University Press, 1978.

Mehta, Uday Singh. *Liberalism and Empire: A Study in Nineteenth-Century British Liberal Thought*. Chicago: University of Chicago Press, 1999.

Meiroku Zasshi: Journal of the Japanese Enlightenment. Translated by William R. Braisted. Cambridge, Mass.: Harvard University Press, 1976.

Melching, Willem, and Wyger Velema, eds. *Main Trends in Cultural History: Ten Essays*. Amsterdam: Rodopi, 1994.

Mendel, Douglas H., Jr. "Ozaki Yukio: Political Conscience of Modern Japan." *Far Eastern Quarterly* 15(3) (May 1956):343–356.

Mill, John Stuart. *On Liberty*. In *Three Essays*, 1–141. Oxford: Oxford University Press, 1975.

Miller, Frank O. *Minobe Tatsukichi: Interpreter of Constitutionalism in Japan*. Berkeley: University of California Press, 1965.

Miller, Roy Andrew. *The Japanese Language*. Chicago: University of Chicago Press, 1967.

Minear, Richard H. *Japanese Tradition and Western Law: Emperor, State, and Law in the Thought of Hozumi Yatsuka.* Cambridge, Mass.: Harvard University Press, 1970.

———. "Nishi Amane and the Reception of Western Law in Japan." *Monumenta Nipponica* 28(2) (1973):151–175.

Minegishi Kentarō. *Kinsei mibun ron.* Tokyo: Azekura shobō, 1989.

Mitani Hiroshi. "A Protonation-State and Its 'Unforgettable Other'—The Prerequisites for Meiji International Relations." In *New Directions in the Study of Meiji Japan,* ed. Helen Hardacre, with Adam L. Kern, 293–310. Leiden: Brill, 1997.

Mitsukuri Rinshō. "Bakkuru-shi no Eikoku kaikashi yori shōyaku." *Meiroku zasshi,* no. 7 (5/1874):4a-6a.

———. "*Riboruchī* no setsu." *Meiroku zasshi,* no. 9 (6/1874):2b-4b and no. 14 (7/1874):3a-5b.

Miyagawa Tōru. "Nihon keimō shisō no kōzō—minken giin mondai o chūshin toshite." In *Meiji keimō shisō shū,* ed. Ōkubo Toshiaki, 424–436. Tokyo: Chikuma shobō, 1967.

———. "Nihon no keimō shisō." In *Kōza: Kindai shisō shi,* vol. 9: *Nihon ni okeru seiyō kindai shisō no jūyō,* ed. Kaneko Masashi and Ōtsuka Hisao, 113–147. Tokyo: Kōbundō, 1959.

Miyakoshi Shin'ichirō, ed. *Nihon kensei kiso shiryō.* Tokyo: Giin seijisha, 1939.

Mori Arinori. "Kaika daiichi hanashi." *Meiroku zasshi,* no. 3 [4/1874]:1.

———. *Life and Resources in America.* [Washington, D.C.]: privately printed, [1871].

———. *Religious Freedom in Japan: A Memorial and Draft of Charter.* [Washington, D.C.]: privately printed, [1872].

———. "Saishō ron." *Meiroku zasshi,* no. 8 (5/1874):2–3 and no. 27 (2/1875):1–3.

———. "Shūkyō." *Meiroku zasshi,* no. 6 [4/1874]:6a-12b.

Mori Kazutsura. *Kindai Nihon shisōshi josetsu: shizen to shakai no ronri.* Kyoto: Kōyō shobō, 1984.

Morioka Kenji. "Kaika ki hon'yaku sho no goi." In *Kindai no goi,* ed. Satō Kiyoji, 63–82. Tokyo: Meiji shoin, 1982.

———. [*Kaitei*] *Kindaigo no seiritsu: goi hen.* Rev. ed. Tokyo: Meiji shoin, 1991.

Motoyama Yukihiko. "Bunmeikaika ki ni okeru shin chishikijin no shisō—Meirokusha no hitobito o chūshin toshite." *Jinbun gakuhō* 4 (1954):45–84.

———. *Proliferating Talent: Essays on Politics, Thought, and Education in the Meiji Era,* ed. J.S.A. Elisonas and Richard Rubinger. Honolulu: University of Hawai'i Press, 1997.

Mukihara Norio. "Bunmeikaika ron." In *Iwanami kōza—Nihon tsūshi,* vol. 16: *Kindai,* pt. 1, 251–290. Tokyo: Iwanami shoten, 1994.

Mulligan, Lotte, Judith Richards, and John Graham. "Intentions and Conventions: A Critique of Quentin Skinner's Method for the Study of the History of Ideas." *Political Studies* 27(1) (March 1979):84–98.

Muraoka Tsunetsugu. *Studies in Shintō Thought.* Translated by Delmer M. Brown and James T. Araki. New York: Greenwood Press, 1988.

Mutel, Jacques. "The Modernization of Japan: Why Has Japan Succeeded in Its Modernization?" In *Europe and the Rise of Capitalism,* ed. Jean Baechler, John A. Hall, and Michael Mann, 136–158. Oxford: Blackwell, 1988.

Nagai Michio. *Kindaika to kyōiku.* Tokyo: Tokyo Daigaku shuppanbu, 1969.

———. "Mori Arinori: Pioneer of Modern Japan." In *Higher Education in Japan: Its Take-off and Crash*, trans. Jerry Dusenbury, 166–196. Tokyo: University of Tokyo Press, 1971.

Nagamine Hideki, trans. [John Stuart Mill.] *Daigi seitai* (1875). In *Meiji bunka zenshū*, 2nd ed., vol. 3: *Seiji hen.* Tokyo: Nihon hyōron shinsha, 1955.

Nagao Ryūichi. "Nishi Amane ni okeru ningen to shakai." In *Nihon hō shisōshi kenkyū*, 5–34. Tokyo: Sōbunsha, 1981.

Nagashima Daisuke. *Ran-Wa Ei-Wa jisho hattatsu shi.* Tokyo: Kōdansha, 1970.

Nagatsuka Sōtarō, comp. *Minkenka hitsudoku—shuken ron san* (1882). In *Meiji bunka zenshū*, vol. 5: *Jiyū minken hen*, 309–352. Tokyo: Nihon hyōronsha, 1927.

Najita, Tetsuo. "Ambiguous Encounters: Ogata Kōan and International Studies in Late Tokugawa Osaka." In *Osaka: The Merchants' Capital of Early Modern Japan,* ed. James L. McClain and Wakita Osamu, 213–242. Ithaca: Cornell University Press, 1999.

———. *Japan: The Intellectual Foundations of Modern Japanese Politics.* Chicago: University of Chicago Press, 1974.

———. "Presidential Address: Reflections on Modernity and Modernization." *Journal of Asian Studies* 52(4) (November 1993):845–853.

———. "Some Reflections on Idealism in the Political Thought of Yoshino Sakuzō." In *Japan in Crisis: Essays on Taishō Democracy*, ed. Bernard S. Silberman and H. D. Harootunian, 29–66. Princeton: Princeton University Press, 1974.

———. *Visions of Virtue in Tokugawa Japan: The Kaitokudō Merchant Academy of Osaka.* Chicago: University of Chicago Press, 1987.

Najita, Tetsuo, and Irwin Scheiner, eds. *Japanese Thought in the Tokugawa Period: Methods and Metaphors.* Chicago: University of Chicago Press, 1978.

Nakae Chōmin, trans. [Jean-Jacques Rousseau.] *Minyaku yakkai.* In *Meiji bunka zenshū*, 2nd ed., vol. 3: *Seiji hen.* Tokyo: Nihon hyōron shinsha, 1955.

Nakamura Keiu. "Fuku Inoue sonkenkun sho." *Tōyō gakugei zasshi*, no. 19 (4/1883):512–514.

———. "Gi taiseijin josho." In *Meiji keimō shisō shū*, ed. Ōkubo Toshiaki, 281–283. Tokyo: Chikuma shobō, 1967.

———. "Jinmin no seishitsu o kaizōsuru setsu." *Meiroku zasshi*, no. 30 (2/1875): 7–8.

———. "Kangaku fukahai ron." *Tōkyō gakushi kaiin zasshi* 9(4) (5/1887):33–68.

———. *Keiu bunshū*. Tokyo: Yoshikawa kōbunkan, 1903.

———. "Seigaku ippan." *Meiroku zasshi*, no. 12 (6/1874):9a and no. 15 (8/1874): 2b-4b.

———. "Seikyō mu mujun no hei." In *Keiu bunshū*, vol. 13:16–17. Tokyo: Yoshikawa kōbunkan, 1903.

———. "Shina fukabu ron." *Meiroku zasshi*, no. 35 (4/1875):1–3a.

———. "Shisho sodoku no ron." *Tōkyō gakushi kaiin zasshi* 3(2) [1880–1881]: 6–15.

———. "Zenryō naru bo o tsukuru setsu." *Meiroku zasshi*, no. 33 (3/1875):1–3.

Nakamura Keiu, trans. [John Stuart Mill.] *Jiyū no ri* (1871). In *Meiji bunka zenshū*, vol. 5: *Jiyū minken hen*, 1–84. Tokyo: Nihon hyōronsha, 1927.

———. [Samuel Smiles.] *Saikoku risshi hen*. Tokyo: Ginkadō, 1888.

Nakamura Kichiji. *Nihon shakai shi gaisetsu*. Tokyo: Usui shobō, 1947.

Neumann, Franz. *The Democratic and the Authoritarian State*, ed. Herbert Marcuse. Glencoe: Free Press, 1957.

Nichi-Ran gakkai [Numata Jirō et al.], ed. *Yōgakushi jiten*. Tokyo: Yūshōdō, 1984.

Nihon kuni kokken an [1880–1881?]. Transcribed by Miura Kaneyuki. In *Meiji bunka zenshū*, 3rd ed., vol. 10: *Shōshi hen*, pt. 2:418–430. Tokyo: Nihon hyōronsha, 1968.

Nihongo no reikishi. Vol. 6: *Atarashii kokugo e no ayumi*, ed. Shimonaka Kunihiko, 2nd ed. Tokyo: Heibonsha, 1976.

Nishi Amane. *Fisuserinku-shi bankoku kōhō*. Edo: n.p., 1868.

———. *Fisuserinku-shi bankoku kōhō*. In *Nishi Amane zenshū*, ed. Ōkubo Toshiaki, vol. 2:3–102. Tokyo: Munetaka, 1962.

———. *Hyakugaku renkan/Encyclopedia*. In *Nishi Amane zenshū*, ed. Ōkubo Toshiaki, vol. 4. Tokyo: Munetaka shobō, 1981.

———. *Hyakuichi shinron*. In *Nishi Amane zenshū*, ed. Ōkubo Toshiaki, vol. 1:232–289. Tokyo: Munetaka, 1960.

———. *Kenpō sōan*. In *Nishi Amane zenshū*, ed. Ōkubo Toshiaki, vol. 2:197–237. Tokyo: Munetaka, 1962.

———. "Kokumin kifū/Nashonaru kerekutoru ron." *Meiroku zasshi*, no. 32 (3/1875):1–3.

———. "Kyōmon ron." *Meiroku zasshi*, no. 4 [4/1874]:5b-8b, no. 5 [4/1874]:3b-6a, no. 6 [4/1874]:2a-3a, no. 8 (5/1874):6b-8a, and no. 12 (6/1874):1–3a.

———. "Yōji o motte kokugo o shosuru no ron." *Meiroku zasshi*, no. 1 [3/1874]:1–10a.

Nishida Taketoshi. *Meiji jidai no shinbun to zasshi*. Tokyo: Shibundō, 1961.

Nishikawa Nagao. *Kokkyō no koekata—hikaku bunkaron josetsu*. Tokyo: Chikuma shobō, 1992.

Nishimura Shigeki. "Chingen issoku." *Meiroku zasshi*, no. 3 [4/1874]:1b-2a.

———. "Jishujiyū kai." *Meiroku zasshi*, no. 37 (5/1875):1b-2b.

———. "Kaika no do ni yotte kai monji o hassubeki no ron." *Meiroku zasshi*, no. 1 [4/1874]:10b-12.

———. *Nihon kōdō ron* (1887). In *Meiji keimō shishō shū*, ed. Ōkubo Toshiaki, 369–402. Tokyo: Chikuma shobō, 1967.

———. *Shōgaku shūshin kun* (1880). In *Nihon kyōkasho taikei—Kindai hen*, vol. 2: *Shūshin*, pt. 2, ed. Kaigo Tokiomi, 6–37. Tokyo: Kōdansha, 1962.

———. "Shūshin chikoku futamichi arazu ron." *Meiroku zasshi*, no. 31 (6/1875): 3b-6.

———. "Tenkan setsu." *Meiroku zasshi*, no. 43 (11/1875):1–4.

———. "Zanbōritsu - shinbun jōrei o hinansu" (11/1875). In *Shinbun shūsei Meiji hennen shi*, ed. Nakayama Yasumasa, vol. 2:444–445. Tokyo: Honpō shoseki, 1982.

Nishio Mitsuo. "*Saikoku risshi hen* no furigana ni tsuite." In *Kindaigo kenkyū*, ed. Kindaigo gakkai, vol. 2:473–488. Tokyo: Musashino shoin, 1968.

Norman, E. H. *Origins of the Modern Japanese State: Selected Writings of E. H. Norman*, ed. John W. Dower. New York: Random House, 1975.

Norman, Jerry. *Chinese*. Cambridge: Cambridge University Press, 1988.

Numata Jirō. *Yōgaku*. Tokyo: Yoshikawa kōbunkan, 1989.

———. *Yōgaku denrai no rekishi*. Tokyo: Shibundō, 1966.

Obata Tokujirō, trans. [Alexis de Tocqueville.] *Jōboku jiyū no ron*. In *Meiji bunka zenshū*, vol. 5: *Jiyūminken hen*, 127–136. Tokyo: Nihon hyōronsha, 1927.

Ochiai Hiroki. "Meiji zenki no rikugun kashi to jiyūminken." *Jinbun gakuhō*, no. 74 (3/1994):37–65.

Ogyū Sorai. *The Political Writings of Ogyū Sorai*. Translated by J. R. McEwan. Cambridge: Cambridge University Press, 1969.

Öhman, Suzanne. "Theories of the 'Linguistic Field.'" *Word* 9 (1953):123–134.

Okabe Keigorō. *Bunmeikaika hyōrin* (1875). In *Meiji bunka zenshū*, vol. 24: *Bunmeikaika hen*, 239–240. Tokyo: Nihon hyōronsha, 1967.

Okamoto Isao. *Meiji shosakka no buntai: Meiji bungo no kenkyū*. Tokyo: Kasama shoin, 1980.

Ōkubo Toshiaki. *Bakumatsu ishin no yōgaku*. Tokyo: Yoshikawa kōbunkan, 1986.

———. *Meiji no shisō to bunka*. Tokyo: Yoshikawa kōbunkan, 1988.

———. *Meirokusha kō*. Tokyo: Rittaisha, 1976.

———, ed. *Kindaishi shiryō*. Tokyo: Yoshikawa kōbunkan, 1965.

Ōkuni [Nonoguchi] Takamasa. *Shinshin kōhō ron* (1867). In *Nihon shisōshi taikei*, vol. 50: *Hirata Atsutane, Ban Nobumoto, Ōkuni Takamasa*, ed. Tahara Tsuguo et al., 493–511. Tokyo: Iwanami shoten, 1973.

Ono Azusa. "Kenri no zoku." In *Meiji shisō shū*, ed. Matsumoto Sannosuke, vol. 1:181–183. Tokyo: Chikuma shobō, 1976.

———. "Waga seijijō no shugi." In *Meiji shisō shū*, ed. Matsumoto Sannosuke, vol. 1:184–207. Tokyo: Chikuma shobō, 1976.

Ono Hideo. "Meiji shoki ni okeru shuppan jiyū no gainen." *Shinkyū jidai* 2(4–5) (1926):83–92.

Ooms, Herman. *Tokugawa Village Practice: Class, Status, Power, Law*. Berkeley: University of California Press, 1996.

Osatake Takeki. *Nihon kensei shi taikō*. 2 vols. Tokyo: Nihon hyōronsha, 1938–1939.

Ōta Aito. *Meiji Kirisutokyō no ryūiki: Shizuoka bando to bakushin tachi*. Tokyo: Tsukiji shokan, 1979.

Oto Shigeru [Uryū Tora]. *Keimō chie no kan*. Tokyo: n.p., [1872].

Ōtsuki Akira. *Kinsei Nihon no jugaku to yōgaku*. Kyoto: Shibunkaku, 1988.

Ōtsuki Fumihiko. "Gairaigo genkō." *Gakugei shirin* 17 [nos. missing] (2/1884): 122–139, (4/1884):370–384, and (6/1884):572–590.

———. *Mitsukuri Rinshō-kun den*. Tokyo: n.p., 1907.

"Ōtsuki Fumihiko hakushi nenpu." *Kokugo to kokubungaku* 5(7) (7/1928):22–82.

The Oxford English Dictionary. 2nd ed. Prepared by J. A. Simpson and E.S.C. Weiner. Oxford: Clarendon Press, 1989.

Ozaki Yukio, trans. [Herbert Spencer.] *Kenri teikō*. In *Ozaki Gakudō zenshū*, vol. 1. Tokyo: Kōronsha, 1956.

Ozawa Saburō. *Bakumatsu Meiji Yasokyō shi kenkyū*. Tokyo: Nihon Kirisutokyō-dan shuppankyo, 1973.

Parsons, Talcott. "A Revised Analytical Approach to the Theory of Social Stratification." In *Class, Status, and Power: A Reader in Social Stratification*, ed. Reinhard Bendix and Seymour Martin Lipset, 92–128. Glencoe: Free Press, 1953.

———. "Society." In *Encyclopedia of the Social Sciences*, ed. E.R.A. Seligman, vol. 13:225–232. New York: Macmillan, 1934.

Passin, Herbert. *Society and Education in Japan*. New York: Columbia University Press, 1965.

Pedlar, Neil. *The Imported Pioneers: Westerners Who Helped Build Modern Japan*. New York: St. Martin's Press, 1990.

Peel, J. D. Y. *Herbert Spencer: The Evolution of a Sociologist*. London: Heinemann, 1971.

Peirce, C. S. *Philosophical Writings of Peirce*. Edited by Justus Buchler. New York: Dover, 1955.

Pitkin, Hanna Fenichel. "Are Freedom and Liberty Twins?" *Political Theory* 16(4) (November 1988):523–552.

Pittau, Joseph. *Political Thought in Early Meiji Japan, 1868–1889*. Cambridge, Mass.: Harvard University Press, 1967.

Pocock, J.G.A. "Virtues, Rights, and Manners: A Model for Historians of Political Thought." *Political Theory* 9(3) (August 1981):353–368.

Pollack, David. *The Fracture of Meaning: Japan's Synthesis of China from the Eighth Through the Eighteenth Centuries*. Princeton: Princeton University Press, 1986.

Pyle, Kenneth B. *The New Generation in Meiji Japan: Problems of Cultural Identity, 1885–1895*. Stanford: Stanford University Press, 1969.

Rai San'yō. *Nihon gaishi*. In *Rai San'yō*, ed. Rai Tsutomu. Tokyo: Chūōkōronsha, 1984.

———. *Nihon seiki*. In *Rai San'yō*, ed. Uete Michiari. Tokyo: Iwanami shoten, 1977.

Ravina, Mark. *Land and Lordship in Early Modern Japan*. Stanford: Stanford University Press, 1999.

———. "State-Building and Political Economy in Early-Modern Japan." *Journal of Asian Studies* 54(4) (November 1995):997–1022.

Renan, Ernest. "What Is a Nation?" Translated by Martin Thom. In *Nation and Narration*, ed. Homi K. Bhabha, 8–22. London: Routledge, 1990.

Richter, Melvin. "*Begriffsgeschichte* and the History of Ideas." *Journal of the History of Ideas* 48(2) (1987):247–263.

———. "Conceptual History (*Begriffsgeschichte*) and Political Theory." *Political Theory* 14(4) (November 1986):604–637.

———. *The History of Political and Social Concepts: A Critical Introduction*. New York: Oxford University Press, 1995.

Roberts, Luke S. "A Petition for a Popularly Chosen Council of Government in Tosa in 1787." *Harvard Journal of Asiatic Studies* 57(2) (December 1997):575–596.

Rostow, W. W. *The Stages of Economic Growth: A Non-Communist Manifesto*. Cambridge: Cambridge University Press, 1960.

Rubin, Jay. *Injurious to Public Morals: Writers and the Meiji State*. Seattle: University of Washington Press, 1984.

Saitō Tsuyoshi. *Meiji no kotoba: higashi kara nishi e no kakehashi*. Tokyo: Kodansha, 1977.

Sakaguchi Sakichi, trans. [Herbert Spencer.] "Fujo no kenri." *Gakugei shirin*, vol. 5 (11/1879):340–354 and (12/1879):451–468.

Sakai, Naoki. *Voices of the Past: The Status of Language in Eighteenth-Century Japanese Discourse*. Ithaca: Cornell University Press, 1991.

Sakamoto Takao. *Kindai Nihon seishin shi ron*. Tokyo: Kōdansha, 1996.

———. *Meiji kokka no kensetsu, 1871–1890*. Tokyo: Chūōkōronsha, 1999.

———. *Shijō-dōtoku-chitsujo*. Tokyo: Sōbunsha, 1991.

Sakatani Shiroshi. "Amakudari setsu." *Meiroku zasshi*, no. 35 (4/1875):3–8a and no. 36 (5/1875):1–6a.

———. "Seikyō no utagai." *Meiroku zasshi*, no. 22 (12/1874):4–5 and no. 25 (12/1874):3b-6.

———. "Shitsugi issoku." *Meiroku zasshi*, no. 11 (6/1874):7–9.

———. "Yō seishin issetsu." *Meiroku zasshi*, no. 40 (8/1875):5–8 and no. 41 (8/1875):5b-8.

Sanada Shinji. *Hyōjungo wa, ikani seiritsu shita ka?* Tokyo: Sōtakusha, 1991.

Satō Kiyoji. *Kokugo goi no rekishiteki kenkyū*. Tokyo: Meiji shoin, 1971.

Satō Masayuki. "'Kojin no shūgōtai toshite no shakai' toiu kangaekata no teichaku ni hatashita shoki shakaika no yakuwari." *Shakaika kyōiku kenkyū*, no. 68 (1993):18–29.

Satō Shōsuke. *Yōgaku shi no kenkyū*. Tokyo: Chūōkōronsha, 1980.

Satō Tōru. *Bakumatsu-Meiji shoki goi no kenkyū*. Tokyo: Ōfūsha, 1986.

Scalapino, Robert A. *Democracy and the Party Movement in Prewar Japan: The Failure of the First Attempt*. Berkeley: University of California Press, 1953.

———. "Ideology and Modernization—The Japanese Case." In *Ideology and Discontent*, ed. David E. Apter, 93–127. New York: Free Press; London: Collier-Macmillan, 1964.

Schwantes, Robert S. "Christianity versus Science: A Conflict of Ideas in Meiji Japan." *Far Eastern Quarterly* 12(2) (February 1953):123–132.

Screech, Timon. *The Western Scientific Gaze and Popular Imagery in Later Edo Japan: The Lens Within the Heart*. Cambridge: Cambridge University Press, 1996.

Seeley, Christopher. *A History of Writing in Japan*. Leiden: Brill, 1991.

Sekiwa Masamichi. "Kaika to kaika no sensō" (1884.9.28). In *Nihon kindai shisō taikei*, vol. 12: *Taigaihen*, ed. Shibahara Takuji et al., 304–307. Tokyo: Iwanami shoten, 1988.

Shigeno Yasutsugu. "Kangaku yoku seisoku ikka o mōke, shōnen shūsai o erami, Shinkoku ni ryūgaku seshimubeki ronsetsu." *Tōkyō gakushi kaiin zasshi*, no. 4 [1880]:77–93.

———. *Wayaku bankoku kōhō*. Kagoshima: n.p., 1870.

Shimaji Mokurai. "Sanjō kyōsoku hihan kenpakusho." In *Gendai Nihon shisō taikei*, vol. 7: *Bukkyō*, ed. Yoshida Kyūichi, 61–70. Tokyo: Chikuma shobō, 1965.

Shimizu Usaburō. "Hiragana no setsu." *Meiroku zasshi*, no. 7 (5/1874):8–10.

Shimoide Junkichi. *Meiji shakai shisō kenkyū*. Tokyo: Asano shoten, 1932.

Shinbun shūsei Meiji hennen shi, ed. Nakayama Yasumasa (1934–1936). Tokyo: Honpō shoseki, 1982.

Shindō Sakiko. *Meiji jidai go no kenkyū: goi to bunshō*. Tokyo: Meiji shoin, 1981.

———. "Meiji shoki no furigana." In *Kindaigo kenkyū*, ed. Kindaigo gakkai, vol. 2:489–504. Tokyo: Musashino shoin, 1968.

Shively, Donald H. "Nishimura Shigeki: A Confucian View of Modernization."

In *Changing Japanese Attitudes Toward Modernization*, ed. Marius B. Jansen, 193–241. Princeton: Princeton University Press, 1965.

Skinner, Quentin. *The Foundations of Modern Political Thought: Volume One: The Renaissance*. Cambridge: Cambridge University Press, 1978.

———. *Liberty Before Liberalism*. Cambridge: Cambridge University Press, 1998.

———. "Meaning and Understanding in the History of Ideas." *History and Theory* 8 (1969):3–53.

———. "A Reply to My Critics." In *Meaning and Context: Quentin Skinner and His Critics*, ed. James Tully, 260–281. Princeton: Princeton University Press, 1988.

———. "'Social Meaning' and the Explanation of Social Actions." In *The Philosophy of History*, ed. Patrick Gardiner, 106–126. Oxford: Oxford University Press, 1974.

Snell-Hornby, Mary. *Translation Studies: An Integrated Approach*. Amsterdam: John Benjamins, 1988.

Sōgō Masaaki and Hida Yoshifumi. *Meiji no kotoba jiten*. Tokyo: Tōkyōdō, 1986.

Sonoda Hidehiro. "Gun-ken no bushi—bushi mibun kaitai ni kansuru ichi kōsatsu." In *Bunmeikaika no kenkyū*, ed. Hayashiya Tatsusaburō, 35–76. Tokyo: Iwanami shoten, 1979.

Sonoda Hidehiro, Hamana Atsushi, and Hirota Teruyuki. *Shizoku no rekishi shakaigaku-teki kenkyū*. Nagoya: Nagoya Daigaku shuppankai, 1995.

Soviak, Eugene. "The Case of Baba Tatsui: Western Enlightenment, Social Change, and the Early Meiji Intellectual." *Monumenta Nipponica* 18 (1963):191–235.

———. "On the Nature of Western Progress: The Journal of the Iwakura Embassy." In *Tradition and Modernization in Japanese Culture*, ed. Donald H. Shively, 7–34. Princeton: Princeton University Press, 1971.

Spaulding, Robert M. "The Intent of the Charter Oath." In *Studies in Japanese History and Politics*, ed. Richard K. Beardsley, 1–36. Ann Arbor: University of Michigan Press, 1967.

Spence, N.C.W. "Linguistic Fields, Conceptual Systems, and the *Weltbild*." *Transactions of the Philological Society* (1961):87–106.

Spencer, Herbert. *Social Statics: The conditions essential to human happiness specified, and the first of them developed*. New York: Schalkenbach Foundation, 1995.

Spengler, Joseph J. "Theory, Ideology, Non-Economic Values, and Politico-Economic Development." In *Tradition, Values, and Socio-Economic Development*, ed. Ralph Braibanti and Joseph J. Spengler, 3–56. Durham: Duke University Press; London: Cambridge University Press, 1961.

Spitzer, Leo. "Geistesgeschichte vs. History of Ideas as Applied to Hitlerism." *Journal of the History of Ideas* 5 (1944):191–203.

Steiner, George. *After Babel: Aspects of Language and Translation.* London: Oxford University Press, 1975.

Stern, John Peter. *The Japanese Interpretation of the "Law of Nations," 1854–1874.* Princeton: Princeton University Press, 1979.

Sugi Kōji. "Jinkan kōkyō." *Meiroku zasshi,* no. 19 (10/1874):6b-8b.

Sugimoto Tsutomu. *Kokugogaku to Rangogaku/Japanese Linguistics and Dutch Linguistics.* Tokyo: Musashiya shoin, 1991.

———. *Sugimoto Tsutomu Nihongo kōza,* vol. 6: *Gairaigo to Nihongo.* Tokyo: Ōfūsha, 1980.

———. *Zuroku Rangaku kotohajime.* Tokyo: Waseda Daigaku shuppanbu, 1985.

Sugimoto Tsutomu, comp. *Nihon Eigo bunka shi shiryō.* Tokyo: Yasaka shobō, 1985.

Suzuki Shūji. *Bunmei no kotoba.* Hiroshima: Bunka hyōron, 1981.

———. *Kanji—sono tokushitsu to kanji bunmei no shōrai.* Tokyo: Kōdansha, 1978.

———. *Nihon kango to Chūgokugo.* Tokyo: Chūōkōronsha, 1981.

Suzuki, Takao. "Writing Is Not Language, or Is It?" *Journal of Pragmatics* 1(4) (1977):407–420.

Suzuki Yuichi, trans. [Albany de Fonblanque.] *Eisei ikan* (1868). In *Meiji bunka zenshū,* 2nd ed., vol. 3: *Seiji hen.* Tokyo: Nihon hyōron shinsha, 1955.

Takagi Hiroshi. *Kindai tennōsei no bunkashiteki kenkyū: tennō shūnin girei, nenchūgyōji, bunkazai.* Tokyo: Azekura shobō, 1997.

Takahashi Kamekichi. *Tokugawa hōken keizai no kenkyū.* Tokyo: Senshinsha, 1932.

Takahashi Masao. *Nishimura Shigeki.* Tokyo: Yoshikawa kōbunkan, 1987.

Takaya Tatsukuni and Nakamura Keiu. *Bankoku kōhō reikan.* N.p.: Saibi kōzō, 1876.

Takikawa Masajirō. *Nihon hōsei shi.* Rev. ed. Tokyo: Kadokawa shoten, 1959.

Tanaka Hiroshi. "The Development of Liberalism in Modern Japan: Continuity of an Idea—From Taguchi and Kuga to Hasegawa." *Hitotsubashi Journal of Social Studies* 21 (1989):259–268.

———. *Kindai Nihon to "riberarizumu."* Tokyo: Iwanami shoten, 1993.

Tanaka, Stefan. "Imaging History: Inscribing Belief in the Nation." *Journal of Asian Studies* 53(1) (February 1994):24–44.

———. *Japan's Orient: Reordering Pasts into History.* Berkeley: University of California Press, 1993.

Tao, De-min. "Shigeno Yasutsugu as an Advocate of 'Practical Sinology' in Meiji Japan." In *New Directions in the Study of Meiji Japan,* ed. Helen Hardacre, with Adam L. Kern, 373–386. Leiden: Brill, 1997.

Taoka Ryōichi. "Nishi Shūsuke *Bankoku kōhō.*" *Kokusaihō gaikō zasshi* 71 (5/1972):1–57.

Thelle, Notto R. *Buddhism and Christianity in Japan: From Conflict to Dialogue, 1854–1899.* Honolulu: University of Hawai'i Press, 1987.

Tipps, Dean. "Modernization Theory and the Comparative Study of Societies:

A Critical Perspective." *Comparative Studies in Society and History* 15 (March 1973):199–226.

Tocqueville, Alexis de. *Democracy in America.* Translated by George Lawrence; edited by J. P. Mayer and Max Lerner. New York: Harper & Row, 1966.

Toews, John E. "Intellectual History After the Linguistic Turn: The Autonomy of Meaning and the Irreducibility of Experience." *American Historical Review* 92(4) (October 1987):879–907.

Tokutomi Sohō. *The Future Japan.* Translated and edited by Vinh Sinh. Edmonton: University of Alberta Press, 1989.

———. *Shōrai no Nihon.* In *Tokutomi Sohō shū,* ed. Uete Michiari, 50–114. Tokyo: Chikuma shobō, 1974.

Tōkyō daigaku hyakunen shi: Tsūshi. Tokyo: Tokyo Daigaku, 1984.

Tokyo-Yokohama mainichi shinbun. "*Jinken shinsetsu* o hyōsu." In *Meiji bunka zenshū,* vol. 5: *Jiyū minken hen,* 410–427. Tokyo: Nihon hyōronsha, 1927.

Toriumi Yasushi. *Meiroku zasshi to kindai Nihon.* 2 vols. Tokyo: Nihonhōsō shuppan kyōkai, 1994–1995.

Toury, Gideon. *In Search of a Theory of Translation.* Tel Aviv: Tel Aviv University, Porter Institute for Poetics and Semiotics, 1980.

Tōyama Shigeki. *Meiji ishin.* Rev. ed. Tokyo: Iwanami shoten, 1972.

———. "Meiroku zasshi." *Shisō,* no. 447 (9/1961):117–128.

———. "Reforms of the Meiji Restoration and the Birth of Modern Intellectuals." *Acta Asiatica* 13 (1967):55–99.

Toyama Shōichi. "Futatabi *Jinken shinsetsu* chosha ni tadashiawasete Supenserushi no tame ni en o toku." In *Meiji bunka zenshū,* vol. 5: *Jiyū minken hen,* 431–437. Tokyo: Nihon hyōronsha, 1927.

———. "*Jinken shinsetsu* no chosha ni tadashiawasete shinbun kishano mugaku wo gasu." In *Meiji bunka zenshū,* vol. 5: *Jiyū minken hen,* 427–431. Tokyo: Nihon hyōronsha, 1927.

———. "Kanji o haishi Eigo o shi ni okosu wa kyō no kyūmunari." *Tōyō gakugei zasshi,* no. 33 (1884.6.25):70–75.

———. "Kanji o haisubeshi." *Tōyō gakugei zasshi,* no. 30 (1884.3.25):307–312 and no. 31 (1884.4.25):7–12.

———. *Minken benwaku.* In *Meiji bunka zenshū,* vol. 5: *Jiyū minken hen,* 213–229. Tokyo: Nihon hyōronsha, 1927.

———. "Rōmajikai o okosu no shui." *Tōyō gakugei zasshi,* no. 39 (1884.12.25):228–232.

———. "Rōmaji o shuchōsuru mono ni tsugu." *Tōyō gakugei zasshi,* no. 34 (1884.6.25):104–106.

———. "Shakaigaku no genri o daisu" (1882). In Toyama Shōichi, Yatabe Ryōkichi, and Inoue Tetsujirō, *Shintaishi shō: shohen,* 31–34a. Tokyo: Sekai bunko, 1961.

Tsuchida Mitsufumi. *Meiji-Taishō no shingo-ryūkōgo*. Tokyo: Kadokawa shoten, 1983.

Tsuda Mamichi. "Fūfu dōken ben." *Meiroku zasshi*, no. 35 (4/1875):8–9.

———. "Jinsai ron." *Meiroku zasshi*, no. 30 (2/1875):4–5b.

———. "Jōyoku," *Meiroku zasshi*, no. 34 (4/1875):8b-9a.

———. "Kaika o shinzuru hōhō o ronzu." *Meiroku zasshi*, no. 3 [4/1874]:7a-8b.

———. "Shinbunshi ron." *Meiroku zasshi*, no. 20 (11/1874):1–2b.

———. "Shuppan jiyū naran koto o nozomu ron." *Meiroku zasshi*, no. 6 [4/1874]:1–2a.

———. *Taisei kokuhō ron* (1868). Tokyo: Tōyōsha, 1875.

Tsutsumi Koshiji. *Bankoku kōhō yakugi*. N.p., 1868.

Tully, James H. "Review Article: The Pen Is a Mighty Sword: Quentin Skinner's Analysis of Politics." *British Journal of Political Science* 13(4) (October 1983):489–509.

Twine, Nanette. "The Genbunitchi Movement: Its Origin, Development, and Conclusion." *Monumenta Nipponica* 33(3) (Autumn 1978):333–356.

———. *Language and the Modern State: The Reform of Written Japanese*. London: Routledge, 1991.

Ueki Emori. "Danjo no dōken." In *Ueki Emori senshū*, ed. Ienaga Saburō, 149–186. Tokyo: Iwanami shoten, 1974.

———. "Hinmin ron." In *Ueki Emori senshū*, ed. Ienaga Saburō, 115–146. Tokyo: Iwanami shoten, 1974.

———. "Jinmin no kokka ni taisuru seishin o ronzu." In *Meiji shisō shū*, ed. Matsumoto Sannosuke, vol. 1:169–178. Tokyo: Chikuma shobō, 1976.

———. "Meirei no moji wa jiyū dōken to heikō suru mono ni arazu." In *Ueki Emori shū*, ed. Ienaga Saburō et al., vol. 3:238–240. Tokyo: Iwanami shoten, 1990.

———. *Minken jiyū ron*. In *Jiyūjiji gannen no yume*, ed. Ide Magoroku, 10–31. Tokyo: Shakai hyōronsha, 1991.

———. *Minken jiyū ron—nihen kangō*. In *Ueki Emori shū*, ed. Ienaga Saburō et al., vol. 1:125–160. Tokyo: Iwanami shoten, 1990.

———. *Nihon kuni kokken an*. In *Jiyūjiji gannen no yume*, ed. Ide Magoroku, 110–112. Tokyo: Shakai hyōronsha, 1991.

———. "Shogen." In *Ueki Emori shū*, ed. Ienaga Saburō et al., vol. 3:83–85. Tokyo: Iwanami shoten, 1990.

———. *Tenpu jinken ben*. In *Meiji bunka zenshū*, vol. 5: *Jiyū minken hen*, 463–482. Tokyo: Nihon hyōronsha, 1927.

Umeda Yoshihiko. "Shūkyō hō ni tsuite—Edo bakufu kara Meiji seifu e." *Shintō shūkyō* no. 26 (11/1961):37–55.

Unger, J. Marshall. "The Very Idea: The Notion of Ideogram in China and Japan." *Monumenta Nipponica* 45(4) (1990):391–411.

Verwayen, F. B. "Tokugawa Translations of Dutch Legal Texts." *Monumenta Nipponica* 53(3) (Fall 1998):335–358.

Voloshinov, V. N. *Marxism and the Philosophy of Language*. Translated by Ladislav Matejka and I. R. Titunik. New York: Academic Press, 1973.

Walthall, Anne. *Social Protest and Popular Culture in Eighteenth-Century Japan*. Tucson: University of Arizona Press, 1986.

Ward, Robert E. "Political Modernization and Political Culture in Japan." *World Politics* 15(4) (July 1963):569–596.

Watanabe Hiroshi. "About Some Japanese Historical Terms." Translated by Luke S. Roberts. *Sino-Japanese Studies* 10(2) (April 1998):32–42.

———. *Kinsei Nihon shakai to sōgaku*. Tokyo: Tokyo Daigaku shuppankai, 1985.

Watanabe Kazuyasu. *Meiji shisō shi: jukkyō teki dentō to kindai ninshiki ron*. 2nd ed. Tokyo: Perikansha, 1985.

Watanabe, Masao. *The Japanese and Western Science*. Translated by Otto Theodor Benfey. Philadelphia: University of Pennsylvania Press, 1988.

Watanabe Shūjirō. *Meiji kaika shi*. Tokyo: Matsui suji, 1880.

Wheaton, Henry. *Elements of International Law*. 2nd ann. ed. Edited by William Beach Lawrence. Boston: Little, Brown, 1863.

———. *Elements of International Law*. 6th ed. Boston: Little, Brown, 1855.

[Wheaton, Henry.] *Wanguo gongfa*. [Translated by W.A.P. Martin.] Reprinted as *Bankoku kōhō*. Edo: Kaiseijo, 1865.

White, James W. "State Growth and Popular Protest in Tokugawa Japan." *Journal of Japanese Studies* 14(1) (1988):1–25.

Wieger, Léon. *Chinese Characters: Their Origin, Etymology, History, Classification, and Signification. A Thorough Study from Chinese Documents*. Translated by L. Davrout. 2nd ed. (1927). New York: Dover, 1965.

Wierzbicka, Anna. *Understanding Cultures Through Their Key Words: English, Russian, Polish, German, and Japanese*. New York: Oxford University Press, 1997.

Williams, Raymond. *Keywords: A Vocabulary of Culture and Society*. New York: Oxford University Press, 1976.

Wilson, Robert A. *Genesis of the Meiji Government in Japan, 1868–1871*. Berkeley: University of California Press, 1957.

Wolf, Eric R. "Inventing Society." *American Ethnologist* 15(4) (November 1988):752–761.

Yaguchi Shigeo. "Meiji izen ni okeru gairaigo no on'yaku." *Gairaigo kenkyū* 4(2) (1/1938):49–72.

Yamamoto Masahide. *Genbunitchi no rekishi ronkō*. 2 vols. Tokyo: Ōfūsha, 1971 and 1981.

———. *Kindai buntai hassei no shiteki kenkyū*. Tokyo: Iwanami shoten, 1965.

———, ed. *Kindai buntai keisei shiryō shūsei*. 2 vols. Tokyo: Ōfūsha, 1978–1979.

Yamamuro Shin'ichi. "Form and Function of the Meiji State in Modern East Asia." *Zinbun*, no. 34 (1999):179–196.

———. *Hōsei kanryō no jidai: kokka no sekkei to chi no rekitei*. Tokyo: Mokutakusha, 1984.

———. *Kindai Nihon no chi to seiji: Inoue Kowashi kara taishūengei made*. Tokyo: Mokutakusha, 1985.

Yamashita, Samuel Hideo. "Reading the New Tokugawa Intellectual Histories." *Journal of Japanese Studies* 22(1) (Winter 1996):1–48.

Yamashita Shigekazu. "Ono Azusa to Igirisu seiji shisō." In Takeda Kiyoko et al., *Igirisu shisō to kindai Nihon*, 125–161. Tokyo: Kitaki shuppan, 1992.

———. *Supensā to Nihon kindai*. Tokyo: Ochanomizu shobō, 1983.

Yanabu Akira. *Hon'yaku to wa nani ka?—Nihongo to hon'yaku bunka*. 2nd ed. Tokyo: Hōsei Daigaku shuppankyoku, 1985.

———. *Hon'yakugo no ronri*. Tokyo: Hōsei Daigaku shuppankyoku, 1972.

———. *Hon'yakugo seiritsu jijō*. Tokyo: Iwanami shoten, 1982.

Yanagida Izumi. "*Shakai heiken ron* yakusha—Matsushima Kō den." In *Meiji shoki hon'yaku bungaku no kenkyū* (*Meiji bungaku kenkyū*, vol. 5). Rev. ed., 358–370. Tokyo: Haruakisha, 1961.

Yano Fumio. *Jinken shinsetsu bakuron*. In *Meiji bunka zenshū*, vol. 5: *Jiyū minken hen*, 391–410. Tokyo: Nihon hyōronsha, 1927.

Yasumaru Yoshio and Fukaya Katsumi, eds. *Minshū undō*. (*Nihon kindai shisō taikei*, vol. 21.) Tokyo: Iwanami shoten, 1989.

Yatabe Ryōkichi. "Rōmaji o motte Nihongo o tsuzuru no setsu." *Tōyō gakugei zasshi*, no. 7 (4/1882):127–130 and no. 8(5/1882):151–152.

Yoda Yoshiie. *The Foundations of Japan's Modernization: A Comparison with China's Path Towards Modernization*. Translated by Kurt W. Radtke. Leiden: Brill, 1996.

Yokoyama Toshio. "*Setsuyōshū* and Japanese Civilization." In *Themes and Theories in Modern Japanese History: Essays in Memory of Richard Storry*, ed. Sue Henny and Jean-Pierre Lehmann, 78–98. London: Athlone, 1988.

Yoshida Kanehiko. "Jisho no rekishi." In *Kōza: Kokugo shi*, vol. 3: *Goi shi*, by Sakakura Atsuyoshi et al., 503–537. Tokyo: Taishūkan, 1971.

Yoshino Sakuzō. "Waga kuni kindaishi ni okeru seiji ishiki no hassei." In *Yoshino Sakuzō Hakase: Minshushugi ron shū*, vol. 8: *Meiji bunka kenkyū*, 11–100. Tokyo: Shinkigensha, 1948.

Zlateva, Palma. "Translation: Text and Pre-Text: 'Adequacy' and 'Acceptability' in Crosscultural Communication." In *Translation, History, and Culture,* ed. Susan Bassnett and André Lefevere, 29–37. London: Pinter, 1980.

Index

accessibility. *See* translation

Aikokusha (Patriotic Association), 166, 168, 169, 171, 175

analogs (compound signs), 6, 76–82, 85, 87, 123, 141, 163, 184; cumulative resolution of, 79–80, 81; substitutive resolution of, 80–81

Ariga Nagao, 51–52, 54, 172

Austin, John, 66, 141

authenticity. *See* translation

authoritarianism, 42–43, 58, 94, 95, 100, 105, 131, 146, 180; as encouraging servility, 32, 55, 57, 178. *See also* tutelage of the people

autonomy, 97, 99–100, 103, 107, 139, 186

Baba Tatsui, 138, 172, 173, 245n. 93; history of natural right, 138

Bansho shirabesho, 10, 62, 192n. 9, 237n. 18

Begriffsgeschichte, 7–8, 25–30, 184; "horizon of expectations," 8, 29

Bellah, Robert, 20

Bentham, Jeremy, 66

Blacker, Carmen, 16, 17, 39

Blackstone, William, 129, 141

Bluntschli, Johann Kaspar, 108, 128, 139, 141, 142

Bodin, Jean, 95

bourgeoisie, 5, 33–34, 40, 42; self-representation as civil society, 158–162, 164, 165

Buckle, Thomas Henry, 33, 45

Buddhism, 58, 108–110

bunka, 33, 38, 203n. 16; as German *Kultur*, 38, 187. See also *bunmeikaika*

bunmei, 27, 33, 84, 85; *bunmei no iki*, 8. See also *bunmeikaika*

bunmeikaika, 2–3, 12–13, 33–39, 40, 60, 63, 192n. 13, 202n. 13; *bunmei* versus *kaika*, 33, 42–43; histories of, 15–18, 35–36; multiple terms for, 33; parodies of, 36–37; as a softening of manners, 37, 202n. 14; translated as "civilization and enlightenment," 38–40. *See also* civilization; development; Westernization

Chambers, William and Robert, 129, 154, 159–161; *Political Economy*, 62, 76, 159

15, 36, 90, 115–118; centralized bureaucracy, 10, 186; Education Law (1872),
69, 158; Ministry of Education, 15,
35, 59, 69, 90, 91, 187; oligarchy, 10–
12, 114, 129, 131, 151, 153, 165, 181, 186;
policy of "uniting politics and religion," 108–110; role in supervising
religion, 108, 114; threat of "officials'
rights," 133, 150–151; Three Standards
of Instruction (1872), 108–110
Meiji Restoration, 10, 15, 40, 55, 61, 147,
152, 159, 167; as temporal shift, 144
Meiji Six Society. *See* Meirokusha
Meiji state, constitutional form of, 130,
140
Meiroku zasshi, 13–15, 45, 49, 92, 128
Meirokusha, 13–15, 32, 35, 40–43, 45–
49, 56, 60, 110, 112, 115, 119, 124, 134,
166, 176, 240n. 50
Mill, John Stuart, 5, 22, 95, 97, 104, 136,
137, 154, 239n. 37; *Considerations on
Representative Government*, 132, 133,
167; on liberty of the press, 114, 116;
on middle-class interference with
individual liberty, 106, 163; *On Liberty*, 1, 3, 13, 62, 76, 95, 96, 131, 133,
159; on religious belief, 107–108; on
self-protection of society, 105
minken, 123, 131, 132, 133, 135, 147–148,
150; as translation for *droit civil,*
229n. 37
Minoura Katsundo, 117, 234n. 82
Mitsukuri Rinshō, 41, 45, 124, 229n. 37,
240n. 50
Miyagawa Tōru, 15
modernity, 16, 26, 178, 194n. 20
modernization theory, 2–3, 16–17, 19–
21, 193n. 18
monarchy, 94, 131–132, 142–143; monarchical privilege, 142; monarch's right
(kunken), 131
morality, 101, 104, 109–114, 127, 128,

175, 178, 188, 208n. 58; moral agency,
99–100; moral hierarchy, 156–158,
181, 187. *See also* duty; loyalty
Mori Arinori, 14, 38, 187, 221n. 35; contract marriage, 134; in debate over
duty of scholars, 44–45; on national
religion, 113, 223n. 55; *Religious Freedom in Japan,* 111
movement to establish a national
assembly, 11, 23–24, 115, 123, 130,
132, 135, 140, 164–171, 181, 184,
196n. 43, 220n. 30; stratifying versus
unifying strategies, 166–171

Nagamine Hideki, 132
Nagasaki interpreters, 9, 53
Nagata Tomoyoshi, 70–75
Najita Tetsuo, 17, 25
Nakae Chōmin, 145, 233n. 75
Nakamura Keiu, 13, 14, 41, 92, 117, 119,
164; as defender of China and Chinese learning, 50, 52–55; encouragement of Christianity, 106–107, 111–
113, 222n. 50; interpretation of society, 162–164, 238n. 30; *Jiyū no ri*
(translation of J. S. Mill's *On
Liberty*), 62, 76, 86, 89, 96, 101–107,
115, 128, 134, 162; on liberty of the
press, 115, 117; on national character,
55–58; *Saikoku risshi hen* (translation
of Smiles' *Self-Help*), 13, 14, 49, 62,
76, 78, 86, 89, 161; translation habits
of, 86; translation words for "society," 162–164
Napoleon III, 116
nation, 134, 148, 160, 171, 181, 185–187;
as mediating individual and state,
149, 185; national character, 33,
55–60, 208n. 61; national language
(kokugo), 33, 49–50, 88; national
religion, 108, 112–113; terminology
for, 149, 185, 241n. 60

national assembly, 12, 13, 44, 84, 115, 117, 130, 133, 139, 142–143, 145, 146, 148, 150, 154, 167, 185. *See also* movement to establish a national assembly

nationalism, 23, 58, 74–75

native learning *(kokugaku)*, 65, 109

neologisms, 62, 82. *See also* loanwords; translation words

newspaper debate on sovereignty (1881–1882), 87, 130, 138–146, 150

Nishi Amane, 13, 14, 45, 64–65, 124; in debate over duty of scholars, 44–45; in debate over freedom of religion, 56, 110–111; differentiating right and principle, 128; *Fisuserinku-shi bankoku kōhō*, 98, 126; *Hyakugaku renkan/Encyclopedia*, 76–79, 86; *Hyakuichi shinron*, 66; on national character, 57; "On Writing Japanese with the Western Alphabet," 45–48, 62, 76; on problems of translation, 82–84, 86; on the rights of states and individuals, 126–127, 129; use of analogs, 76–82, 87

Nishimura Shigeki, 47, 119; *Elementary Instruction in Ethics*, 59–60; on ethics instruction, 55–60; on government control of the press; 116, 117–118; on the ignorance of the people, 45, 47, 49, 187; on natural versus social liberty, 119–120

Norman, E. H., 15

Numa Morikazu, 140

Obata Tokujirō, 139

Ochiai Hiroki, 185

Ogyū Sorai, 156

Ōishi Masami, 145

Ōkubo Toshiaki, 16

Ōkubo Toshimichi, 131, 140, 157, 165

Ōkuma Shigenobu, 131, 172

Ōkuni Takamasa, 65–66

Ono Azusa, 145, 172, 237n. 20

Oto Shigeru. *See* Uryū Tora

Ōtsuki Fumihiko, 63, 85, 88, 92, 215n. 42

Ozaki Yukio, 172, 173, 233n. 68

Parliament (Britain), 142. *See also* national assembly

Parsons, Talcott, 19, 21

participation in government, 60, 95, 121, 129, 135, 148, 152, 167–168. *See also* people's right(s); tutelage of the people

people, the, 1, 44, 94, 153–154; as a problem of representation, 170–171; the problem of their ignorance, 13–14, 31, 45, 49, 57, 148, 167, 186; range of translation words for, 160, 162; as represented in the movement for a national assembly, 166–168; versus government, 4, 44, 104, 105, 131, 150–151, 167–168, 178–181; as "we," 168. *See also* four divisions of the people; samurai

people's right(s) *(minken)*, 94, 119, 123, 129, 132, 139, 146, 150, 152, 175, 184, 185; differentiated from popular sovereignty, 134–135, 139, 151–152; linked to state right, 135, 147–152, 169; people's civil rights, 122, 124, 130, 132; people's right to consitute a government, 124, 132, 133; people's right to participate in government, 133–134, 146, 148, 169, 171. *See also* movement to establish a national assembly; rights

Perry Expedition to Japan, 8–9, 46, 64, 103, 149, 185

personal freedoms and rights, 42,

scholars: duty of, 42–45; scholarly journals in Meiji period, 13–15, 90, 92
science, as goal of Westernization, 12,
52, 54, 112, 180, 188
scientific certitude in progress, 176–178
self-determination, 96, 99, 186
self-government, 99; as goal of revolution, 103. *See also* autonomy
self-mastery. *See* autonomy
selfishness, 96, 101, 103, 105, 220n. 21
semantic (lexical) field theory, 28–29
semantic transparency, 5–6, 18–25, 27,
63, 190n. 2
semantics, 27–29, 184
semiotic theory, 6, 79–82; materiality
of words, 27–29; type versus token,
27–28, 63–64, 93, 190n. 3. *See also*
analogs; denotation; loanwords;
meaning; translation words
shakai, 30, 84–85, 154, 158, 161, 170–173,
179, 184
Shigeno Yasutsugu, 53
Shimaji Mokurai, 110
Shimeikai, 140
Shimizu Usaburō, 13, 14, 48–49, 62
Shintō, 108–110
shuken, 87, 123, 126, 127, 138
signs and sign theory. *See* analogs; semiotic theory
Skinner, Quentin, 18, 25–27, 29
Smiles, Samuel, 154, 159–160; *Self-Help*,
13, 14, 49, 59, 62, 79, 159
society, 1, 5, 30, 95, 184; as an abstraction of the "people," 153, 170–171,
177; appearance in proposals for a
national assembly, 170; as "body
politic," 154, 159, 162; as "corporation," 161, 162, 164; differentiated
from government, 160, 163–164, 179;
history of concept in English, 154–
155; as object of scientific inquiry,
172, 180–181; as root of "socialism,"

176, 181; as site of class divisions in
West, 155, 177, 179, 180; as the social
milieu of the individual, 154, 159;
translation words for, 160–163, 172–
173, 238n. 30, 238n. 33, 239n. 35,
243n. 70. *See also* bourgeoisie; civil
society; people; working class
sociology of values, 19–21
Soejima Taneomi, 166, 167
Sonoda Hidehiro, 157, 158
sovereignty, 1, 4, 140–146, 150–151, 185;
contrasted with royal prerogatives,
142; of Japan's emperors, 138, 140,
141, 143–145, 184; location in a constitutional polity, 122, 130, 142–144;
newspaper debate on (1881–1882),
130, 138–146; philological relation
to sovereign, 139, 141; popular sovereignty, 117, 139, 141; as power to
establish law, 139, 142; as state right,
139, 145; translation words for,
86–87, 141–143
Spencer, Herbert, 95, 160, 171–182,
243n. 69; on natural rights, 173; on
social evolution, 137, 154, 166, 173,
174–180, 243n. 72, 244n. 84; *Social
Statics*, 131, 173, 174, 175, 176, 180,
245n. 93; "The Rights of Women,"
176, 179, 245n. 90; works translated
into Japanese, 171, 176
state right, 15, 66, 123, 127, 135, 138, 139,
146, 147–150, 169, 173, 176–177, 186
status *(mibun)*, 148, 155–158, 167, 168,
181
sub- and super-script. *See* analogs
Sugimoto Tsutomu, 209n. 2
"survival of the fittest," 136, 181

Taguchi Ukichi, 92
Taishō democracy, 23, 135, 185
Taiwan Incident of 1874, 50, 53, 115,
206n. 44

About the Author

Douglas Howland is an associate professor of history at DePaul University and author of *Borders of Chinese Civilization: Geography and History at Empire's End* (Duke University Press, 1996). *Translating the West* was written during a fellowship at the Woodrow Wilson International Center for Scholars. During the academic year 2000–2001, Professor Howland was a member of the Institute for Advanced Study, Princeton, where he was at work on a book manuscript about the reception of John Stuart Mill in East Asia.